Tourism and Inequ...

Problems and Prosp...

D0531293

THE LEARNING CENTRE
HAMMERSMITH AND WEST
LONDON COLLEGE
GLIDDON ROAD
LONDON W14 9BL

WITHDRAWN

This book is dedicated to Shannay and Toby, in the hope that the inequalities in and through tourism will be reduced by the time they come to book their first holiday.

Tourism and Inequality

Problems and Prospects

———————————

Edited by

Stroma Cole

University of the West of England

and

Nigel Morgan

University of Wales Institute, Cardiff

www.cabi.org

338.4791 TOU

CABI is a trading name of CAB International

CABI Head Office	CABI North American Office
Nosworthy Way	875 Massachusetts Avenue
Wallingford	7th Floor
Oxfordshire, OX10 8DE	Cambridge, MA 02139
UK	USA
Tel: +44 (0)1491 832111	Tel: +1 617 395 4056
Fax: +44 (0)1491 833508	Fax: +1 617 354 6875
E-mail: cabi@cabi.org	E-mail: cabi-nao@cabi.org
Website: www.cabi.org	

A catalogue record for this book is available from the British Library, London, UK.

Library of Congress Cataloging-in-Publication Data

Tourism and inequality : problems and prospects / edited by
  Stroma Cole, Nigel Morgan.
    p. ; cm.
  Includes bibliographical references and index.
  ISBN 978-1-84593-662-4 (hardback alk. paper)
  ISBN 978-1-84593-690-7 (pbk.: alk paper)
 1. Tourism. 2. Tourism--Sociological aspects. I. Cole, Stroma, 1962-
  II. Morgan, Nigel. III. Title.

  G155.A1T58934862 2010
  306.4'.819--dc22

                              2010019057

ISBN-13: 978 1 84593 662 4 (hardback)
ISBN-13: 978 1 84593 690 7 (paperback)

Commissioning editor: Sarah Hulbert
Production editor: Kate Hill

Typeset by Columns Design Ltd, Reading, UK.
Printed and bound in the UK by MPG Books Group.

Contents

Contributors

Frances Brown is a freelance editor and author. She was editor of *Tourism Management* from 1987 to 1996 and is on the editorial board of *Tourism Recreation Research*. She has also lectured in the UK and abroad on publishing tourism research, and was guest editor of a recent special issue on tourism of *Third World Quarterly*.

Dr Sheena Carlisle is Senior Lecturer in Tourism Management, and Programme Director for Undergraduate Tourism at the University of Wales Institute, Cardiff. Her research interests include: political economy of tourism in developing countries; fair trade and pro-poor tourism; small and medium enterprise (SME) development and partnership models in destination management.

Dr Stroma Cole is a senior lecturer in Tourism Geography at the University of the West of England. With research interests in responsible tourism development in less developed countries, the anthropology of tourism, and the link between tourism and human rights, she is an activist researcher critiquing the consequences of tourism development. Stroma is Chair of Tourism Concern: see http://www.tourismconcern.org.uk for further details.

Associate Professor Simon Darcy is Research Director in the School of Leisure, Sport and Tourism at the University of Technology, Sydney. He teaches, researches and has published in the areas of social participation patterns, public policy, environmental planning and inclusive planning practices for marginalized groups. Since incurring a spinal cord injury, Simon is a power wheelchair user and has been active in the advocacy and research of issues facing people with disabilities.

Jenny Eriksson studied Human Rights at the Institution of Global Studies at Gothenburg University, Sweden. In 2008 she undertook research for Tourism Concern's report 'Putting Tourism to Rights' and in 2009 researched Swedish tour operators and corporate responsibility and human rights for the Swedish network on fair travel 'Schyst Resande'. She is author of the site http://www.fairtourism.org, which discusses human rights related issues in tourism.

Dr Tim Gale is a senior lecturer in Tourism Geography at the University of the West of England, Bristol. His research interests include the decline and restructuring of cold-water resorts, new forms of tourism production and consumption (e.g. cyber- and eco-tourism; urban beaches), and environmental sustainability and tourism development.

Dr Kevin Griffin is the Head of Tourism at the School of Hospitality Management and Tourism in the Dublin Institute of Technology. Having studied teaching, tourism organization and historic settlement, and having previously worked in a number of geography departments, he has a broad range of interests in the tourism, heritage and sustainability areas. His interests in social tourism link with his research into sustainable and religious tourism and are developed from his volunteer work in the provision of holidays.

C. Michael Hall is Professor in the Department of Management at the University of Canterbury, New Zealand; Docent in the Department of Geography, University of Oulu, Finland; and visiting professor at the Linnaeus University School of Business and Economics, Sweden.

Derek Hall was trained in geography and social anthropology, and he has a doctorate in urban social and political geography. Together with Frances Brown he co-wrote *Tourism and Welfare: Ethics, Responsibility and Sustained Well-being*, published by CAB International in 2006.

Dr Freya Higgins-Desbiolles is a lecturer in tourism in the School of Management, University of South Australia. She holds degrees in politics and international relations and has 10 years working experience in development and development education. Her research in tourism has included a focus on the concerns of host communities, the impacts of tourism, indigenous tourism and justice through tourism. She has recently worked with indigenous Australian communities and Palestinians on projects fostering the use of tourism for community benefit.

Angela Kalisch is Senior Lecturer in Tourism Management at the University of Gloucestershire. Between 1999 and 2002, she was organizing international research on Fair Trade in Tourism and Corporate Social Responsibility at the UK-based Non-Governmental Organization (NGO) Tourism Concern. She is currently updating this work for her PhD.

Dr Dorothea Meyer is Senior Lecturer at Sheffield Hallam University, UK. Her research is investigating how tourism can be used as a tool for poverty reduction. While her current research is mainly focused on Africa, she also works in Europe, Asia and the Pacific. Previously, Dorothea worked for the tourism team at Overseas Development Institute (ODI).

Dr Lynn Minnaert is a research fellow and lecturer at the University of Westminster. Her research focuses on social tourism in the UK and Europe, and on social sustainability in the tourism and events industry.

Nigel Morgan is Professor of Tourism Studies at the University of Wales Institute, Cardiff. He writes on destination brands, tourism, social justice and citizenship, and hopeful tourism scholarship. His next book will be the second edition of *The Critical Turn in Tourism Studies*, edited with Irena Ateljevic and Annette Pritchard.

Polyp is an activist and full time cartoonist/illustrator/prop builder for a wide range of campaign groups and NGOs. His work can be seen at http://www.polyp.org.uk. His ambitious graphic novel, *Speechless – World History Without Words*, is published by New Internationalist and Friends of the Earth International. See http://www.speechlessthebook.org for further details.

Annette Pritchard is Professor of Critical Tourism Studies and Director of the Cardiff School of Management's Welsh Centre for Tourism Research at the University of Wales Institute, Cardiff. She researches on tourism and gender, hopeful tourism scholarship, and destination brands. She is an editorial board member of the *Journal of Tourism and Cultural Change*, *Tourism and Hospitality Research* and the *Annals of Tourism Research*.

Bernadette Quinn is a human geographer. She lectures in the School of Hospitality Management and Tourism, Dublin Institute of Technology. Her research interests include tourism and cultural change, festivals and events, and tourism and social justice. Her work has been published in a number of journals including *Social and Cultural Geography*, *Urban Studies* and *Annals of Tourism Research*.

Victoria Richards is a qualified rehabilitation officer and has worked with and for people with visual impairment in public sector and charity organizations. She is pursuing a University of Wales Institute, Cardiff-funded doctoral study of the tourism experiences of people with visual impairment at the Welsh Centre for Tourism Research in the Cardiff School of Management.

Jacqueline Sánchez Taylor is a lecturer at the University of Leicester. She has undertaken extensive ethnographic research on sex tourism with a particular focus on female sex tourism. Her research and publications have focused on theoretical questions about the intersections of race, gender, sexuality, age and economic inequalities in the global sex trade.

Dr Diane Sedgley is Senior Lecturer in Tourism at the University of Wales Institute, Cardiff. Her research interests focus on under-empowered and discriminated against groups in society, and she has published on the tourism and leisure activities of older people, people with disabilities and gay and lesbian consumers.

Jennie Small is a senior lecturer in the School of Leisure, Sport and Tourism at the University of Technology, Sydney. Her specific research interest is tourist behaviour from a critical tourism approach, focusing on equity and social justice issues in tourism. Her research publications relate to embodiment, gender, disability, obesity, age and the life course.

Jane Stacey is a researcher and lecturer in the School of Hospitality Management and Tourism, Dublin Institute of Technology. Her research interests include social justice and equality issues in tourism, sustainability, education and cultural tourism. She also conducts applied research projects on behalf of public sector agencies, industry associations and private commercial organizations.

Foreword

_____

As someone who has spent their entire working life fighting for equal rights for all people and working to develop stronger communities, I was struck by the evidence and arguments in this edited volume by Stroma Cole and Nigel Morgan about the prevalence of inequality and discrimination in the tourism industry. Fortunately, this book also points to tourism's potential to act as a powerful force for reducing inequality and positive community development through social inclusion initiatives that incorporate poverty alleviation and fair trade and ethical practices that support human rights.

As the editors point out in their introduction, analysis of the causes of inequality in tourism is not new. The seasonal and low-skilled labour markets in tourism lead to temporary employment at non-liveable wages without the usual health and other employee benefits. Often black and ethnic minority workers confront barriers when entering management or other higher-paying jobs. The room cleaning, garden tending, kitchen worker and waitress jobs are filled disproportionately by low-skilled female employees. Women are also exploited in sex tourism, with pervasive issues of abuse and human rights. These inequalities can create dual economies in local communities, one for wealthier tourists and the other for impoverished local workers. In addition, tourism destinations and accommodations are rarely easily accessible for people with physical disabilities.

Tourism can also create local jobs in communities devastated by mining or manufacturing closures and in low-income countries seeking to build businesses and jobs on natural beauty and historical heritage. Tourists not only stay in hotels, they also use the transportation system, frequent cafes and restaurants and go shopping. Tourism can attract foreign investment and real estate development.

The editors and authors of this volume seek solutions to reconcile these economic benefits of tourism with reducing inequality and injustice. The contributions are representative of wider tourism studies that challenge us to think about the critical importance of equality and social justice in economic development. The authors argue for social tourism for low-income groups, the role of welfare in tourism, and changes in the fair trade and ethical practices of the tourism industry. Human rights, fairness and equity are too important for any industry to exempt itself from these universal values.

Two of the book's main audiences are tourism students and educators – the first are the future tourism professionals, practitioners and policy makers, and the second are those most responsible for embedding ethics, values and stewardship in teaching and learning practice. I am acutely aware of the importance of education and attitudinal change in bringing about social progress. I hope that this book will lead the way in encouraging both groups to not only reflect on the importance of humanism, respect and responsibility in the classroom, but also to transform the world of tourism in practice.

Dr Cherry Short, CBE
Assistant Dean for Global and Community Initiatives
School of Social Work
University of Southern California

Acknowledgements

An edited textbook is a long project that requires the support and involvement of a range of people in order to come to fruition. The editors would like to thank first and foremost the contributors for their hard work and dedication to this project. We would also like to thank the ESRC for funding the seminar series out of which this book has grown, and the reviewers who took time to read the proposal and sample chapters and make comments. We would like to thank the staff at CABI, especially Sarah Hulbert, for her patience and belief that we could make it happen. We would like to express our gratitude to the tourists and workers who have shared their stories upon which many cases in this book have been built. Last but not least, we would like to say thank you to our partners, Annette and Brian, for their patience and support.

Stroma Cole
Bristol
Nigel Morgan
Cardiff
April 2010

Acronyms

ADB	Asian Development Bank
ASSET	Association of Small Scale Enterprises in Tourism
ATG	alternative tourism group
AUSAID	Australian Government Overseas Aid Programme
BITS	Bureau Internationale du Tourisme Social
BRIC	Brazil, Russia, India and China
CBT	community-based tourism
CRS	computer reservation systems
CRZ	coastal regulation and buffer zones
CSR	corporate social responsibility
DBSA	Development Bank Southern Africa
DfID	UK Department for International Development
DfT	Department for Transport
EC	European Commission
ECOT	Ecumenical Coalition on Tourism
EU	European Union
FCO	Foreign and Commonwealth Office
FDI	foreign direct investment
FHA	Family Holiday Association
FLO	The International Fair Trade Labelling Organization
FOC	flag of convenience
FTO	Federation of Tour Operators
FTTSA	Fair Trade Tourism in South Africa
GATS	general agreement on trade in services
GDP	gross domestic product
GDS	global distribution systems
GRI	global reporting initiative
GTA	Gambia Tourism Authority
GTZ	Gesellschaft fuer Technische Zusammenarbeit
GX	Global Exchange
HDI	Human Development Index
HIV	human immunodeficiency virus
IBLF	International Business Leaders Forum

ICCPR	International Covenant on Civil and Political Rights
ICESCR	International Covenant on Economic, Social and Cultural Rights
ICIDH	International Classification of Impairments, Disabilities and Handicap
IFC	International Finance Corporation
ILO	International Labour Organization
IMF	International Monetary Fund
(I)NGO	(international) non-governmental organization
ISEC	International Society for Ecology and Culture
ISM	International Solidarity Movement
ITC	International Trade Centre
ITF	International Transport Workers Federation
ITO	international tour operator
KfW	Kreditanstalt fuer Wiederaufbau
LDC	least developed country
LEDC	less economically developed country
MDG	millennium development goals
MEDC	more developed country
NGO	non-governmental organization
NTS	national travel survey
NZAID	New Zealand's International Aid and Development Agency
ODI	Overseas Development Institute
OECD	Organization for Economic Co-operation and Development
OTG	official tourist guide
PPG	pro-poor growth
PPT	pro-poor tourism
PRSP	poverty reduction strategy papers
QoL	quality of life
R&R	rest and recreation
RNIB	Royal National Institute of Blind People
RTP	Responsible Tourism Partnership
SAP	Structural Adjustment Programmes
SL	sustainable livelihoods
SME	small and medium enterprise
SMME	small, medium and micro-enterprise
SNV	Netherlands Development Organization
SRI	socially responsible investment
TDA	tourism development area
TIG	tourism interventions group
TNC	transnational corporations
TRP	Tsunami Rehabilitation Programme
UDHR	Universal Declaration of Human Rights
UK	United Kingdom
UN	United Nations
UNCTAD	United Nations Commission on Trade and Development
UNWTO	United Nations World Tourism Organization
UPAIS	Union of Physically Impaired Against Segregation
USAID	United States Agency for International Development
VCA	value chain analysis
VSO	voluntary service overseas
WSF	World Social Forum
WTO	World Trade Organization
WTTC	World Travel and Tourism Council

Introduction: Tourism and Inequalities

Stroma Cole and Nigel Morgan

As its title suggests, this book seeks to make a distinctive contribution to the tourism and inequality debate, not only through its investigation of how and why tourism contributes to and reflects social inequality, but crucially through its exploration of the ways in which tourism can be a means to reduce social inequality or alleviate its impact. As such, it is firmly located within 'hopeful tourism scholarship', an emerging paradigm within the field, which advocates linking critical thinking, pedagogy and action to achieve more just societies in and through tourism (Ateljevic *et al.*, 2007a; Ren *et al.*, in press). Tourism is frequently described as one of the world's fastest growing industries and a new source of wealth creation in deprived regions and less developed nations. Recently, however, emphasis on its economic benefits has been countered by increasing concerns over the uneven nature of such economic development, serious questions about the environmental sustainability of the tourism industry and disquiet at the negative social and cultural impacts of tourism. These concerns have been expressed by academics, policy makers and practitioners, and have been raised in relation to different scales: individual well-being, family structure, community development and national identity (Botterill and Klemm, 2006, 2007). In both tourism-generating regions and in tourism-receiving communities, tourism is part of wider social, economic, political, ecological and cultural processes, and the goal of this volume is to unpick these complex processes in order to expose the relationships between tourism and inequality; more than this, however, its contributors also review international examples of socially responsible tourism to provide a stock of good practice cases for tourism students, educators, practitioners and activists.

Tourism has always been a site for and a contributor to social inequality (e.g. Morgan and Pritchard, 1999; Walton, 2005) but as tourism expands at a seemingly insatiable pace, the inequalities become increasingly evident and so too does the need for more complex and nuanced understandings of them. During an ESRC seminar series on Tourism Inequality and Social Justice in 2007, the level of interest and the number of researchers actively engaged in research about tourism and inequality became apparent. The individual seminars each examined inequality from a different perspective and those who attended them came from a variety of backgrounds, including academia, the public and private sectors, third sector organizations and a range of non-governmental organizations or NGOs. The academics came from a broad range of different disciplines and fields of study beyond tourism, including leisure studies, psychology, sociology, anthropology, geography and cultural studies, and while this volume is not in any way intended to be representative of the seminars, they certainly provided its genesis and many of these disciplines are reflected in the following chapters.

Of course, analysis of inequality is not new and there is a well-developed literature on exclusion, inequality and social justice within many of tourism studies' underpinning disciplines, most notably geography and sociology (Barry, 2005; Pogge, 2007), much of it traversed in the following chapters. Similarly, scholars working across the broad fields of leisure and sports studies have undertaken extensive research into inequality and exclusion in leisure and sport provision and participation (Roberts, 2006). Such research has addressed spatial, social, cultural and economic inequalities, the mutually informing nature of such inequalities and the ways in which inequality is experienced differently in relation to cultural context, social class, gender, ethnicity, age and disability. To date, however, there has been limited synthesis of existing research relating to all these different forms of inequality, exclusion or injustice and how they relate to tourism (thus, contributions such as Hall and Brown, 2006, and Burns and Novelli, 2008, cover some but not all of these areas). At the same time, on the other hand, reflecting broader theoretical debates in social sciences, there is a clear sense that tourism as a field of research and an area of study is maturing and demonstrating a 'critical turn' – a shift in thought that provides opportunities for more critical engagement with the major environmental, socio-cultural and political issues facing the world (Ateljevic *et al.*, 2007b). As a result, there is a growing demand for volumes such as the present one, which focus on issues of ethics, citizenship and justice as they relate to tourism in an intellectually rigorous and thought-provoking way.

Such issues are of increasing interest not only to the growing tourism student body in the more economically developed countries (MEDCs) of the world but also in the less economically developed countries (LEDCs) who are seeing exponential growth in tourism and a consequent growth in tourism education provision. The need for a single volume that is accessible and above all affordable to today's diverse student body was the rationale behind this book. While it was written to appeal primarily to undergraduates, we hope that the book will also open new intellectual doors for masters-level students and offer stimulating reading for doctoral students, academics and reflexive practitioners. Thus, the volume endeavours to provide an accessible exploration of tourism's role as a site of injustice and its potential to address inequality. It seeks to extend debates and discourses prominent elsewhere to tourism studies, where research on inequality and social justice has lacked the visibility seen in other disciplines and subject fields. Across its 12 chapters, a wide range of inter-related forms of inequality and routes towards social justice are addressed. These include, but are not limited to, relations of class, nation, ethnicity, race, gender, disability and age, as they relate to social justice initiatives incorporating poverty alleviation, social inclusion, fair trade, ethics and human rights.

Tourism and Inequalities

For most people in MEDCs, having a holiday or a vacation is considered a feature of their everyday lifestyles, it is part of what they do and there is a well developed literature on the benefits that can be derived from taking a holiday (e.g. Minnaert *et al.*, 2006, 2009). Everyone can derive some benefit from taking a holiday (many of which are listed in Table I.1) and such breaks from routine are especially important in affirming relationships with family and friends, particularly for children (Hazel, 2005; Hilbrecht *et al.*, 2008). However, while many of us can and do enjoy some or all of these advantages, most people cannot, indeed it is estimated that less than 5% of the world's population currently participate in international air travel (Peeters *et al.*, 2006). What is particularly pertinent in all this of course is that it is usually those who are most in need of the benefits of a holiday (e.g. children and adults living in poverty, lone parents, individuals with disabilities and chronic, terminal and mental illnesses and those who care for such individuals), who are least likely to be able to have one.

Since the early 1970s, scholars working broadly in leisure and sports studies have explored in considerable detail exactly which groups in societies are least likely to

Table I.1. The benefits of holidays.

Recreational pleasure	Respite from the exigencies of modern life
Educational awareness	Enhancing and maintaining one's cultural capital
Self-actualization	Improved quality of life
Self-esteem	Material for narrating self-identity
Mutual interaction	Making new friends
Reinforcement of group and family relations	Subject of family narratives
Relief from time and place	Investment in well-being

participate fully in cultural life, which encompasses sport, leisure and the arts (Critcher *et al.*, 1995; Haworth and Veal, 2004; Cushman *et al.*, 2005). Yet, after more than 30 years of scholarship in tourism enquiry, the field has nothing like a comparable literature in scale, scope or longevity, such has been tourism's focus on technically useful, management and performance-driven investigation, which has little interest in those who cannot access tourism products and services. Clearly, some groups are excluded from participation in tourism as a result of socio-economic disadvantage (Hughes, 1991) but exclusion and marginalization also results from discrimination, cultural prejudice and fear. For example, studies have shown that racial prejudice and institutional racist practices restrict ethnic minority citizens from enjoying tourism experiences to the full and thereby limit them from achieving full rights to social forms of citizenship (Stephenson, 2006). Such discrimination and prejudice encompasses all aspects of tourism; for instance, the promotion and marketing of holidays by major tour operators is perceived negatively by British Asians who consider that holidays in such brochures are 'for white people' (Klemm and Kelsey, 2004). Demonstrating how human status characteristics (such as gender, race, class, sexuality, age, ethnicity and ability) form layers and points of oppression and empowerment, the same tourism brochures not only exclude British Asians but have also been described as marginalizing women in 'a world dominated by male heterosexual marketing fantasies' (Pritchard and Morgan, 2000: 899).

If gendered and racialized exclusion and marginalization (see Chapters 4 and 7, this volume) results from discrimination, cultural prejudice and fear, there are 'genuine problems and challenges which can attach to having bodies/psyches that are different from mainstream "norms"' (Butler and Parr, 1999: 2), such as ageing or disabled bodies. There have been calls for the tourism industry (and other areas such as environmental and product design) to adopt universal design principles. Universal design is a paradigm that extends the concept of accessibility and barrier-free environments to incorporate intergenerational and lifespan planning; it recognizes the nexus between ageing, disability and the continuum of ability of people over lifespan and much more. Universal design:

> ... is the design of products and environments to be usable by all people, to the greatest extent possible, without the need for adaption or specialized design...The intent of the universal design concept is to simplify life for everyone by making products, communications, and the built environment more usable by more people at little or no extra cost. The universal design concept targets all people of all ages, sizes and abilities.

(Center for Universal Design, 2010)

These issues are examined in depth in Jennie Small and Simon Darcy's chapter, which analyses inequalities for people with mobility disability. Their chapter highlights how it is society that disables people, a theme continued in Chapter 2 by Victoria Richards, Nigel Morgan, Annette Pritchard and Diane Sedgley. Taken together, these two chapters expose how ableist power geometries (Kitchin and Law, 2001) prevent people with disabilities from fully participating in and contributing to tourism, and reveal how disability interacts with age to create further inequalities.

Disability also intersects with poverty and gender in this regard – for example as Richards *et al.* (Chapter 2) point out, over 80% of people with low or no vision in the UK of working age are unemployed, while the impacts of disabilities are felt disproportionately by the populations of LEDCs, particularly women who have less access to medical care. As disparity of income is one of the commonest causes of inequality, it is not surprising that it features in many of the chapters in this volume. Chapters 3 (Michael Hall) and 8 (Lynn Minnaert, Jane Stacey, Bernadette Quinn and Kevin Griffin) discuss poverty in the MEDCs context. Taking a relativist view of poverty as equating to exclusion from participation in a significant part of contemporary life, at the European level the inability to afford a 1-week annual holiday is an indicator of material deprivation (see Chapter 3), and since 2003 the UK government has used this as a measurement of child poverty (see Chapter 8). Chapters 4, 5, 6, 7 and 10 explicitly analyse poverty in the LEDC context. Here, we are discussing tourism production and consumption in a framework of absolute poverty as much of the population in many of these tourism receiving countries exist on less than a US$ a day. Thus Stroma Cole and Jenny Eriksson (Chapter 7) relate Gladys's story, a woman who has to walk for over an hour to work an 8-h shift during which she is not allowed to eat or drink at any point. At least this woman has a job, unlike many of the 'bumsters' in The Gambia (Chapter 5) or the women and children who have nothing left to sell other than their bodies (Chapter 4).

Tourism, Inequalities and Prospects

Analyses of the causes of inequality in tourism and how they relate to wider international systems of political and economic dependency relations are not new (e.g. de Kadt, 1979; Harrison, 2001). The underlying causes of inequity relating to unjust global systems, unfair international trade agreements, the workings of transnational corporations and the neoliberal capitalist system are reviewed by various authors in this volume (see especially Chapters 9 and 10). However, while they review previous contributions to this debate, the contributors to this volume move the discussion forward in a number of new ways. To see a problem is an easy task, but to understand multi-faceted problems is a much more complex but essential undertaking if we are to begin to find solutions. As editors of this book, neither of us wanted to produce a collection that simply scoped and reviewed the problems of tourism and inequality; we wanted to produce a thought-provoking and accessible text that also engaged with prospects for greater equality. Thus, while the power dynamics of international politics are rehearsed here, the contributors urge us to see these relations through new lenses, to appreciate their complexities and to demand more in-depth understanding.

This is true of all of the chapters in different ways as their authors go beyond examining the problems to ask 'what can be done' and 'is there another way'? Thus, in Part I, Darcy and Small (Chapter 1) and Richards *et al.* (Chapter 2) argue that equality legislation needs to be combined with enforcement, education and attitudinal change to create more inclusive environments, while Hall (Chapter 3) calls on us to understand mobility and accessibility as being imbued with values that are central to human well-being and a sustainable society. In Part II, Jacqueline Sánchez Taylor's (Chapter 4) examination of sex tourism contends that a deeper understanding of the interlocking processes of globalization, legislation, race and gender inequalities is required to develop a more fine-grained understanding of the growing phenomena of sex tourism. Similarly, Sheena Carlisle (Chapter 5) exposes not only the causes of inequality for Gambians but also examines some excellent examples of how marginalized groups can be included in the benefits of tourism. Angela Kalisch (Chapter 6) is overtly critical of neo-liberal capitalism, which has continued the colonial legacy and created unequal relations between rich and poor nations, but offers an alternative in the form of a fair trademark for tourism. Stroma Cole and Jenny Eriksson (Chapter 7) investigate the human rights of citizens in tourism destinations and go on to provide a strong argument for companies to include human rights as part of their corporate social responsibility (CSR) agenda. Derek Hall and Frances Brown (Chapter 9) lay out the case for welfare-positive tourism, and the chapters by Minnaert *et al.* and Tim Gale (Chapters 8 and 11) provide compelling evidence of the benefits of social tourism, while that by Dorothea Meyer (Chapter 10) moves beyond causes of inequity to examine solutions in the form of pro-poor tourism (PPT), and Freya Higgins-Desbiolles (Chapter 12) explores both the causes and effects of inequality and injustice in tourism before examining how they can be reduced through justice tourism.

Structure of the Book

Taken as a group, the book's contributors draw on a range of disciplines and case studies to provide unique perspectives on social justice and inequality in tourism from the consumers' and producers' perspectives. The disciplinary perspectives of its contributors include sociology, cultural studies, media studies, geography, anthropology, history and tourism management, and they illustrate their arguments with international case studies drawn from countries including Australia, England, Ethiopia, Belgium, the Caribbean, Eire, France, The Gambia, Kenya, Palestine, New Zealand, Thailand, the USA and Wales. This book is divided into three parts. Following this introduction, the first examines social inequalities from the tourist consumer's perspective; the second explores inequalities as experienced by the tourism producers; and the third part consists of a series of chapters that review initiatives to reduce or alleviate the impact of inequalities for both consumers and producers. It should be noted, however, that these distinctions are somewhat artificial, as individuals can be both producers and consumers of tourism; furthermore, while the book is structured in this way, there is overlap within and between parts; for example, while Sheena Carlisle's chapter examines marginalization in The Gambia, it also provides some excellent cases of how, in partnership with various international organizations, the Gambians are overcoming their social exclusion and pursuing a more equal form of tourism.

The first part of the book consists of three chapters that examine inequality from the perspective of those who want to take part in tourism. Each chapter calls for a more nuanced understanding of the complexities of non-participation in tourism and argues that the answers to why people are excluded lie beyond economic poverty and include cultural prejudice, discrimination and fear. Jennie Small and Simon Darcy's chapter examines the social inequality of tourists with mobility disabilities. Critical of the commonly used medical approach to disability, the authors encourage a social approach that conceptualizes disability as a product of the dis-enabling social environment and prevailing attitudes. The chapter provides the concepts necessary for a fuller understanding of disability. Using Australia as a case study, the chapter unpicks The Disability Discrimination Act and explores the complaints that have been raised since the Act became law in 1992, 27% of which were in the tourism and hospitality sectors. The chapter concludes that legislation alone is not enough to effect change and that political will, enforcement and education, together with changes in attitudes and behaviours, are required before this form of inequality can be combated.

These themes are reinforced in the next chapter written by Victoria Richards, Nigel Morgan, Annette Pritchard and Diane Sedgley, which focuses on their research on the tourism experiences of people with low or no vision in the UK. Their chapter demonstrates how, when the sighted world fails tourists with visual impairment through organizations' inabilities to provide staff training and inclusive physical environments, those individuals' tourism (and life) experiences are circumscribed. In such situations, many people with visual impairment prefer to remain at home and forgo the benefits of tourism rather than negotiate the anxiety and stress of travel in an unsympathetic, unaccommodating sighted world. Richards, Morgan, Pritchard and Sedgley conclude that the challenge for the tourism industry is to identify these customers, analyse their service needs in more depth and treat them with respect and dignity, to learn new skills, to be creative and then to truly apply that knowledge holistically.

The final chapter in Part I by Michael Hall links the topic of inequality with mobility and discusses the 'mobility gap' between those with privilege and plenty and those whose deprivation is acute. Using evidence from National Surveys in the UK, EU, USA and New Zealand Hall provides evidence of how social and economic inequality limit access to travel and tourism and how the car is the most significant factor affecting travel. In his chapter, Hall calls on us to understand mobility and accessibility as being imbued with values that are central to human well-being and a sustainable society. He concludes that if tourism studies are to embrace social justice then we need to understand how tourism opportunities are part of the overall life chances of individuals and appreciate how these are constituted and reproduced.

The second part of the book examines the social inequalities experienced by people in tourism destinations. While this adds to an already large body of existing literature these chapters all take new perspectives. In the first, Jacqueline Sánchez Taylor argues that hitherto sex tourism has been examined within the framework of gender inequalities and is better understood through the prism of race, globalization, agency *and* gender. Her chapter examines how sex tourism today involves men and women, the formal and informal sectors and overt prostitution and 'friendships'. Examining case study material from the Dominican Republic and Jamaica, Jacqueline Sánchez Taylor explores the links between sex tourism and globalization, the law and race. She argues that economic, gender, race and age inequalities all interlock in the diversity and complexity of sexual-economic exchanges between tourists and locals.

The next chapter, written by Sheena Carlisle, examines tourism in Africa's smallest state, The Gambia. Following her provision of the background to the economic situation in The Gambia, Carlisle goes on to examine the barriers that marginalize local people from full participation in tourism development in beach enclave tourism. She illustrates how the inequalities result from a lack of access to certain areas, poor access to water and electricity, limited marketing, and a difficulty adhering to licensing rules and international legislation, and demonstrates how the resulting marginalization and social exclusion has led to the well known problem of 'bumsters'. Carlisle then examines the role of ASSET (Association of Small Scale Enterprises in Tourism) who work to include local businesses and provides examples of how the Gambians are rising above their social exclusion. Finally, the chapter concludes by demonstrating how by working in partnership, some of the barriers can be overcome and a more inclusive equal form of tourism can be pursued.

Chapter 6 is written by Angela Kalisch and examines the complexities of developing a fair trade mark for tourism. After presenting the backdrop of unfair, unequal, neo-colonial exchange that has given rise to the present capitalist tourism economy, her chapter explores issues of corporate power and the problems of unfair international trade agreements. Kalisch then explores tourism certification in general before examining Fair Trade certification in particular. She exposes the rationale and philosophy behind the Fair Trade in Tourism Network and the criteria it developed. Kalisch concludes that a market instrument such as a Fair Trade kite mark cannot change the root causes of poverty and inequality in isolation but might succeed in bringing about changes in values and a greater commitment to social justice.

The final chapter in Part II analyses how, despite tourism's ability to alleviate poverty and bring dignity, it frequently does the reverse and so abuses the human rights of the people in destinations. Stroma Cole and Jenny Eriksson demonstrate how the political economy of tourism means that the rights of the tourists to rest and travel override the most basic human rights of others, and argue that by regarding tourism as a system rather than an industry we can gain a more appropriate approach to understanding human rights abuses in the tourism context. Their chapter uses examples of labour, privacy, water and housing rights from a variety of international cases to illustrate how holidays for some bring about poverty and destitution for others. The chapter ends on the business case for including human rights as part of social performance indicators in a company's CSR report.

As we have made clear above, this book is not just about how and why tourism contributes to social inequality. It also examines how tourism can be a route to alleviate social inequality and reduce its impacts, both for the consumers and for the producers of tourism, for those that take holidays and for those in destination communities that provide the products and services consumed by the holiday-makers. The third and final part of the book thus examines the prospects for reducing inequalities in and through tourism. Lynn Minnaert, Jane Stacey, Bernadette Quinn and Kevin Griffin begin with their chapter on social tourism – initiatives that aim to include groups in tourism that would otherwise be excluded on the basis that tourism is a right and promotes integration, knowledge and personal development. Their chapter explores the social and economic benefits for social tourism for the individuals involved and for society at large and, after reviewing examples of social tourism from various European countries, the authors explore the impacts of social tourism based on research in Eire and the UK. Their work illustrates how holidays provide participants with a much-needed break, improve family relations, create new social networks, enhance self-esteem and lead to the development of new skills and improved behaviour. The authors conclude their chapter with compelling social, economic and policy arguments for social tourism and their evidence suggests that tourism can be used to reduce inequality as well as to bring wider social and economic benefits.

In the second chapter of this part, Derek Hall and Francis Brown advocate using a 'welfare approach' to the study of tourism to enhance its benefits and reduce its negative impacts. Their chapter acknowledges the challenges of welfare-positive tourism while examining the need to explore the ethical dilemmas, nature of responsibilities and welfare trade-offs of and between the many different stakeholders in tourism. After placing welfare in its philosophical context the authors examine how tourism contributes to the well-being and welfare enhancement of tourists. They then take McKercher's 'fundamental truths about tourism' and Fennell's 'five paradoxes of tourism' as their starting point for examining CSR and industry responsibilities in tourism, before turning their attention to welfare considerations in destinations.

Following this, Dorothea Meyer's chapter examines the origins and ideas behind PPT. She begins her chapter with the meanings of poverty in LEDCs and then examines how tourism can be used to reduce poverty through two intertwined approaches: pro-poor growth and sustainable livelihoods. Meyer then evaluates how these strategies have been put into practice by focusing on the accommodation sector. She notes how PPT is not without its critics and explores these critiques before examining how this approach to reducing inequalities can be taken forward in tourism development.

The next chapter is Tim Gale's analysis of urban beaches, a phenomenon that has become a feature of many European cities in the summer months, with the aim of providing an alternative recreational space for residents on low incomes. Gale's chapter extends the discussion of social tourism in Chapter 8 to encompass the urban beach as a means of addressing, or compensating for, non-participation in leisure travel by the least mobile in society. He focuses on Paris Plage and Bristol Urban Beach and thought provokingly concludes that such 'tourism/leisure' spaces may increase in popularity as the era of uncomplicated long distance leisure travel comes under threat from climate change, economic downturn and global insecurities.

The final chapter of this third part of the book explores 'justice tourism'. After briefly examining tourism and injustice and how the discrepancies in wealth, power and status are particularly apparent in tourism encounters, Freya Higgins-Desbiolles considers the limited contributions to the discussion of the ethics of tourism and looks at theories of global justice and how these could be linked to tourism. Her chapter then goes on to examine how tourism can be used to bring about social justice. She describes a continuum of justice tourism, from responsible tourism at one end to transnational solidarity activism at the other. The chapter provides four case studies: tours offered by a human rights group; support for the Palestinians; the International Solidarity Movement; and a solidarity activist, Rachel Corrie. Throughout her contribution, Higgins-Desbiolles explores the ambiguities and difficulties of justice through tourism and concludes that global solidarity tourism can help change our ethical understandings.

We said at the beginning of this introduction that this book is located within the hopeful tourism scholarship paradigm. Being a hopeful scholar or a transformative advocate matters when taking on research in tourism, in that your position (whether it is based on anti-oppression, social justice, pro-woman, advocacy of emancipation or self-determination, or any other similar worldview) influences every aspect of the research process. Thinking about your research and those with whom you co-create that research (including your participants, co-researchers and your audiences) from a critical point of view sharpens your ethical approach to a project. Above all, taking on research as a hopeful scholar means that we all should consider the wider impacts of our research – whether we are an undergraduate or postgraduate student or a more established researcher and educator. We hope that this book will be of value to anyone who is thinking about, practising or using such tourism research. Of course there are gaps and omissions, as this volume is not intended as a comprehensive textbook but rather as a collection of explorations into tourism and inequality – that, after all, is the nature of any project – it is never and nor should it be complete. We urge you to read, learn, get engaged, get thinking and get active but above all, be hopeful for a more socially responsible future for tourism practice.

References

Ateljevic, I., Morgan, N. and Pritchard, A. (2007a) Editors' introduction: promoting an academy of hope in tourism enquiry. In: Ateljevic, I., Pritchard, A. and Morgan, N. (eds) *The Critical Turn in Tourism Studies: Innovative Research Methodologies.* Elsevier, Oxford, UK, pp. 1–10.

Ateljevic, I., Pritchard, A. and Morgan, N. (eds) (2007b) *The Critical Turn in Tourism Studies: Innovative Research Methodologies.* Elsevier, Oxford, UK.

Barry, B. (2005) *Why Social Justice Matters.* Polity Press, Cambridge, UK.

Botterill, D. and Klemm, M. (eds) (2006) Introduction: tourism and social inclusion. *Tourism, Culture and Communication* 6, 1–5.

Botterill, D. and Klemm, M. (2007) Editorial overview: special issue on tourism and social inclusion – part B. *Tourism, Culture & Communication* 7, 1–4.

Burns, P. and Novelli, M. (2008) *Tourism Development, Growth and Inequalities.* CAB International, Wallingford, UK.

Butler, R. and Parr, H. (1999) New geographies of illness, impairment and disability. In: Butler, R. and Parr, H. (eds) *Mind and Body Spaces: Geographies of Illness, Impairment and Disability.* Routledge, London, pp. 1–25.

Center for Universal Design (2010) http://www.design.ncsu.edu/cud/about_ud/udprinciplestext.htm (accessed 10 April 2010).

Critcher, C., Bramham, P. and Tomlinson, A. (eds) (1995) *Leisure Sociology: A Reader*. E & FN Spon, London.

Cushman, G., Veal, A.J. and Zuzanek, J. (eds) (2005) *Free Time and Leisure Participation: International Perspectives*. CAB International, Wallingford, UK.

de Kadt, E. (1979) *Tourism: Passport to Development?* Open University Press, Oxford, UK.

Hall, D. and Brown, F. (2006) *Tourism and Welfare: Ethics, Responsibility and Sustainable Well-Being*. CAB International, Wallingford, UK.

Harrison, D. (2001) Introduction. In: Harrison, D. (ed.) *Tourism in the Less Developed World: Issues and Cases*. CAB International, Wallingford, UK, pp. 1–22.

Haworth, T.A. and Veal, A.J. (eds) (2004) *Work and Leisure*. Routledge, London.

Hazel, N. (2005) Holidays for children and families in need: an exploration of the research and policy context for social tourism in the UK. *Children & Society* 19, 225–236.

Hilbrecht, M., Shaw, S.M., Delamere, F.M. and Havitz, M.E. (2008) Experiences, perspectives, and meanings of family vacations for children. *Leisure/Loisir* 32, 541–571.

Hughes, H. (1991) Holidays and the economically disadvantaged. *Tourism Management* 12, 193–196.

Kitchin, R. and Law, R. (2001) The socio-spatial construction of (in)accessible public toilets. *Urban Studies* 38, 287–298.

Klemm, M.S. and Kelsey, S. (2004) Ethnic groups and the British travel industry: servicing a minority? *Service Industries Journal* 24, 115–128.

Minnaert, L., Maitland, R. and Miller, G. (2006) Social tourism and its ethical foundations. *Tourism Culture & Communication* 7, 7–17.

Minnaert, L., Maitland, R. and Miller, G. (2009) Tourism and social policy: the value of social tourism. *Annals of Tourism Research* 36, 316–334.

Morgan, N. and Pritchard, A. (1999) *Power and Politics at the Seaside: The Development of Devon's Seaside Resorts in the Twentieth Century*. University of Exeter Press, Exeter, UK.

Peeters, P., Gossling, S. and Becken, S. (2006) Innovation towards sustainability: climate change and aviation. *International Journal of Innovation and Sustainable Development* 1, 184–200.

Pogge, T. (ed.) (2007) *Freedom from Poverty as a Human Right: Who Owes What to the Very Poor?* Oxford University Press, Oxford, UK.

Pritchard, A. and Morgan, N. (2000) Privileging the male gaze. Gendered tourism landscapes. *Annals of Tourism Research* 27, 884–905.

Ren, C., Pritchard, A. and Morgan, N. (In press). Constructing tourism research: A critical enquiry. *Annals of Tourism Research*.

Roberts, K. (2006) *Leisure in Contemporary Society*, 2nd edn. CAB International, Wallingford, UK.

Stephenson, M. (2006) Travel and the 'freedom of movement': racialised encounters and experiences among ethnic minority tourists in the EU. *Mobilities* 1, 285–306.

Walton, J.K. (ed.) (2005) *Tourism Histories: Representation, Identity and Conflict*. Channel View, Clevedon, UK.

1 Tourism, Disability and Mobility

Jennie Small and Simon Darcy

Introduction

In more economically developed countries, tourism is considered part of the modern experience with all people having the right to travel. None the less, there are many groups of people who do not take holidays or do not fully participate in the holiday experience for reasons such as low income, ethnicity, sexual orientation, gender, body size and disability. This chapter focuses on disability, in particular mobility, and argues that people with disabilities should expect the same rights to citizenship and the same quality of life as the non-disabled, which include the right to travel and participate in leisure activities (United Nations, 1993). Exclusion from full participation equates to social inequality. The United Nation's (2006) *Convention of the Rights of People with Disabilities* has been signed by all but a few nations and provides a philosophical agreement that people with disability should not be discriminated against in any areas of citizenship. However, how each nation state implements such a convention is left to its own discretion. A number of nations including the USA, Australia and the UK have taken a legislative approach to enshrining the principles of disability rights within their legal systems. A review of legislation can be a guide to examine the relative position of disability within tourism. The chapter commences with a general overview of disability demographics, different approaches to disability and the concepts required for an understanding of the disability experience. Using Australia as a case study, it reviews the implementation of the United Nations (UN) Convention through the 17-year history (1993–2008) of the *Disability Discrimination Act 1992*. An examination of complaint cases highlights the specific experiences of social inequality experienced by people with mobility disability.

Disability Demographics

Disability is a part of the diversity of human communities rather than a deviation from an objective norm. All communities contain individuals with disabilities with the World Health Organization (WHO) (1997) and the UN (2009b) estimating that an average 10% of the population have a disability. This equates to 650 million people with disabilities living in the world today. The World Health Organization forecasts that there will be one billion people with disabilities living in the world by 2050, an increase of 350 million. These figures are estimates based on disability statistics collected from the minority of nations who collect this information. World Bank statisticians recognize that: the operational definitions for collecting this information vary widely depending on whether from a census or a specific disability survey; there is a cultural context to collecting this information where self-identification of disability is problematic in developing nations; and the conceptualizations of disability are dynamic and evolving (Metts, 2004). Despite these caveats, there are significant numbers of people identified with disabilities in nation states with sizeable domestic and outbound tourism markets. There are major implications for the developing BRIC nations of Brazil, Russia, India and China. Figure 1.1 presents the best available disability statistics and proportions of people with disabilities in nation states where this information is collected.

The WHO's International Classification of Impairments, Disabilities and Handicap's (ICIDH) (1997, 2001) framework and the statistical data collection for the nation states identify that approximately half of all disabilities are identified as 'physical disabilities' that affect a person's activities of daily living including mobility, self-care and communication. The following discus-sion focuses on the mobility component of 'physical disabilities'. To develop a greater understanding of the definitions of physical disability and the mobility dimension of access (discussed in full later), see the *Australian Institute of Health and Welfare* paper, which presents a very clear articulation of this dimension of access (Wen and Fortune, 1999).

Within these estimates is a well understood nexus between the increasing numbers of seniors and the increasing rates of disability as people age over the lifespan. As Darcy and Dickson (2009) established, a 'whole-of-life approach' identifies that at any time 30% of the community has some form of disability or access need: this includes families with young children and those experiencing temporary disabling sporting injuries and other medical conditions. This is discussed later in relation to the argument for universal design.

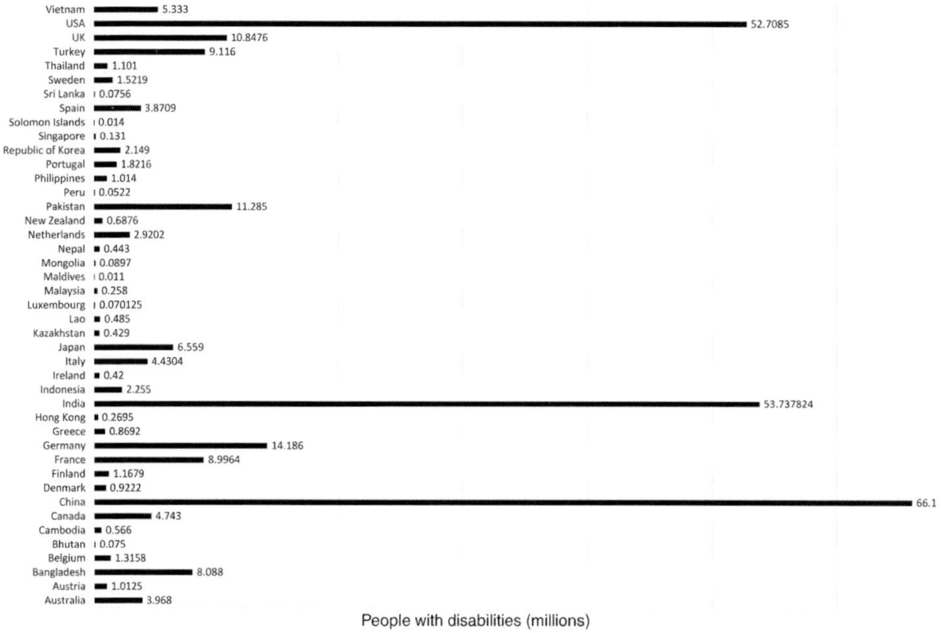

Vietnam ▬ 5.333
USA ▬▬▬▬▬▬▬▬▬▬▬▬▬▬▬▬▬▬▬▬▬▬▬▬▬▬▬▬▬▬▬▬▬▬▬▬▬ 52.7085
UK ▬▬ 10.8476
Turkey ▬ 9.116
Thailand ▪ 1.101
Sweden ▬ 1.5219
Sri Lanka ı 0.0756
Spain ▬ 3.8709
Solomon Islands ı 0.014
Singapore ı 0.131
Republic of Korea ▬ 2.149
Portugal ▪ 1.8216
Philippines ▪ 1.014
Peru ı 0.0522
Pakistan ▬▬ 11.285
New Zealand ▪ 0.6876
Netherlands ▬ 2.9202
Nepal ▪ 0.443
Mongolia ı 0.0897
Maldives ı 0.011
Malaysia ▪ 0.258
Luxembourg ı 0.070125
Lao ▪ 0.485
Kazakhstan ▪ 0.429
Japan ▬▬ 6.559
Italy ▬▬ 4.4304
Ireland ▪ 0.42
Indonesia ▪ 2.255
India ▬▬▬▬▬▬▬▬▬▬▬▬▬▬▬▬▬▬▬▬▬▬▬▬▬▬▬▬▬▬▬▬▬▬▬▬▬▬ 53.737824
Hong Kong ▪ 0.2695
Greece ▬ 0.8692
Germany ▬▬▬ 14.186
France ▬ 8.9964
Finland ▪ 1.1679
Denmark ▪ 0.9222
China ▬▬▬ 66.1
Canada ▬ 4.743
Cambodia ▪ 0.566
Bhutan ı 0.075
Belgium ▪ 1.3158
Bangladesh ▬ 8.088
Austria ▪ 1.0125
Australia ▬ 3.968

People with disabilities (millions)

Fig. 1.1. Nation states' disability populations (adapted from Darcy and Dickson, 2009).

Approaches to Disability: Medical Approach, Social Approach and Embodiment

Two broad approaches to an understanding of disability are the medical and the social approaches. The medical approach is founded on the 'personal tragedy theory of disability' (Oliver, 1996). Here the focus is on the individual and his/her impairment (functional/psychological losses). It is the fault of the individual because of, for example, blindness, deafness, paralysis, mental health issues etc. that they cannot participate fully in social life. This discourse views able-bodiedness as the social norm and, hence, excludes the 'abnormal' (people with impairments) from citizenship. For example, a tourist to Sydney who is a wheelchair user may not be able to access all public areas of Sydney Opera House. The medical model would explain this inability of access as related to the medical condition – paralysis. Social approaches to conceptualizing disability challenge that disability is the result of an individual's impairment, their 'personal tragedy' (Oliver, 1996) and instead conceptualize disability as the product of the disabling social environment and the prevailing attitudes (Barnes, 1996). The individual's embodiment (their impairment) is not the cause of the person's exclusion but rather it is the oppressive social environment and attitudes that produce disability (Oliver, 1996; Goggin and Newell, 2005).

The social approach places disability on the social, economic and political agendas. Returning to the example of the tourist in a wheelchair at Sydney Opera House, the reason that the tourist is prevented from accessing all of the public areas is that the building was constructed without lifts/ramps to all areas, as these were not considered socially necessary in the design of the building. The social approach recognizes that the 'normal activities and roles' are informed by the dominant medical model of disability and this socially constructed environment creates disabilities on top of the person's impairment. The social structures are a product of historical development and cannot be divorced from their cultural context. The cultural context involves both a material and ideological transformation of the way people with impairments are treated by society. As Gleeson (1999: 13) comments, society has in the past changed its attitude towards institutional oppression of other groups in society, such as women and indigenous groups, 'while continuing to ignore the material hardships and injustices to which they are subjected'.

The Union of Physically Impaired Against Segregation (UPAIS) was the first to articulate that the social model distinguishes between *impairment* and *disability* (UPAIS, 1975):

- impairment – part of an individual's embodiment; and
- disability – social disadvantage that is the product of the disabling social environment and attitudes.

'It is the disabling social practices that transform the individual's *impairment* (embodiment) into a disability' (Small and Darcy, 2010). To understand disability, one needs to focus on disabling barriers, hostile social attitudes and the material relations of power.

It can be seen that the social model is more emancipatory than the medical model. None the less, according to Shakespeare and Watson (2001), there are three central criticisms of the social model. These criticisms focus on impairment, the impairment/disability dualism and the issue of individual identity. They highlight that impairment and disability are not dichotomous but are different places and times on a continuum. They suggest that disability should not be reduced to just a medical condition or to just social barriers alone, as it is more complex. Our lived experiences are corporeal/embodied and we need to take both impairment and social structures into account. For example, the tourist with mobility impairment may suffer from fatigue related to the impairment. No matter how accessible a tourist site is for a tourist with an impairment, the fatigue will/can prevent the individual from full participation. Shakespeare and Watson conclude that an *embodied ontology* offers a starting point for disability studies to begin to develop a more adequate social theory of disability creating a space and place for embodiment within the social paradigm. 'In effect, the embodied ontology challenges the dichotomies of impairment/disability and illness/health and offers a model that intertwines structure and agency' (Small and Darcy, 2010).

Concepts Required for an Understanding of Disability

As identified in Fig. 1.2 below, we propose that an understanding of disability requires knowledge of four concepts: types or dimensions of disability; levels of support needs; access enablers; and universal design. These four concepts and their inter-dependence form the basis of a comprehension of disability and tourism and hence, what is known as *accessible tourism*. As Packer *et al.* (2006) suggest, there is a complex interplay between the individual, the environment and the tourism context, which demonstrates how people with disabilities can be excluded in tourism. At one or more of these interfaces, people can become marginalized through a series of structural constraints that may require a series of institutional responses to provide an enabling tourism environment (Darcy, 2002).

Relatively little research has empirically examined how these interfaces create social inequality with most research on disability and tourism limited to a focus on people with physical disabilities who require mobility access, for example Israeli's (2002) study, which identified some seven basic considerations for destination site accessibility for mobility. However, as identified by Packer *et al.*'s (2006) research, accessible tourism is more complex. To this end, Darcy (2002; 2009) identified impairment, independence, level of support needs and aids used as statistically significant determinants of a

person's likelihood to travel and how often they travelled. Studies by Burnett and Bender-Baker (2001) and Darcy (1998) on travel criteria of people with mobility disabilities found that the level of support needs was an important way to segment disability travel. Similarly, Bi *et al.* (2007) found that level of support needs and functional ability were major influences on tourists' perceptions of accessibility and attitudinal barriers to transport, accommodation, hospitality and attractions.

In summary, the literature suggests that the disability/dimensions of access, the support needs and the accessibility of the environment (enablers) are important to understanding the tourist experiences of people with disabilities. Each of these concepts is now considered prior to extending this understanding to universal design.

Disability and Dimensions of Access

Traditionally, disability has been largely understood through medical approaches in the definition, categorization and statistical collection of data on disability outlined by the WHO's ICIDH. As stated above, within these approaches there is a focus on the

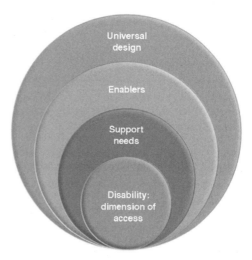

Fig. 1.2. Concepts for an understanding of disability (Small and Darcy, 2010).

disabling medical conditions of individuals (WHO, 2002b). Within the frameworks of classification, there are literally thousands of conditions that can be diagnosed for the individual's lack of ability. However, this type of information does not provide meaningful direction to creating enabling environments.

These shortcomings of the ICIDH have been recognized by many commentators including the UN Convention on the Rights of People with Disabilities (2006). Policy makers have attempted to provide a better categorization to understand the practical requirements of creating an enabling environment. For example, the way that disability is defined under national disability discrimination legislation focuses far more on the dimensions of disability as an outcome of their access needs. As such, the Australian *Disability Discrimination Act 1992*'s definition of disability aggregates major dimensions rather than focusing on individual conditions. In doing so, it identifies: physical (mobility); sensory (hearing and vision); intellectual; psychiatric; neurological; learning, physical disfigurement; and the presence in the body of disease-causing organisms. Darcy in interpreting the ICIDH-1 (World Health Organization, 1997) stated that the access needs of tourists with disabilities could be reduced to three dimensions of access: physical; sensory; and communication (Darcy, 1998). In subsequent research (Darcy, 2009), these dimensions of access were expanded to include:

- mobility;
- vision;
- hearing;
- cognitive/learning – involving issues of speech or understanding;
- mental health;
- sensitivities – including respiratory, food and chemical; and
- other.

The advantage of the above conceptualization is that the focus is on the provision of the broad dimensions for access to create enabling environments, as advocated by social approaches to disability (Oliver, 1990, 1996; Thomson, 1997; Thomas, 1999; Swain *et al.*, 2004; Thomas, 2007).

Level of Support Needs

Another factor that contributes to a greater understanding of disability is an individual's level of support requirements. Any individual has needs in everyday living. The level of support needs of individuals with mobility disabilities can be identified on a continuum. At one end of the continuum are those who live independently in the community with no support required while at the other extreme are those who require a high level of one-on-one support 24 h a day. The level of an individual's support needs directly affects their social participation. In disability statistics, this has been referred to as the relative 'severity' of a person's disability or their functional ability (WHO, 2002a). For the purposes of this chapter, this approach can be referred to as a 'medical' conceptualization that focuses on 'loss' experience and attributes this loss as the reason for reduced social participation. The level of support needs is generally described in the following terms: independent (no support needs); low; medium; high; very high (requires 24-h support).

Access Enablers

The discussion so far has focused on the intersection between disability and level of support needs and has shown the complexity of an understanding of disability. A further layer to this understanding can be found through the disability studies literature, which seeks to change disabling environments to enabling environments (Swain *et al.*, 2004) by focusing attention on the lived experience of people with disabilities and the barriers that they face in their everyday living. Access enablers for those with a mobility impairment can be conceptualized in three broad categories:

- Adaptive or assistive technology that maximizes the abilities of people with disabilities: this may include mobility equipment such as wheelchairs, walking frames etc.
- Environmental or structural enablers: these are well articulated through the access and mobility codes for building. In their most basic form, enablers require a continuous pathway for people with mobility impairment to experience environments seamlessly. Basic inclusions to enable mobility include ramps, lifts and accessible toilets.
- Attitudes/behaviour of others: a significant area of consideration goes beyond adaptive equipment and environmental enablers to challenge disabling attitudes towards people with disabilities. The literature on attitudes and behaviour is substantial with a number of applications in the tourism literature (Daruwalla and Darcy, 2005) in regard to attitudes to customer service and employment (van Lin *et al.*, 2001; Ross, 2004; Slonaker *et al.*, 2007).

Universal Design

Universal design is a paradigm that incorporates intergenerational and lifespan planning, recognizing the nexus between ageing, disability and the continuum of ability of people over their lifespan (Aslaksen *et al.*, 1997; Steinfeld and Shea, 2001). Universal design has been defined as:

> … the design of products and environments to be usable by all people, to the greatest extent possible, without the need for adaptation or specialized design…The intent of the universal design concept is to simplify life for everyone by making products, communications, and the built environment more usable by more people at little or no extra cost. The universal design concept targets all people of all ages, sizes and abilities.
>
> (Center for Universal Design, 2003)

Universal design is based on seven principles to facilitate equitable access across the lifespan (Preiser and Ostroff,

2001; Center for Universal Design, 2003, 2005):

- Principle 1: Equitable Use.
- Principle 2: Flexibility in Use.
- Principle 3: Simple and Intuitive Use.
- Principle 4: Perceptible Information.
- Principle 5: Tolerance for Error.
- Principle 6: Low Physical Effort.
- Principle 7: Size and Space for Approach and Use (Center for Universal Design, 2009).

The implication of this design approach is that access would become central to a design rather than an add-on for compliance reasons. As indicated in Fig. 1.3, it is not only those with access needs who benefit but all users as a universally designed environment considers occupational and safety issues, making it a safer environment for all. There has been a call for the tourism industry to adopt universal design principles as a foundation to achieving greater social sustainability (Rains, 2004; Walsh, 2004).

Figure 1.4 below illustrates a universally designed water playground with level access in Cairns, Queensland, that provides an equality of experience for children with or without mobility disabilities.

With this brief understanding of the underlying concepts that require consideration in understanding accessible tourism, the chapter now moves to examine tourism and disability in Australia.

Tourism and Disability in Australia

Australia is one of the few countries with national tourism statistics that provides a comparison between the tourism participation of the general population and people with disabilities. As outlined by Dwyer and Darcy (2008) and shown in Fig. 1.5, people with disabilities, when compared with the general population, travel at the same rate for day trips but at a much lower rate than the general population for overnight domestic travel (21% less) and international

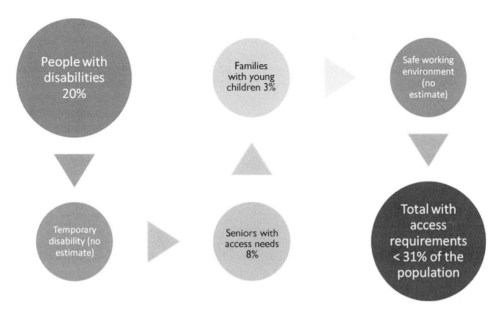

Fig. 1.3. Universal design beneficiaries (proportion of Australians) (Darcy and Dickson, 2009).

Fig. 1.4. Universal design water playground in Cairns, Queensland (©Darcy 2005, with permission).

travel (51% less). This is despite progress in the past 25 years in removing barriers in the transport, accommodation and attraction sectors. An explanation for the difference between the two groups in domestic and international travel is continued inequality in the provision of accessible air travel and hotel accommodation (Darcy *et al.*, 2008).

The level of social inequality is further exacerbated by the dimension of disability and access for the traveller. As Fig. 1.6 shows, people with impairments related to mental health, vision, speech, physical affecting arms and/or legs, hearing, general physical and acquired brain injury/stroke travel significantly less than the non-disabled. These figures are illuminating but

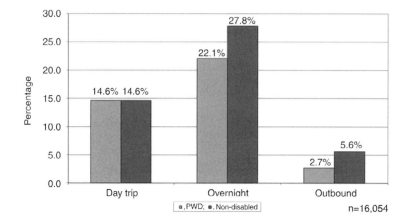

Fig. 1.5. Comparative travel patterns (Dwyer and Darcy, 2008).

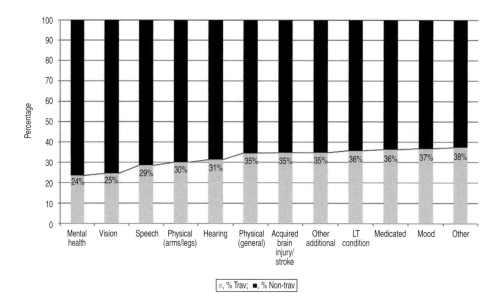

Fig. 1.6. Impairment by traveller (n=5741). From Darcy (2003), based on the 1998 Bureau of Tourism Research's Domestic Tourism Monitor.

do not provide an understanding of where tourism inequality exists.

People with disabilities do not cite their impairment as a reason for non-participation but instead a series of structural constraints (Darcy, 2003). This suggests the social construction of the tourism environment is the major deterrent to full tourism citizenship. However, the

tourism industry has a history of resistance to provide enabling environments and positive customer service initiatives (Daruwalla and Darcy, 2005), preferring to perceive that people with disability do not want to travel rather than question industry's preconceptions and lack of knowledge on how to assist tourists with a disability. These findings are supported by the complexity of constraints identified by Daniels *et al.* (2005) in analysing the 'travel tales' of people with disabilities.

A key finding of the research into the tourist experiences of people with a disability is that travel is a highly anxious experience (Darcy, 1998; Packer *et al.*, 2008):

> Travelling with a disability is a never ending nightmare, hell on Earth, indescribable, nerve wracking, stomach churning, unbelievably expensive experience [Tourist with a mobility impairment].
>
> (Darcy, 1998, p. 44)

The remainder of the chapter discusses the intersection between human rights, disability and tourism inequality and reviews the operation of the disability legislation to understand the ways in which people with mobility disabilities experience discrimination within the tourism sector.

Human Rights, Disability and Tourism Inequality

Central to the UN human rights declarations was the recognition that people with disabilities should enjoy the rights of citizenship of its signatory nations. The UN provides the foundation of citizenship through the international framework of human rights of which the UN's *Convention on the Rights of People with Disabilities* (2006) is the most recent addition. Each country operationalizes these rights under its own legislative and policy frameworks. Given the various UN conventions over the years, it is surprising that only 40 countries have introduced specific disability discrimination legislation (United Nations, 2009a). Table 1.1 shows a chronology of disability discrimination legislation for a sample of countries.

It is through these frameworks that governments resource and regulate their implementation of the UN Convention as a way to empower people with disabilities to achieve all their rights of citizenship. Yet, as Hutchison (1997: 3) notes, human rights is only part of establishing citizenship. Hutchison acknowledges that 'Rights and responsibility, empowerment, inclusion, and "getting a life" are all important' but 'citizenship is much more than each of these separate components added together ... It is a more tangible concept that includes all of these things, but something more. It is at the core of what it is to be human'.

The chapter now examines the framework that ensures equality of experience before the law of those with disabilities and the general population. It does so by reviewing the Australian context of implementing the UN Convention through the 17 years experience of having a disability discrimination legislation in place. In the first instance, the framework is reviewed so that the mechanisms for implementing the Disability Discrimination Act are understood. The remainder of the chapter then specifically examines the major areas of social inequality in tourism for people with mobility disabilities.

Table 1.1. National disability discrimination legislation.

Year	Country	Legislation
1990	USA	Americans with Disabilities Act
1990	China	The Law of People's Republic of China on the Protection of Disabled Persons
1992	Australia	Disability Discrimination Act
1995	UK	Disability Discrimination Act
1995	India	Persons with Disabilities (Equal Opportunities, Protection of Rights and Full Participation) Act
1996	Costa Rica	Law No. 7600 on Equality for Persons with Disabilities
1996	Hong Kong	Disability Discrimination Ordinance (1996)

Source: United Nations (2009a); UN ESCAP (2008).

Australian Human Rights Commission[1] and the *Disability Discrimination Act 1992*

Half of all complaint cases lodged to the Australian Human Rights Commission are based on *disability* discrimination. The *Disability Discrimination Act 1992 [Comm]* became the first Australian disability-specific human rights legislation where previously disability had been part of state-based antidiscrimination legislation together with gender, age and race. For a full explanation of the way that the Disability Discrimination Act operates across the cultural industries, see Darcy and Taylor (2009). The premise of the Disability Discrimination Act was that disability discrimination happens when a person with a disability is treated less fairly than someone without a disability. Discrimination can be direct or indirect. Direct discrimination occurs when the person with a disability is treated less favourably than a person without disability, in circumstances that are not materially different. An example would be a wheelchair user refused permission by the ticket seller to enter a particular tourist attraction because of their disability. Indirect discrimination occurs when a person with a disability is required to comply with a condition, to which the person cannot comply because of the disability, and is thus disadvantaged. An example would be when the wheelchair user is unable to access the tourist attraction because of a step at the entrance. Implicit in the Act is the expectation that, in both cases, *reasonable adjustments* should be made for the person with the disability to ensure the person is not treated less favourably than someone without a disability.

As Fig. 1.7 shows, there are five strategies used by the Disability Discrimination Act to achieve the objectives of the Act:

1. To eliminate, as far as possible, discrimination against persons on the ground of disability in the areas of: (i) work, accommodation, education, access to premises, clubs and sport; and (ii) the provision of goods, facilities, services and land; and (iii) existing laws; and (iv) the administration of Commonwealth laws and programs.

2. To ensure, as far as practicable, that persons with disabilities have the same rights to equality before the law as the rest of the community.

3. To promote recognition and acceptance within the community of the principle that persons with disabilities have the same fundamental rights as the rest of the community.

The strategies of education, public enquiries, Disability Action Plans, Disability Standards and complaint cases/Federal court actions are all used to challenge underlying institutional inequalities in Australian society and promote fuller participation in citizenship by people with disabilities (Jones and Basser Marks, 1999). Each of these strategies will now be examined to assess the level of engagement of the tourism sector.

Education

Central to the objectives of the Disability Discrimination Act is the ongoing education of the public about disability discrimination. While disability awareness training has taken place within organizations and regions, it has largely gone on without formal documentation and evaluation. One study which has tested the impact of disability awareness training in

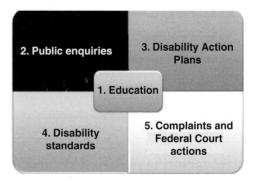

Fig. 1.7. Disability Discrimination Act strategies.

the tourism industry (Daruwalla and Darcy, 2005) has shown the positive impact of such training.

Public enquiries

The Australian Human Rights Commission has the power in the Disability Discrimination Act to call a public inquiry for matters or issues deemed to be a concern for many people in the community. This fulfils the role of a class action without the need for individuals formally to take an action. This power has been used only infrequently. Relevant to tourism, is the public inquiry into accessible taxis in NSW (Human Rights and Equal Opportunity Commission, 2002).

Disability Action Plans

Disability Action Plans seek to provide a strategic approach to identifying disabling practices and environments within organizations and provide an enabling outcome-based framework for addressing identified access issues. Disability Action Plans are voluntary for state and Commonwealth government although they were strongly recommended by the Human Rights and Equal Opportunity Commission, the Commonwealth Attorney General's Department and a number of state government departments. From mid-2009 there were 599 plans registered with the Australian Human Rights Commission (Australian Human Rights Commission, 2009a). Of the Commonwealth and state tourism authorities, only Tourism NSW (2000) has lodged a Disability Action Plan. As part of the Disability Action Plan strategies, all staff have completed a disability awareness-training programme (Daruwalla and Darcy, 2005). Tourism Victoria developed a draft document under the Disability Action Plan provisions and circulated it for comment but did not release it publicly (Tourism Victoria, 2007). Only one specific tourism-related business in the hospitality sector

lodged a Disability Action Plan. It did so as a means to protect the organization from a complaint case while building work was planned (Access Solutions, 2008). The transport sector has been the most active in developing Disability Action Plans following the development of a disability standard in accessible public transport by the Attorney General's Department.

Disability Standards

The Disability Discrimination Act provides the power for the Attorney General to instigate research for consultation concerning the development of Disability Standards. The premise was that Disability Standards provide a higher level of certainty for developers and operators and, hence, reduce delays and costs that may arise from the complaints system (Human Rights and Equal Opportunity Commission, 1993). Since the inception of the Disability Discrimination Act, two standards have been progressed. First, the Disability Standard for Accessible Public Transport (Commonwealth Attorney General's Department, 2001a, 2001b). This Disability Standard has recently undergone a 5-year review, which has cautiously shown a steady improvement in the accessibility of public transport albeit with variations between the government and private sector providers. The submissions to the inquiry showed air travel and charter operations still lag behind and create significant disadvantage for people (including tourists) with disabilities. More recently, there have been prolonged negotiations for the Draft Disability Standard for Access to Premises to harmonize the Building Codes of Australia and the Disability Discrimination Act (Commonwealth Attorney General's Department, 2009a, 2009b). The Australian Buildings Codes Board discussion paper outlined the issues surrounding the DDA, the Building Codes of Australia review, and AS1428 (Australian Building Codes Board, 2001). A delay of some 7 years from the original discussion paper to the Draft of these Disability Standards was partly related to the industry resistance to the provisions about the proportion of accessible class 3 hotel and motel accommodation (Innes, 2006; House of Representatives Standing Committee on Legal and Constitutional Affairs, 2009). A major area of contention is the make-up of the Australian Building Codes Board where the disability perspective is cast as an outsider, as there is no representative on the board itself or on the Building Codes Committee. Hence, decision-making power is controlled by the building industry rather than having direct input from the disability sector or the Australian Human Rights Commission.

Complaints and Federal Court Actions

By far the main strategy used by people with disabilities to redress their discrimination is complaint cases and Federal court actions. Under the Disability Discrimination Act, people with a disability have the right of complaint when they believe they have been discriminated against. Ninety five per cent of complaints brought to the Human Rights and Equal Opportunity Commission (now known as the Australian Human Rights Commission) are dealt with through staff investigation and conciliation (Hastings, 1995, 1997). Depending on the nature of the complaint, conciliation may result in: payment of damages; job reinstatement or job promotion; an apology; changes in policies or practices; and/or some other outcome. If complaints cannot be resolved through conciliation then the people with disabilities can ask for the complaint to go to a Human Rights and Equal Opportunity Commission hearing (pre-2000) or have the complaint heard by the Federal Court of Australia (post-2000). The advantage of a Federal court decision is that it is binding on the parties, whereas a Human Rights and Equal Opportunity Commission/Australian Human Rights Commission ruling is not (Hastings, 1995). As Thornton (2000) believes, a weakness of the

complaint system is the confidentiality of the process that individualizes the outcomes rather than contributing towards the challenging of the social norms of discrimination through the public reporting of outcomes. *Brandy vs Human Rights and Equal Opportunity Commission* (1995 HCA PLPR 19) determined that it was unconstitutional for the Human Rights and Equal Opportunity Commission formally to hear complaints and make binding decisions. Therefore, all complaints requiring an enforceable, legally binding and public decision must be heard by the Federal Court of Australia. Unfortunately, the Federal court is also a cost jurisdiction where any individual bringing a court action may not only have their own costs of representation to bear but also have costs of the other party awarded against them. There has been a drop in the number of Federal court actions under the Disability Discrimination Act since the cost jurisdiction was introduced.

Darcy and Taylor (2009) reviewed the implementation of the Disability Discrimination Act since 1993 when over 7000 complaint cases had been lodged (an average of 575 per year). Just under half of the complaints cases each year are for employment, followed by goods/services/facilities (25%), and access to premises (7%) (Human Rights and Equal Opportunity Commission, 2007). Only the summaries of a small number (421) of complaints are made publicly available because of confidentiality agreements. As Table 1.2 shows, when the sectoral areas were analysed, tourism and hospitality accounted for 27% of all cases. Of these, airlines attracted the most cases followed by accommodation and hospitality.

Through examining complaints, one can understand how tourists with mobility disability experience social inequality. It is recognized that these tourists might also have additional impairments that require further provisions for accessibility. The complaints included below are those specifically related to mobility disability and the tourist experience. An examination of the complaint case outcomes identifies

Table 1.2. Complaint cases.

Sector	Frequency	Percentage
Sport or recreation	27	6.5
The arts/leisure	44	10.6
Tourism	73	17.6
Hospitality/clubs	41	9.9
Retail/supermarkets	30	7.2
Local and Commonwealth government	62	14.9
Other	138	33.3
Total	415	100.0

Source: Darcy and Taylor (2009).

that discrimination occurs in many sectors of the tourism industry: transport; accommodation; tourist attractions; and tours (Australian Human Rights Commission, 2009b). In analysing the complaint cases of those with a mobility disability, three themes emerge:

- lack of accessible infrastructure;
- inadequate information provision; and
- lack of inclusive customer service provisions.

Although not included below, local residents' complaints to the Human Rights and Equal Opportunity Commission, which relate to their experiences in their home region, may also be relevant to those who visit this region. For example, complaints about local restaurants, local buses and trains, railway stations, parking spaces, shopping centres, cinemas, theatres, festivals, swimming pools, beaches, banks, ATMs, footpaths, etc., are also relevant to the tourist with a mobility disability who visits these sites and wants to use these facilities and services. No doubt there are many complaints by tourists with a mobility disability that have not been formally submitted because of a number of factors including the temporary nature of visitation as well as the time, money and emotional resources required to submit and see a complaint through to its end. All complaints' summaries below are direct quotes from the Australian Human Rights Commission complaint case register (2009b).

Lack of accessible infrastructure

Since tourism requires travel and a stay of at least one night away from home, accessibility of transport and accommodation are *essential* for tourism to take place. At the destination, accessible public transport, accessible day trips and tours, and accessible tourist attractions and restaurants are required to ensure tourists with a mobility disability can fully participate in the tourist experience. The following complaints relate to inclusion of steps instead of ramps, height of counters, inaccessible toilet facilities, a heavy door to be opened, and narrow doorways and corridors.

- A man with a mobility impairment complained that a budget airline's terminal building was inaccessible because the entrance was by steps with no ramp access is *(sic)* provided. The complaint was settled when the airline agreed to install ramps and review other access features (2001, transport).
- A man who uses a wheelchair complained that airline club lounge facilities were inaccessible. The complaint was settled with an agreement to include a section of the reception desk at a lower height and to install tables with a variety of heights within the club (2001, transport).
- A woman with a mobility impairment complained that a caravan park did not have accessible toilet facilities. The complaint was settled when the park advised that accessible facilities were

being constructed (2002, access to premises).

- A man whose wife uses a wheelchair complained that on a holiday cruise they had booked, although initial boarding and cabin arrangement were accessible, access had been impossible or unsafe at ports along the way. The complaint was settled with payment of over $4000 to refund fares and other expenses, an apology and an agreement for the company's disability access officer to meet with the complainants to discuss services and procedures for passengers with disabilities (2006, transport).

- A woman who uses a wheelchair complained that on a visit to Sydney she had been unable to access a coffee shop as both entrances had steps. The respondent indicated that there were difficulties with providing access as the premises had heritage value, but agreed to raise the matter with the Australian Heritage Commission (which provides information on upgrading heritage premises for access). The complaint was settled with an agreement to provide ramp access at one of the entrances (2004, access to premises).

- A man who has a mobility impairment resulting from childhood polio complained that a new museum building had a step in the path from the disability parking spaces, and heavy manual glass entrance doors. This meant he could not enter the building unless another member of the public came along and held the doors open. The respondent agreed, as a short-term measure, to re-site the disability parking to a position adjacent to a lift and accessible entrance on the lower level of the building. As a longer term solution, the respondent agreed to find funds to alter the mechanism of the main entry doors and replace them with automatic sliding doors (2001, access to premises).

- A man who uses a wheelchair for mobility complained of restricted wheelchair accessibility on a rail operator's long-distance services because of dimensions

of doors, corridors and toilet doors. In conciliation, the complainant accepted undertakings that while it would not be feasible to modify the carriages concerned to provide access as desired, the operator provided a narrow wheelchair that did allow access to the train; new carriages would be accessible; and the operator would consult with the complainant on any feasible minor modifications (2000, transport).

- A woman lodged a complaint against a state railway authority regarding lack of accessible toilets on stations throughout that state. The rail authority advised that there was a plan in place to make stations accessible by 2020 in accord with proposed transport standards and that the station nearest the complainant's home, a main transit station, was scheduled for conversion by July 1997, although this plan did not include an accessible toilet. The complainant proposed the installation of portable toilets as an interim step but was advised this was impracticable because of the need to remove waste, security issues and so on. In December 1996, the rail authority agreed to build a permanent accessible toilet within the station. This was completed in early March 1997 and the complainant confirmed that she was satisfied with the outcome (1997, transport).

- A woman who uses a wheelchair complained that a wildlife viewing centre had been permitted to move from an accessible to an inaccessible venue. The matter was settled with payment of financial compensation and agreement by the venue to install suitable access (2004, goods, services and facilities).

'Accessible' infrastructure if poorly constructed is not accessible.

- A woman who uses a wheelchair complained that her local council, which had approved construction of a motel with disability access, had failed to note on final inspection that a number of features of the accessible suite were not in fact accessible to people who use wheelchairs and that a disabled parking space was lacking. The matter was settled when the council advised that rectification of the motel access features had been arranged, and that staff had increased their vigilance on access issues (2000, access to premises).

Inadequate information provision

For tourists with a mobility disability, much time and effort goes into the planning of a holiday. The tourism industry needs to provide accurate information to enable appropriate decisions to be made. As stated by Small and Darcy (2010), 'The general accessibility of properties, the associated facilities and the specific criteria of rooms and bathrooms require detailed and accurate information provision, communication and marketing'. Unfortunately, 'research has consistently shown that information about tourism accommodation was not available, was not provided accurately when requested or was misunderstood by the managers and staff interacting with guests' (Murray and Sproats, 1990; Gallagher and Hull, 1996; Upchurch and Seo, 1996; Turco *et al.*, 1998; Ray and Ryder, 2003; Darcy, 2004; Daniels *et al.*, 2005; Small and Darcy, 2010). The following complaints stem from the provision of inaccurate information.

- A woman whose husband has had both legs amputated complained that a harbour cruise that the couple had booked was not wheelchair accessible without assistance, although she had been assured when booking that access was provided. The complaint was settled when the operator agreed to update its website and other information to ensure that accurate information was provided on the requirements for access to its boats (2003, goods, services and facilities).
- A woman who uses a wheelchair complained that a holiday room for herself and her family was not accessible despite assurances when booking. There was a step at the door and the

bathroom was not wheelchair accessible. The respondent advised that it had not been clear from the booking request that fully independent access was required. The complaint was settled with an apology, an agreement to purchase a portable ramp and payment of compensation (2002, accommodation).

- A woman who uses a wheelchair complained that after she had booked a hotel room online with a request for an accessible room, she had been advised there were in fact six steps at the hotel entrance. The complaint was settled when the hotel agreed to change its online information to indicate the lack of independent access and to offer staff assistance with access where required (2004, accommodation).

Customer service attitude

Tourism is a service-based industry that needs to understand that people with disabilities must be treated equally before the law. Customer service issues have been highlighted in a number of complaint cases. Complaints provide an insight into the need for disability awareness training for customer service staff. In some instances the discrimination toward people with disabilities is direct and conscionable. In other cases it involves less favourable treatment where a person with a disability is not treated in the same manner as the non-disabled.

- A man who uses a wheelchair complained that he had been refused travel by an airline unless accompanied by a carer, although he had previously flown alone with no problems. The complaint was settled when the airline agreed to provide a letter confirming the complainant could travel independently (2005, transport).
- A man who uses a manual wheelchair complained that an airline had advised that he would not be able to travel on certain flights. The complaint was

settled when the airline apologised and advised that its information systems had been improved to make clearer to staff what limitations there were on its ability to carry some powered chairs and not on folding manual chairs (2007, public transport).

- The daughter of a woman who has had a stroke and uses a wheelchair complained that she had been discriminated against on the basis of the mother's disability when she booked cabins on a cruise boat. Only outside cabins, which were higher priced, were accessible, and there were also access problems with an associated tour. After a conciliation conference the complaint was settled with an agreement to reimburse the cost of the tour and improve accessibility information (2001, goods, services and facilities).
- A man who uses a wheelchair complained that he had been discriminated against by being charged an additional fee for use of the accessible accommodation at some holiday cottages. The matter was settled without admission of liability when the new owners of the cottages advised that no such additional fee would be charged by them (1995, accommodation).

Conclusion

Social inclusion occurs when all individuals can participate fully in tourism. As the above discussion indicates, there are many tourists, including those with a mobility disability, who are excluded from participating, or from participating fully, in tourism as a consequence of lack of accessible infrastructure, poorly constructed 'accessible' infrastructure, inadequate information provision and/or lack of inclusive customer service provisions. This chapter has focused on Australia, a country with a 17-year history of disability discrimination legislation. While the discussion is specific to Australia, there are universal themes of social exclusion that

are mirrored across the other more economically developed countries and also the less economically developed countries. As other marginalized groups like women, indigenous people and homosexuals have found, formal declarations, and even legislation, do not in themselves guarantee social justice or equality. Rather, there is the requirement for political will, enforcement, education and changes in social and cultural attitudes and behaviour. This is not a simple task or a straightforward process and is often not fully recognized or understood by many of the organizations that are, or should be, involved and affected.

Questions

1. Think of a tourism attraction in your home town. What are the mobility provisions for access? How could the attraction adopt universal design principles to achieve greater social sustainability?

2. Research the website of the attraction and its printed promotional material. What information is provided on mobility access? Is there adequate information for a person with a mobility disability to consider visitation?

3. Access the archives of your local newspaper and search on the words (*disabled*, or *disability and access*). Select an article that describes a significant access issue that has occurred in your local area. What were the major areas of contention? Has there been an outcome to this issue?

Learning Activity – Local Council Access Committee

Contact your local Council and determine whether the Council has an *Access Committee* of professionals who consider access-related matters or a committee of local people with disabilities who perform a role. If it does, organize to attend the next Access Committee meeting. Go prepared to find out what provisions (e.g. accessible parking, toilets, etc.) are available for supporting accessible tourism environments in your area. Find out who the members of the access committee are and how they can support your efforts to be inclusive in planning the local environments through networks, service providers, information etc. Make enquiries as to how the information discussed in the Access Committee gets incorporated and implemented within Council decisions, policies and procedures. Provide an example of a successful accessible environment outcome – provide photos where appropriate.

If Council does not have an Access Committee, identify who within Council has the major responsibilities for dealing with access-related issues. Interview them about how access-related issues are incorporated into Council decisions, policies and procedures (adapted from Darcy and Daruwalla, 2002).

Notes

[1]Previously known as the Human Rights and Equal Opportunity Commission (HREOC).

References

Access Solutions (2008) Coast Hotel Coffs Harbour: Disability Action Plan For completion by December 2010. http://www.hreoc.gov.au/disability_rights/action_plans/Register/register.html

Aslaksen, F., Bergh, S., Bringa, O.R. and Heggem, E.K. (1997) *Universal Design: Planning and Design for All.* The Norwegian State Council on Disability, Oslo.

Australian Building Codes Board (2001) Disability Discrimination Act (DDA) – Disability Standard on Access to Premises Directions Report. Australian Building Codes Board, Canberra.

Australian Human Rights Commission (2009a) Disability Action Plan Register. Australian Human Rights Commission. http://www.hreoc.gov.au/disability_rights/action_plans/Register/register.html (accessed 20 September 2009).

Australian Human Rights Commission (2009b) Disability Discrimination Act Complaints Cases Register and Decisions. http://www.hreoc.gov.au/disability_rights/decisions/decisions.html (accessed 7 November 2009).

Barnes, C. (1996) Theories of disability and the origins of the oppression of disabled people in western society. In: Barton, L. (ed.) *Disability and Society: Emerging Issues and Insights.* Longman, New York, pp. 40–59.

Bi, Y., Card, J.A. and Cole, S.T. (2007) Accessibility and attitudinal barriers encountered by Chinese travellers with physical disabilities. *International Journal of Tourism Research* 9, 205–216.

Burnett, J.J. and Bender-Baker, H. (2001) Assessing the travel-related behaviors of the mobility-disabled consumer. *Journal of Travel Research* 40, 4–11.

Center for Universal Design (2003) Universal Design Principles. http://www.design.ncsu.edu/cud/about_ud/about_ud.htm (accessed 13 September 2004).

Center for Universal Design (2005) Universal Design Principles. http://www.design.ncsu.edu/cud/about_ud/about_ud.htm (accessed 20 May 2009).

Center for Universal Design (2009) Universal Design Principles. http://www.design.ncsu.edu/cud/about_ud/about_ud.htm (accessed 20 May 2009).

Commonwealth Attorney General's Department (2001a) *Disability Standards for Accessible Public Transport.* AGPS, Canberra.

Commonwealth Attorney General's Department (2001b) *Disability Standards for Accessible Public Transport Guidelines.* AGPS, Canberra.

Commonwealth Attorney General's Department (2009a) Draft Disability (Access to Premises – Buildings) Standards 2009. http://www.ag.gov.au/premisesstandards (accessed 2 December 2008).

Commonwealth Attorney General's Department (2009b) Disability (Access to Premises – Buildings) Standards Guidelines 2009. http://www.ag.gov.au/premisesstandards (accessed 2 December 2008).

Daniels, M.J., Drogin Rodgers, E.B. and Wiggins, B.P. (2005) 'Travel tales': an interpretive analysis of constraints and negotiations to pleasure travel as experienced by persons with physical disabilities. *Tourism Management* 26, 919–930.

Darcy, S. (1998) *Anxiety to Access: Tourism Patterns and Experiences of New South Wales People with a Physical Disability*. Tourism New South Wales, Sydney.

Darcy, S. (2002) Marginalised participation: physical disability, high support needs and tourism. *Journal of Hospitality and Tourism Management* 9, 61–72.

Darcy, S. (2003) Disabling journeys: the tourism patterns of people with impairments in Australia. Paper presented at the Riding the Wave of Tourism and Hospitality Research, CAUTHE – Southern Cross University, Lismore, 5–8 February.

Darcy, S. (2004) Disabling journeys: the social relations of tourism for people with impairments in Australia – an analysis of government tourism authorities and accommodation sector practices and discourses. Forthcoming Ph.D., University of Technology, Sydney, Sydney. http://epress.lib.uts.edu.au/dspace/handle/2100/260.

Darcy, S. (2009) Inherent complexity: disability, accessible tourism and accommodation information preferences. *Tourism Management*. Published online doi:10.1016/j.tourman.2009.08.010.

Darcy, S. and Daruwalla, P.S. (2002) Inclusive special event planning for people with disabilities. In Harris, R. and Allen, J. (eds) *Regional Event Management Handbook*. The Australian Centre for Event Management (UTS) and the Department of Industry, Science and Resources, Sydney, pp. 91–103.

Darcy, S. and Dickson, T. (2009) A whole-of-life approach to tourism: the case for accessible tourism experiences. *Journal of Hospitality and Tourism Management* 16, 32–44.

Darcy, S. and Taylor, T. (2009) Disability citizenship: An Australian human rights analysis of the cultural industries. *Leisure Studies* 28, 419–441.

Darcy, S., Cameron, B., Dwyer, L., Taylor, T., Wong, E. and Thomson, A. (2008) Technical report 90064: Visitor accessibility in urban centres. http://www.crctourism.com.au/BookShop/BookDetail.aspx?d=626.

Daruwalla, P.S. and Darcy, S. (2005) Personal and societal attitudes to disability. *Annals of Tourism Research* 32, 549–570.

Dwyer, L. and Darcy, S. (2008) Chapter 4 – Economic contribution of disability to tourism in Australia. In Darcy, S., Cameron, B., Dwyer, L., Taylor, T., Wong, E. and Thomson, A. (eds) Technical Report 90040: Visitor accessibility in urban centres. Sustainable Tourism Cooperative Research Centre, Gold Coast, pp. 15–21.

Gallagher, J.M. and Hull, A.H. (1996) Cruise ship accommodations for passengers with physical limitations due to disability or age. *American Journal of Occupational Therapy* 50, 685–687.

Gleeson, B. (1999) *Geographies of Disability*. Routledge, London.

Goggin, G. and Newell, C. (2005) *Disability in Australia: Exposing a Social Apartheid*. University of New South Wales Press, Sydney.

Hastings, E. (1995) *Clarification of High Court decision about the enforcement of HREOC determinations*. HREOC, Sydney.

Hastings, E. (1997) *FounDDAtions: Reflections on the First Five Years of the Disability Discrimination Act in Australia*. Human Rights and Equal Opportunity Commission, Sydney.

House of Representatives Standing Committee on Legal and Constitutional Affairs (2009) Access All Areas: Report of the Inquiry into Draft Disability (Access to Premises – Buildings) Standards. http://www.aph.gov.au/house/committee/laca/disabilitystandards/report.htm

Human Rights and Equal Opportunity Commission (1993, 1 December 2001) Issues Paper: Disability Standards under the Disability Discrimination Act. www.hreoc.gov.au/disability_rights/standards/issues93.htm (accessed 23 December 2001).

Human Rights and Equal Opportunity Commission (2002) Report: Inquiry into the NSW wheelchair accessible taxi service. www.hreoc.gov.au/disability_rights/inquiries/taxi/direction.htm

Human Rights and Equal Opportunity Commission (2007) Annual Report. Human Rights and Equal Opportunity Commission, Sydney.

Hutchison, P. (1997) Citizenship – Setting the Scene (Keynote Address). Paper presented at the Citizenship … beyond Disability Conference, Brisbane, 10–12 October, pp. 3–17.

Innes, G. (2006) Building access and no holiday for the disabled, Website, *The Daily Telegraph*, 21 January.

Israeli, A. (2002) A preliminary investigation of the importance of site accessibility factor for disabled tourists. *Journal of Travel Research* 41, 101–104.

Jones, M. and Basser Marks, L.A. (1999) Disability rights and law in Australia. In Jones, M. and Basser Marks, L.A. (eds) *Disability, Divers-ability and Legal Change*. Kluwer Law International, London, pp. 189–208.

Metts, R. (2004) Disability and Development. Background Paper prepared for the Disability and Development Research Agenda Meeting. Report to the World Bank, Washington, DC.

Murray, M. and Sproats, J. (1990) The disabled traveller: tourism and disability in Australia. *Journal of Tourism Studies* 1, 9–14.

Oliver, M. (1990) *The Politics of Disablement*. Macmillan, Houndmills, Basingstoke.

Oliver, M. (1996) *Understanding Disability: From Theory to Practice*. Macmillan, Houndmills, Basingstoke.

Packer, T., McKercher, B. and Yau, M. (2006) Understanding the complex interplay between tourism, disability and environmental contexts. FINADAPT Working Paper 11. Finnish Environment Institute, Helsinki.

Packer, T., Small, J. and Darcy, S. (2008) *Technical Report 90044: Tourist experiences of individuals with vision impairment*. Sustainable Tourism Cooperative Research Centre, Gold Coast, Queensland, Australia.

Preiser, W.F.E. and Ostroff, E. (2001) *Universal Design Handbook*. McGraw-Hill, New York.

Rains, S. (2004) Universal design and the international travel & hospitality industry. Paper presented at the Designing for the 21st Century III, Rio de Janeiro, 7–12 December.

Ray, N.M. and Ryder, M.E. (2003) 'Ebilities' tourism: an exploratory discussion of the travel needs and motivations of the mobility-disabled. *Tourism Management* 24, 57–72.

Ross, G.F. (2004) Ethics, trust and expectations regarding the treatment of disabled staff within a tourism/hospitality industry context. *International Journal of Hospitality Management* 23, 523–544.

Shakespeare, T. and Watson, N. (2001) The social model of disability: an outdated ideology? In Barnartt, S.N. and Mandell Altman, B. (eds) *Exploring Theories and Expanding Methodologies*. JAI Press, Stamford, CT, Vol. 2, pp. 9–28.

Slonaker, W.M., Wendt, A.C. and Baker, B. (2007) Employment discrimination in the restaurant industry. *Cornell Hotel and Restaurant Administration Quarterly* 48, 46–58. doi: 10.1177/0010880406297591.

Small, J. and Darcy, S. (2010) Understanding tourist experience through embodiment: the contribution of critical tourism and disability studies. In Buhalis, D., Darcy, S. and Ambrose, I. (eds) *Accessible Tourism: Concepts and Issues*. Channel View, Clevedon, pp. 1–25.

Steinfeld, E. and Shea, S.M. (2001) Fair housing: toward universal design in multifamily housing. In: Preiser, W.F.E. and Ostroff, E. (eds) *Universal Design Handbook*. McGraw-Hill, New York, pp. 35.31–35.13.

Swain, J., Finkelstein, V., French, S. and Oliver, M. (2004) *Disabling Barriers – Enabling Environments*, 3rd edn. Sage, London.

Thomas, C. (1999) *Female Forms: Experiencing and Understanding Disability*. Open University Press, Buckingham.

Thomas, C. (2007) *Sociologies of Disability and Illness: Contested Ideas in Disability Studies and Medical Sociology*. Palgrave Macmillan, Houndmills, Basingstoke.

Thomson, R.G. (1997) *Extraordinary Bodies: Figuring Physical Disability in American Culture and Literature*. Columbia University Press, New York.

Thornton, M. (2000) Neo-liberalism, discrimination and the politics of resentment. In Jones, M. and Marks, L.A.B. (eds) *Explorations on Law and Disability in Australia*. Federation Press, Leichhardt, NSW, pp. 8–27.

Tourism New South Wales. (2000) *Disability Action Plan: 1 January 2000 to 31 December 2002*. Tourism New South Wales, Sydney.

Tourism Victoria. (2007) *DRAFT – Victorian Accessible Tourism Plan*. Tourism Victoria. http://www.tourism.vic.gov.au/images/assets/All_TXT/VicAccessibleTourismPlanAppendix1-2007Draft.txt

Turco, D.M., Stumbo, N. and Garncarz, J. (1998) Tourism constraints – people with disabilities. *Parks and Recreation Journal* 33, 78–84.

UN ESCAP (2008) Disability at a glance: a Profile of 28 Countries and Areas in Asia and the Pacific, Vol. 2002. http://www.unescap.org/esid/psis/disability

United Nations (1993) *Standard Rules on the Equalization of Opportunities for Persons with Disabilities (General Assembly resolution 48/96)*. United Nations, Geneva.

United Nations (2006) Convention on the Rights of Persons with Disabilities, New York. http://www.un.org/esa/socdev/enable/rights/convtexte.htm: United Nations General Assembly A/61/611, 6 December 2006.

United Nations (2009a) Enable. http://www.un.org/disabilities/, 2 June 2009.

United Nations (2009b) Fact Sheet on Persons with Disabilities (Media Release). http://www.un.org/disabilities/default.asp?id=18 (5 January 2009).

UPAIS (1975) *Fundamental Principles of Disability*. Union of Physically Impaired Against Segregation and The Disability Alliance, London.

Upchurch, R.S. and Seo, J.W. (1996) Civic responsibility and market positioning: complying with the Americans with Disabilities Act. *Facilities* 14(5/6).

van Lin, M., Prins, R. and Zwinkels, W. (2001) The employment situation of disabled persons in the EU. © EIM Zoetermeer, Commissioned by DG Employment and Social Affairs.

Walsh, C.J. (2004) Rio de Janeiro Declaration on Sustainable Social Development, Disability & Ageing. Paper presented at the Designing for the 21st Century III – an international conference on universal design, Rio de Janeiro, 7–12 December.

Wen, X. and Fortune, N. (1999) *The Definition and Prevalence of Physical Disability in Australia.* Australian Institute of Health and Welfare, Canberra.

World Health Organization (1997) *International Classification of Impairments, Disabilities and Handicaps (ICIDH).* World Health Organization, Geneva.

World Health Organization (2001) *International Classification of Functioning, Disability and Health (ICIDH-2).* World Health Organization, Geneva.

World Health Organization (2002a) *ICF CHECKLIST: Version 2.1a, Clinician Form for International Classification of Functioning, Disability and Health.* World Health Organization, Geneva.

World Health Organization (2002b) *Towards a Common Language for Functioning, Disability and Health – ICF.* World Health Organization, Geneva.

2 Tourism and Visual Impairment

Victoria Richards, Nigel Morgan, Annette Pritchard and Diane Sedgley

Introduction

Disability is a neglected subject within tourism enquiry and studies that examine the travel-related experiences of people with visual impairment (and those of their families and friends who might travel with them) are even more scarce, with some notable exceptions (e.g. Small *et al.*, 2007; Richards *et al.*, in press; Darcy and Small, this volume). An estimated 314 million people worldwide (Box 2.1) live with low vision and blindness (http://www.vision2020.org) and a moral imperative exists to explore the barriers that prevent participation in tourism and to understand the positive impact tourism experiences can have on an individual's emotional and physical well-being, self-esteem, self-confidence, quality of life, identity and social inclusion. As Tourism for All UK (2009) notes:

> Tourism is important to our lives, giving us something to look forward to, time to enjoy our families, a chance for adventure, or perhaps some time to ourselves, to recover, and acquire memories of happy times. In the past, some of us have encountered barriers to our participation in tourism – those with disabilities, older people, carers of young people or disabled or older relatives ...

This chapter discusses the tourism experiences of visually impaired individuals and explores the positive role tourism can play in their lives. Taking research undertaken in the UK to illustrate the argument, it also outlines the key barriers to participation in tourism for individuals with visual impairment. These barriers are discussed as:

- individual barriers (emotional, psychological, (in)dependence);
- social barriers (awareness, staff and decision makers);
- environmental barriers (physical access, accessible information, transport).

The chapter begins by briefly discussing the wider tourism and disability context before

---

Box 2.1. Global visual impairment facts.

An estimated 314 million people worldwide live with low vision or blindness. Of these, 45 million are blind and 269 have low vision.

- 145 million people have low vision problems, which could be rectified by eye glasses;
- 90% of blind people live in low income countries;
- 80% of low vision problems are correctable or preventable;
- two-thirds of people who are blind or have low vision are women;
- without effective intervention, the numbers of people who suffer from blindness is expected to increase by 76 million worldwide by 2020.

Source: http://www.vision2020.org

---

focusing particularly on the tourism requirements of individuals with visual impairment. We take a person-centred focus in the chapter and explain how it is essential to appreciate a visually impaired person's life journey in order to understand their tourism experiences and requirements. For example, a person who has been blind from birth has a very different experience with visual impairment than someone who becomes blind later in life. Finally, we attempt to raise awareness of the needs and citizenship rights of visually impaired people. Throughout the chapter we use a variety of terms to describe people with no or low vision including 'blind', 'partially sighted', 'vision and visually impaired' and 'people with sight problems' (uncorrectable vision), as these terms are used interchangeably by the statutory and voluntary sectors. It is important to underline at the outset, however, that our emphasis is firmly on the necessity for the travel and tourism sectors to treat people as individuals rather than as a homogeneous group defined by negative terms such as 'the blind' or 'the visually impaired.' This is not mere 'political correctness' but challenges essentializing attitudes and stereotypes that are reflected in and expressed through language.

Disability, Rights and Tourism

Tourism researchers and educators have barely scratched the surface of disability – there are relatively few research papers, doctoral studies or textbooks in the field that focus on the subject and its importance is rarely taught in tourism-related undergraduate or postgraduate programmes. Having said this, there has been more engagement with the topic since 2000, most evident in the work of the Australian academic Simon Darcy (Darcy, 2002; Darcy and Taylor, 2009; Darcy and Buhalis, 2010). Other recent relevant studies include those of:

- Shaw and Coles (2004), which examines disability and the UK tourism industry;

- Miller and Kirk (2002), which discusses disability legislation;
- Hunter-Jones (2004), which examines the barriers to holidaying for young cancer patients;
- Daruwalla and Darcy (2005), which explores personal and societal attitudes towards disability;
- Ozturk *et al.* (2007), which assesses the Turkish tourism industry's ability to meet the needs of people with disabilities;
- Williams and Rattray (2005), Shi (2006), and Williams *et al.* (2006), which all evaluate the accessibility of the web to individuals with disabilities.

Within this tourism and disability literature, studies that examine the holiday experiences of people with visual impairment and their families are rare. Examples include the studies by Packer *et al.* (2007), Yau *et al.* (2004), Poria *et al.* (2010) and Small *et al.* (2007). The first three are qualitative studies of the experiences of individuals with mobility and visual impairments in Hong Kong and Israel, while the latter investigates the tourism experiences of those who are vision impaired in Western Australia and focuses on the types of holidays taken and positive and negative experiences. These proved to be related to: preparation and accessing information; navigating the physical environment; the knowledge and attitudes of others.

Putting Disability in Focus

Despite the emergence of work on tourism and disability, this kind of research remains on the margins of tourism scholarship. This is the case despite the growing strength of the disability rights movement and moves in the last decade in more developed economies to enact legislation to ensure that the needs and rights of people with disabilities are considered. For example, in 1999, the then recently elected UK Labour Government launched a new tourism strategy that signalled a commitment to help 'the elderly, people with disabilities, single parent families, families with young children, carers and people on low incomes who find difficulty in taking holidays or leisure breaks' (DCMS, 1999: 79). One of the key objectives of this strategy was to widen access to tourism opportunities for these disadvantaged groups, while at the local level in the UK authorities are also seeking to use tourism to combat social exclusion (http://www.lga.gov.uk/lga/tourism).

The 1995 Disability Discrimination Act also brought increased political and economic attention to the tourism sector (Shaw and Coles, 2004), a piece of legislation that was further strengthened by the 2005 Disability Discrimination Act, which requires premises such as tourist attractions and accommodation operations to take reasonable steps to ensure that their facilities are accessible to people with disabilities (Box 2.2). Such discrimination legislation was further streamlined in 2010 when the UK's new Equality Bill became law (http://www.equalityhumanrights.com/legislative-framework/equality-bill/). At the same time, a range of initiatives from the EU are concerned to improve the rights of disabled persons and persons with reduced mobility when travelling. For instance, European Regulation (EC) 1107/2006, which came into full force in July 2008, imposes obligations on airlines, travel agents and tour operators not to refuse a reservation or boarding on the grounds of disability except on the grounds of safety or where it is physically impossible (for further information, see http://www.dft.gov.uk/transportforyou).

In the USA, Hotels.com and Expedia.com, two of the world's leading online travel companies, have recently agreed to add features to their online travel reservation systems so that travellers with disabilities can use their online services to search for and reserve hotel rooms that have the accommodation they need. As a result of the settlement of a class action lawsuit in California, these two online travel companies will now gather information about hotels' accessibility features and incorporate that information into their websites so that travellers can both search for hotels with rooms that offer the particular accommodations they need, and make special requests online to book those accessible rooms. Each special request will be given individual consideration by a trained customer service representative, who will work with the customer to accommodate his or her needs. These new features will be rolled out during 2010 (http://www.icdri.org/legal/HotelsCom_Settlement.htm). Yet despite this increasing legal recognition of the

---

Box 2.2. The Disability Discrimination Act (DDA) 2005.

In December 1997, the UK Government established the Disability Rights Task Force, an independent body comprising members from disability organizations, the private and public sectors and trade unions, to advise it on how best to meet its 1997 manifesto commitment to look at securing comprehensive and enforceable civil rights for disabled people. In December 1999, the Task Force published its final report to Government: *From Exclusion to Inclusion*, which recommended a number of major extensions to the 1995 Disability Discrimination Act which had already made it 'unlawful to discriminate against a disabled person in relation to employment, the provision of goods, facilities and services ....' The 2005 Act made several new provisions, including:

- introducing a new duty on public authorities 'requiring them to have due regard to the need to eliminate harassment of and unlawful discrimination against disabled persons, to promote positive attitudes towards disabled persons, to encourage participation by disabled persons in public life, and to promote equality of opportunity between disabled persons and other persons';
- introducing new provisions regarding transport accessibility;
- amending the definition of disability in respect of people with mental illnesses and deeming 'people with HIV infection, multiple sclerosis, or cancer to be disabled for the purposes of the DDA'.

Source: Explanatory Notes to Disability Discrimination Act 2005 Chapter 13, available at: http://www.opsi.gov.uk/acts/acts2005/en/ukpgaen_20050013_en_1.htm

transport and tourism industries' responsibilities to people with disabilities, relatively little research exists in this area in relation to disability, particularly the challenges facing people with vision impairment when they travel.

In recent decades, disability activists have worked hard to challenge traditional perspectives on disability and activists and academics discuss elsewhere the emergence of the disability movement and the politics of disability (Oliver, 1990, 1995, 2004; Finkelstein, 2004). Simply put, academic engagement with disability has been dominated by two models – the 'medical model' of disability and the 'social model' of disability. These provide frameworks for understanding the way in which people with impairments experience disability. Until relatively recently, the medical model of disability dominated how people with disabilities were treated by society. In this model, people with disabilities were seen as 'ill', in need of medical attention and welfare, people who were unable to participate fully in the world and therefore needed to be excluded from it (Barnes and Mercer, 2005).

Disabled people were depersonalized, institutionalized and hidden away from a society that saw no real need for change. During the 1970s, however, disability activists began to challenge such views and focus on a 'disabling society', which excluded people with disabilities from full participation in all aspects of society. This challenge to disability, oppression and exclusion produced the politics of disablement (Oliver, 1990) reflected in the social model of disability, which 'by providing a different way of looking at ourselves and others, establishes everyone is equal and demonstrates that it is society which erects barriers' (Disability Awareness in Action, 2009). More recently, commentators have suggested that we need a framework for analysis, which takes into account the relationship between our bodies, selves and environments. They argue that bodily experiences involve struggling with both social barriers and the effects of an impairment (Thomas, 2002).

This embodiment perspective urges space for the corporeal, embodied nature of experiences in the social paradigm (Shakespeare and Watson, 2001). In essence, it requires us to recognize that disability is part of the human condition and that societies are not divided between able bodied and disabled people since the former are simply temporarily able people who (through accident, illness or ageing) will join the ranks of the latter from time to time or permanently.

In this chapter, we advocate critical and emancipatory disability research in order to promote people with disabilities' individual and collective empowerment and their full participation in society as a human right. The universal establishment of human rights is the single most important political development of recent decades and approaches based on human rights principles and the social model of disability are 'mutually reinforcing' (Bickenbach, 2001: 567). Both are founded on values of equality, dignity, respect and social justice and central to our approach is 'the consideration of the individual and their impairment within the socially constructed disability environments' (Darcy and Taylor, 2009: 420).

Understanding Visual Impairment

Around 20% of UK adults have some form of disability, around half of whom are over state pension age and that figure is set to increase dramatically in the near future as the population ages (by 2030 over a third of the population of Europe is expected to be over 65 years of age). Of these individuals, around 8.7 million people have hearing difficulties, approximately half a million are wheelchair users and around two million people have a sight problem (Department for Work and Pensions 2006 and The European Commission 2003). Of all the senses, people fear losing their sight the most; indeed, in a UK opinion poll, 90% of the respondents said this (Stephens, 2007), and yet wider society demonstrates very little awareness of the psychological and emotional impacts of sight loss, which can and often do lead to depression, loneliness and anxiety (Stephens, 2007). People with sight problems come from differing backgrounds and varying lifestyles and each person is affected by sight problems in their own individual way – it is not the same experience for everyone.

Its impacts also vary, as sight loss is not a linear process and can involve periods of deterioration and improvement, even on a daily basis. Sight loss is more complex than most people realize and individuals have differing experiences of 'seeing' (Fig. 2.1) – meaning that any one-size fits all solutions are problematic. In essence, there exists a vision loss continuum, where full sight and no sight are the extremes. The majority of people with visual impairments have some useful vision as only around 140,000 British people have no vision, of whom 3000 were born blind. Visual impairment is caused by disease, as a result of an accident,

deterioration related to age or it can be congenital. Partial sight can be confusing and frustrating at the same time, because a partially sighted person often frequently misinterprets what he or she sees and a sighted person processes mixed messages about how much someone can or cannot see, often resulting in misplaced judge-ments (RNIB, 1998).

In addition to the eye condition, vision is also affected by other factors including lighting levels, tiredness or lack of colour contrast. The most severe sight problems can lead to someone being certified by an ophthalmologist as 'severely visually impaired' or 'sight impaired.' At this stage in the UK, the individual can then register with their local social services department. Every day 100 more people start to lose their sight in the UK and one in 12 of us will become blind or partially sighted by the time we are 60, rising to one in six by the time we reach 75 (RNIB, 2003). Thus, more than any other disability, loss of sight is associated with old age and the

Fig. 2.1. Impressions of different eye conditions. (a) Perfect vision; (b) macular degeneration; (c) glaucoma; and (d) retinis pigmentosa. Reproduced courtesy of Wales Council for the Blind (2008).

older we are the more chance there is that we will develop some problems with our vision.

The Potentialities of Travel

There is a real danger that individuals with visual impairment may disengage from the many possibilities and potentialities of life that sighted people take for granted because of the ways in which our everyday environments marginalize and disable them, whether this is socially, economically or politically. In our sighted world, most people would empathize with the newly blind woman who asked the blind-from-birth poet, memoirist and academic Stephen Kuusisto 'Why travel anywhere if you can't see?' (Kuusisto, 2006: preface, x). Yet, this is to underestimate severely just how much pleasure a visually impaired person can derive from a holiday. In his book *Eavesdropping*, Kuusisto describes a world of soundscapes, which a sighted person would barely register. He vividly portrays how he goes sightseeing by ear in places as varied as Iceland and Venice and although he can only see slivered fragments and patterns, he makes clear how colourful the sensory experience of travel can be for him.

Tourism consists of a range of embodied, sensual and emotional encounters and while visual appreciation is undoubtedly part of the tourist experience, it is just one element of those encounters and its impact is entwined with those of the other senses. Tourism as it is commonly understood and practiced is a form of commoditized pleasures and these – whether tastes, touches, smells, sounds, spectacles or sensations – are sensual and embodied (Pritchard and Morgan, in press). We experience and enjoy the world through our sense organs – for instance, studies reveal the central role that taste and smell play in tourism experiences (e.g. Dann and Jacobsen, 2003; Small, 2007). Indeed, smells and tastes (both pleasant and unpleasant) evoke memories and are often synonymous with places we've visited and the tourist experience should be seen as a series of corporeal, embodied encounters that embrace all the senses. The warmth of the sun on our skin, the call of seabirds, the smell of unfamiliar food markets, the sights and sounds of a bustling city or the taste of exotic foodstuffs are all typical memories of holiday times.

Many visually impaired people can make use of their remaining vision supplemented by their other senses (particularly touch and sound) and their kinaesthetic skills (being able to sense and feel something). Thus, they can feel the wind and coldness while on holiday in the mountains; experience the sensations of swimming in the sea or a pool; and feel the different textures and surfaces at museums and historic sites. As we will discuss in the next section of the chapter, however, although there are significant benefits and enjoyment to be gained from travelling, there are also genuine problems and challenges that arise when society and the tourism industry in particular fail to understand the needs and requirements of individuals who have bodies that differ from mainstream 'norms'.

The Challenges of Travelling with a Visual Impairment

Many individuals with visual impairment travel with sighted family members and friends, particularly those who rely heavily on being guided, particularly in unfamiliar surroundings. For such people, disability organizations such as the Royal National Institute for the Blind (RNIB; http://www.rnib.org.uk) produce guides to specialist accommodation for potential tourists and information on catering for people with disabilities for providers. However, independent travel is not always a practical option and many individuals with special needs have difficulty accessing and using mainstream or even specialist tourism providers.

To assist with this, day trips, short breaks and longer holidays are also organized by social groups who arrange stays in mainstream or specialist accommodation, and there are also a range of organizations that offer travel opportunities specifically catering for people with vision problems. Within the UK vision impairment network of voluntary organizations, for example, several organizations such as Action for Blind People, The Royal Blind Society and Torch Trust have hotels specifically catering for visually impaired people. Vitalise is a charity that provides holidays for disabled people and particularly visually impaired people who benefit from the assistance of sighted guides. In addition, a number of commercial companies (e.g. http://www. traveleyes-international.com) have become very successful in offering holidays further afield, again with sighted guides allowing single people the opportunity to travel.

Conversations with Individuals with Visual Impairment

The next part of the chapter is based on our research with individuals with visual impairment in the UK (Richards *et al.*, forthcoming). In eight focus groups and during semi-structured interviews and conversations with several families, we explored the benefits of holidays, the reasons why individuals perhaps did not participate in tourism and their experiences of travel and tourism providers and services.

All of those who had travelled spoke of the many pleasures and benefits they derived from holidays and breaks away from home. Their experiences had much in common with those of sighted people and included social interaction, warmer climates, relaxation, experience of other cultures and countries and a change from routine environments. It was evident that the majority of the participants had taken some form of holiday, short break or day trip, although members of organized social groups had done so more regularly as those groups tended to arrange formal tourism

activities as part of their social role. What was immediately apparent, however, was the genuine challenges that travel posed for visually impaired people and their accompanying friends and family. While many of these issues overlap, we discuss them under the headings of person-centred, societal and environmental barriers (Fig. 2.2).

Person-centred barriers

Our research reveals that individuals with no or low vision repeatedly feel disregarded and ignored. Moreover, they feel that they are treated as one homogeneous group of people, not as individuals with their own personalities and backgrounds who simply happen to be visually impaired. One woman described how even when she is out with her friends (who one would imagine would be sympathetic to her needs) they talk about her in the third person and say things like 'let's put her over there.' These reactions can have severe repercussions on an individual's perceptions of their own worth and value, even leading some to withdraw from everyday life. As another person commented, 'because my eyes look perfect in front they [i.e. other people] don't believe that I'm blind so I'm getting that I don't want to go out sometimes.'

The individuality of ways of seeing and functioning among visually impaired people was a key theme throughout our research. Individuals spoke of how they create their own coping strategies to enable them to function or to disguise the fact that they have a visual difficulty. As one participant commented: 'not everyone has got a [total] sight loss [there are] ... different levels of sight.' Participants spoke of how they felt 'a fraud', as many sighted people can only relate to stereotypical notions of how a visually impaired person should look (Box 2.3). A guide dog owner who was usually accompanied by her husband on holidays commented that her white cane and guide dog act as visual clues to people

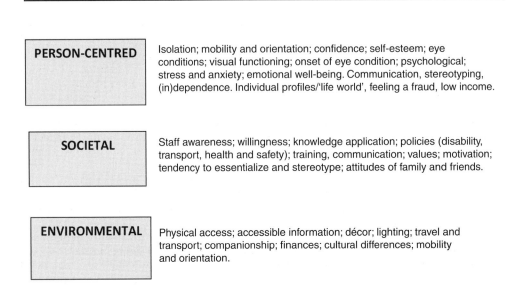

PERSON-CENTRED	Isolation; mobility and orientation; confidence; self-esteem; eye conditions; visual functioning; onset of eye condition; psychological; stress and anxiety; emotional well-being. Communication, stereotyping, (in)dependence. Individual profiles/'life world', feeling a fraud, low income.
SOCIETAL	Staff awareness; willingness; knowledge application; policies (disability, transport, health and safety); training, communication; values; motivation; tendency to essentialize and stereotype; attitudes of family and friends.
ENVIRONMENTAL	Physical access; accessible information; décor; lighting; travel and transport; companionship; finances; cultural differences; mobility and orientation.

Fig. 2.2. Barriers to participation in tourism for individuals with visual impairment.

that she has difficulty in seeing, otherwise they complain that she is receiving preferential treatment: 'If you've a cane or a dog, people are more open to you, otherwise they don't always understand you've got something wrong.'

Societal barriers

All of the visually impaired individuals who took part in the research discussed here consistently spoke of the need for awareness training for staff, family, friends and the population as a whole. Awareness training focuses on how visual impairment affects all the different aspects of people's lives; it is based on gaining an understanding of how a person experiences the world by provoking thoughts and ideas among participants as well as learning practical skills (Wales Council for the Blind, 2008). The research participants also spoke about their decisions in different situations to reveal and highlight their disability and of the fact that they often felt conscious of 'not looking blind.' Many commented that some tourism and hospitality staff may never have come

across a visually impaired person in their personal and professional life and had no idea how to interact with a person with sight problems. One of the sighted volunteers we spoke to commented: 'I mean it's not their fault [the staff], none of us know until we actually start working; we are not aware of the problems if we don't have them ourselves.'

All of the participants suggested that a lack of awareness of the needs of people with disabilities was a major issue, which usually resulted in service providers acting on myths and stereotypes; for them a simple solution was for the tourism industry to train staff to know how to interact with people with no or low vision (Box 2.4). Some blind and partially sighted people use 'cues' such as white canes as much to identify to others that they are visually impaired as for their own benefit. In the focus groups we held, there were several discussions about misunderstandings around the white stick, its meaning and purpose, the way it is used in different countries, and how providing written material in Braille is regarded as the 'proverbial response' of the industry to the needs of a visually impaired person: '... it's

Box 2.3. Martin's story.

Martin is 53 years old and lives with his wife. He is registered blind and volunteers for a local society for the blind. When he was in his thirties, he was diagnosed with retinitis pigmentosa, which affected his peripheral vision (so he has tunnel vision). His sight is worse at night and in dark areas, and he has diffi-culty with bright light, thus his remaining vision is very variable. Martin does make the most of the vision he has but finds life frustrating when sighted people lack awareness about issues affecting visually impaired people. At times Martin needs to wear dark glasses to avoid glare and he uses a long white cane at night to help him get around (he has been trained to use it). At other times, particularly in unfa-miliar areas, his wife guides him. Even though he has come to terms with his visual impairment and found different ways of doing things, each day continues to be a challenge.

Martin and his wife continue to enjoy a winter skiing holiday and a summer break in September visiting their daughter who lives overseas. This short description is written by Martin:

We travel by air to both our winter and summer destinations. Because it can be quite stressful at the airport we have booked assistance so that they can organize our luggage and get us through quicker to the departure lounge and on and off the plane. It seems to vary unfortunately and I do feel very frustrated when they turn up with a wheelchair and insist that I sit in it. I can walk – I just require guiding. It makes me feel like a fraud because other people think you can't walk either.

We've always loved skiing even when our daughter was with us. Nowadays my wife really has to keep an eye on me. We don't just bomb off anymore, sometimes she goes first and gives me instructions but we've also been working as a team going down together where she has a tape in her bag playing music which I follow. Although I am virtually totally blind with the glare of the snow I still appreciate the atmosphere and thrill of the air whizzing past me as I descend.

On summer holidays we are both pretty active as I can't bear to sit around by a pool. We both enjoy historical locations, scenery and all sorts. My wife is very good at describing things to me, however I appreciate it for myself when for example I can touch exhibits or use an audio-described tour of a castle and so on. I can appreciate scenery to some degree, not the detail but I can make out colours, use my other senses such as smell and sound.

Box 2.4. Issues to think about when meeting a person with a visual disability.

- It is always appropriate to offer your help but do not be surprised if the individual would prefer 'do it himself/herself'.
- If you are helping and not sure what to do, just ask the person. A gentle touch on his/her elbow will indicate to a person with a visual disability that you are speaking to him/her.
- If you are walking with a person who is blind do not take that person's arm; rather let that person take your arm.
- Being visually impaired is not a hearing disability so there is no need to shout. Neither is it a speech disability. If you have a question for the person with a visual disability, ask him/her – not their com-panion.
- Do not worry about substituting words for 'see', 'look', or even 'blind'. Do not avoid them where these words fit. You can talk about blindness itself, when you both feel comfortable about it.
- When you meet a person with a visual disability you know, mention your name. It is difficult to recognize voices unless you happen to have a very distinctive one.

like all these Braille signs. They say "oh we've got all our signs in Braille" which is all very well [but] unless you know where to look for the sign how are you going to read the Braille?'

Although many sighted people are aware of Braille, few probably realize that only 4% of visually impaired people can actually read it while many more people with low vision would prefer large print, audio formats, mobile phones, e-mail and accessible web pages (Wales Council for the Blind, 2008). Braille is a writing system based on a combination of raised dots but if they are flattened or stored underneath other heavy items, the dots will be compressed, thus rendering it useless. Yet as one visually impaired participant noted, a restaurant they visited they had a Braille menu but as the waiter habitually kept it in his back pocket and sat on it, it was of no use.

Environmental barriers

While many sighted people might think that the main barriers that prevent people with sight difficulties accessing tourism facilities and services are physical (and indeed much of the legislative effort has focused on improving accessibility), those individuals who took part in this study considered physical access important but not to the same extent as staff awareness. The major access issues for visually impaired people include clear edging of steps, good colour contrast of surfaces, suitable lighting, contrasting handrails and clear signage. Taking lighting as an example, several people spoke of the inconvenience caused by the 'mood' lighting of many restaurants and hotels. For individuals whose low vision is compounded by partial or total hearing loss (dual sensory loss), this creates particular problems, leaving them feeling anxious and afraid, uncertain of what to expect and how to cope, even when they are guided by a sighted person. Access to information was also a topic of great discussion and consternation and most of our participants had difficulties reading travel information signs, screens and reading holiday publicity.

Small *et al.* (2007) note that navigating the physical environment becomes an essential element of tourism trips for those with visual impairment, whether they are travelling alone or with others. Our participants pointed out that effective mobility in familiar and unfamiliar environments depended on their abilities to memorize routes, use environmental clues and deal with obstacles and hazards

along the way (Box 2.5). One individual described how unfamiliar terrain affected her and her partner:

> We'd love to go on coach trips but when we get off the coach we don't know where to go and I can't read signs. If people give me directions I can't follow them – 'just go down there and turn right' [doesn't help], I don't find it a lot of fun really.

Planning a holiday if one or more of the party is visually impaired takes more time and consideration (Small *et al.*, 2007). Our participants agreed that taking holidays in the UK has become much easier as a result of the Disability Discrimination Acts of 1995 and 2005, while visiting some overseas destinations where access issues are challenging remains difficult. However, they felt that travel agents had inadequate information on accommodation and could not guarantee whether hotels and similar facilities were vision impairment or disability friendly. This meant that they have to undertake more in-depth research themselves before booking. The priority for families where one or more of their number has a sight problem are that accommodation has to be physically accessible, offer communicating or family rooms and is conveniently located to places of interest. Many such families are unable to book last-minute holiday deals and they feel that specialist holidays charge a disability premium. Several individuals commented that in general holidays are more expensive for people needing additional requirements. This is especially problematic as the majority of visually impaired people in the UK are over 60 and retired, while 83% of those of working age are unemployed (RNIB, 2009).

In addition to such considerations of each person's needs, issues of stereotyping and a lack of information are important to people with vision impairment. People with sight problems and other disabilities are often perceived as the passive person in a group and thus totally reliant on others, yet of course they are often also fathers, mothers, husbands and wives and have others who are relying on them.

Box 2.5. Lucy's story.

Lucy is 15 years old and lives with her mother and father. Lucy was born totally blind and is registered blind. She attends mainstream school with additional learning support in Braille and mobility skills (getting around the school using a long cane). As a family, they have an annual summer holiday and other times of the year visit friends and family. Other holiday opportunities have been through visual impairment support organizations. Lucy's holiday interests are being with her parents in a warmer climate, by a beach or pool and to speak and hear a foreign language. Her parents enjoy being active, walking and running; however, Lucy's experience is their priority. Lucy's mother plans the holidays and chooses the most appropriate places to suit Lucy.

This year they decided on Spain; however, the accommodation provider could not guarantee a triple room and therefore without wanting to risk any anxiety, Lucy's mother chose Portugal as the destination where the hotel was more accommodating. They flew from their local airport. The following is a short description written by Lucy's mother:

> Our holiday in Brisa Sol, Albufeira, Portugal. At Cardiff airport we asked for assistance and it was a very positive experience. We were checked in without queuing and fast tracked through security. A gentleman took Lucy and guided her up to the plane. At the airport in Portugal the gentleman dealing with the transfer took the cases so I could guide Lucy. Either things have improved with this over the years or maybe we now know how to play the system, to ask for and get the assistance we need.

> The pavements in Albufeira were very narrow and bumpy – made out of small uneven tiles while there were cars parked everywhere on the pavements. There were very steep hills down to the old town, which was very impractical for Lucy. There were always massive queues for taxis and no way of pre booking them even for disabled so we had to make do trying to walk it, not the best experience. The land train was very expensive and it would help if there was a reduction for the disabled. Things were quite spaced apart and we often had to walk on the road as the pavements weren't wide enough for people to pass.

> In the hotel there were only handrails on parts of the stairs and then they stopped and started again further down, they were also only on one side. This confused Lucy. Meal times in the hotel were always pretty stressful as it was so busy. We asked to be seated at a table nearest the buffet so that we wouldn't be too far away from Lucy when getting her food. I also spent the first few days trying to orientate Lucy around the hotel but she got fed up with it and started to complain that she was supposed to be on holiday and all she was doing was working. She eventually refused and I gave up because I wanted us to have a relaxing holiday.

There are also perceptual barriers (of self, one's appearance and the perceptions of others) and the desire to strike a balance between being treated as a 'normal' family and requesting additional assistance is felt by many, which can be compounded by other people's perceptions and judgements. People with visual impairment need to be guided in unfamiliar places but as we have said above, many self-identify their disability by carrying a white stick more for the benefit of others as sighted people can misjudge situations. For example, one woman commented that she was more likely to carry a white stick at the airport 'but it is easier to carry a cane so that other people understand why you have jumped the queue and have a concession.'

Conclusion

As we have seen in this chapter, people with visual impairments are first and foremost individuals and members of the community and their impairment should be accommodated in every policy area (Wales Council for the Blind, 2003). Tourism participation is increasingly being recognized as a right of citizenship by many governments and supranational organizations such as the European Union (EU) and United Nations (UN; Minnaert *et al.*, 2009; Minnaert *et al.*, this volume). The EU recently welcomed Regulation (EC) 1107/2006, which stipulates that: 'disabled people and people with reduced mobility have the same right as any other citizens to free movement' (RNIB, 2009). Similarly, the

UN 2006 Treaty on Rights for the Disabled draws specific attention to the role of cultural activities in promoting citizenship, well-being and life quality. The extent to which such policies are enforced, however, is highly dependent on a responsive tourism industry.

Despite the increasing legislative drive in many countries, people with disabilities still participate significantly less in cultural life around the world – which encompasses tourism, sport, the arts and leisure (Darcy and Taylor, 2009). We have seen here how, when the sighted world fails tourists with visual impairment through organizations' inabilities to provide staff training and inclusive physical environments, those individuals' tourism (and life) experiences are circumscribed. Thus, many visually impaired people prefer to remain at home and forgo the enjoyments of tourism rather than negotiate the anxiety and stress of travel in an unsympathetic, unaccommodating sighted world. This in turn is compounded by the attitude of many sighted people that people with low vision derive limited enjoyment from travelling – the 'why travel if you cannot see' attitude.

People are disabled more by poor design, inaccessible services and other people's attitudes than by their impairment but personal issues of identity and self-perception also play a vital part. In understanding people's experiences we would do well to remember that impairment is part of the human condition and 'able-bodiedness' is a temporary state as all of us will be 'disabled' at some point in our lives. This simple switch of mindset provides us with an alternative way of seeing and of addressing the holiday experience for people with low vision that is inclusive rather than exclusive and reactive. The challenge for the tourism industry is to identify these customers, analyse their service needs in more depth and treat them with respect and dignity, to learn new skills, be creative and truly apply that knowledge holistically.

Discussion Questions

1. Urry's (1990) 'tourist gaze' is one of the most influential concepts in tourism studies. How has this influenced our view of the embodied nature of tourism experiences?
2. Identify and discuss the key barriers to tourism that a visually impaired tourist might experience.
3. Under the Disability Discrimination Acts (or similar legislation in your country) what 'reasonable adjustments' should tourism organizations make to their services and facilities for visually impaired tourists?

References

Barnes, C. and Mercer, G. (2005) Disability, work and welfare: challenging the social exclusion of disabled people. *Work, Employment and Society* 19, 527–554.
Bickenbach, J.E. (2001) Disability, human rights, law and policy. In: Albrecht, G.L., Seelman, K.D. and Bury, M. (eds) *The Handbook of Disability Studies*. Sage, London, pp. 565–584.
Dann, G.M.S. and Jacobsen, J.K.S. (2003) Tourism smellscapes. *Tourism Geographies* 5, 3–25.
Darcy, S. (2002) Marginalised participation: physical disability, high support needs and tourism. *Journal of Hospitality and Tourism Management* 9, 61–72.
Darcy, S. and Buhalis, D. (2010) *Accessible Tourism: Concepts and Issues*. Channel View, Clevedon, UK.
Darcy, S. and Taylor, T. (2009) Disability citizenship: an Australian human rights analysis of the cultural industries. *Leisure Studies* 28, 419–442.
Daruwalla, P.S. and Darcy, S. (2005) Personal and societal attitudes to disability. *Annals of Tourism Research* 32, 549–570.
DCMS, *Tomorrow's Tourism: a Growth Industry for the New Millennium*, February 1999. Available at: http://www.culture.gov.uk/pdf/tomorrows_tourism.pdf
Department for Work and Pensions (2006) and The European Commission (2003), available at http://www.disabilitywales.org (accessed 2 November 2008).
Disability Awareness in Action (2009) Available at http://www.daa.org.uk/?page=newsletter (accessed 10 October 2009).

Finkelstein, V. (2004) Representing disability. In Swain, J., French, S., Barnes, C. and Thomas, C. (eds) *Disabling Barriers – Enabling Environments*, 2nd edn. Sage, London, pp. 13–20.

Hunter-Jones, P. (2004) Young people, holiday-taking and cancer – an exploratory analysis. *Tourism Management* 25, 249–258.

Kuusisto, S. (2006) *Eavesdropping – a Life by Ear*. W.W. Norton & Company, New York.

Miller, G. and Kirk, E. (2002) The Disability Discrimination Act: time for the stick. *Journal of Sustainable Tourism* 10, 82–88.

Minnaert, L., Maitland, R. and Miller, G. (2009) Tourism and social policy: the value of social tourism. *Annals of Tourism Research* 36, 316–334.

Oliver, M. (1990) *The Politics of Disablement*. Macmillan and St Martins Press, Basingstoke.

Oliver, M. (1995) *Understanding Disability: from Theory to Practice*. MacMillans, Basingstoke.

Oliver, M. (2004) If I had a hammer: the social model in action. In Swain, J., French, S., Barnes, C. and Thomas, C. (eds) *Disabling Barriers – Enabling Environments*, 2nd edn. Sage, London, pp. 7–12.

Ozturk, Y., Yayli, A. and Yesiltas, M. (2007) Is the Turkish tourism industry ready for a disabled customer's market? The views of hotel and travel agency managers. *Tourism Management* 29, 382–389.

Packer, T.L., McKercher, B. and Yau, M. (2007) Understanding the complex interplay between tourism, disability and environmental contexts. *Disability and Rehabilitation* 29, 281–292.

Poria, Y., Reichel, A. and Brandt, Y. (2010) Blind people's tourism experiences: an exploratory study. In: Darcy, S. and Buhalis, D. (eds) *Accessible Tourism: Concepts and Issues*. Channel View, Clevedon, UK, pp. 191–205.

Pritchard, A. and Morgan, N. (In press) Tourist bodies, transformation and sensuality. In Wagg, S. and Brabham, P. (eds) *Unforbidden Fruit: the New Politics of Pleasure and Leisure*. Palgrave, Basingstoke.

Richards, V., Pritchard, A. and Morgan, N. (In press) (Re)envisioning tourism and visual impairment. *Annals of Tourism Research*.

Royal National Institute for the Blind (1998) *Within Reason: Access to Services for Blind and Partially Sighted People*. RNIB, London.

Royal National Institute for the Blind (2003) *Museums, Galleries and Heritage Sites: Improving Access for Blind and Partially Sighted People. The Talking Images Guide*. RNIB and Vocaleyes, London.

Royal National Institute of the Blind (2009) Talking point, what's in a word? *NB The Sight Loss and Eye Health Magazine* Issue 40, April, 18–20. RNIB, London.

Shakespeare, T. and Watson, N. (2001) The social model of disability: an outdated ideology? In Barnett, S.N. and Mandell, B. (eds) *Exploring Theories and Expanding Methodologies*. JAI Press, Stamford, CT, pp. 9–28.

Shaw, G. and Coles, T. (2004) Disability, holiday making and the tourism industry in the UK: a preliminary survey. *Tourism Management* 25, 397–403 (EJournal, accessed 25 February 2009).

Shi, Y. (2006) The accessibility of Queensland information centres' websites. *Tourism Management* 27, 829–841.

Small, J. (2007) The emergence of the body in the holiday accounts of women and girls. In Pritchard, A., Morgan, N., Ateljevic, I. and Harris, C. (eds) *Tourism and Gender: Embodiment, Sensuality and Experience*. CAB International, Wallingford, pp. 73–91.

Small, J., Darcy, S. and Packer, T. (2007) Beyond a visual gaze: tourist experiences of individuals with vision impairment. *2nd International Critical Tourism Studies Conference*, Split, Croatia.

Stephens, J. (2007) The emotional well-being of blind and partially sighted people. Available at http://www.guidedogs.org.uk (accessed July 2008).

Thomas, C. (2002), The disabled body. In Evans, M. and Lee, E. (eds) *Real Bodies. A Sociological Introduction*. Palgrave, Basingstoke, pp. 64–78.

Tourism for All (2009) Available at http://www.tourismforall.org.uk/index.htm (accessed 18 March 2010).

Urry, J. (1990) *The Tourist Gaze*. Sage, London.

Vision2020 (2010) Available at http://www.Vision2020.org (accessed 17 March 2010).

Wales Council for the Blind (2003) *Manifesto from Visually impaired People in Wales*. WCB, Cardiff.

Wales Council for the Blind (2008) Awareness Training. Available at http://www.wcb-ccd.org.uk/projects/awarenesstraining (accessed 12 October 2008).

Williams, R. and Rattray, R. (2005) UK hotel webpage accessibility for disabled and challenged users. *Tourism and Hospitality Research* 5, 255–267.

Williams, R., Rattray, R. and Grimes, A. (2006) Meeting the online needs of disabled tourists: an assessment of UK-based hotel websites. *International Journal of Tourism Research* 8, 59–73.

Yau, M., McKercher, B. and Packer, T.L. (2004) Travelling with a disability: more than an access issue. *Annals of Tourism Research* 31, 946–960.

3 Equal Access for All? Regulative Mechanisms, Inequality and Tourism Mobility

C. Michael Hall

This chapter focuses on those who are relatively immobile because of the economic and other structural and regulative mechanisms, such as class, race, gender and religion, which affect the economic and social capital of individuals in society and therefore their life chances, with respect to tourism related mobility. It primarily focuses on the allocation of economic resources as a central regulative mechanism of tourism mobility but other forms of regulation are noted, and is divided into three main sections: first, a discussion of inequality in relation to concepts of tourism mobilities; second, the use of national travel survey data to illustrate the way in which mobility is unevenly distributed in society and the strong relationship of those mobilities to economic unevenness. British, EU, American and New Zealand data are used to illustrate how poverty and lack of car access in particular affects leisure mobility, while New Zealand data is also expanded with reference to findings from a qualitative assessment of access to tourism and leisure mobility. Finally, the chapter concludes by stressing the importance of connecting social exclusion to understandings of leisure mobility and how restricted activity space may serve as an indicator of social justice.

Tourism is often portrayed in terms of fun, freedom and access (Wang, 2000). Holidays are supposedly becoming ever more accessible to consumers, via growth in personal income as well as the emergence of budget airlines and advances in technology. Indeed, the serial reproduction of tourism as fun and easily available has become one of the central elements of the representation of tourism in destination promotion (Tapachai and Waryszak, 2000). However, while a substantial amount of attention is paid by the tourism industry and tourism researchers as to how image can be maintained and made even more appealing (e.g. Govers *et al.*, 2007; Tasci and Gartner, 2007), the reality is that tourism is an idealized commodity that is only accessible to some.

Tourism is therefore part of a 'mobility gap' in which the 'hypermobile' or 'kinetic elite' travel ever more frequently while many do not travel far for leisure or business at all (Gössling *et al.*, 2009). For example, it is estimated that the percentage of the world's population participating in international air travel is in the order of just 2–3% (Peeters *et al.*, 2006). At a global scale, accessibility and mobility have long-been regarded as integral to the development process (e.g. Addo, 1995). In the African context, Pirie (2009: 22) has also powerfully noted:

> The mobility gap may match the wide differentials of income and life chances on the continent; it is surely rooted in and expresses gaps in privilege and plenty. The condition presupposes what might be termed a 'mobility morality'. Super-mobile people are at one end of the mobility scale. At the

other extreme are Africans stranded in rural villages where mobility deprivation is acute. They are the kinetic underclass.

Pirie (2009: 21) also concludes that the 'way we act on, and the way we think, talk and write about, geographical mobility needs reconceptualizing in terms of fairness, equity, environmental justice, and human rights'. Yet issues of who do not travel and why receives only passing interest in most mainstream tourism research, leading Hall (2005a) to claim that tourism studies as it is currently constituted is probably the only discipline to study the rich – as you have to be relatively wealthy in time and money to be able to travel for leisure. But leaving such sanguine aside, the dominant discourse in tourism focuses on the 'given' of mobility and movement

rather than immobility and issues of social and economic exclusion are more likely to be dealt with in relation to destination communities under the umbrella of pro-poor tourism than the exclusion of potential consumers from tourism opportunities per se.

Nevertheless, for much of the 20th century there was a government as well as academic concern with access to travel and recreation for much of the developed world under the rubric of 'social tourism'. Social tourism can be defined as 'the relationships and phenomena in the field of tourism resulting from participation in travel by economically weak or otherwise disadvantaged elements of society' (Hunzinger, quoted in Murphy, 1985: 23). Social tourism involves the extension of the

---

Box 3.1. Case study: immobility, inequality and preparedness for natural disasters.

Natural disasters often illustrate the relative mobility of a population. In the case of natural disasters such as cyclones or even tsunamis, the capacity to respond to a disaster warning and get people to safety is not just a matter of providing warnings and having civil defence in place but it is also an issue of the capacity of people to evacuate. Mobility in this case includes factors such as transport infrastructure as well as access to cars and public transport.

Many coastal tourism destinations are increasingly at threat from natural disasters because of environmental change while some regions, such as the Caribbean and the South Pacific, have long been vulnerable to the effects of hurricanes and cyclones (Hall, 2005a). Cuba is especially vulnerable to natural disaster because of its location and has a diversity of potential natural disasters, including hurricanes, non-tropical depressions, tropical storms, tropical cyclones and severe local storms, along with earthquakes and droughts. However, planning for natural disasters is integral to the economic and social life of Cuba at all political levels. On several occasions, United Nations (UN) officials have pointed to Cuba as a model for countries preparing for hurricanes and other natural disasters (Berjamo, 2006). Part of Cuba's preparedness is ensuring that public transport to safety infrastructure is available for those who do not own their own car or who are infirm as well as for visitors to the country. This has meant that Cuba has experienced a very low loss of life from hurricanes in recent years compared with other countries in the region.

In contrast, there were almost 1500 deaths as a result of the impact of Hurricane Katrina in Louisiana in 2005. The Hurricane has also led to the permanent migration of many people away from New Orleans. With respect to the impacts of the Hurricane in terms of disaster preparedness, Katrina emphasized how immobility affects the capacity of people to evacuate. As Guidotti (2006: 223) observed:

> Katrina revealed the great divide that remains between people living next to one another but differing in the clustered characteristics of race, poverty, immobility and ill-health … Those who lacked the resources, who could not fend for themselves, who were left behind, who happened to be sick were almost all African-American, and therefore so were the ones who died.

Indeed, the images of those who remained in New Orleans immediately after Katrina had hit, were mainly of the poor, Black population who were without personal car access (Atkins and Moy, 2005). However, there were also many tourists who were unable to leave as well (Rhoads et al., 2006), which also created substantial negative publicity (e.g. BBC News, 2005). This is all the more remarkable as tourism was, and still is, of major economic importance to New Orleans and so the economy of the city depended on mobility, yet it did not have a strategy in place to cater adequately for those who were relatively immobile because of income or circumstance.

benefits of holidays to economically margin-alized groups, including the unemployed and single-parent families, as well as, in certain cases, pensioners and people with disabilities. According to Murphy (1985: 24), social tourism had 'become a recognized component and legitimate objective for modern tourism. By extending the physical and psychological benefits of rest and travel to less fortunate people it can be looked upon as a form of preventative medicine'. Haulot (1981: 212) further extended this perspective by noting that: 'Social tourism ... finds justification in that its individual and collective objectives are consistent with the view that all measures taken by modern society should ensure more justice, more dignity and improved enjoyment of life for all citizens'.

Some four decades on from the enthusiasm of Murphy and Haulot for social tourism, the landscape of modern tourism has changed. Neoliberal policy settings and new positionings as to the role of the state in society, including relative to state involvement in welfare provision and social equity via tourism opportunities, means that the state's role in tourism is primarily perceived in most western policy circles as one of enhancing promotion rather than provision for the less well off in society. This is not to suggest that social tourism is non-existent. The Bureau Internationale du Tourisme Social (BITS), an international non-profit organization that promotes social tourism, continues to undertake work in the area, including encouraging the European Parliament to support a pilot project on social tourism in 2009 (BITS, 2009). But the relative size of the budget, one million Euros, compared with other tourism promotion initiatives is perhaps also a good indication of the relative policy influence of social tourism.

Not only has the policy terrain of the linkage between tourism and social and economic inequality shifted, so has the intellectual terrain. Access to tourism opportunities is not a significant research question for most English language tourism academics except when it comes to concerns over increasing consumption or expanding the market. The framing of the access issue has therefore moved from being understood in social and political terms to one that is perceived as a market issue. These are clearly generalizations as to intellectual and policy shifts, exceptions can always be located, yet it does also suggest that neoliberal ideas as to the role of the state, the market and the individual influence not just policy settings but also the body of tourism knowledge and how problems are defined (Bramwell and Lane, 2005). Indeed, one of the great ironies of the study of tourism in the first decade of the 21st century is that despite the adoption by some of the concept of mobility, there is relatively little attention to the less mobile in contemporary society. Moreover, as this chapter will emphasize, the mobility gap is not just an issue of the less developed countries but is actually intrinsic to those in the developed as well.

Inequality and the Mobile Turn

The 'mobility turn' in tourism has been shared with other social science fields, leading Cresswell (1997: 360) to comment:

> Everyone is travelling in the field of 'theory' today. Metaphors of movement parade across the pages of cultural theorists, social theorists, geographers, artists, literary critics. Mobility is the order of the day. Nomads, migrants, travellers and explorers inhabit a world where nothing is certain or fixed. Tradition and rootedness have the smell of death'.

Sheller and Urry (2003) have also used the metaphor of mobility to revise notions of globalization:

> [which] can be seen in terms of global fluids constituted of waves of people, information, objects, money, images, risks and networks moving across regions in heterogeneous, uneven, unpredictable and often unplanned shapes. Such global fluids demonstrate no clear point of departure, just de-territorialized movement, at certain speeds and different levels of viscosity with no necessary end-state or purpose.

(Sheller and Urry, 2003: 117)

Mobility has also come to be strongly associated with cosmopolitanism and modernity (Szerszynski and Urry 2006). For Wang (2000):

> travel distinguishes 'us', the modern, from 'others' who are not modern. 'We' travel for pleasure and fun because 'we' are moderns. 'They' don't travel because 'they' are socially and economically constrained from doing so, and hence are still outside the modern lifestyle. Therefore, tourism, especially mass tourism, is an indicator of the affluence brought about by modernity and its associated lifestyles. The rate of national participation in tourism becomes one of the indicators of a demarcation between the traditional and the modern.
>
> (Wang, 2000: 29)

Yet, the 'new mobility paradigm' (Sheller and Urry, 2006) has also been subject to substantial critique. Numerous authors, including Tsing (1998), Favell (2001), Coles *et al.* (2004, 2005) and Hall (2005b, 2005c), have all emphasized that the identification of mobility, interconnection and relatedness greatly predated the late 20th century. As Tsing (1998: 356) noted, 'if older ... frameworks were unable to handle interconnection and mobility, this is a problem with the frameworks and a reason for new ones but not the mirror of an evolutionary change in the world'. Yet, perhaps most fundamentally, and especially critical for the present chapter, has been the relative lack of understanding of the unevenness of mobility and its function as a scarce resource. Bauman (1998: 2) recognized, that 'mobility climbs to the uppermost among the coveted values – and the freedom to move, perpetually a scarce and unequally distributed commodity, fast becomes the main stratifying factor of our late-modern or postmodern times'. Indeed, a damning critique of the new fashion of mobility by Favell (2001) emphasized that:

> To assess really the extent or nature of movement, or indeed even to see it sometimes, you have in fact to spend a lot of the time studying things that stand still: the borders, institutions and territories of nationstates; the sedimented 'home' cultures of people that do not move. Nothing stands

still in Urry's [2000] world: his first 'rule' is 'to develop through appropriate metaphors a sociology that focuses on movement, mobility and contingent ordering, rather than upon stasis, structure and social order (Urry, 2000).
>
> (Favell, 2001: 391–392)

From such a perspective, fixity, immobility and stasis are therefore just as important to consider as mobility. Of course, the dichotomy of mobility/immobility is extremely artificial. Nothing ever stands completely still. Instead, mobility should be understood in a relative sense (Hall, 2005a; Adey, 2006). But the reasons underlying the relative mobility of people do need to be part of the broader understandings of tourism, especially as mobility appears constitutive of identity as well as constituting a form of social capital, which can also have implications for economic capital formation. As Giddens (1984: xxv) commented, 'Time–space "fixity" also normally means social fixity; the substantially "given" character of the physical milieux of day-to-day life interlaces with routine and is deeply influential in the contours of institutional reproduction'.

Giddens's observations grew out of his interest in the work of Torsten Hägerstrand and other geographers on space–time movements and activity spaces from the mid-1960s on. Although arguably somewhat underappreciated by those in tourism studies, there is a substantial body of literature in geography that examines time geography and its relationship to accessibility and welfare, including with respect to personal mobility (Hall, 2005a). For example, Kenyon *et al.* (2002: 210–211) argue that there is a 'mobility dimension to exclusion', that relates to:

> [the] process by which people are prevented from participating in the economic, political and social life of the community because of reduced accessibility to opportunities, services and social networks, due in whole or in part to insufficient mobility in a society and environment built around the assumption of high mobility.

Therefore, rather than treat tourism mobility as something that emerges out of 'lifestyle' that is framed as being constituted separately from such regulatory mechanisms as poverty, race, gender and class (e.g. Laws and Thyne, 2004; Gross *et al.*, 2008; Chen *et al.*, 2009), this chapter aims to interrogate the extent to which tourism opportunities are constrained by economic and temporal capacities that are often embedded in such mechanisms. The next section seeks to provide evidence from national surveys of how economic and social inequalities limits access to tourism and travel before going on to provide a brief case study of non-participation in tourism in New Zealand.

Constraints of Participation in Leisure Travel and Tourism

One of the most substantial deficiencies in tourism studies is the relative lack of research on what constrains people from engaging in tourism. This is despite a well-developed literature on the subject in leisure studies, which is strongly theoretically based (see Hinch and Jackson, 2000; Hudson and Gilbert, 2000; Hall, 2005a, 2005b; Nyaupane and Andereck, 2008; McKercher, 2009, for notable exceptions). Constraints can take various forms, including physical constraints such as disability and perceptions of a destination as dangerous or risky. However, central to the present discussion are the constraints that are regulative mechanisms that position individuals relative to economic, temporal and cultural capital as well as what can be termed mobility capital (Gustafson, 2006).

The strength of some of the regulative constraints on travel and tourism are seemingly downplayed in tourism transport and travel data in much of the developed world. National tourism statistics focus strongly on those who participate in leisure travel (and other forms of tourist mobility) compared with those who do not. In one sense, this perhaps should not be surprising, as many of the agencies that provide tourism data as in international and domestic tourism surveys are doing so

in order to identify ways in which greater profit-oriented consumption can be encouraged at both firm and destination level. In contrast, national transport surveys do tend to include overt discussions of social inclusion and accessibility, often because in many developed countries such data is extremely important for public transport planning. Therefore, arguably some of the best insights into equality of access for tourism and leisure mobility can be derived from some of the national transport and travel survey data that is available.

United Kingdom

Poverty is a major determinant of travel behaviour as it affects the capacity to travel by different transport modes as well as the capacity to own personal transport such as a car. The car is the dominant form of transport for tourism in the UK, with 73% of trips using a private car for the longest part of the journey from home to the destination in 2008, public transport is only used for 18% of holiday trips (VisitBritain *et al.*, 2009). In Great Britain, the 2008 National Travel Survey (NTS) (Department for Transport (DfT), 2009) indicated that 51% of households in the lowest income quintile had no car compared with 11% in the highest income quintile (Table 3.1), although the survey did also note that 'the gap in car availability between high and low income households is narrowing as car ownership increases among low income households' (DfT, 2009: 1). In 2008, 43% of respondents to the NTS aged 17 and over in the lowest income quintile lived in households with no car compared with 8% in the highest income quintile. There is also a significant gender difference in the availability of adults to a personal car with 22% of all females not having access compared with 17% of males. As would be expected, this also greatly reflects differences in possession of a driving licence with 81% of males having full car driving licences compared with 65% of females (DfT, 2009). Significantly, car

Table 3.1. Household car availability in Great Britain by household income quintile (2008).

	No car	One car	Two cars	Three or more cars	All households	Persons in household without a car[a]
Lowest real income level (%)	51	39	8	2	100	43
Second level (%)	36	46	15	3	100	29
Third level (%)	16	51	27	6	100	12
Fourth level (%)	11	40	40	8	100	9
Highest real income level (%)	11	39	41	9	100	8
All income levels (%)						19
All households (%)	25	43	26	6	100	

Source: Derived from Department for Transport (2009).
[a]Figure does not add up to 100% because of rounding.

availability and access is also differentiated by ethnic group, the proportion of people aged 17 and over living in a household with a car was very similar among people of Indian background (84%), Pakistani background (82%) and white British people (83%). However, 54% of adults of black African background, 63% of other ethnic groups, 64% of white other and 67% of Caribbeans lived in a household with a car (Table 3.2). Such figures potentially suggest the interrelationships of economic and cultural reproduction in affecting the mobility opportunities of individuals.

The 2008 NTS indicates that commuting and business travel accounted for 19% of all trips and 28% of the average

distance travelled, while visiting friends and other leisure (including holidays and day trips) accounted for 31% and 40%, respectively. Unfortunately, these figures have not been broken down by income. However, there is a clear relationship between household income and the number of trips taken as well as the distance travelled. In 2008, on average people in the highest income quintile group made 24% more trips than those in the lowest income quintile group and travelled two and a half times further (10,290 versus 4112 miles per person) (DfT, 2009) (Table 3.3). Car access is the most significant factor affecting travel in every income quintile. Households with access make more trips and travel further

Table 3.2. Personal car access by ethnic group in Great Britain for aged 17+ (2005–2008) (%).

Ethnic group	Persons in households without a car	Persons in households with a car				All persons
		Main driver	Other driver	Non-driver	All	
White British	17	57	13	13	83	100
White other	36	38	13	12	64	100
Indian	16	46	15	22	84	100
Pakistani	18	40	14	28	82	100
Other Asian background	32	32	7	29	68	100
Caribbean	33	42	9	16	67	100
African	46	31	6	16	54	100
Other (mixed, other Black, Chinese or other ethnic group)	37	36	10	17	63	100
All groups	19	55	12	13	81	100

Source: Derived from Department for Transport (2009).

Table 3.3. Travel by household income quintile by number of trips and distance travelled in Great Britain, 2008.

	Lowest real income	Second level	Third level	Fourth level	Highest real income	All income levels
Trips per person per year by main mode						
Walk	271	230	228	200	181	221
Bicycle	15	16	15	17	16	16
Car driver	225	334	438	497	536	410
Car passenger	199	219	252	240	218	227
Other private transport	11	14	15	13	10	13
Bus and coach	107	88	55	48	35	66
Rail	15	14	17	29	59	27
Taxi and minicab	13	14	9	9	11	11
Other public transport	2	2	1	2	2	2
All modes	860	931	1,032	1,054	1,069	992
Distance per person per year by mode						
Walk	204	186	200	186	191	193
Bicycle	34	36	40	49	51	42
Car driver	1,469	2,277	3,297	4,432	5,845	3,494
Car passenger	1,466	1,783	2,023	2,275	2,268	1,974
Other private transport	90	138	182	187	137	149
Bus and coach	537	454	327	334	199	367
Rail	223	290	370	626	1,348	570
Taxi and minicab	55	52	40	45	79	54
Other public transport	34	26	40	127	172	80
All modes	4,112	5,241	6,519	8,261	10,290	6,923

Adapted from Department for Transport (2009).

than those without. In 2008, 49% of trips among the lowest income group were by car compared with 71% among the highest. The British level of car ownership in lower income households is comparable with the wealthier EU members, but lower than newer EU members.

European Union

Table 3.4 indicates the percentage of European households that cannot afford a personal car because of household income levels (below 60% of median equivalized income). To enable comparisons between households of different sizes and across the EU Member States, equivalized incomes are defined as the household's total disposable income divided by its 'equivalent size'. A quotient is attributed to each household member (including children) on the basis of

the Organization for Economic and Co-operative Development (OECD) modified scale. A weight of 1.0 is given to the first adult, 0.5 to other persons aged 14 or over who are living in the household and 0.3 to each child aged less than 14 (Eurostat, 2010b). Possession of a personal car has been adopted as one of the indicators of the 'Material Deprivation Rate' by the Indicators Sub-Group of the Social Protection Committee at the European Commission, so as to complement monetary measures of living standards with some non-monetary measures in monitoring poverty and social exclusion at EU level (Zaidi, 2010). Such an indicator suggests that mobility capacity is therefore a potential component of measures of material deprivation and are significant for tourism and leisure mobility because of the extent to which vehicle access is identified as dominating leisure travel throughout the developed world (e.g. Axhausen, 2001;

Table 3.4. Enforced lack of a personal car and capacity to afford a 1-week annual holiday in the European Union (% of population below 60% of median equivalized income).

Geographical area	Enforced lack of a personal car					Capacity to afford a 1-week annual holiday
	2004	2005	2006	2007	2008	2007
European Union (27 countries)	na	na	na	22	20	65
European Union (25 countries)	na	20	18	17	17	–
European Union (15 countries)	na	16	14	14	14	–
New Member States	na	38	38	35	30	–
Euro area	na	16	14	14	14	–
Belgium	25	27	25	25	23	58
Bulgaria	na	na	na	67	48	98
Czech Republic	na	44	45	43	37	73
Denmark	30	27	28	24	23	23
Germany	na	26	17	17	18	55
Estonia	46	48	37	39	34	87
Ireland	25	26	26	24	21	42
Greece	20	19	16	19	16	76
Spain	12	12	10	10	11	58
France	14	13	13	11	15	63
Italy	9	8	8	8	8	71
Cyprus	na	9	8	8	5	82
Latvia	na	55	52	47	43	91
Lithuania	na	51	43	29	26	89
Luxembourg	7	9	7	9	10	39
Hungary	na	41	44	42	37	90
Malta	na	8	8	9	6	83
Netherlands	na	17	18	20	19	35
Austria	16	14	15	20	24	58
Poland	na	36	35	33	28	89
Portugal	25	24	25	28	20	89
Romania	na	na	na	75	64	97
Slovenia	na	13	14	16	14	64
Slovakia	na	38	47	48	38	84
Finland	25	29	30	28	27	47
Sweden	14	14	15	14	11	35
UK	na	14	13	14	14	43
Iceland	8	8	5	6	6	28
Norway	24	25	17	20	21	18

Eurostat (2010a, 2010b).

Cao and Mokhtarian, 2005; Hall, 2005a; Tourism Australia, 2009).

The EU also include the capacity to afford a 1-week annual holiday as part of its indicators of material deprivation. Within the EU-27, almost two-thirds of those at risk of poverty were unable to afford a 1-week annual holiday (65%). By type of household, single parents with dependent children had the highest relative incapacity to afford a 1-week holiday (76%) (Eurostat, 2010b). The inclusion of the holiday affordability indicator reflects that holidays are regarded within the EU as being part of a decent life. Guio (2009: 3) notes that to be a Eurostat indicator of 'lifestyle deprivation', an item should 'reflects the lack of an ordinary living pattern common to a majority or large part of the population in the European Union and most of its Member States'. Significantly, she reports EU survey data that suggests that 49% of people consider holidays as absolutely necessary or necessary. This is just below that of a telephone (51%), car (56%) and a television (65%).

The UK and EU experiences emphasize that poverty is strongly related to a relative lack of mobility, whether measured as trips, distance travelled or even the speed of travel (as the availability of mode of transport will affect the speed at which point to point journeys can be made). Such relative lack of mobility affects not only access to work opportunities and services but also leisure and tourism opportunities. These relationships also strongly emerge in US travel data.

United States

In the USA, driving is the dominant travel mode across all income levels. However, as in the UK, household income has a significant influence, especially at the upper and lower levels, on mode choice. Long-distance travel data from the 2001 US national household travel survey provides some significant insights into longer-distance day-tripping and tourism travel

(Table 3.5). Although personal vehicle is the dominant mode for all long-distance travel, the percentage of trips made by driving declines substantially for those with incomes over US$75,000 annually. For those above that income level, 84% of long-distance trips are made by driving, below that level more than 91% of long-distance trips are made by driving. High-income households have a greater capacity to switch modes of transport for long-distance travel with those with incomes in excess of US$75,000 making nearly 14% of their long-distance trips by air, compared with only 3–5% of trips by those households below that income level. In contrast, those with household incomes below $25,000 are more likely to make trips by bus than those at the higher income levels (Bureau of Transportation Statistics, 2006).

The results of the 2001 travel survey reflected those of the 1995 survey. As in other national travel surveys, there is an increase in long-distance trip generation with income, with the trip generation rate almost tripling in the transition from the very-low-income group to the very-high-income group (Georggi and Penyala, 2001). Whereas 46% of the lowest income group households made zero long-distance trips, just 17% of the highest income group did so. At the time of the 1995 survey, about 30% of the low-income population lived in a household without a vehicle, with vehicle availability being an important determinant of long-distance travel. The trip rate per

Table 3.5. Percentage of long-distance trips by mode for US household income groups (2001).

Mode	Less than US$25K	Standard error	US$25K-$49K	Standard error	US$50-$74K	Standard error	US$75K+	Standard error
Personal vehicle	92.2	0.81	93.3	0.40	91.7	0.55	83.9	0.63
Air	3.0	0.34	3.8	0.29	5.3	0.39	13.7	0.61
Bus	3.8	0.57	2.1	0.19	2.0	0.29	1.5	0.19
Train	0.7	0.22	0.6	0.18	0.8	0.22	0.8	0.15
Other	0.3	0.28	0.1	0.05	0.3	0.14	0.2	0.05
Total	100.0		100.0		100.0		100.0	

Only trips for which transportation mode and household income can be determined are tabulated.
Column totals may not add to 100% because of rounding (United States Department of Transportation (2001) and Bureau of Transportation Statistics (2006)).

person of low-income households without a vehicle was about a third that of people in low-income households with one vehicle, and about a quarter that of people in such households with two or more vehicles. On average, low-income people made 1.6 long-distance person trips in 1995 compared with 3.9 trips for the entire population. The non-low-income population as a whole made 4.4 trips annually, with persons in households with medium-low income making 2.6 trips a year, medium-high income 4.2 trips and high income 6.3 trips (Mallett, 2001).

New Zealand

In New Zealand, the most recent publication from the national travel survey at the time of writing does not report on the relationship between household income and travel (Ministry of Transport, 2009a), although as elsewhere in the developed world, the car is the dominant mode of transport overall. For social and holiday motivations, it accounts for 82% of all travel, which is marginally higher than its use for work. The country's domestic tourism survey indicates that the car is the dominant mode of transport for domestic travellers, with over 90% of visitors to most destinations using a car, while the vast majority of day trips (more than 95%) are also conducted by car (Ministry of Tourism, 2006). Previous New Zealand studies have indicated a relationship between personal income and travel and reinforce the notion that high-income people spend more time travelling and travel further than low-income people (Ministry of Transport, 2008). Approximately 8% of New Zealand households do not have access to a motor vehicle (a drop of 5% since 1986), although there is a growing percentage of the population that sees private transport cost as a barrier to use. In 2002 the figure was 19%; by 2006 it had reached 46% (Ministry of Transport, 2009b). The New Zealand domestic travel survey also examines the reasons for not travelling. If a survey respondent reports no day or overnight

trips during the specified recall period (1 week for day trips and 1 month for overnight trips), they are asked a series of questions about why they did not travel. In the 2005 survey, 25% of people cited being too busy as their main reason for not travelling, up from 23% in 1999, while around 19% responded that they did not travel because they had no reason to. Approximately 5% say they did not travel because of no money and 6% because of bad health. Overall, around 60% of domestic travel survey respondents in each year do not report a day or overnight trip within the specified recall period (Ministry of Tourism, 2006). However, one of the difficulties in examining non-travel is the extent to which a stated rationale given by respondents may be different from actual reasons (McKercher, 2009).

A series of interviews conducted by the author within New Zealand on 'staycations' (narrowly interpreted as leisure holidays taken in the home environment but also understood as any holiday period or opportunity that is spent at home) reinforces the connection between income levels and leisure travel opportunities. A series of 14 interviews had been conducted by the time of writing. A common theme across nearly all participants is that leisure travel opportunities remain restricted in line with other social and economic opportunities, such as maintaining social contacts and employment opportunities. Where overnight travel is undertaken, it is usually because of family reasons and, in a number of cases, the cost of the trip has been met in whole or part by other family members. In one case, this included international travel to the UK for 4 weeks, which was paid for by the participant's son, and a week-long trip to another town in the South Island paid for by the daughter. Yet apart from that, the participant had not travelled at all since losing car access. Usual leisure-related travel tended to be highly localized, with the bus or walking being more commonly utilized than a car. Staying at home during school or other holidays was therefore regarded as an economic necessity as opposed to a social preference. Although visiting friends and family was seen as an opportunity for travel, a comment such as 'you still have be able to afford to get there' was common, while several interviewees noted 'that they 'didn't want to impose' and would not stay overnight unless invited.

Perhaps one of the most interesting aspects of the conversations with participants was the extent to which the desire for a 'real holiday' was regarded as being extremely attractive. Several respondents used the notion of 'escape', with one commenting: '... I would just love a break from just trying to make ends meet. I don't even need to go to one of those places you see on TV like Bali or the Gold Coast. Even a few days in a caravan by the beach would suit me.' Interestingly, the idea that domestic holidays had become less affordable was shared by several participants who noted that the 'old-fashioned' holiday at a public holiday park or camping ground had disappeared: 'It's got more expensive now. I used to be able to stay in a caravan or holiday park or even park-up near the beach. Now they've been closed or gone up-market.'

Yet for a number of respondents, while the idea of a holiday – even a relatively short distance away – was attractive, they emphasized that one of the difficulties in trying to have a holiday was structural, in that the nature of their employment (usually part-time or casual) meant that they felt it difficult to take time off, partly for income reasons but also because they were concerned as to whether their employer would look less favourably on them. Clearly, at a period of economic downturn, perceived job security therefore became a factor affecting decisions to requesting 'time off' from employers. The results of the interviews, even though limited, suggest that while the relationship between low-income earners and relative lack of travel opportunities hold, the relative immobility is not necessarily because of an absence of interest. Several respondents believed that a holiday would improve their health and overall wellbeing.

The perceived loss of cheap holiday locations is also possibly not unjustified as many beach-front campgrounds have been closed and/or converted to residential or more formal accommodation use (Collins and Kearns, 2010), but perhaps more significantly, the interviews suggest that leisure travel opportunities are restricted by regulative mechanisms such as occupation and the nature of employment as well as relative lack of income as well.

Conclusions

In their article of social exclusion, mobility and access, Cass *et al.* (2005: 539) argued that 'much of the literature on social exclusion ignores its "spatial" or "mobility" related aspects'. Apart from the obvious lack of recognition of studies of the spatial dimensions of social exclusion by geographers, this notion can be turned around so that perhaps, more accurately, we could suggest that much of the literature on mobility excludes its social exclusion-related aspects. This is especially so with respect to tourism mobility. Yet, as this chapter has illustrated, mobility is unevenly distributed and the number of trips, distance travelled, speed of travel and mode of travel – some of the key determinants of the activity spaces and networks of individuals – are substantially affected by income levels. Income is not the sole explanatory variable – the life chances of individuals including with respect to tourism opportunities are also affected by cultural and economic reproduction and capital – but it is a critical one.

Any attempt to relate conceptions of tourism to social justice needs to do so with respect to both the production and consumption of tourism opportunities. As has been suggested above, the terrain of understanding on tourism with respect to both policy and the academy has been strongly influenced by neoliberal thinking in the role of the state, the market and the individual. This has meant that the social justice policy agenda in tourism has often been more geared by some policy actors to the use of tourism as a market implement for 'pro-poor' tourism development and the encouragement of economic liberalization (Schilcher, 2007), rather than being positioned within a broader understanding of human welfare and economic equality issues. Moralizing mobility with respect to equality should therefore, as Pirie (2009: 33) observes, 'not be construed as pathologizing mobility or preaching immobility. Rather, bringing mobility into the orbit of ethics signals that geographical mobility should be considered a more precious asset whose use needs tempering.' The challenge is to start contesting the purposes and practices of mobility and seeing its study not as a technical–rational drive for efficiency in a market of consumers but understanding mobility and accessibility being imbued with values that are central to human well-being and a sustainable society.

Access to new communication technologies is often proposed as a response to problems of mobility access. However, such new technologies are not a solution, even if it can be accepted that virtual leisure communities are a substitute for physical leisure and tourism mobility. Instead, they are also unevenly distributed and even where low-income households may have Internet access, the quality of such access is typically not as great as higher income brackets (Fitzpatrick, 2003). Rather than giving rise to an experience of constant mobility and 'anytime–anywhere' availability, low-income individuals and households continue to face limitations

and exclusions that profoundly constrict the potential leisure 'mobility' afforded by these devices (Ureta, 2008). Instead, 'solutions' need to be found within the broader context of economic and welfare policies.

The activity spaces of poorer members of society are significantly smaller than those of wealthier members. This is not to suggest that lower-income groups should become hyper-mobile, but it is to note, along the lines of Kenyon *et al.* (2002), that reduced accessibility to facilities, goods and services, including those relating to leisure and tourism opportunities, are significant dimensions and factors of social exclusion (Schönfelder, 2006). The size and structure of the leisure and tourism activity space of individuals may potentially act as a highly political indicator of social justice. If tourism studies is to embrace social justice as a significant concept for its work, then it needs to understood not in terms of expanding the market but how tourism and leisure opportunities are part of the overall life chances of individuals and how these are constituted and reproduced.

Questions

1. Why might inequalities in access to mobility in terms of income level also be related to differences in access on the basis of ethnic group or gender?
2. Why are the activity spaces of individuals related to their life chances?
3. Should the capacity to afford a 1-week annual holiday be an indicator of material deprivation?

References

Adey, P. (2006) If mobility is everything then it is nothing: towards a relational politics of (im)mobilities. *Mobilities* 1, 75–94.

Addo, S.T. (1995) Accessibility, mobility and the development process. *Institute of African Studies: Research Review* 11, 1–15.

Atkins, D. and Moy, E.M. (2005) Left behind: the legacy of hurricane Katrina. *British Medical Journal* 331, 916–918.

Axhausen, K.W. (2001) Methodological research for an European survey of long-distance travel. In: *Personal Travel: The Long and Short of It, Conference Proceedings*, 28 June–1 July 1999, Washington, D.C., TRB Transportation Research Circular E-C026. Transportation Research Board, Washington DC, pp. 321–342.

Bauman, Z. (1998) *Globalization: Human Consequences.* Polity Press, Cambridge.

BBC News (2005) British tourists 'flee Superdome'. 2 September. Available at: http://news.bbc.co.uk/2/hi/uk_news/england/wear/4208792.stm (accessed 25 January 2006).

Berjamo, P.M. (2006) Preparation and response in case of natural disasters: Cuban programs and experience. *Journal of Public Health Policy* 27, 13–21.

Bramwell, B. and Lane, B. (2005) Editorial: sustainable tourism research and the importance of societal and social science trends. *Journal of Sustainable Tourism* 13, 1–3.

Bureau Internationale du Tourisme Social (BITS) (2009) The European Parliament approves a pilot project on social tourism, Press Release, 20 January 2009. BITS, Brussels.

Bureau of Transportation Statistics (2006) *Long Distance Transportation Patterns: Mode Choice.* Bureau of Transportation Statistics, Washington, DC.

Cao, X. and Mokhtarian, P.L. (2005) How do individuals adapt their personal travel? Objective and subjective influences on the consideration of travel-related strategies for San Francisco Bay Area commuters. *Transport Policy* 12, 291–302.

Cass, N., Shove, E. and Urry, J. (2005) Social exclusion, mobility and access. *Sociological Review* 53, 539–555.

Chen, J.S., Huang, Y. and Cheng, J. (2009) Vacation lifestyles and travel behaviours. *Journal of Travel & Tourism Marketing* 26, 494–506.

Coles, T., Duval, D. and Hall, C.M. (2004) Tourism, mobility and global communities: new approaches to theorising tourism and tourist spaces. In: Theobold, W. (ed.) *Global Tourism*, 3rd edn. Heinemann, Oxford, pp. 463–481.

Coles, T., Hall, C.M. and Duval, D. (2005) Mobilising tourism: a post-disciplinary critique. *Tourism Recreation Research* 30, 31–41.

Collins, D. and Kearns, R. (2010) 'Pulling up the tent pegs?' The significance and changing status of coastal campgrounds in New Zealand. *Tourism Geographies* 12, 53–76.

Cresswell, T. (1997) Imagining the nomad: mobility and the postmodern primitive. In: Benko, G. and Strohmayer, U. (eds) *Space and Social Theory: Interpreting Modernity and Postmodernity*. Blackwell, Oxford, pp. 360–379.

Department for Transport (2009) *Transport Statistics Bulletin, National Travel Survey: 2008.* A National Statistics Publication produced by Transport Statistics, Department for Transport. Department for Transport, London.

Eurostat (2010a) Enforced lack of a personal car (last updated 17 February 2010). Available at: http://nui.epp.eurostat.ec.europa.eu/nui/show.do?dataset=ilc_mddu05&lang=en (accessed 27 February 2010).

Eurostat (2010b) *Combating Poverty and Social Exclusion. A Statistical Portrait of the European Union 2010.* Eurostat European Commission, Luxembourg.

Favell, A. (2001) Migration, mobility and globaloney: metaphors and rhetoric in the sociology of globalization. *Global Networks* 1, 389–398.

Fitzpatrick, T. (2003) Introduction: new technologies and social policy. *Critical Social Policy* 23, 131–138.

Georggi, N.L. and Pendyala, R.M. (2001) Analysis of long-distance travel behavior of the elderly and low income. In In: *Personal Travel: The Long and Short of It, Conference Proceedings*, 28 June–1 July 1999, Washington, D.C., TRB Transportation Research Circular E-C026. Transportation Research Board, Washington DC, pp. 121–150.

Giddens, A. (1984) *The Constitution of Society: Outline of the Theory of Structuration.* University of California Press, Berkeley, CA.

Govers, R., Go, F.M. and Kumar, K. (2007) Promoting destination image. *Journal of Travel Research* 46, 15–23.

Guidotti, T.L. (2006) Hurricane Katrina: an American tragedy. *Occupational Medicine* 56, 222–224.

Guio, A-C. (2009) What can be learned from deprivation indicators in Europe? Paper presented at the Indicator Subgroup of the Social Protection Committee, 10 February 2009. EUROSTAT methodological and working paper. Eurostat, Luxembourg.

Gössling, S., Ceron, J-P., Dubios, G. and Hall, C.M. (2009) Hypermobile travelers. In: Gössling, S. and Upham, P. (eds) *Climate Change and Aviation*. Earthscan, London, pp. 131–149.

Gross, M.J., Brien, C. and Brown, G. (2008) Examining the dimensions of a lifestyle tourism destination. *International Journal of Culture, Tourism and Hospitality Research* 2, 44–66.

Gustafson, P. (2006) Place attachment and mobility. In: McIntyre, N., Williams, D. and McHugh, K. (eds) *Multiple Dwelling and Tourism: Negotiating Place, Home and Identity*. CAB International, Wallingford, UK, pp. 17–31.

Hall, C.M. (2005a) *Tourism: Rethinking the Social Science of Mobility*. Pearson, Harlow.

Hall, C.M. (2005b) Reconsidering the geography of tourism and contemporary mobility. *Geographical Research* 43, 125–39.

Hall, C.M. (2005c) Time, space, tourism and social physics. *Tourism Recreation Research* 30, 93–8.

Haulot, A. (1981) Social tourism: current dimensions and future developments. *Tourism Management* 2, 207–12.

Hinch, T. and Jackson, E.L. (2000) Leisure constraints research: its value as a framework for understanding tourism seasonability. *Current Issues in Tourism* 3, 87–106.

Hudson, S. and Gilbert, D. (2000) Tourism constraints: the neglected dimension in consumer behaviour research. *Journal of Travel & Tourism Marketing* 8, 69–78.

Kenyon, S., Lyons, G. and Rafferty, J. (2002) Transport and social exclusion: investigating the possibility of promoting inclusion through virtual mobility. *Journal of Transport Geography* 10, 207–219.

Laws, E. and Thyne, M. (eds) (2004) *Hospitality, Tourism, and Lifestyle Concepts: Implications for Quality Management and Customer Satisfaction*. Haworth Press, Binghamton, NY.

Mallett, W.J. (2001) Long-distance travel by low-income households. In: *Personal Travel: The Long and Short of It, Conference Proceedings*, 28 June–1 July 1999, Washington, D.C., TRB Transportation Research Circular E-C026. Transportation Research Board, Washington DC, pp. 169–177.

McKercher, B. (2009) Non-travel by Hong Kong residents. *International Journal of Tourism Research* 11, 507–519.

Ministry of Tourism (2006) *New Zealand Domestic and Outbound Travel Patterns*. Ministry of Tourism, Wellington.

Ministry of Transport (2008) *1997/98 Travel Survey Highlights – Personal Income and Travel*. Available at: http://www.transport.govt.nz/research/Pages/199798TravelSurveyHighlights-PersonalIncomeandTravel.aspx (accessed 10 December 2009).

Ministry of Transport (2009a) *How New Zealanders Travel: Trends in New Zealand Household Travel 1989–2008*. Ministry of Transport, Wellington.

Ministry of Transport (2009b) *Transport Monitoring Indicator Framework* (TMIF). Available at: http://www.transport.govt.nz/ourwork/tmif/ (accessed 10 December 2009).

Murphy, P.E. (1985) *Tourism: A Community Approach*. Methuen, New York.

Nyaupane, G.P. and Andereck, K.L. (2008) Understanding travel constraints: application and extension of a leisure constraints model. *Journal of Travel Research* 46, 433–439.

Peeters, P., Gössling, S. and Becken, S. (2006) Innovation towards tourism sustainability: climate change and aviation. *International Journal of Innovation and Sustainable Development* 1, 184–200.

Pirie, G.H. (2009) Virtuous mobility: moralising vs measuring geographical mobility in Africa. *Afrika Focus* 22, 21–35.

Rhoads, J., Mitchell, F. and Rick, S. (2006) Posttraumatic stress disorder after Hurricane Katrina. *The Journal for Nurse Practitioners* 2, 18–26.

Schönfelder, S. (2006) Urban rhythms – modelling the rhythms of individual travel behaviour, unpublished dissertation. University of Dortmund, Dortmund.

Schilcher, D. (2007) Growth versus equity: the continuum of pro-poor tourism and neoliberal governance. *Current Issues in Tourism* 10, 166–193.

Sheller, M. and Urry, J. (2003) Mobile transformations of 'public' and 'private' life. *Theory, Culture & Society* 20, 107–125.

Sheller, M. and Urry, J. (2006) The new mobilities paradigm. *Environment and Planning A* 38, 207–226.

Szerszynski, B. and Urry, J. (2006) Visuality, mobility and the cosmopolitan: inhabiting the world from afar. *British Journal of Sociology* 57, 113–131.

Tasci, A.D.A. and Gartner, W.C. (2007) Destination image and its functional relationships. *Journal of Travel Research* 45, 413–425.

Tapachai, N. and Waryszak, R. (2000) An examination of the role of beneficial image in tourist destination. *Journal of Travel Research* 39, 37–44.

Tourism Australia (2009) *Transport Fact Sheet 2009*. Tourism Australia, Canberra.

Tsing, A. (1998) The global situation. *Cultural Anthropology* 15, 327–360.

United States Department of Transportation (2001) *National Household Travel Survey, Long-distance file, 2001*. US Department of Transportation, Research and Innovative Technology Administration, Bureau of Transportation Statistics, Federal Highway Administration, Washington, DC.

Ureta, S. (2008) Mobilising poverty? Mobile phone use and everyday spatial mobility among low-income families in Santiago, Chile. *The Information Society* 24, 83–92.

Urry, J. (2000) *Sociology Beyond Societies*. London: Routledge.
VisitBritain, VisitScotland, Visit Wales and Northern Ireland Tourism Board. (2009) *United Kingdom Tourism Survey 2008*, produced by TNS Travel & Tourism. VisitBritain, London.
Wang, N. (2000) *Tourism and Modernity: A Sociological Analysis*. Elsevier Science/Pergamon, Oxford.
Zaidi, A. (2010) *Poverty Risks for Older People in EU Countries – An Update*. Policy Brief, January. European Centre for Social Welfare Policy and Research, Vienna.

4 Sex Tourism and Inequalities

Jacqueline Sánchez Taylor

In academic as well as popular usage, the term 'sex tourism' has generally been used to refer to tourism that is linked to commercial sex, as opposed to sex with other tourists or non-commercial sexual experience with local partners. As such, it is shaped by, and can serve to reproduce, a number of different though often intersecting forms of inequality. This chapter begins by considering the global political and economic context in which sex tourism has developed, and then explores its connections to inequalities structured along lines of gender, race, age and class.

Global Political and Economic Inequalities

Until the 1980s, tourism research was a relatively small and specialist field, and within this, links between sex and tourism attracted very little research attention. From the late 1980s, however, a small number of feminists began to express concern about 'sex tourism', using the term to refer to mass prostitution, which was linked, directly or indirectly, with the development of tourism in 'Third World' countries. Wendy Lee (1991: 141) argued that 'tourism and prostitution are now a "package commodity" marketed on an international scale'. Key early texts on the topic include Cynthia Enloe's (1989) *Bananas, Beaches and Bases*, which focused on links between the military's masculinist ideology and the sexual exploitation of women and Than

Dam Truong's (1990) *Sex, Money and Morality*, which explored the political economy of sex tourism in Thailand. A number of other studies of militarized prostitution and sex tourism in South-east Asia appeared in the early 1990s, showing how foreign economic and military interventions had played a crucial role in the development of sex tourism in the region (Heyzer, 1986).

In Thailand, as in several other South-east Asian countries, a period of 'economic colonialism and militarization in which prostitution is a formalized mechanism of dominance' has been a key stage in the development of sex tourism (Hall, 1994: 151). With the encouragement of the World Bank, tourist development policy in Thailand in the 1970s attempted to maximize profits by capitalizing on accommodation and 'entertainment' facilities, which had been put in place to serve US military personnel on 'Rest and Recreation' (R&R) (Truong, 1990). Indeed, the close links between militarization and economic colonialism are illustrated by the fact that it was 'World Bank President Robert McNamara, who had been US Secretary of Defense when the R&R contracts with Thailand were signed' who went to Bangkok in 1971 'to arrange for the bank's experts to produce a study of Thailand's postwar tourism prospects' (Bishop and Robinson, 1998: 98). While prostitution may have existed before the R&R contracts, militarization played major role in developing the sex industry in the region. On the one hand, the US military sanctioned and facilitated the existence of brothels to meet the assumed 'physical necessities' of the troops (Sturdevant and Stoltzfus, 1992), while on the other, the local business community, international businesses and the military sought to profit from the many small-scale operations (Truong, 1990).

It is estimated that from the 1960s to the mid-1970s, thousands of local women and girls were engaged in prostitution serving the thousands of American men in service in South-east Asia. Lee (1991) estimated that in Thailand between 1966 and 1974, the number of 'special job workers', a euphemism for prostitute, increased from 1246 to over 7000, while some 20,000 'entertainment' establishments nationwide generated over US$20 million (Truong, 1990). A similar expansion of sexual services occurred in other countries such as the Philippines (Ofreneo and Ofreneo, 1998) and South Korea (Mitter, 1986; Hall, 1992; Leheny, 1995). Korean women were even trained for Japanese businessmen in their new role as 'Kisaeng girls', to further the government's economic plan:

> Prospective Kisaeng are given lectures by a male university professor on the crucial role of tourism in South Korea's economy before they get their licenses. And South Korean ministers have praised the sincerity of girls who have contributed to their fatherland's economic development.
>
> (Mitter, 1986: 64)

Sturdevant and Stoltzfus (1992) observed that R&R centres became models for tourist 'playgrounds' and the development of the tourist prostitution industry in Asia. Entry into the tourist market for many South-east Asian countries rested on exploiting the existing entertainment infrastructure created by and for the US military for quick foreign exchange. Generous incentives were given to foreign investors which resulted in many of the girlie bars, go-go bars and sex floor shows being foreign owned and run. The red light areas and brothel districts that became most famous among tourists were those developed by this kind of 'sexpatriate' involvement and investment (e.g. the Soi Cowboy area and Pat Pong Road in Bangkok).

Thus early research on sex tourism tended to:

- emphasize the links between foreign military and economic interventions and the development of sex tourism in South-east Asia; and
- focus almost exclusively on male tourists' consumption of sexual services provided by female sex workers in the formally organized 'sex sector' (i.e. in business establishments such as brothels, go-go bars, massage parlours).

However, it was soon noted that:

- tourist-related prostitution in developing countries (in South-east Asia as well as other regions) can actually take many forms;
- sexual–economic exchanges between locals and tourists have emerged as a highly visible feature of tourism in locations where *no* such sex industry existed, for instance, The Gambia, Brazil and Cuba; and
- tourist-related sexual exchanges take place in the informal sex industry as well as the formally organized sex industry.

As O'Connell Davidson (2005) observes, structural adjustment driven by global economic policies has created a 'surplus' labouring population, as well as driving down wages of those in work in many less economically developed countries (LEDCs). This has encouraged large numbers of ordinary people to turn to the informal economic sector in search of ways to earn a living, or supplement or substitute for impossibly low-waged employment. Though sex tourism involves only a minority of local and migrant persons, expatriates and tourists in any given setting, it is none the less the case that prostitution and other forms of informal economic activity that take place around tourists are an important part of the tourism economy in developing countries such as Africa, Latin America, the Caribbean and South Asia, as well as in South-east Asia (e.g. Dahles, 1998; Phillips, 1999; Ratnapala, 1999; Ford and Wirawan, 2000; Sánchez Taylor, 2001; Cabezas, 2004; Nyanzi

Fig. 4.1. Massages on the beach in the Dominican Republic. This is just one of the informal activities that take place on the beach. Others include selling trinkets and drinks, shoe-shine boys, providing taxi services, braiding hair, etc.

et al., 2005). Sex tourism has also emerged alongside tourist development in a number of East European and newly independent states following the collapse of the Soviet Union and the fall of the Berlin wall. It was again fuelled by economic and political instability and inequalities, and often entailed the growth of informal and open-ended prostitution as much as the development of a formally organized sex sector (Clift and Carter, 2000).

Indeed, research has increasingly drawn attention to the fact that sites of sex tourism in developing countries are often distinguished not simply or necessarily by the existence of a large, diverse, formally organized sex industry, but more particularly by the existence of a busy informal sex sector and can straddle both the formal and informal sectors.

The sexual exchanges that take place in the informal tourist-related sector tend to resemble non-commercial sexual relationships, as local women often act in ways that are taken to signify genuine affection, for instance holding hands, kissing, walking arm in arm, sharing a bed and providing some form of intimacy (O'Connell Davidson,

1995), making these relationships difficult to categorize as straightforward prostitution. This is made even more complicated when some of those who engage in open-ended prostitution would identify themselves as 'sex workers', but rather enter into sexual relationships with tourists to supplement their income if they already have jobs, or in the hope of a chance to migrate through friendship/marriage to a tourist. As will be seen below, this has important implications for tourists' subjective perceptions of the meanings of sexual–economic exchanges with locals, and so for their willingness to engage in such exchanges.

Sex Tourism and Gender Inequality

The vast majority of sex workers in tourist-related prostitution are women and the vast majority of clients who travel for sex are men. Many of those seeking to theorize sex tourism have therefore focused on the patriarchal power structures that underpin women's entry into prostitution and men's desire and economic capacity to consume

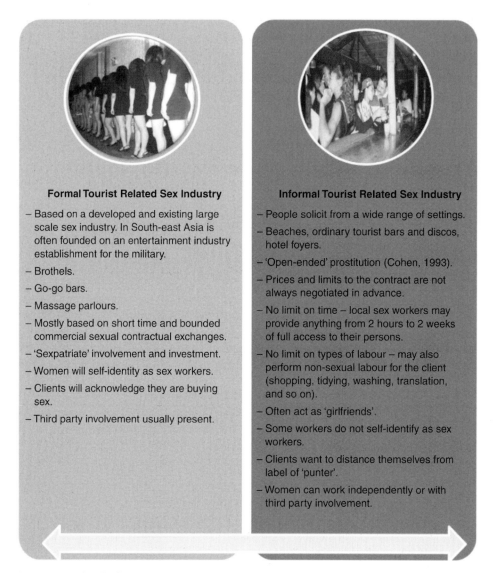

Formal Tourist Related Sex Industry

– Based on a developed and existing large
  scale sex industry. In South-east Asia is
  often founded on an entertainment industry
  establishment for the military.

– Brothels.

– Go-go bars.

– Massage parlours.

– Mostly based on short time and bounded
  commercial sexual contractual exchanges.

– 'Sexpatriate' involvement and investment.

– Women will self-identity as sex workers.

– Clients will acknowledge they are buying
  sex.

– Third party involvement usually present.

Informal Tourist Related Sex Industry

– People solicit from a wide range of settings.

– Beaches, ordinary tourist bars and discos,
  hotel foyers.

– 'Open-ended' prostitution (Cohen, 1993).

– Prices and limits to the contract are not
  always negotiated in advance.

– No limit on time – local sex workers may
  provide anything from 2 hours to 2 weeks
  of full access to their persons.

– No limit on types of labour – may also
  perform non-sexual labour for the client
  (shopping, tidying, washing, translation,
  and so on).

– Often act as 'girlfriends'.

– Some workers do not self-identify as sex
  workers.

– Clients want to distance themselves from
  label of 'punter'.

– Women can work independently or with
  third party involvement.

Fig. 4.2. Formal and informal tourist-related sex industry.

sexual services. Prostitution has more
generally been theorized by radical feminists as first and foremost an expression of
male patriarchal power and female powerlessness (Barry, 1995; Jeffreys, 1997).
Patriarchal structures ensure men's political
dominance over women at national level,
and global policies and development often
reflect and further reinforce gender
inequalities. Many analysts have therefore
been keen to explore how regimes of gender

and questions of gender inequality shape
sex tourism, and have emphasized the
following as common factors precipitating
women and girls' entry into prostitution in
sex tourist destinations in LECDs:

• Gender inequality restricts women and
  girls' opportunities for education and
  employment. Many girls in LEDCs are
  not sent to school and instead have to
  look after the home and younger siblings.

Girls are not encouraged to take on skilled work and are excluded from many sectors of a gendered labour market shaped by essentialist ideas. Women and young girls are usually found in low-paid jobs like domestic work, hairdressing and sewing.

- Changing employment patterns have made men's work more unskilled, low-paid and casual. This has lead to a breakdown of the traditional family institution, as men can no longer afford to support families or have to leave to search for work. This has resulted in women becoming head of households, often supporting children and other vulnerable family members.
- The lack of sex education, educational opportunities and the belief that young women only become recognized adults through having a child results in a high rate of teenage pregnancy. Young girls and women are often left as the sole providers for their child and have to find ways to provide financially for their children from a limited number of options.
- Strict gendered systems governed by religious or state apparatus and essentialist ideas about sexuality shapes the sexual behaviour and identity of women. Girls and women are traditionally encouraged to remain virgins until they marry, and sex outside marriage or deviant sexual behaviour is heavily stigmatized. Once a woman becomes sexually active outside marriage, women are often regarded as 'fallen women', which reinforces their exclusion and can lock them into prostitution.

Gender and Male Demand for Sex Tourism

Researchers have also examined links between gender inequalities and the demand for sex tourism (Kruhse-Mount Burton, 1995; O'Connell Davidson, 1995, 2001). Radical feminist writers (who are more generally concerned to demonstrate that female prostitution has its basis in, and serves to reproduce, patriarchal power relations, e.g. Barry, 1995; Hughes, 2000; Raymond, 2004) often draw on the findings of such research to support the argument that 'Prostitution tourists seek to buy subordination when they travel' (Jeffreys, 2009: 151). There is certainly evidence that some male tourists travel to LEDCs with the explicit and conscious intention of buying sexual services because they know that first, commercial sex is cheap in these countries, and second, the array of different forms of commercial sex on offer is wide, so that there is a very high level of 'consumer choice'. In sex tourist destinations in LEDCs, prostitutes work from a huge variety of settings – brothels, bars, restaurants, massage parlours, escort agencies, karaoke joints, discos, hotels, streets, beaches, golf courses, to name but a few – and customers can enter into a range of different transactions with them: 'short-time' deals (an hour or two with the prostitute), 'overnight' deals (up to 24 h) and 'long-haul' deals (lasting anywhere between a few days to a few weeks). O'Connell Davidson and Sánchez Taylor (2005) have referred to the type of tourist who travels specifically in search of cheap, plentiful and diverse opportunities for commercial sexual experience as 'hard-core sex tourists'.

There are a number of travel clubs and Internet websites that are run by and for such hard-core male sex tourists. O'Connell Davidson (2001: 7–8) describes one of these clubs as follows:

> Travel and the Single Male (TSM) ... is one of several similar organizations run by and for male sex tourists, [and] boasts some 5,000 members, most of whom are white Americans. TSM publishes a guidebook (Cassirer, 1992) and sells club membership for US$50 per annum. Members receive a quarterly newsletter, discounts in some hotels and brothels, and most importantly, are provided access to the TSM Internet site. This provides information on travel and prostitution in various countries around the world, access to soft-core pornographic photographs of female sex workers from those countries, two message boards and a chat room for members to swap 'sexperiences', views, news and

handy travel tips ... Though its organizers and members would not describe it as a political organization, the ethos of TSM is aggressively heterosexist, deeply misogynist and profoundly racist, and the club thus expresses and promotes a particular worldview, as well as a particular form of travel.

The worldview and sexual ambitions of hard-core male heterosexual sex tourists is well captured in the passage below, taken from a posting on TSM's website and describing Boca Chica, a resort town in the Dominican Republic that was famed for sex tourism in the 1990s (this website has now joined together with the World Sex Guide to form the 'World Sex Achieves', an adult discussion forum for sex tourists).

> Boca is a place of [Western] men's dreams and [Western] women's nightmares. It finds the heart of desire within all of us. Boca ... is a place where sexual fantasies become commonplace. A place where you can go into your room with a pack of multi-colored girls and no one will blink twice. A place where an older man can convince himself that the young girl rotating on his lap cares for him and understands his needs more than the women from his homeland. It's a place where men come for lust and sometimes end up confusing it for love. It's where a man can be a star in his own adult videos. It's a place where a young pretty girl once offered me sex for a [plate of] lasagna. It's a place where every woman you see whether whore or maid or waitress, young or old, can be bought for a few hundred pesos. It's a place where you can have a girl, her sisters and her cousins.

> (Travel & the Single Male message board, 19 March 1998)

If we restrict our focus to the kind of hard-core heterosexual male sex tourist who would join a club like TSM, then the radical feminist argument that sex tourism 'is fundamentally about the commercialization of women's subordination' (Jeffreys, 2009: 151) seems to hold good. Hard-core male heterosexual sex tourists do 'express quite clearly their desires to purchase sexual servants to compensate for the infuriating rise of women's equality in many rich countries' (Jeffreys, 2009: 151). However, not all tourists who enter into sexual–

economic exchanges with local people in sex tourist destinations fit this bill. Many of them did not travel with the explicit intention of buying sex from prostitutes; many of them do not even recognize the sexual–economic relationships they enter into with local people as a form of prostitution; and not all of them are heterosexual men.

In a survey of 661 German men who had had sex with one or more local women or girls in Thailand, the Philippines, Kenya, Brazil and the Dominican Republic, Kleiber and Wilke (1995) found that only a minority, 22%, described themselves as 'sex tourists'. As Gunther (1998: 71) observes, the curious phenomenon of sex tourism without sex tourists rests on the fact that many settings of tourism-oriented prostitution allow 'for a personal, noneconomic and self-serving "framing" ... of the tourist–prostitute relationship'. O'Connell Davidson (2005) notes that these findings are partly explained by the fact that the open-ended and non-contractual nature of informal sector prostitution allows tourists to delude themselves about the commercial basis of their sexual interactions: instead of having to go into a brothel or to negotiate a deal in advance (two things that are often viewed as integral to 'prostitution'), they can pick up a 'freelance' by using the same scripts that they use in non-commercial encounters ('Can I get you a drink?', 'Would you like to have dinner with me?', 'Do you want to come up to my room?'). The whole process can be interpreted as confirming a mutual attraction, and the client can then construct the act of giving money to the prostitute not as payment for services rendered, but as a gesture of friendship, generosity or compassion. Indeed, even when tourists realize that the local person is engaged in a form of prostitution, they do not necessarily come to understand themselves as 'clients' or 'customers' of sex workers. Instead, they often tell themselves they are 'helping' the local person out. O'Connell Davidson (2005) illustrates this with the following extract from a guidebook for gay male sex tourists to Thailand:

Many Westerners are troubled about the idea of paying a young man for his time or sex, seeing it as pure prostitution, but this is an oversimplification. In Thailand, as in other less-developed countries, you will be considered a higher-status person... with obligations to those less fortunate than yourself.

(Hammer, 1997: 18)

In most sites of sex tourism in LEDCs, what is recognizable as prostitution (brief, businesslike, cash for sex exchanges) shades off into other, still temporary but, much more loosely organized and open-ended sexual–economic exchanges, and these in turn can shade off into longer-term sexual and romantic relationships, even marriage. Male tourists are not necessarily drawn to these more open-ended forms of sexual–economic exchange by a conscious desire to dominate, control or exploit the local person. Some enter into these relationships precisely because they appear to be romantic and 'genuine', rather than economic (Seabrook, 1996). It also the case the women who enter into these relationships are also looking to distance themselves from the label of sex worker, and looking for romance and using their relationship as a strategy to migrate (Brennan, 2004; Yea, 2005). Little attention has been paid to this in commentary on male sex tourism, and yet studies of women tourists who enter into sexual–economic exchanges with local men very often assume that they are motivated by a desire for romance, as opposed to a desire for control over 'sexual servants'.

Gender and Romance Tourism

If sex tourism is understood to encompass a wide range of sexual–economic exchanges, as opposed to simply the purchase of commodified sexual services in brothels or red light areas, then there is research to show that women can also be 'sex tourists'. However, the behaviour of North American, Australian, European and Japanese women who have sex with local men in LEDCs is often interpreted in a very different way

from that of their male tourist counterparts. Tourist women have sometimes been sympathetically described as 'lonely women' whose 'economic and social ability to travel alone is being exploited by Caribbean tourism' and the 'beach boys' who either offer them the possibility of a 'holiday romance' or 'sexual harassment' (Momsen, 1994: 116). Indeed, few studies refer to the phenomenon of 'female sex tourism', but prefer instead the term 'romance tourism' (Momsen, 1994; Pruitt and LaFont, 1995; Meisch, 1995; Dahles and Bras, 1999). Idea about love and intimacy are part of the narratives used by tourist women to point to the role of courtship, dancing, dining and emotion, which underpin the discourses used by the women (Tornqyist, 2009).

Nor are the activities of local males necessarily viewed as 'prostitution'. Heidi Dahles and Karin Bras (1999), for example, argue that their study of female tourists and local men in Indonesia does not try to look at the activities of the men from the point of view of prostitution. Instead, they consider relations between the two groups as an 'inversion' and transgression of usual gender norms of both the West and Eastern cultures, in that local young men have sex with older, Western tourist women, who are their economic superiors. They argue that it is important to understand the cultural meanings attached to these interactions within the context of a wider subsistence strategy. They note the men's 'romantic and sexual behaviour':

The men's activities are regarded as just one part of a 'hustling' strategy in which they continue to have gender power, even if they do not have economic, racial, aged or social power in the tourist setting. The patterns of 'romantic overtures' that emerge in Indonesia are similar to those in tourist areas in the Caribbean, which are again often interpreted as a phenomenon very different from male sex tourism. In her study of beach boys in Barbados, for example, Joan Phillips (1999:186) also stresses the entrepreneurial side of hustling as part of local men's masculinity and further states that 'hustling can be viewed as the exploitation of white females by young black Barbadians' and has to be understood as a part of their entrepreneurial strategies to make a living as well as to secure their future. Romancing the tourist seems to be the major economic strategy of these boys who are labelled 'romantic entrepreneurs' (1999: 281).

Researchers rarely draw attention to the similarities between female tourists' so-called 'romance tourism' and the informal tourist-related prostitution that involves local women and tourist men. Thus, although research evidence from a number of different countries produces a fairly consistent picture of how 'beach boys' and 'guides' operate and the nature of their sexual interactions with female tourists, there is no consensus as to whether these interactions should be understood as a form of prostitution or as an expression of 'promiscuity' on the part of both tourist women and local men. Commentators seem uncertain whether these relationships are exploitative, and if so, undecided as to who is exploiting whom.

Gunther's (1998: 71) comment on the paradox of sex tourism without sex tourists rings even more true in relation to women tourists. Few female tourists perceive the economic element of the sexual relationships they form with local men, for local males who use such relationships as a means of earning do not act out a script that is recognizable as 'prostitution'. Instead, they use the scripts that they use in non-commercial, romantic encounters. The romance element is important for female tourists who have relationships with local men as they interpret their experience through highly gendered and heterosexual commonsense understandings of both 'courtship' and 'prostitution'. Through the lens of this commonsense understanding, only women and homo-sexual men can be prostitutes, and only men can be prostitute-users. Within this essentialist framework, women cannot be sexually active/predatory but only passive/preyed upon. The idea of a woman using prostitutes therefore becomes something of an oxymoron (Sánchez Taylor, 2006), and it is because ethnographic researchers who have studied female sex tourism tend to draw on the subjective meanings that participants attach to their sexual behaviour and relationships that they have found it so difficult to define or categorize relationships

Fig. 4.3. 'Chatting up' scenes on Caribbean beaches.

between tourist women and local men. It has been labelled 'romance tourism' in opposition to male 'sex tourism' and researchers have focused on questions of intimacy and romance rather than sex work.

However, research by Sánchez Taylor (2001) highlights problems with this distinction. A survey of 240 tourist women in Jamaica and the Dominican Republic provided an insight into how women understood their sexual encounters with local men. The data showed that almost a third of the sample (75 women) had engaged in one or more sexual relationships with local men during the course of their holiday. The women who had entered into sexual relationships with local men were not a homogenous group in terms of background characteristics. They ranged in age from girls in their late teens to women in their sixties, though women in the 30–40 age group were the most likely to have had sex with local men. They tended to come from regions that traditionally send male sex tourists, i.e. North America and Europe. In terms of racial identities, respondents who had entered into sexual relationships with local men more or less mirrored the composition of the sample as a whole, which is to say the vast majority were white.

The majority of the women who had entered into sexual relationships while on holiday stated that they had formed only one such relationship. However, 27% of women reported entering into sexual relationships with two or more partners.

These women were virtually all on return visits to the country. Albuquerque (1999) refers to such women as 'veteran female sex tourists', that is, women who regularly visit the same tourist destination to pursue sexual relationships with local men. This profile is very similar to male sex tourists who are repeat visitors to sex tourist destinations.

Although about a quarter of respondents to the survey said that they had been approached by a gigolo, not one said that they had taken up the offer of commercial sex. This is interesting considering that about 60% did acknowledge providing cash or buying gifts, meals, etc. for their boyfriends. Women were also more likely to describe their sexual encounters and relationships as 'holiday romances' rather than describing them as 'purely sexual'. They used the term 'holiday romance' in a fairly flexible way, however. It covered everything from a one-night stand to relationships that lasted a week or a month or even a year. One woman stated that she had three 'holiday romances' in the space of a week.

The key point, however, is that these survey respondents did not perceive their sexual encounters with local men as prostitute–client transactions, but rather used the notion of 'romance' to interpret them as non-commercial.

Sánchez Taylor's (2001, 2006) interview research further found that it is important for both tourist women and local men to construct their sexual encounters/relationships as something other than

Table 4.1. Female tourists' descriptions of their sexual relationships with local men (Sánchez Taylor, 2001).

Description of relationship	Jamaica, % (*n*=52)	Dominican Republic, % (*n*=23)	Both countries, % (*n*=75)
Holiday romance	42	26	39
Real love	13	39	22
Purely physical	4	9	3
Both physical and holiday romance	13	4	12
Long term	6	4	5
Several types	10	4	8
Other	10	9	8
No Response	2	4	3

'prostitution', a label that would dishonour both parties. Although the power relations that usually exist in heterosexual sexual encounters are inverted (in sex tourist destinations in LEDCs, tourist women are often older, and always more economically powerful than their male partners), neither female tourists nor local men wished to be seen as transgressing the gendered norms of sexual behaviour for men and women. By tapping into existing essentialist ideas about gender, sexuality and prostitution, they can explain their sexual encounters without having to consider the asymmetries of power that exist between them.

Interestingly, sexual–economic relationships between local men and tourist women are not legally or socially constructed as 'prostitution' in the host country either. Where local women who engage in such relationships with tourist men are viewed as prostitutes and as such frequently subject to harassment, arrest and imprisonment, as well as often extortion, violence and rape by police officers (Brennan, 2004; Cabezas, 2004; O'Connell Davidson, 2005), in most LEDCs, local men who enter into relationships with tourist women are not subject to legal control or police surveillance.

The idea that tourist women who have sex with local men are 'romance tourists' while tourist men who have sex with local women are 'sex tourists' reflects a number of assumptions that are not straightforwardly supported by research. In particular, this gendered distinction between romance and sex tourism:

- overlooks similarities between open-ended prostitution as practised by local men as well as women, and similarities between the way in which both male and female tourists (mis)understand it;
- relies on a gender essentialist model of sexuality within which women are always passive receptors or victims of male sexual attention;
- downplays the significance of the immense economic and political power that female as well as male tourists enjoy relative to local people;
- also deflects attention from the significance of racism and racial power for sexual encounters between tourists and locals in LEDCs.

Sex Tourism and Racial Inequalities

An analysis of the demand for sex tourism cannot be complete without a consideration of sexualized racism. In the case of hard-core male heterosexual sex tourists, this is starkly visible – they often refer to the local women they have sex with as 'LBFMs' or 'Little Brown Fucking Machines', a term

Fig. 4.4. A mural in a bar for tourists run by an expatriate German in Sousa.

coined by American GIs stationed in Southeast Asia and employed as a catch-all category encompassing any female 'other' not deemed to be either white or 'African' (O'Connell Davidson and Sánchez Taylor, 1999). But sexualized racism also plays an important role in allowing ordinary tourists to frame 'sex tourism' as 'not-really-prostitution'.

When tourists spend their time in resorts and *barrios* where tourist-related prostitution is widespread, they constantly encounter what appear to them as hedonistic scenes – local 'girls' and young men dancing 'sensuously', draping themselves over and being fondled by Western tourists, drinking and joking with each other and so on; 'fit' young local men playing on the beach and 'hitting' on tourist women. Instead of seeing the relationship between these scenes and their own presence in the resort, sex tourists tend to interpret all this as empirical vindication of Western ideologies of 'non-Western peoples living in idyllic pleasure, splendid innocence or Paradise-like conditions – as purely sensual, natural, simple and uncorrupted beings' (Kempadoo, 1996: 76). Western sex tourists (and this is true of black as well as white sex tourists) argue that sex is more 'natural' in 'Third World' countries, that prostitution is not really prostitution but a 'way of life'.

This also helps to explain how men and women who are not, and would not dream of buying sexual services from a prostitute back home can happily practice sex tourism. Racism allows the sex tourist to distance themselves from traditional forms of prostitution – the sex workers are not really like prostitutes and so they themselves are not really like clients. Also the prostitution contract is not like the Western prostitution contract, and so does not really count as prostitution.

It further points to the complex interrelations between discourses of gender, 'race' and sexuality. To begin with, the supposed 'naturalness' of prostitution in the 'Third World' actually reassures the Western male sex tourist of his 'racial' and/or cultural superiority. Thus we find that sex tourists continue a very traditional Western discourse of travel which rests on an imagined opposition between the 'civilized' West and the 'barbarous' other (Brace and O'Connell Davidson, 1996). In 'civilized' countries, only 'bad' women become prostitutes to earn 'easy money', but in the 'Third World' which is perceived as a corrupt and lawless place where people exist in a state of nature, 'nice girls' may be driven to prostitution in order to survive.

In this, we see that sex tourism is not only about sustaining a male identity as some radical feminists have argued. For some white men it is also about sustaining a white identity. Sexualized-racisms help the sex tourist to attain a sense of control over himself and 'others' as engendered and 'racialized' sexual beings. Here it is important to recognize the subtle (or not so subtle) variations of racism employed by white Western men.

The sex tourists interviewed by Sánchez Taylor and O'Connell Davidson in the Caribbean are not a homogeneous group in terms of their 'race' politics, and this reflects differences of national identity, age, socio-economic background and racialized identity. One clearly identifiable subgroup comprises of white North American men aged upwards of 40, who espouse a white supremacist world view and consider black people their biological, social and cultural inferiors. They use the word 'nigger' and consider any challenge to their 'right' to use this term as 'political correctness' – as one sex tourist complained, in the States 'You can't use the N word, nigger. Always when I was raised up, the only thing was the F word, you can't use the F word. Now you can't say cunt, you can't say nigger'.

For men like this, black women are imagined as the embodiment of all that is low and debased, they are 'inherently degraded, and thus the appropriate partners for degrading sex' (Shrage, 1994: 158). As unambiguous 'whores' by virtue of their 'racialized' identity, they may be briefly and anonymously used, but they are not sought out for longer term and/or quasi-romantic commercial sexual relationships.

But not all Western sex tourists to the Caribbean buy into this kind of overt, denigrating racism. In fact, many of them are far more strongly influenced by what might be termed 'exoticizing' racisms. Younger white Europeans and North Americans, for example, have been much exposed to such racisms through the Western film, music and fashion industries, which retain the old-school racist emphasis on blackness as physicality, but repackage and commoditize this 'animalism' so that black men and women become the ultimate icons of sporting prowess, 'untamed' rebelliousness, 'raw' musical talent, sexual power and so on (Hooks, 1992, 1994; Young, 1996; Kempadoo, 2004). As a consequence, many young (and some not so young) white Westerners view blackness as a marker of something both 'cool' and 'hot'.

It is also the case that female tourists use racialized discourses to distance themselves from the idea that they are buying sex. Interview work with female tourists show very clearly that notions of 'racial' otherness and difference play a key role in allowing women tourists, as much as their male counterparts, to ignore imbalances of age and economic power between themselves and their local sexual partners. Racist ideas about black men being hypersexual and unable to control their sexuality enabled them to explain to themselves why such young and desirable men would be eager for sex with older, and/or often overweight women, without having to think that their partners were interested in them only for economic reasons. Only women who had entered into a series of brief sexual encounters began to acknowledge that 'it's all about money'.

Female sex tourists also shared similar highly racialized fantasies about power and control. While some women wanted to experience sex with a black 'other' that they imagined as their inferior without anyone back home finding out, others wanted a more exotic experience where they had total control. Female sex tourists often refer to tourist destinations they visit as 'lala land' or 'fantasy islands'. They are places where they can transgress sexual boundaries that are restricted at home. They can have sex with ethnic and racial 'others' or have sex with lots of men or have sex with younger men with no one finding out.

It also allows some tourists to experience positive encounters with the 'others' because the local people live up to the stereotypes they have of other ethnic/racial groups. As one British sex tourist to Cuba argued, black people in Britain are 'very stand-offish … They stick to their own, and it's a shame, because it makes divisions'. What a delight it is for men like this to holiday in the Caribbean, then, where poverty, combined with the exigencies of tourist development ensure that they are constantly faced by smiling, welcoming black people who act as their guides and friends that they can then 'help out' if they chose to.

Sex Tourism and Inequalities of Age

In the early 1990s, media and policy attention was increasingly paid to 'child sex tourism', presented as a phenomenon in which Western men travel as tourists, or take up permanent or temporary residence in poor and developing countries in order to gain sexual access to local children. Cases of 'paedophile'-tourists have been documented in a wide range of countries and regions, including Sri Lanka (Ratnapala, 1999; Seabrook, 2001), Goa (O'Connell Davidson and Sánchez Taylor, 1996), Thailand (Montgomery, 2001; Seabrook, 2001), Cambodia (Foggo, 2002), the Philippines (Lee-Wright, 1990), the Dominican Republic (de Moya and Garcia, 1999) and Costa Rica (Aguilar, 1994).

In popular discourse, child sex tourism is constructed as a discrete and neatly bounded problem, something that can be separated from the more general phenomenon of tourism, and even from sex tourism involving adults. To speak of child sex tourism is to conjure up visions of paedophiles and child molesters, and campaigns against 'child sex tourism' have been primarily concerned with preventing foreign paedophiles from travelling to sex tourist destinations to abuse prepubertal children.

The United Nations (UN) defines the 'child' as a person aged anywhere from 0 to 18, however. Children at different ages have different levels of physical and psychological development and the UN definition thus spans children who are completely and absolutely dependent on older carers through to children who are completely independent (and may have their own children). Within any given country, children are further divided by gender, class, race, ethnicity and/or 'caste', and nationality. 'Children' are therefore not a homogeneous group and this has implications for analysing both children's presence in prostitution and demand for their services. As O'Connell Davidson (2005) explains, although there is evidence of a very small niche market serving the desires of paedophile tourists in some LEDCs, the majority of children in the sex trade around the world (whether serving the tourist market or any other market segment) are teenagers aged between 14 and 18, rather than prepubertal children. These older teenagers typically work alongside adult sex workers in tourist areas and serve ordinary tourist customers rather than catering for 'paedophiles' or 'child molesters'. If we are to work with the UN definition of a child, then 'child sex tourism' is not merely a problem of paedophilia and questions about who pays children for sex and why are more complicated than popular discourse allows.

Questions about why persons under the age of 18 enter into sexual–economic exchanges are also more complicated than popular discourse suggests. It is not always a case of children being physically forced into prostitution by a ruthless and exploitative adult (Montgomery, 2001; O'Connell Davidson, 2005). Factors that push children into the sex industry include:

- economic disadvantage;
- homelessness;
- abuse;
- lack of adequately paid employment opportunities;
- the need to support other family members;
- racism;
- homophobia.

Teenagers can also migrate to tourist areas not because they are abused or starved, but simply in the hope of having a more exciting and adventurous life and escaping the tedium of everyday existence in rural areas of LEDCs. Once in a tourist area, they trade sex in order to subsist (O'Connell Davidson and Sánchez Taylor, 1996).

In other words, children's presence in the tourist-related sex trade has as much, if not more, to do with a complex mix of structural inequalities than to do with questions of individual morality, and O'Connell Davidson (2005) argues that campaigns against 'child sex tourism deflect attention from this fact'. Instead of questioning the tourism industry more generally, or thinking about global political and economic inequalities, or about the ideas and attitudes that encourage and foster all forms of sexual exploitation, the focus is limited to the need for stronger and stricter law enforcement against paedophiles who travel abroad (see also Chapter 7).

Sex Tourism and the Intersections of Inequalities

For women, men and children in LEDCs, sexual–economic exchanges with tourists (whether highly commoditized or open-ended and diffuse) may represent a means by which to subsist or supplement an impossibly low income, or a way in which to access a lifestyle that would otherwise be closed to them, or a means by which to further other goals, including migration to a richer country. Globalization has facilitated the growth of sex tourism and shapes the types of relationships that take place and the way that some bodies are commodified for sexual consumption for others to consume (Wonders and Michalowski, 2001). As such, it is just one part of an international sex industry that is increasingly important to the global economy that reproduces and reinforces global and local inequalities to create particular 'sexscapes' (Brennan, 2004).

There is a sense in which we could say that class inequalities are fundamental in determining who becomes involved in such exchanges with tourists. Elite and middle class women, men and children in LEDCs do not need to enter into such exchanges in order to subsist or improve their life-chances. But class intersects with gender, race, age and nationality to create hier-archies of power and opportunity within both the formal *and* the informal tourism economy in LEDCs, hierarchies that link to macro level factors, including:

- gender-discriminatory social practices;
- race ideas (and in the Caribbean, in particular, colonialism's legacy of a 'pigmentocracy');
- immigration, tax and prostitution law and law enforcement practice;
- patterns of foreign investment in tour-ism.

The nature of individuals' involvement in sex tourism and the benefits (if any) derived from such involvement are strongly linked to their position within these hierarchies.

In general, the formal and informal tourism economy offer more plentiful and more lucrative economic opportunities to males, whether local or migrant, or adult or child, than to their female counterparts. This increases women and girls' vulner-ability to prostitution, which in turn creates still more economic openings for men, who can supplement their income by procuring prostitutes, including child prostitutes, for tourists. Legal measures to control informal economic activity in tourist resorts can also differentially affect local and migrant men and women's experience. For example, O'Connell Davidson and Sánchez Taylor (2001) found that in the late 1990s, both Jamaica and the Dominican Republic enacted legislation against 'tourist hustling', and introduced licensing systems for ambu-lant vendors and tourist guides. These measures consolidated existing inequalities in the informal tourism sector. In the Dominican Republic, they increased Haitian workers' vulnerability to harassment and deportation, and in both Jamaica and the Dominican Republic, they buttressed gender divisions in the informal economy.

In particular, they reinforced the beach – a prime location for informal tourist-related economic activity – as a largely male terrain. Only those who obtained a vendor's license or whose presence there was linked to their formal employment now had 'legitimate' access to the beach, and these trades/jobs were male dominated (e.g. lifeguard, watersports promoter, boat hand). Access to the beach meant access to tourists, and so to 'hustle', which included procuring prostitutes for tourists and/or entry into sexual–economic exchanges. In both countries, local men involved in drug selling and procuring claimed that corrupt police officers extorted money from them in exchange for turning a blind eye to their activities, adding yet another dimension to the process of informalization.

Because measures to control informal economic activity restricted women's access to the beach, they simultaneously created openings for men to act as intermediaries between female prostitutes and tourist clients. The policing of prostitution in both Jamaica and the Dominican Republic had much the same effect. Though Dominican law formally tolerates prostitution to a much greater degree than Jamaican law, law enforcement practice was remarkably similar in each country. It focused heavily upon female prostitutes who solicit in the streets and other public spaces, rather than on any abuse or exploitation of female prostitutes by third parties that may have been occurring. This kind of policing made solicitation by independent prostitutes a more high-risk activity, and so encouraged dependence on procurers, pimps and other third parties. The research also found that law enforcement in both countries often itself involved serious violations of women and children's civil and human rights, and that existing law enforcement practice did not help to protect children from com-mercial sexual exploitation.

Class, gender and the stigma against and criminalization of female prostitution all intersect to make it more likely that women will end up in various forms prostitution in tourist resorts in LEDCs, but men can also be disadvantaged within local labour markets because of their immigration status and/or race, as well as class. They too can therefore end up entering into sexual–economic exchanges with tourists as a means of subsisting or supplementing low wages. In LEDCs, poor economic conditions mean that household strategies for economic survival often include deploying children's income-generating capacities, and that there are also children who have to support themselves independently. Children are therefore also present in the informal tourism economy (Black, 1995). However, age discrimination means that it is the least economically rewarding activities, such as bottle collecting, and fruit and sweet selling, which are undertaken by the young. Child labour is also highly gendered. Those working in non-sexualized outdoor activities are predominantly male, while girl children's involvement in the informal economy in many LEDCs is more likely to take the form of domestic work in private households, and/or assisting adult relatives in home-based enterprises such as souvenir production, baking, laundry, and so on. Very often, girl children in domestic work and boy children in occupations such as shoeshine and beach/street vending are vulnerable to sexual abuse, both by locals and tourists.

The absence of alternative means of subsistence means that teenage girls are also found working alongside adult women in the mainstream sex industry, but they are often less able than adult women to enforce condom-use, and more vulnerable to being cheated of payment by clients.

Sex Tourism and Tourism

There is long historical association between travel and sex, an association that has strengthened and diversified with the development of the tourism industry. There are now a number of European and North American holiday destinations renowned for a rich and uninhibited 'nightlife', within which tourists find many opportunities for sex with other tourists; there are tourist destinations in both the affluent and the developing world famed for their commercial sex industries (such as Amsterdam and Bangkok); and there are destinations where 'holiday romances' between tourists and locals are reputed to be commonplace. Because the relationship between tourism and sex is close but multifaceted, the term 'sex tourism' is not as easy to define as it may first appear, and the problem cannot be fully resolved by defining 'sex tourism' as 'prostitution-tourism', because, as has been seen in this chapter, sexual–economic relationships between tourists and local/migrant persons range from brief and explicit cash-for-sex exchanges that both parties understand as 'prostitution', through more open-ended, diffuse exchanges, to relationships that are understood by both parties to be 'romantic' despite the asymmetry of economic power between them. It is actually very difficult to draw a sharp line between tourists' experience of commercial and non-commercial sex. It is also important to recognize that in some cases, local/migrant people pursue relationships with tourists for reasons that are simultaneously economic and sexual. For example, in countries that are profoundly homophobic and opportunities for same-sex sexual contact extremely limited, gay tourists can represent an accepting and similar haven for local gay people who are not socially accepted.

Deciding who counts as 'a sex tourist' is also difficult. Are sex tourists people who travel with the explicit and conscious intention of consuming commercial sexual services, or should we also count those who select a holiday destination for other reasons but then proceed to enter into some kind of a sexual–economic exchange with a local person? Definitions of sex tourism are invariably theory-impregnated, reflecting broader assumptions about gender and sexuality (Opperman, 1998; Ryan and Hall, 2001).

This chapter has approached sex tourism as a phenomenon involving sexual–economic exchanges between tourists and locals/migrants in LEDCs, ranging from straightforward prostitution contracts to more diffuse short- or long-term sexual relationships that have some economic element to them. Viewed as such the chapter has argued it is premised on, shaped by and serves to reproduce several forms of inequality. As Truong (1990) put it in her ground-breaking study of sex tourism in Thailand:

> the emergence of sex tourism and sex-related entertainment is an articulation of a series of unequal social relations, including North–South relations, and relations between capital and labour, male and female, production and reproduction. This articulation has been induced by capital and state interests and therefore cannot be considered as an outcome of a policy mistake, or an effect of uncontrollable poverty. Rather, it is evoked by an interplay between external and internal economic and political forces.
>
> (Truong, 1990, 129)

Truong examined the connection between the international tourist industry and the development of the local tourist sex sector. She showed how the rapid growth of the tourist trade has been designed by international financing sources and political institutions, which encouraged tourism development projects in indebted countries desperate for foreign exchange. Host countries are left to supply cheap, preferably non-unionized labour and provide attractive incentives to encourage foreign companies to invest in tourism while predominantly foreign owned hotels, tour operators and airlines supplied the capital, knowledge and experience and reaped the profits. Within this framework, women's labour and sexuality have become important commodities to tourism in general, and not simply to 'sex tourism'.

Women are a cheap source of labour for the hotel and service sectors, and as Noeleen Heyzer (1986: 54) notes, while tourism created a variety of jobs, employment opportunities within tourism are gendered in ways that mean:

> jobs for young women are usually concentrated in public relations, in the promotional aspects of tourism, as cashiers and waitresses, in traditional entertainment, in new entertainment and servicing including sexual services demanded by visitors and by business tourists, the bulk of whom are men.

However, though gender inequality is integral to the tourism industry, 'Interwoven in this basic gender hierarchy are the spectres of race, class and nationality' (Chant and McIlwaine, 1995: 217), and sex tourism in particular rests 'on a peculiar and unstable combination of sexuality, nationalism, and economic power' (Leheny, 1995: 381).

Conclusion

The line between tourism and sex tourism (including child sex tourism) is not easily drawn. Tourist development in LEDCs brings together tourists and locals in a profoundly unequal way, and 'ordinary' tourists – whether women or men – as well as hard-core sex tourists can take sexual advantage of the inequalities and asymmetries of power that underpin and are reproduced by tourism.

Questions

1. What factors have contributed to the development of sex tourism in particular holiday destinations?
2. Can a distinction be made between female 'romance tourism' and male 'sex tourism'?
3. What roles do sexualized racism play in constructing bodies for sexual consumption and 'fantasy islands'?

References

Aguilar, M. (1994) Alarma corrupcion de menores en Puntareas. *Sucesos,* San José, Costa Rica.

Albuquerque, K., (1999) Sex, beach boys and female tourists in the Caribbean. In: Dank, B.M. and Refinetti, R. (eds) *Sex Work and Sex Workers: Sexuality and Culture,* Volume II. Transaction, New Brunswick, New Jersey.

Barry, K. (1995) *The Prostitution of Sexuality.* New York University Press, New York.

Bishop, R. and Robinson, L. (1998) *Night Market: Sexual Cultures and the Thai Economic Miracle.* Routledge, London.

Black, M. (1995) *In the Twilight Zone: Child Workers in the Hotel, Tourism and Catering Industry.* International labour Office, Geneva.

Brace, L. and O'Connell Davidson, J. (1996) Desperate debtors and counterfeit love: Hobbesian world of the sex tourist. *Contemporary Politics* 2(3), 55–78.

Brennan, D. (2004) *What's Love Got to Do with It? Transnational Desires and Sex Tourism in the Dominican Republic.* Duke University Press, Durham, NC.

Cabezas, A. (2004) Between love and money: sex, tourism and citizenship in Cuba and the Dominican Republic. *Signs: Journal of Women in Culture and Society* 29, 987–1015.

Cassirer, B. (1994) *Travel and the Single Male* (Newsletter). TSM Publishing, Channel Island, CA.

Chant, S. and McIlwaine, C. (1995) *Women of Lesser Cost: Female Labour, Foreign Exchange and Philippine Development.* Pluto Press, London.

Clift, S. and Carter, S. (eds) (2000) *Tourism and Sex: Culture, Commerce and Coercion.* Pinter, London.

Dahles, H. (1998) Of birds and fish: street guides, tourists, and sexual encounters in Yogyakarta, Indonesia. In: Oppermann, M. (ed.) *Sex Tourism and Prostitution: Aspects of Leisure, Recreation and Work.* Cognizant Communication Corporation, Sydney.

Dahles, H. and Bras, B. (1999) Entrepreneurs in romance: tourism in Indonesia. *Annals of Tourism Research* 26, 267–293.

Enloe, C. (1989) *Bananas, Beaches, Bases.* Pandora, London.

Foggo, D. (2002) The approach is unchanging: 'You want young girl, little girl?' *Sunday Telegraph,* 15 September 2002: http://www.ratanak.org/media_reports.cfm

Ford, K. and Wirawan, D. (2000) Tourism and commercial sex in Indonesia. In: Clift Cassell, S. and Carter, S. (eds) *Tourism and Sex.* Pinter, London, pp. 91–108.

Gunther, A. (1998) Sex tourism without sex tourists. In: Oppermann, M. (ed.) *Sex Tourism and Prostitution: Aspects of Leisure, Recreation and Work.* Cognizant Communication Corporation, Sydney.

Hall, C.M. (1992) Sex tourism in South East Asia. In: Harrison, D. (ed.) *Tourism and the Less Developed Countries.* John Wiley & Sons, London.

Hall, C.M. (1994) Gender and economic interests in tourism prostitution: the nature, development and implications of sex tourism in South-East Asia. In: Kinnard, V. and Hall, D. (eds) *Tourism: A Gender Analysis.* John Wiley & Sons, Chicester.

Hammer, D. (1997) *Thai Scene.* Gay Men's Press, Swaffham.

Heyzer, N. (1986) *Working Women in South-East Asia: Development, Subordination and Emancipation.* Open University, Milton Keynes.

Hooks, B. (1992) Selling hot pussy. In: *Black Looks: Race and Representation.* Turnaround, London.

Hooks, B. (1994) *Outlaw Culture: Resisting Representation.* Routledge, London.

Hughes, D. (2000) Welcome to the rape camp. Sexual exploitation and the Internet in Cambodia. *Journal of Sexual Aggression* 6, 29–51.

Jeffreys, S. (1997) *The Idea of Prostitution.* Spinifex Press, North Melbourne.

Jeffreys, S. (2009) *The Industrial Vagina. The Political Economy of the Global Sex Trade.* Routledge, London.

Kempadoo, K. (1996) Prostitution, marginality and empowerment: Caribbean women in the sex trade. *Beyond Law* 5, 69–84.

Kempadoo, K. (2004) *Sexing the Caribbean: Gender, Race and Sexual Labor.* Routledge, New York.

Kleiber, D. and Wilke, M. (1995) *Aids, Sex und Tourismus: Ergebnisse einer Befragung deutscher Urlauber und Sextouristen.* Nosmos-Verlagsgesellschaft, Baden-Baden.

Kruhse-Mount Burton, S. (1995) Sex tourism and traditional Australian male identity. In Lanfont, M., Allcock, J.B. and Bruner, E.M. (eds) *International Tourism: Identity and Change.* Sage, London.

Lee, W. (1991) Prostitution and tourism in South East Asia. In: Redcliff, M. and Sinclair, M.T. (eds) *Working Women: International Perspectives on Labour and Gender Ideology.* Routledge, London.

Lee-Wright, P. (1990) *Child Slaves.* Earthscan, London.

Leheny, D. (1995) A political economy of sex tourism. *Annals of Tourism Research* 22, 367–384.

Mitter, S. (1986) *Common Fate, Common Bond: Women in the Global Economy.* Pluto Press, London.

Meisch, L. (1995) Gringas and otavalenos: changing tourists relations. *Annals of Tourism Research* 22, 441–462.

Momsen, J. (1994) Tourism, gender and development in the Caribbean. In: Kinnaird, V. and Hall, D. (eds) *Tourism: A Gender Analysis.* John Wiley & Sons, Chichester.

Montgomery, H. (2001) *Modern Babylon? Prostituting Children in Thailand.* Berg, Oxford.

Nyanzi, S., Rosenberg-Jallow, O., Bah, O. and Nyanzi, S. (2005) Bumsters, big black organs and olde white gold: embodied racial myths in sexual relations of Gambian beach boys. *Culture, Health and Sexuality* 7, 557–569.

O'Connell Davidson, J. (1995) British sex tourists in Thailand. In: Maynard, M. and Purvis, J. (eds) *(Hetero) Sexual Politics.* Taylor & Francis, London.

O'Connell Davidson, J. (2001) The sex tourist, the expatriate, his ex-wife and the 'other': the politics of loss, difference and desire. *Sexualities* 4, 5–24.

O'Connell Davidson, J. (2005) *Children in the Global Sex Trade.* Polity, Cambridge.

O'Connell Davidson, J. and Sánchez Taylor, J. (1996) *Child Prostitution and Sex Tourism: Goa.* ECPAT, Bangkok.

O'Connell Davidson, J. and Sánchez Taylor, J. (1999) Fantasy islands: exploring the demand for sex tourism. In: Kempadoo, K. (ed.) *Sun, Sex and Gold: Tourism and Sex Work in the Caribbean.* Rowman and Littlefield, Oxford.

O'Connell Davidson, J. and Sanchez Taylor, J. (2001) *Tourism and the Commercial Sexual Exploitation of Children in Jamaica and the Dominican Republic,* with Julia O'Connell Davidson. Save the Children Sweden, Stockholm.

O'Connell Davidson, J. and Sánchez Taylor, J (2005) Travel and taboo: heterosexual sex tourism to the Caribbean. In: Bernstein, E. and Schaffner, L. (eds) *Regulating Sex: The Politics of Intimacy and Identity.* Routledge, London.

Ofreneo, R. and Ofreneo, R. (1998) Prostitution in the Philippines. In: Lim, L.L. (ed.) *The Sex Sector: The Economics and Special Bases of Prostitution in Southeast Asia.* International Labour Office, Geneva.

Oppermann, M. (1998) *Sex Tourism and Prostitution: Aspects of Leisure, Recreation and Work.* Cognizant Communication Corporation, Sydney.

Phillips, J. (1999) Tourist-oriented prostitution in Barbados: the case of the beach boy and the white female tourist. In Kempadoo, K. (ed.) *Sun, Sex and Gold: Tourism and Sex Work in the Caribbean.* Rowman and Littlefield, Oxford.

Pruitt, D. and LaFont, S. (1995) For love and money: romance tourism in Jamaica. *Annals of Tourism Research* 22, 422–440.

Ratnapala, N. (1999) *Tourism in Sri Lanka.* Sarvodaya Vishva Lekha, Sri Lanka.

Raymond, J. (2004) Prostitution on demand. *Violence Against Women* 10, 1156–1186.

Ryan, C. and Hall, C.M. (2001) *Sex Tourism: Marginal People and Liminalities.* Routledge, London.

Sánchez Taylor, J. (2001) Dollars are a girl's best friend. *Sociology* 35, 749–764.

Sánchez Taylor, J. (2006) Female sex tourism: a contradiction in terms. *Feminist Review* 83, 42–59.

Seabrook, J. (1996) *Travels in the Skin Trade: Tourism and the Sex Trade.* Pluto, London.

Seabrook, J. (2001) *Travels in the Skin Trade: Tourism and the Sex Industry.* Pluto Press, London.

Shrage, L. (1994) *Moral Dilemmas of Feminism: Prostitution, Adultery and Abortion.* Routledge, London.

Studevant, S. and Stoltzfus, B. (1992) *Let the Good Times Roll: Prostitution and the U.S. Military in Asia.* The New Press, New York.

Tornqvist, M. (2009) Troubling romance tourism: reflections from an ethnographic work on tango travels to Buenos Aires. Paper presented to Feminist Research Methods Conference, University of Stockholm. http://www.kvinfo.su.se/femmet09/papers.htm

Truong, T.D. (1990) *Sex Money and Morality: Prostitution and Tourism in South-East Asia.* Zed Books Ltd, London.

Wonders, N.A. and Michalowski, R. (2001) Bodies, borders, and sex tourism in a globalized world: a tale of two cities – Amsterdam and Havana. *Social Problems* 48, 545–571.

Yea, S. (2005) Labour of love: Filipina entertainer's narratives of romance and relationships with GIs in US military camp towns in Korea. *Women's Studies International Forum* 28, 456–472.

Young, L. (1996) *Fear of the Dark.* Routledge, London.

5 Access and Marginalization in a Beach Enclave Resort

Sheena Carlisle

Introduction

This chapter highlights some of the significant barriers that cause marginalization in a beach enclave resort in a less economically developed country (LEDC). Reasons for marginalization of the local business community and freedom of citizens to interact with the tourism industry are explained in the context of political, legislative and socio-economic structures by drawing on the case study of the Senegambia beach enclave resort. The chapter also emphasizes the importance of the local tourism industry to adhere to international trading rules and regulations such as the EU Directive on Package Holidays 1992, licensing rules and quality standards. Against this legislative background, other local economic factors of an LEDC economy, where there is a lack of access to capital, trained staff and marketing outlets, are common challenges for local businesses.

Drawing on a larger empirical study carried out between 2001 and 2007 in The Gambia for a doctoral study examining the political economy of small-scale business development in Gambian Tourism, the chapter highlights the importance of distribution of tourist's wealth at the destination. The fieldwork and research encompassed extensive Participant Action Research, focus groups, interviews and consultancy work with the trade Association of Small-scale Enterprises in Tourism (ASSET), the Responsible Tourism Partnership (RTP)

and the Gambia Tourism Authority (GTA). Significantly, tourist expenditure in a country classified as being among the poorest countries of the world, ranking 156th out of 177 countries in the 2005 UNDP Human Development Index (HDI) is an important part of tourism analysis in an LEDC context.

In 2000, grassroots action began to improve local business involvement with the tourism industry and The Gambia is unique in how ASSET is trying to overcome some of the challenges highlighted in this chapter. It is demonstrated how ASSET is essentially working on behalf of small local businesses and the 'informal sector' to increase their status and position within the industry via advocacy, training, marketing and networking. In addition, it is also demonstrated how the tourism industry could address some of the structural problems characteristic of the tourism supply chain that manifest at the local level and how responsible and sustainable tourism principles are beginning to challenge the innate social exclusion to which beach tourism can contribute; by finding methods of increasing collaboration rather than isolating residents and local businesses, a more responsible tourism industry may be able to unfold.

The Gambian Economy

The Gambia may be considered a microstate because of its size as the smallest

African country, with an area of 10402 km^2, a population of 1.6 million and a GDP per capita of US$376 (World Bank, 2007). Below is a list of some key socio-economic factors that impact on tourism as a development strategy:

- 70% of population engaged in subsistence farming;
- 30% literacy rate (World Bank, 2008);
- 10% unemployment (World Bank, 2008);
- 5% inflation rate (2009 Economic Freedom Index);
- tourism contributes 13% of GDP (Master Plan Study, 2005);
- GDP per capita US$377 (UN Data country profile, 2007);
- exports: US$12.7 million; imports: US$307 million;
- tourism provides approximately 10,000 people with jobs, estimated increase to 35,000 in 2020 (Master Plan Study, 2005);
- net foreign exchange earnings are projected to increase from an estimated US$40 million in 2004 to US$130 million in 2020 (Master Plan Study, 2005);
- poor infrastructure capacity.

LEDC microstates often experience constraints of economic development because of their limited range of resources and narrowly specialized economies, which are based on one or two agricultural commodities. Subsequently, microstates can have difficulty influencing terms of international trade to manage and control their open economies to their full advantage, and employment opportunities are often missed because of a narrow range of local skills and problems of matching local skills and jobs. Because of its small GDP per capita, The Gambia faces problems in establishing import substitution industries because of inflation and international inbound tourism is a favoured option to boost the economy and improve balance of payments.

The morality and exclusivity of how international tourism operates at destinations with a poverty status becomes questionable where there is a lack of an adequate social welfare system to support the majority of residents in their health, education and housing needs, while also providing luxury comfort to tourists. Significantly for developing countries, tourism generated foreign earnings of more than US$260 billion in 2007 (UNWTO, 2009), more than six times higher than in 1990. Tourism is also one of the major export sectors of poor countries and the leading source of foreign exchange in 46 of the 49 LEDCs (UNWTO, 2006). Therefore what is of importance is how the tourism industry and local governments can create more opportunities to increase the local benefits from tourism and ensure wider economic sustainability through linking tourism with development objectives.

Since the 1960s, newly independent African countries have been encouraged to pursue a form of trade that could depend on the abundant natural and cultural resources Africa has. Instead of developing an industrialized base that could substitute imports, a more outward approach was initially encouraged by the neo-liberalist way of thinking, which encouraged global market orientation, reduced government intervention and encouraged the further development of primary exports (Bianchi, 2002). Tourism was seen as a labour intensive product rather than a capital-intensive product (Mihalic, 2002: 106), thereby increasing employment opportunities. Significantly, Europeans set the precedent for tourism in Africa for other Europeans rather than tourism being developed for and by Africans themselves (Harrison, 2001). Tourism in developing countries was also largely a result of the modernization process occurring in Western Europe and America, which continues to allow people to take rest and relaxation away from their homes and work environment (Krippendorf, 1987; Lickorish and Jenkins, 1991; Holloway, 2002). Harrison (2001: 41) noted that the top ten African destinations that receive the highest earnings from tourism are those countries that were most settled by Europeans and are the most accessible. The proliferation of colonial legacies also contributed to the nature of tourism development (Harrison, 2001), where:

> Patterns of colonial settlement, most pronounced where natural resources were plentiful, prompted the development of roads, railways, and the infrastructure of travel that enabled traders, hunters, soldiers, administrators, missionaries and adventurers to move with variable degrees of comfort across sub-Saharan Africa. They set the pattern for future tourism development.
>
> (Harrison, 2001: 15)

Those countries that were less colonized and also those with political instability and military violence have a relatively minor share in international tourism arrivals.

Other factors that encourage governments to pursue tourism as a development strategy include the ability to gain foreign exchange earnings from Foreign Direct Investment (FDI) and tourism taxes that should assist balance of payments and external accounts leading to better ratings in international financial markets, and providing easier access to loans and investment capital. Foreign exchange earned could also pay for imported goods needed for the industry and help to develop a modern image and improve reputation. However, this depends on the level of export earnings, debt repayments and the health of domestic markets.

The search for the unusual, the primitive and the exotic, popular in the early 20th century by anthropologists, explorers and missionaries, parallels the search for pleasure and sunshine, which have become key motivating factors fuelling the demand for tourism in exotic places (Azarya, 2004). The exotic smiling, sun, sea and sand image used to promote LEDCs has dominated tourism brochures (Echtner and Prasad, 2003) and the commodification of cultures via cultural performances, demonstrations and museums has not always provided the economic returns that a community expects through participation in a globalized tourism industry. Cornelissen (2005) analyses a political economy of image making for tourism in South Africa and challenges international tour operators'

(ITO) manipulation of destinations to produce images that fit their production and consumption system and represents a narrow perspective of what South Africa has to offer, ignoring its people and local businesses that support emerging black African entrepreneurship as opposed to the predominantly white-owned tourism businesses. This careful selection of what tourists are encouraged to see and not see can limit opportunities for local economic gain from tourists.

Social Exclusion and Enclaves in an LEDC context

In order to understand *how* to alleviate marginalization in tourism it is important to address barriers resulting from the beach enclave model and increase opportunities for inclusive decision making, stakeholder collaboration and local action that respects local needs not only tourist needs. Often the concerns surrounding marginalization are closely related to how a lack of access leads to being made marginal within the beach enclave model. The following list highlights core access issues common to LEDCs in tourism:

- marginalization from decision making;
- difficulty to access capital to enhance domestic investment;
- difficulty to purchase land because of substantial increases in land prices related to tourists buying second homes;
- heightened security for tourists leading to poor access to beach areas for domestic leisure purposes;
- strict planning regulations that can reduce domestic investment in tourism;
- lack of skills;
- limited access to water and electricity (compared with tourists);
- difficulties with integrating a tourist culture that highlights significant differences in moral values and beliefs;
- difficulty to find work outside of the tourist season;
- dependency upon tourists to fund business or development projects.

It is such extensive lists of challenges that urgently require collaboration between the international tourism industry, national governments, non-governmental organiza- tions (NGOs) and business associations, communities and tourists to be able to address these challenges when developing policies and strategies. The phenomenon and popularity of an enclave resort has been a hallmark development of modern tourism as ITOs such as TUI and Thomas Cook have grown in their ownership of key supply chain services and become more sophisticated in the promotion and development of the enclave product. A definition of an enclave is:

> ... an area of a country, region or city that is occupied by people ethnically or culturally distinct from their neighbours. Enclave tourism often refers to geographically isolated and closed-off resorts containing all tourism facilities and services required by tourists, and thus encouraging them to stay inside and spend within the compounds of the enclave.
>
> (Pro-poor Tourism, 2008)

Enclaves may also include all-inclusive resorts where tourists pre-pay for food, beverage and services as part of the holiday price (e.g. Sandals in the Caribbean) or entire destinations such as the Maldivian Islands (Pro-poor Tourism, 2008). All- inclusive and beach package enclaves offering bed and breakfast and half board have become an important product and pricing strategy for many ITOs. Although the high prices charged for tourists are often beyond the means of local residents and domestic markets, there is an increas- ing trend in regional business and confer- ence tourism where local elites and public sector workers utilize tourism facilities. A number of authors have criticized the impacts of enclave tourism strategies that focus primarily on one type of tourism product in LEDCs, notably Mbaiwa (2003, 2005), who critiqued safari tourism in Botswana and explains how tourism in the Okavango Delta has many characteristics of beach enclave tourism only in a safari context, where there is a low level of local involvement in running profitable tourism

enterprises and high levels of foreign ownership of lodges, which add minimal value to the local economy, except via low- paid staffing costs. Sindiga (1999) critiqued beach enclave tourism in Kenya for similar reasons. Both authors highlight the chal- lenges surrounding a reliance on foreign capital and foreign ownership to support the development of enclave tourism. FDI is also supported by the General Agreement on Trade in Services (GATS; see Chapter 6, this volume) and may use the cheap labour available while also charging western rates for their products and services. Such dependency upon foreign investment capital can create animosity and disparity among citizens living adjacent to enclave areas and Mbaiwa (2005) calls for increased entrepreneurship and destination sectoral linkages to increase economic opportunities from enclave tourism.

Frietag (1994) provided a detailed analysis of the impact of the all-inclusive beach resorts in the Dominican Republic, which in turn have restricted the spread of economic development throughout the country. Pattullo (1996) also demonstrates the implicit marginality that is felt by the local Caribbean community, living adjacent to beach resorts, and the segregated nature of the all-inclusive holiday. All-inclusive visitors are perhaps most commonly known for living in a 'tourist bubble', where they rarely go out into the local community and only stay within the confines of the hotel grounds consuming their pre-paid drinks and meals.

Other authors who have criticized tourism in LEDCs as being primarily in the interests of Western European travel com- panies, polarizing development and focus- ing on externally led development strategies include Bianchi (2002), Britton (1982), Scheveyns (2002), and Sharpley and Telfer (2002). However, in 2007, the United Nations Commission on Trade and Develop- ment (UNCTAD) published a report that researched the nature and impact of FDI in Tunisia, Kenya, Bhutan, the Dominican Republic, Morocco, Sri Lanka and the United Republic of Tanzania. From destin- ation to destination, there are varying degrees of how FDI effectively collaborates with local businesses and communities (see the Sheraton collaboration example with the Tourist Taxi Association in Gambia in Box 5.2). Through FDI, it is argued that in some destinations it has brought positive policy implications, improved the image of the destination and increased product diversification, which can compliment domestic investment. Improved access to training, better working conditions and an increase in balance of payments to a destination may also come as a result of FDI. In some cases, FDI can help raise standards through advanced systems and quality control, though it is also recognized that some foreign investments have perpetuated low standards, inherent in some forms of mass tourism. The report argues that the impact of FDI is therefore mixed in terms of the potential for adding value to a destination. According to the report, it recommends that: 'To take full advantage of FDI as a catalyst and a complement to domestic investment, a coherent and integrated policy framework is essential' (UNCTAD, 2007). However, it is recognized that this is not a simple task because of the long value chain that involves the provision of services by many providers. In addition to this, it is important to understand the contribution and impact of the local elite, government-owned tourism facilities and 'Southern' corporations, which have capitalized on opportunities for investment in tourism.

Akama and Keiti (2007) carried out a study of resident and local business attitudes towards beach enclave resort development and the challenges preventing collaboration and integration with the tourism industry. Here, consequences of foreign ownership of tourism facilities are highlighted as a key challenge for the international industry to work more collaboratively with the local business community. Duijnhoven and Roessingh (2005) also explain the frustration felt by local business communities in the Dominican Republic, as they compete with large ITOs and their preferential trading structures. Britton's (1982) classic diagram

of a beach enclave trading structure (Fig. 5.1), which illustrates the relationship between peripheral and metropolitan economies, represents the predominant power and influence that flow from ITOs and national governments to local destination communities. Although outside social and technological influences and western imports are an integral part of enclaves and can create enclave industrialization and externally oriented growth strategies (Lockhart and Drakkis-Smith, 1993), the model does not detail local social and economic contexts or grassroots initiatives that have sought to challenge external powers or government planning.

The enclave model extensively utilized by ITOs is characteristic of many worldwide tourism destinations. Significantly, the majority of tourists visiting LEDCs do so via a package deal from an ITO such as Thomas Cook or TUI to an enclave area. In The Gambia, 80% of tourists arrive on a package deal organized by multinational tour operators (Government of Gambia Statistics, 2006). This is related to convenience, price and travel style, which remains attractive to many customers across the globe (Milne and Ateljevic, 2001: 378). Some of the characteristics of mass tourism that ITOs capitalize upon whether in LEDCs or Southern Europe are:

- seasonal collective consumption by undifferentiated tourists;
- demands for familiarity by tourists;
- undifferentiated standardized products and services where tourists seek familiarity in facilities and experiences across the globe;
- economies of scale via ownership of key supply chain providers, i.e. airlines, hotels, travel agents; and
- highly competitive pricing.

Within such enclave structures, financial capital, micro-credit or revolving loan facilities to help develop indigenous enterprises compete with foreign-owned establishments are often not a priority included in tourism development strategies (ILO, 2008). The enclave model has thus

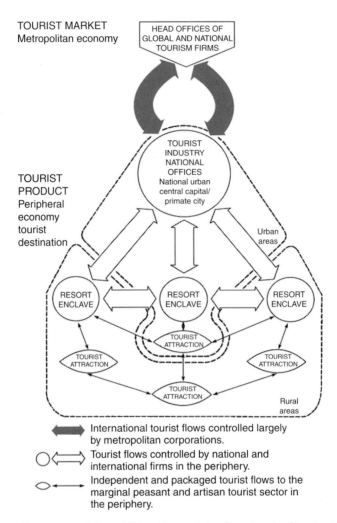

TOURIST MARKET
Metropolitan economy

HEAD OFFICES OF
GLOBAL AND NATIONAL
TOURISM FIRMS

TOURIST
INDUSTRY
NATIONAL
OFFICES
National urban
central capital/
primate city

TOURIST
PRODUCT
Peripheral
economy
tourist
destination

Urban
areas

RESORT
ENCLAVE

RESORT
ENCLAVE

RESORT
ENCLAVE

TOURIST
ATTRACTION

TOURIST
ATTRACTION

TOURIST
ATTRACTION

TOURIST
ATTRACTION

Rural
areas

International tourist flows controlled largely by metropolitan corporations.

Tourist flows controlled by national and international firms in the periphery.

Independent and packaged tourist flows to the marginal peasant and artisan tourist sector in the periphery.

Fig. 5.1. Enclave trading structure (Britton, 1982, with permission from *Annals of Tourism Research*).

contributed to spatial segregation where the focus has primarily been on providing facilities for tourists in order to implement the main features of mass tourism as described above.

Extensive vertical and horizontal integration within the tourism supply chain increases ITO control of the mainstream beach package holiday and therefore the amount of out of pocket expenditure of tourists at their destination becomes vital. However, the use of local businesses becomes problematic when ITOs are distinctly aware of the need to adhere to EU Package Holiday Directive, 1992 legislation, which stipulates the need for strict compliance with consumer protection laws and health and safety requirements. This restricts the scope of partnerships that they are able to forge at the destination with the small and medium enterprise (SME) and informal sector.

The Role and Value of ASSET

Established in 2000, ASSET now has a body of 70 members from tourist guides to elite ecotourism ventures, see http://www.asset-gambia.com, which highlights the diversity of facilities and services on offer to tourists outside of the beach package holiday hotel. According to Mowforth and Munt (2003: 111), 'techniques which allow for consultation and participation [of those people adversely affected by tourism development] are still young in their development'. ASSET is considered an exceptional example with such a varied membership body working on strategies to increase the inclusion of local businesses and 'local people' within the tourism industry via stakeholder collaboration and implement the Responsible Tourism Policy of The Gambia. This has partly been achieved through membership of the RTP, a multi-stakeholder collaboration that is advocating for best practice in responsible tourism and supporting legislation. Led by the GTA, members include: ASSET, The Travel and Tourism Association (representing ground tour operators in The Gambia), the Gambian Hotel Association (GHA) and the British Federation of Tour Operators (FTO).

ASSET is working extensively to increase value within the SME sector via:

- *Value retention* – keeping tourism earnings in the country and minimizing leakages;
- *Value addition* – maximizing linkages within the national value chain;
- *Value creation* – generating new value within the sector (Bah, 2006; Mitchell and Faal, 2007).

Such value enhancement can compliment development objectives in tourism by applying a 'pro-poor tourism approach' to destination management (see Chapter 10, this volume) through direct livelihoods effects on the poor, such as tourism jobs, small tourism enterprises and employment in other complimentary and linking industries, i.e. food and construction. In turn this may also help to develop alternative export sectors such as agricultural exports via Gambia is Good (GiG) (see Box 5.1) and entrepreneurship,

training and infrastructure development, which impacts directly upon citizens.

Essentially, the extent to which tourism benefits in these areas depends on the extent of planning, decision making and inclusivity of policy and practice of destination management. Subsequently, the interrelationship between marginalization and successful inclusion of local people often relies upon a full understanding of how linkages, empowerment and benefits can develop, matched with the necessary policies to implement these strategies. It is in these areas that ASSET has strived to exert influence on behalf of its members since its establishment.

Mitchell and Faal (2007) researched the value of internationally operated tourism in The Gambia, demonstrating the importance of tourism for people's livelihoods, notably via the important tourist expenditure in resorts, with an average of £26 per day per tourist (Master Plan, 2005) where 14% of expenditure within the total Gambia Tourism Value Chain at the destination is 'pro-poor', particularly shopping and excursions, where tourists utilize the services of the Official Tourist Guide (OTG) Association for day tours and Craft Market Associations for souvenirs. Both organizations are members of ASSET. However, the competition for a tourist's out of pocket expenditure at the destination is a challenge and many supermarkets, where tourists shop for Pringles, alcohol and Cadburys chocolate, are owned by Lebanese not Gambians.

In addition, the regularity for small indigenous businesses to receive money from tourists can be restricted because of the seasonal nature of tourism and the relatively large numbers of people engaged in craft vending, taxi driving and tour guiding, which creates extensive competition for success within a small geographical area. In addition, poor infrastructure and a lack of continuous water and electricity supplies hinder investment and new developments. As well as advocating these concerns to local government and the GTA, ASSET's strategies to raise status and use of small businesses in tourism include development of free training programmes for members, marketing and promotion and implementation of quality standards and codes of conduct for effective business practice. Other services offered to members include advice on product development and assistance with access to grants for business development.

Often these issues are not taken seriously enough by governments as the overall benefits of tourism are seen to outweigh the costs, leaving the international industry to exploit opportunities left open by such structural weaknesses. However, via ASSET and the RTP the GTA are taking steps to address such issues.

Beach Enclave Resort Development at Senegambia

The development of Senegambia beach enclave resort began in 1982 with the building of the Senegambia Beach Hotel, and the subsequent development of cafés, nightclubs, restaurants and supermarkets adjacent to the village of Kololi. It consists of one main road (commonly known as 'The Strip') and another smaller road leading towards the coast (Fig. 5.2). Hotels within the immediate vicinity of the Strip include

the Kololi Beach Club time-share apartments, The Kairaba Hotel, Senegambia Beach, Sarge's Hotel, Mansea Beach and Seaview Hotel, all of which are sourced by ITOs. The majority of restaurants and bars offer an eclectic mix of food and drink from around the globe ranging from Irish, Lebanese, Italian, English, Danish, Chinese and Thai, with their associated owners and managers from the country of origin. Tour operators encourage tourists to visit these foreign-owned restaurants and often have an arrangement with the tour rep to advertise their products to tourists. This is a strategy demonstrated in a First Choice/Thomson map of Senegambia, which included the following phrases in promotion of the various businesses: Paradiso 'Best Pizza in The Gambia', 'More up market restaurants' (with an arrow to a Danish- and English-owned restaurant); 'Right Choice English Brands'; 'Nice to relax and best cheesecake in Gambia' (First Choice Senegambia Tourist Map, 2008). Of the 11 restaurants mentioned on the map, only one is promoted for its African food and no Gambian-owned restaurants are on the map, even though there are several in the enclave. Also on the map, OTGs are referred to as Walking Guides with no detail of their affiliation or what they offer, Tourist Taxis are referred to as Green Taxis and the Craft Market does not state opening times or types of products

Fig. 5.2. Entrance to Senegambia enclave.

available. This demonstrates an unfair playing field within the enclave where foreign businesses are given more access to tourists compared with Gambian-owned. Although the tour operators may argue that tourists demand such foreign goods the Gambian offering and associated benefits should also be provided.

The Butler's Tourism Development Area Lifecycle is utilized here to explain some key characteristics of the resort enclave development of Senegambia. Initially in the 'exploration' stages of tourism development between 1960 and 1970, there were a small number of tourists, mainly Swedes, who ventured to the Gambian coast for the first time using the Swedish tour operator Vingressor. There was little tourist infrastructure and the holiday was dependent on the natural and cultural resources that The Gambia had to offer. In the 'involvement' stage, gradually local and public investment was applied to the tourism industry to fulfil a growing interest by Europeans for a winter sun destination. This led to the 'development' stage, which saw the establishment of a tourist season between October and April supported by ITOs and the Tourism Liaison Board, a new government agency that began tourism planning and marketing in 1970. The Tourism Development Area (TDA) was also established during this time, which allocated the coast of Gambia entirely for the purposes of tourism development. The Senegambia Hotel was built in 1982 by a Swedish investor and the 1980s saw a rapid growth in the number of tourists. This period of Senegambia's growth was characterized by foreign investment and visitors increased from 26,745 in 1983 to 58,026 in 1991 and to 84,758 in 1997. It was not until the early 1990s that other areas along the coast including Kotu, Cape Point and Bakau also started to build hotels that received package holiday tourists.

The growth rates of tourism slowed down in the late 1990s, as visitor arrivals remained at approximately 90,000 for about 8 years. Because of the characteristics of all-inclusives discussed earlier, in September 1999, the Gambian government imple-mented a policy whereby the operation of any all-inclusive holiday package was banned. Pressure from local businesses criticized the lack of benefits that such holidays were bringing to the Gambian economy, local entrepreneurs and small businesses. However, the ban was lifted after a year because of pressure from European tour operators who strongly opposed the ban. Although there are all-inclusive packages available, they are not actively promoted by the GTA and The Gambia is not as renowned for all-inclusives compared with the Caribbean.

In the 'consolidation' stage, new attempts were made to develop new markets through development of an Ecotourism policy, and other more specialist niche markets such as nature and culture tourism and new Eastern European markets were targeted. However, stagnation point was reached between 2000 and 2004, and there was a heavy reliance on repeat visitors. At this time, occupancy rates were low and the Senegambia area appeared outdated with shabby facilities. Also at that time there was substantial coastal erosion around the Senegambia beach area, which affected the beauty and paradise image sold in tourist brochures and a poor image surrounding sex tourism and 'bumsters' (see below) continued to affect tourism promotion despite interest to diversify from the traditional beach product. Despite these issues, it became clear that ITOs were primarily focused on The Gambia as a winter sun beach destination and the Senegambia Strip seemed to epitomize this narrow view of Gambia's tourism potential.

During such periods of stagnation, the enclave resort model significantly high-lights the continuous reference to the fact that large numbers of tourists remained inside the hotel walls and did not integrate effectively with the local business com-munity because of poor information from the hotels and tour operators. Similar observations were made by Duijnhoven and Roessingh (2005) in the Dominican Republic. This propensity for tourists to stay inside a hotel for the duration of a beach holiday without necessarily explor-ing the local area, or perhaps tentatively booking a day tour with the inbound tour company is a key challenge to developing countries. Relaxing all day and 'chilling out' was recorded as a primary motivation to visit The Gambia (Master Plan Study, 2005), a factor that requires innovation and collaboration with the SME and informal sector to create an increased impact upon the local economy (see GiG Case Study, Box 5.1).

More recently, The Gambia has seen a rejuvenation period where foreign and domestic investment in tourism has re-vitalized and mass construction of new hotels, including the five-star Coco Ocean and Sheraton Hotel, new supermarkets, luxury apartments and villas, new restaurants, clubs and casinos. The GTA's statistics indicate a 15% average growth between 2005 and 2007 (107,904, 124,800 and 142,626), which coincided with Africa's 8% increase in visitor arrivals throughout the continent in 2007. (UNWTO, 2009). However, according to the GTA monthly arrival statistics, the 2007/2008 season registered arrivals of 137,832, while the provisional figures for winter 2008/2009 registered 110,039, representing a drop of 20% because of the 'global economic downturn' and tightening of tourists spending money on holidays. The British continue to provide the highest number of arrivals representing 56.3% of the arrivals, followed by the Dutch 8.5%, while Scandinavia accounted for 7.8% (GTA, 2009).

The reduction in tourist numbers also reflects how fewer tourists are staying in the main hotels, and more in privately owned accommodation and rented apartments. This reflects the boom in property investment, time-share properties and tourists buying land (Shaw and Williams, 2004: 194). The full economic impact of this trend in second home tourism in The Gambia has yet to be researched.

Access to Tourists and Tourism

The following section demonstrates how a number of concerns surrounding the theme of *access* characterize the social exclusion of residents and local businesses from the

---

Box 5.1. The Gambia is Good (GiG) project.

The GiG project is a unique and highly successful example of voluntary, public and business sector engagement where Concern Universal and a leading UK-based horticultural business Haygrove are working together with support from DFID's Business Linkage Challenge Fund and the Travel Foundation, to create a sustainable, pro-poor marketing initiative in The Gambia to encourage new agricultural exports and links with the tourism industry. Now in its 4th year, GiG, a marketing company under the umbrella of the Irish NGO Concern Universal, is also working with the Travel Foundation, to lever GiG's impact by promoting responsible business practice in the tourism industry. For many years, the horticultural sector remained marginalized from the hotel and catering sector in The Gambia as it was unable to create linkages with the hotel sector because of extensive challenges including:

- poor quality;
- unsuitable varieties of vegetables for the tourist market;
- lack of storage space and poor transportation services of produce to hotels and restaurants, lack of communication between caterers and farmers;
- lack of knowledge of the catering industry; and
- ineffective farming methods to grow bulk produce.

As a result, much of the hotel demands for food were met outside The Gambia in Senegal, Morocco and Britain. Since GiG's inception, GiG now purchases from nearly 1000 growers, 90% of which are women. Of its core suppliers, a transition has been made from subsistence agriculture to commercial enterprise with a marked improvement in quality, yield and diversification. Women in the most rural communities, where they had previously virtually no cash income, are now making up to £150 per month (Concern Universal, 2009). In the period 2006–2009, GiG growers have increased their income by an average of 500%.

mainstream beach package industry. This occurs in a number of ways, including restrictions for local people into tourist areas, poor access to water and electricity, limited destination-based marketing strategies and difficulty in adhering to strict licensing rules and international legislation. The effect of such access-related difficulties has arguably contributed to enclave exclusiveness, and it is argued that tourist harassment and hassling is one local reaction to such restrictions.

The Tourism Offences Act 2003

Access to tourists in order to sell and promote business is a key problem, particularly as the GTA has only recently provided the first tourist information kiosk at the entrance to the Senegambia Enclave, which presents a key opportunity for local business promotion. Lack of local business promotion has in the past reduced opportunities for linkages to complimentary industries and businesses to allow the multiplier effect to establish itself fully within the destination. Other than OTGs, young unemployed men, known in The Gambia as 'bumsters' who trawl the enclave area looking to befriend tourists and supply a variety of informal guiding services, have become the primary tourist information source. While also pursuing a livelihood, whereby a commission is often sought for introducing the tourist to a particular service or business, bumsters have also received extensive criticism for hassling tourists and creating a bad image for The Gambia by using persuasive tactics to lure tourists into parting with their money, some of which include romance tourism. For many Gambian young men and increasingly women, there is pressure to provide for large extended families and some develop relationships with tourists so that they may pursue their business interests, provide for their family, pay for an education or escape The Gambia to work in Europe or the USA. Such a phenomenon is not uncommon in other beach enclaves in LEDCs such as Goa, Thailand, Mombasa and the Caribbean.

Arguably, the bumsters justify their actions as wanting a share in tourist expenditure and may find it difficult to secure alternative livelihood solutions; however, the methods some bumsters use have provoked complaints and frustration towards ITOs and have turned many tourists away from The Gambia. In turn, this justified ITOs to pressure the government to implement legislation to prevent such harassment, which further entrenched the the enclave model and discourages tourists from exploring local areas (Fig. 5.3).

Access to tourists, particularly by the informal sector comprising of juice pressers, craft sellers, taxi drivers, tourist guides and fruit sellers, is compounded further since there are strict regulations detailed in the Tourism Offences Act of 2003 that stipulate that it is an offence by an employee: 'who, being an employee in a Tourism Development Area, tourist enterprise or in any other place that provides services to tourists, alone or jointly with another person … stalks, insults, intimidates, threatens, begs, harasses or hassles a tourist' (2003: 3). The legislation was established in part to make provision for offences related to tourism and also provides for sexual offences of tourists against children, as well as for prohibition of trafficking in children. However, the legislation is open to differences in interpretation particularly for those trying to approach a tourist to sell a service, which could be interpreted as hassle. This has led to a situation where many of those operating in the informal sector do not know or have not experienced another method of promoting one's business because of the lack of promotion and marketing venues and the desperate need to make a living. The Act is also being enforced to curb bumsters, and anyone who is seen talking to a tourist whether legitimately or not or visiting the beach for recreational purposes could be wrongly arrested.

Significantly, the Master Plan Study (2005) reported that 67% of tourists regarded harassment from bumsters as the main problem in The Gambia. The Master

Fig. 5.3. Harassment or friendship? (Source: S. Dobson.)

Plan also recognized the complexity of the bumster issue and the following was concluded about the phenomenon:

> The bumster problem is an enigma ... Bumsters take their role very seriously ... A needs assessment must be conducted to find out the needs of these young people. The finding of this needs assessment should form the basis of any action concerning the bumster. Attempts to use military force to get them off the beaches is not the answer, what is more enduring and lasting is to embody them with self esteem. Activities that promote their human dignity and self worth based on income earning opportunities should be implemented ...

(Master Plan, 2005: 120)

The GTA are particularly concerned with those tourists who will not return to The Gambia because of the 'unbearable harassment from beach boys and all those who hang around the Banjul International Airport, hotel entrances, restaurants, craft markets, taxi parks, museums and other places frequented by tourists' (excerpt from speech by Director of GTA, 2003). The Youth Responsible Tourism Association (YORTA), an organization recognized by the GTA, which began as a group of Gambian tourism students wanting to help address the problem and has an objective to assist with the elimination of bumsterism through sensitization programmes and awareness campaigns in schools, is a good example of grassroots action to address this complex social trend in tourism. Recent developments within the education department to promote tourism education, and discussion of the positive and negative social impacts of tourism on the national curriculum are also aimed at deterring young people from heading to the beach to pursue tourists.

Marketing and Promotion

As previously mentioned, strongly linked to the factor of access to tourists is the lack of marketing and promotion of venues, and the shortage of National Tourist Information Centres in the resort enclave. This has led to certain prohibitive characteristics of the 'resort enclave' where marketing and promotional opportunities are actively prohibited within hotels as they are expected to patronize the ITO bringing tourists to the hotel, making it hard for local businesses to break the tour operator monopoly and inhibits tourists visiting local business outlets.

The lack of knowledge of tour operator representatives can also affect access to tourists. Often ITOs bring new tour reps to The Gambia each or every other year with very limited knowledge of the country. Although the British-owned tour operator Gambia Experience uses Gambian Reps, they are still restricted by the limited local information allowed in Welcome Meetings. According to the Gambia Experience Destination Manager, the welcome meeting does not allow enough time to promote all local businesses, as there are many other issues to cover. However, there are no other alternatives encouraged such as local guidebooks or local information packs available in hotels other than those compiled by the ITO to promote its tours within Gambia and cursory advice about Gambia. ASSET continues to liaise with hotels to advertise their members; however, not all hotels are willing to promote them. To add to this there is a lack of access to information technology and low literacy levels, which limit use of or knowledge of desk top publishing for producing advertising material. In response to this, ASSET provides computer training to its members.

The lack of written marketing material and a venue to distribute such information concerns all ASSET members as opposed to the direct 'face to face' access issue, discussed previously, which mainly concerns 'informal sector' members. It was for this reason in 2006 ASSET opened an information and bookings centre and cafe in Fajara above a popular bookshop, although knowledge of its existence by package holiday tourists is limited.

A breakthrough in small business collaboration with the beach package holiday product was achieved in 2006 when the Gambia is Good (GiG) Farm, with support from the Travel Foundation and Concern Universal, managed to forge a contract with the UK high-street tour operator First Choice (which merged with the German operator TUI in 2007), to promote a visit to the demonstration farm at Yundum within the itinerary of day trips for First Choice tourists.

Marketing and promotional activities are core to ASSET's activities helping businesses to be known and sell themselves outside of The Gambia. This is achieved through their booking centre, website, brochures, leaflets and targeting alternative markets other than the package holiday tourist including expatriates and NGO workers and their visitors, domestic tourists, special interest tourists and independent travellers.

In 2006, ASSET accommodation members collaborated with World Hotel Link, a website promoting a wide variety of accommodation outlets in order to widen opportunities for promotion on the Internet. Within the corporate strategy, the GTA states that it will set up a comprehensive information service to provide relevant information to tourists and potential investors while in The Gambia. This began in March 2010 when the first information kiosk was opened at the entrance of Senegambia Enclave.

Key to marketing success is the ability for stakeholders to feel they have good access to their targeted market. According to a focus group meeting with the fruit juice pressers, access to hotel guests is an ongoing problem. Hotels with a private beach area for guests request that the juice pressers position themselves 10 m away from the sun beds of the hotel. The security guards actively want to enforce this requirement stipulated by hotels and wish to be seen to be protecting the tourist, while the juice presser is merely offering the tourist juice. Both parties are entitled to be on the beach and yet there is sometimes resentment towards the other perhaps over the degrees of access granted (Fig. 5.4).

The OTGs, who offer day excursions around the local area, also experience a number of difficulties promoting their business and hotel policy varies on attitudes towards them. The Senegambia

Fig. 5.4. Security guard patrolling sunbathing area at rear of Senegambia Hotel.

and Kairaba Hotel is immediately opposite a sheltered area where approximately 50 OTGs are permitted to be stationed and tourists have to approach them. Both hotels do not allow OTGs to enter the hotel, whereas Bungalow Beach Hotel and Kombo Beach in Kotu invite a tour guide representative to attend welcome meetings for the tourists. Some tour operators do promote their services, others do not. According to the National Official Tourist Guide Association (NOTGA), the information that the tourist receives from these tour operators is not always positive information, particularly when some tour operators state that tourist guides are not registered or licensed or do not have liability insurance when they are a registered and licensed government-created body.

Craft market vendors also complained of inaccurate information and lack of promotion by some hotels, as craft markets provide competition to the hotel souvenir shops. Hotels are also accused of over-zealous protection of tourists, emphasizing the possibility of hassle and haggling in the markets. However, occasionally the hotels will invite craftspeople into the hotel to do demonstrations or present their wares to sell within the 'safety' of the hotel grounds. Sometimes hotels also hold fashion shows exhibiting locally made clothes.

Another informal sector group, which struggles for regular business and experiences extensive competition from other transport companies and in-house competition, is the Tourist Taxi Drivers Association (TTA). Key problems include access to sell to tourists and informing tourists of their service so they are aware and trusting of their service. The taxis are situated outside hotel entrances and at the entrance to the hotels and at the entrance to the Strip (Fig. 5.5). The standard and quality of the TTA fleet of taxis does not always encourage tourists and has been an ongoing issue that ASSET has helped to address. Although the GTA licence given to Tourist Taxis requires an MOT certificate, tour operators are often keen to emphasize the lack of liability insurance. The EU Package Holiday Directive 1992 stipulates that any business recommended in resort by an ITO should have liability insurance (discussed in the following section), which generally only large-scale ground tour operators can afford, unlike small-scale businesses or the informal sector.

Liability Insurance

Lack of liability insurance is a major factor contributing to the marginalization of certain groups of small-scale business that deal with tourists and where issues of safety and security are involved. Parallel to this, ASSET has campaigned for their members to aim for increased quality standards in order to improve perceptions of ITOs towards the SME sector. Safety and

Fig. 5.5. Tourist taxis waiting for business at the entrance to Senegambia Strip.

security are primary factors rightly given immense priority by ITOs for their customers because of the threat of litigation as a result of negligence. This relates to any services where the tourist partakes in an activity, for example guiding, or uses transport. For the economic sustainability of large-scale tourism operations operating on a global scale like ITOs and large hotel chains, they have to incorporate liability insurance into their management practice to protect them for any incompetence or mistakes made by their organization that may put the tourist at risk. However, in LEDCs and The Gambia, many businesses cannot afford the cost of liability insurance.

Fundamentally, tour operators will not confidently recommend local services to their customers if they are not convinced that the tourist is adequately protected and safe under the health and safety requirements and conditions of the 1992 EU Package Travel Directive, i.e. a tour operator is not going to put themselves in a position of being sued for giving a tourist inappropriate information that may lead to an accident or unfavourable incident. This is why tour operators and hotels generally do not promote taxis that are old or juice pressers who do not use hot water for washing glasses. However, if the tourist makes an independent decision to travel with a local taxi, it is the choice of the tourist. In an LEDC country context, this has major implications for tourism services and facilities, as there are many situations that could be described as unsafe or unhygienic, which can be influenced by lack of basic infrastructure, lack of capital to reinvest into a business or lack of knowledge or understanding about how a situation could pose a risk. This can be applied to bad roads, poor water supplies and poor sanitation facilities. Ashley *et al.* (2001), Bah (2006) and Mitchell and Faal (2007) all highlight liability insurance as a key limiting factor that hinders tour operator promotion of local businesses. To address this issue, ASSET liaised extensively with GAMSTAR, a leading Gambian insurance company, to help offer affordable insurance to small businesses. A milestone was achieved when ASSET and the TTA collaborated with the new Sheraton Hotel to overcome the suspicion and distrust of the Tourist Taxi service (see Box 5.2).

Box 5.2. Tourist Taxis and the Sheraton Hotel.

Despite Tourist Taxis holding a license from the GTA, these standards were not enough for the newly opened Sheraton Hotel, since the MOT test focuses more on the mechanical and external aspects of the vehicle.

The Sheraton requires that the Green Tourist Taxis not only meet the GTA licensing criteria but those of Sheraton Gambia Hotel Resort and Spa as well. The criteria for consideration as a 'Sheraton Taxi' is comprehensive: drivers seeking to be members of the Sheraton family had to read and accept the Sheraton Gambia Hotel Resort and Spa Code of Conduct drafted by the Director of Public Relations. It states that drivers must be Gambian nationals with valid drivers' license; drivers must wear a uniform consisting of navy blue trousers, pressed white shirt, black belt, black shoes and a Sheraton badge; drivers must be able to understand English; drivers must maintain personal hygiene at all times; drivers must refrain from illegal drug trafficking and use; taxis must have valid license from the GTA and valid insurance, which must include liability insurance, arranged with the support of ASSET and a local insurance broker. The taxi seat upholstery and other conveniences inside the cabin also had to meet Sheraton's five-star standards. Taxi drivers must agree to abide by the code of conduct at all times, if they are selected to serve the hotel.

> In the beginning, it was very difficult to convince my fellow taxi drivers to allow their cars to be inspected by Sheraton. I supported the inspection because I knew that the 5-Star hotel wanted something better than what is normally obtained. The drivers had to refer the matter to the Tourism Authority, because they needed to know why Sheraton wanted to inspect their cars again, after having passed an MOT test.
>
> The Secretary General of the Gambia Tourist Taxi Association
> (Business Challenge Fund DFID, 2007)

The Secretary General is responsible for the supervision of the 22 drivers that have signed the Code of Conduct. He is assisted by a Taxi Controller who is responsible for sending a taxi to the front of the lobby when it is requested by guests through the Sheraton Concierge. The acceptance of the Tourist Taxis by Sheraton is a milestone in the potential for informal sector collaboration with the mainstream tourism sector.

While some taxi drivers within the TTA have been working in the tourism industry for many years, own old cars and cannot afford a new replacement car or expensive repairs, some taxi drivers have newer modern cars, often bought through tourist sponsorship. However, tourists regularly choose to utilize the new over the old for safety reasons. This is causing the long-standing taxi drivers to be marginalized when they have given service to the industry. They are finding it more difficult to accept the changes in law and regulation, which gives precedence to cars that are in good condition, modern and more reliable.

The OTGs do not have liability insurance but they argue that they are a government-supported body and therefore they are protected by government. The craft markets are considering whether they can afford to take out association liability insurance.

Although the liability insurance issue is not yet fully addressed for all members, through encouraging adherence to quality standards, ASSET is contributing to an improved image of the local SME sector, which strives for recognition as key stakeholders in the tourism industry. In addition, they are also targeting alternative markets other than package holiday tourists, including business and conference delegates, expatriates, local elites and special interest tourists.

Conclusion

The chapter has highlighted some core issues and concerns that are common in a beach enclave resort in an LEDC context. It is evident that if beach package tourism is to fit better to responsible tourism principles, a new beach tourism business development model is required that enables the local residents to integrate more effectively with the industry. In order to achieve this, stakeholders need to work together to ensure that marketing opportunities are sought, professional training and education is provided to aspiring citizens, and tourists are sensitized about the variety and diversity of alternative services and facilities available at the local level on arrival in the destination. As the GiG example has demonstrated, ITOs should consider how to form partnerships with local organizations and businesses to widen their economic impact at the destination and support philanthropic and entrepreneurial ventures. By focusing purely upon the smiling, sun, sea and sand beach product and providing facilities and services for international tourists, this can restrict opportunities for income generation at the local level and undermine the important relationship between tourism and development. In order to achieve this product diversification, enhanced local supply chain networks, which support a variety of industries, adherence to international quality standards and searching for alternative markets including domestic and business tourism are vital to reduce dependency upon the beach package holiday tourist. Another area

that requires public and private sector support is professional tourism education and training that assists with development of standards within the industry as well as empowerment to enter middle and senior management positions. In addition, examples of successful local entrepreneurship should be utilized for young people to learn and gain inspiration from. In order to counteract the power of larger businesses with economies of scale, the SME sector can network and share knowledge so that a variety of sectors are able to compete for and access specialized resources and information systems and capitalize upon internal competencies and assets. It is in this way that ASSET is encouraging businesses to work together to overcome factors that cause marginalization and work in partnership with the public sector, hotels and ITOs to address barriers arising from a beach package enclave.

Questions

1. Identify three primary reasons for marginalization at a beach enclave resort.
2. Discuss how harassment and hassle of tourists in an enclave area may be reduced.
3. Explain how ITOs can help with SME development in Gambia.

References

Akama, J.S. and Keiti, D. (2007) Tourism and socio-economic development in developing countries: a case study of Mombassa Resort Kenya. *Journal of Sustainable Tourism* 15, 735–747.

Ankomah, P.K. (1991) Tourism skilled labour: the case of Sub-Saharan Africa. *Annals of Tourism Research* 18, 433–442.

Ashley, C., Boyd, C. and Goodwin, H. (2001) Pro-Poor Tourism: Putting Tourism at the Heart of the Tourism Agenda. Overseas Development Institute (ODI) Report, available at: http://www.oneworld.org/odi/nrp/51.html

Azarya, V. (2004) Globalisation and international tourism in developing countries: marginality as a cultural commodity. *Current Sociology* 52, 949–967.

Bah, A. (2006) Challenges of Tourism for Local Communities. The Gambian Experience. Gambia Tourism Concern Document.

Bianchi, R. V. (2002) A new political economy. In: Telfer, D. and Sharpley, R. (eds) *Tourism and Development: Concepts and Issues.* Channel View, Clevedon, pp. 265–299.

Britton, S. (1982) The political economy of tourism in the third world. *Annals of Tourism Research* 9, 331–358.

Concern Universal (2009) Gambia is Good Initiative. Available at: http://www.concernuniversal.org/index.php?/where_we_work/gambia/gambia_is_good_initiative

Cornelissen, S. (2005) Producing and imaging 'place' and 'people': the political economy of South African International Tourist Representation. *Review of International Political Economy* 12, 674–699.

DFID Business Challenge Fund (2007) *The DFID Business Challenge Fund.* Department of International Development.

Duijnhoven, H. and Roessingh, C. (2005) Small entrepreneurs and shifting identities: the case of tourism in Puerto Plata (Northern Dominican Republic). *Journal of Tourism and Cultural Change* 2, 185–202.

Echtner, C. and Prasad, P. (2003) The context of third world tourism marketing. *Annals of Tourism Research* 30, 660–682.

First Choice Senegambia Tourist Map (2008) First Choice Senegambia Tourist Map. First Choice Publications.

Freitag, T. (1994) Enclave tourism development: for the whom the benefits roll: case study of Dominican Republic problems of resort development. *Annals of Tourism Research* 21, 538–554.

Government of The Gambia (2006) *National Tourism Statistics.* Department of Tourism and Culture.

GTA (2009) *International Tourism Statistics.* Gambia Tourism Authority.

Harrison, D. (2001) *Tourism and the Less Developed World: Issues and Case Studies.* CAB International, Wallingford, UK.

Holloway, J.C. (2007) *The Business of Tourism*, 8th edn. Prentice Hall, Englewood Cliffs, NJ.

Index of Economic Freedom (2009) *Index of Economic Freedom.* The Heritage Foundation, available at: http://heritage.org/index/

Krippendorf, J. (1987) *The Holiday Makers: Understanding the Impact of Leisure and Travel.* Heinemann, London.

Lickorish, L.J. and Jenkins, C.L. (1997) *An Introduction to Tourism.* Butterworth-Heinemann Press, Oxford.

Lockhart, D.G., Drakakis-Smith, D. and Schembri, J. (eds) (1998) *The Development Process in Small Island States.* Routledge, London.

Master Plan (2005) *The Gambia Tourism Master Plan 2005 – 2010.* African Development Bank and Department of Tourism and Culture Publications.

Mbaiwa, J.E. (2003) The socio-economic and environmental impacts of tourism development on the Okavango Delta, north-western Botswana. *Journal of Arid Environments* 54, 447–467.

Mbaiwa, J. (2005) Enclave tourism and its socio-economic impacts in the Okavango Delta, Botswana. *Tourism Management* 26, 157–172.

Mihalic, T. (2002) Tourism and economic development issues. In: Sharpley, R. and Telfer, D.J. (eds) *Tourism and Development: Concepts and Issues.* Channel View, Clevedon, pp. 81–111.

Milne, S. and Ateljivic, I. (2001) Tourism, economic development and the global–local nexus: theory embracing complexity. *Tourism Geographies* 3, 369–393.

Mitchell, J. and Faal, J. (2007) Holiday package tourism and the poor in The Gambia. *Development Southern Africa* 24, 445–464.

Mowforth, M. and Munt, I. (2003) *Tourism and Sustainability: New Tourism in the Third World*, 1st and 2nd edn. Routledge, London.

Pattullo, P. (1996) *The Cost of Tourism in The Caribbean.* Cassell, London.

ProPoor Tourism (2008) International tour operator: roles, practices and implications for developing countries. Sheet No. 10. Pro-Poor Tourism Info Sheets.

Scheyvens, R. (2002) *Tourism for Development: Empowering Communities.* Prentice Hall, Englewood Cliffs, New Jersey.

Sharpley, R. and Telfer, D.J. (eds) (2002) *Tourism and Development: Concepts and Issues.* Channel View, Clevedon, UK.

Shaw, G. and Williams, A.M. (2004) *Tourism and Tourism Spaces.* Sage, London.

Sindiga, I. (1999) *Tourism and African Development: Changes and Challenges of Tourism in Kenya.* Ashgate Publishing, Aldershot, UK.

Tourism Offences Act (2003) Tourism Offences Act. Government of The Gambia.

UN Data Country Profile: The Gambia (2007) Available at: http://data.un.org/CountryProfile.aspx?crName=Gambia

UNCTAD (2007) FDI in tourism: the development dimension. United Nations Commission on Trade and Development Published Report, New York and Geneva.

UNWTO (2006) *Compendium of Tourism Statistics 2000–2004.* UNWTO publication.

UNWTO (2009) *Tourism Highlights 2008.* UNWTO publication.

World Bank (2007) *World Development Indicator.* World Bank Publication, Washington DC.

World Bank (2008) *World Development Indicator.* World Bank Publication, Washington DC.

6 Fair Trade in Tourism – a Marketing Tool for Social Transformation?

Angela Kalisch

Introduction

This chapter critically analyses the potential of a Fair Trade Tourism label to address issues of inequality and injustice in international tourism in less economically developed countries (LEDCs). The analysis is based on the premise that contemporary tourism is integral to the system that drives the global economy, capitalism and free trade. Therefore, the attempt to address injustice in tourism with Fair Trade principles needs to incorporate an analysis of the relationship between capitalism and tourism. The chapter starts with an introduction to tourism as an export trade strategy within the capitalist system, and the key factors contributing to poverty and unequal exchange through tourism development in less developed countries. These factors formed the backcloth to the formation of the ideas on Fair Trade in Tourism in the mid-1990s (Badger et al., 1996; Cleverdon and Kalisch, 2000; Kalisch, 2001, 2002). The approach is thus historical from the outset, underpinning a review of contemporary research on Fair Trade in Tourism that followed on from the earlier work; since Fair Trade is a certification process, the chapter critically explores the issues of certification in tourism, as well as Fair Trade certification in primary commodities.

The International Network on Fair Trade in Tourism, set up in 1999 by the UK non-governmental organization (NGO) Tour-ism Concern, is used as a case study to highlight the outcomes of an international multi-stakeholder consultation process on Fair Trade in Tourism conducted between 1999 and 2002. The purpose of the case study is to illustrate the complexities of developing an international consensus on the key criteria for such a concept; and to emphasize the need for shifting the decision-making process on trade justice from a Eurocentric to a polycentric approach, originating from within the communities that it aims to benefit. The chapter ends with an analysis of the future for Fair Trade in Tourism and the development of a Fair Trade label. It acknowledges the need for pilot initiatives to explore the feasibility of a Fair Trade Tourism label, which could assist with a greater understanding of the complexities of implementation. It suggests that a label might contribute to changing public values and expectations of social justice, but only in conjunction with a long-term strategy, incorporating a wider global movement for more equitable trade in tourism. It concludes that a Fair Trade Tourism label, conceived solely as a marketing tool, would be unlikely to achieve significant development benefits to the poorest communities in more or less developed regions; nor would it significantly change the underlying structures of socio-economic inequality in the context of the structural imbalances of the capitalist economic system, which has shaped the organization of international tourism.

The Political and Socio-economic Context of Fair Trade in Tourism

The international promotion of contemporary tourism has been facilitated by neo-liberal capitalist ideals of free markets and free trade in the context of globalization (Harrison, 1994; Bianchi, 2002; Mowforth and Munt, 2003; Reid, 2003). As transnational corporations (TNCs), the vehicles of globalization, penetrate deep into less developed economies, aided by international trade rules, the risks of exploitation and uneven development have been publicly exposed (Ascher, 1985; Barratt-Brown, 1993; Korten 1995; Britton, 1996; Klein, 2000; Hertz, 2001; Pilger, 2002; Madeley, 2003). As a result, an increasing number of critical consumers has started to demand higher ethical standards in business (Cowe and Williams, 2000; Mintel Market Report, 2001; Tallontire *et al.*, 2001). In response to this growing ethical consumer consciousness, NGOs in Europe and North America have created innovative models of fair and ethical trade, combining business priorities with development goals. Fair Trade and organic labelling of products, certifying adherence to various ethical principles of organic and sustainable production and processing are intended to solicit consumer confidence and commitment to a more ethical international trading system (Barratt-Brown, 1993).

'Fair Trade'-certified products are available on the shelves of the bigger supermarkets in northern Europe and America and include a multitude of commodities, such as coffee, tea, fruit, flowers, wine and cotton used for fashionable Fair Trade clothes. Even Fair Trade towns are being created (Fair Trade Labelling Organization, 2009). In the context of rapid tourism growth in less developed economies contributing to human rights abuses and injustices related to certain tourism developments, the question arises of why it should not also be possible to buy Fair Trade certified holidays. This question has been explored since the mid-1990s by an international network of tourism stakeholders, both profit and non-profit making.

However, apart from a Fair Trade Tourism initiative in South Africa, there is as yet no Fair Trade Tourism label, comparable with Fair Trade commodities, certified by the European Fair Trade Labelling Organization or the UK-based Fair Trade Foundation. The following sections provide an insight into why this might be the case and whether a Fair Trade Tourism label could be effective in the context of social and economic justice in tourism.

Capitalism, unequal exchange and corporate power

The geopolitical expansion and influence of tourism in terms of socio-economic and political structures at global and local levels is immense. It is interlinked with agriculture and food security, in the context of imports and land uses for tourism development; construction and property development; telecommunications, infrastructure and transport systems; healthcare and sanitation. Policies developed in any of these sectors will affect tourism and vice versa. In 2008, international tourism arrivals worldwide were estimated to have reached 922 million. Although the global financial crisis in 2008 caused a sharp drop in arrivals to 600 million in 2009, the long-term trend is still expected to be on the increase to 1.6 billion in 2020 (UNWTO, 2009). This human migration constitutes 23% of the world's population of 6.7 billion, thus 'capitalism is crucially involved in managing and profiting from this massive, temporary and annual migration' (Harrison, 1994: 239).

The tourism system and its worldwide promotion in contemporary times is an integral component of the capitalist ideology that promotes private capital and wealth accumulation through private enterprise, worldwide free markets and free trade. This is done in conjunction with state authorities and international organizations, such as the United Nations and the World Tourism Organization (UNWTO) (Harrison, 1994; Lanfant *et al.*, 1995). Tourism is one of the most important sectors, driving the process of globalization, which, according to Reid (2003: 3) is a force that 'pursues profits over justice'.

Within capitalism, capital accumulation is expected to lead to economic growth at global and state levels through private ownership and barrier-free trade. Market forces are left to determine economic dynamics and social systems. This in turn is deemed beneficial to a society's development (Barratt-Brown, 1995). Some analysts believe that capitalism benefits from accumulation by exploitation, which creates inequality in wealth distribution and uneven development (Barratt-Brown, 1995; Levine, 1988; Mowforth and Munt, 2003). This in turn affects productive capacity. They argue that 'accumulation by consent would need to replace accumulation by exploitation' (Barratt-Brown, 1995: 182). One of the ways in which this could be achieved would be to 'transfer the means of production into social ownership' (Barratt-Brown, 1995: 184).

In clarifying the term exploitation, Levine (1988: 66) focuses on exploitation in exchange:

> an exploitative exchange is first of all an unequal exchange; an exchange in which the exploited party gets less than the exploiting party, who does better at the exploited party's expense. This is intuitively, the sense in which exploitative exchanges are unjust (unfair).

However, he elaborates by highlighting that not all unfair exchanges are exploitative. 'The exchange must result from social relations of unequal power'. This means that the power inequality underlying unequal exchange is often hidden behind an intricate set of complex political, social and economic relations that need to be unravelled in order to redress the equilibrium from an exploitative (unjust) exchange to an equitable (just) exchange.

The concept of power forms a necessary starting point in the analysis whether equitable exchange in international trade in tourism is possible, or how it might occur (Britton, 1996; Bianchi, 2002; Mowforth and Munt, 2003). Capitalism uses the means of political and economic power to dominate and eliminate weaker human

systems, widening the rich–poor divide. Indeed, some ideologues consider inequality as a crucial factor of capitalism's success (Fennell, 2006). As Dr. Michael Iwand, Executive Director of TUI, is quoted as saying: 'Tourism is based on inequality ... and we are living comfortably with it. People in the destinations are asking: send us more' (Fernweh, 2004).

Corporate power in tourism

Tourism's growth and popularity has been based on the fact that it is a business transaction, a complex commodity with exchange value (Burns and Holden, 1995; Watson and Kopachevsky, 1996), whose diverse distributional channels and value chains have been skilfully packaged as a product and traded on the world's markets (Kalisch, 2001). TNCs in tourism control the majority of global tourism trade. They own the key components of the tourism value chain through horizontal, vertical and diagonal integration, both in tourism generating as well as receiving countries. Their influence over demand and buying behaviour (Meyer, 2003), as well as supply, means that they can effectively control a country's economy and they particularly exert considerable influence in small countries or island states with a weak infrastructure and a high dependency on tourism.

The continual process of integration, mergers, take-overs and buy-outs results in the consolidation of a small number of corporate players in command of the majority of tourism markets (Madeley, 1996; Mowforth and Munt, 2003; Souty 2004; Mosedale, 2006). Since 2007, nearly 80% of international tourism trade in the UK is in the hands of just two German conglomerates, who have taken over four of the UK's biggest tourism operators.[1] Such centralized systems, combined with an abundance of competing destinations, translate into unequal trading relationships and overwhelming bargaining power in the negotiation of contracts with local tourism suppliers (Ascher, 1985; Madeley, 1996; Buhalis, 2000; Souty, 2004).

Fig. 6.1. Fair share (see http://www.polyp.org.uk).

A key instrument of power for TNCs, which own a myriad of different operations and companies within the same group, is the method of 'transfer pricing'. Transfer pricing enables integrated corporations to transfer goods and services across frontiers but within the same group. It allows corporations to reduce recorded profits in the countries where they are trading, thus minimizing their tax liabilities and enabling them to repatriate their profits. This system makes it difficult for governments, when calculating tax levels, to verify whether recorded prices relate to world prices or whether they are manipulated for strategic reasons (John, 1997). Recording reduced profits also allows corporations to argue for lowering wage levels in tourism destinations, thereby lowering their prices and increasing their competitive advantage for penetrating new markets. While this method is clearly encouraged and regarded desirable in industry circles (Deloitte, 2008), it is costly for destinations because they can lose out on much needed revenue and on the opportunity to maximize the

multiplier effect from tourism income … 'the manipulation of transfer prices is not considered a fair or legal practice' (John, 1997: 59).

Tourism as a 'tool for development'

Maximizing income from tourism can be a matter of survival for many LEDCs. While many countries have benefited from capitalist driven development, and the human condition is said to have improved more in the last century than in the whole of history (World Bank, 2002), the pattern of wealth and well-being is still greatly uneven between and within nations (World Bank, 2002; Mowforth and Munt, 2003; Reid, 2003; Elliott, 2006). Apart from China and the so-called East Asian Tigers (Taiwan, Korea, Hong Kong and Singapore), where poverty has decreased by almost half (White Paper on International Development, 2000), the gap between rich and poor nations and rich and poor in individual states has widened rather than narrowed; a gap that has doubled since the early 1970s. The average income in the richest 20 countries is 37 times the average in the poorest 20. In Latin America, South and Central Asia and Sub-Saharan Africa, the numbers of poor people have been rising (World Bank, 2002: 3).

Tourism has been promoted as a key economic sector in almost every country of the globe, and, since the 1970s and 1980s, as a 'tool' to generate economic growth and development, particularly in countries at low levels of economic development, with high levels of poverty and limited resources to trade (Scheyvens, 2002; Sharpley and Telfer, 2002; Mowforth and Munt, 2003). Tourism is significant in 11 of the 12 countries that hold 80% of the world's poor living on US$1–2 a day (Cattarinich, 2001). International tourism receipts in developing countries had more than tripled in the decade up to 1995, with an annual average growth rate of 13%. By 2000:

- developing countries had 292.6 million arrivals, an increase since 1990 of nearly 95%;
- the 49 least developed countries (LDCs) had 5.1 million international arrivals and achieved an increase of nearly 75% in the decade; and
- developing countries were attracting an increasing share of global international tourist arrivals up from 20.8% in 1973 to 42% in 2000 (Pro-Poor Tourism, 2004).

Yet, the narrow definition of development in the context of economics and growth has attracted substantial controversy over the past 30 years (de Kadt 1979; Dreze and Sen, 1995; Reid, 2003). Sen (1999), for example, stresses the importance of social support and public regulation in addition to economic interchange. Kanbur suggests that economic growth is crucial for sustaining progress in human development but that such growth appears to be most effective if it is accompanied by an equitable distribution of income (Kanbur, 1990). He argues that social and economic policies, based on criteria of equity and democracy are thus crucial (1990). Britton (1996) contests the

promotion of tourism as a highly ambiguous development strategy for less developed economies. His argument is based on the premise that the 'tourist industry is designed to meet, and arose out of the recreational needs of affluent middle class citizens in the world's rich countries', imbuing metropolitan tourism corporations with the power to control the tourist flow chain (1996: 156). He believes that 'the central problem … for Third World destinations, is the essentially inequitable relationship inherent in this international system …' (1996: 160).

International tourism was largely promoted as an export industry, in the context of Structural Adjustment Programmes (SAPs) and Poverty Reduction Strategy Papers (PRSPs), introduced in the 1980s and in 1996 respectively, by the International Monetary Fund (IMF) and World Bank. Ostensibly they were intended to help countries reduce their debt burden. Yet, they were highly controversial and strongly criticized by civil society for increasing rather than alleviating poverty (Mchallo, 1994; Kalisch, 2001; SAPRIN, 2002; Elliott, 2006).

By the 1980s and 1990s, the majority of LEDCs (many of them former colonies, which had achieved political independence in the 1960s and 1970s) were heavily indebted to the IMF and World Bank as a result of several oil crises in the 1970s (Mchallo, 1994; Cho, 1995) and consequently dependent on aid and donations from more economically developed countries (MEDCs) to help run their economies (Mchallo, 1994; Girvan, 1999).

> … Dwindling financial reserves, uncontrolled inflation, rising debt obligations, declining productivity, declining export earning capacity, and growing social instability typified conditions in a number of countries.
>
> (Mchallo, 1994: 90)

Foreign currency was urgently needed to service the debts, and this could only come from the reduction in public expenditure and the promotion of exports. Tourism was considered the obvious solution to expand the export sector. SAPs incorporated policies for a reduction in public expenditure, increased privatization of public assets, export promotion and foreign investment. The consequences of such policies included greater inequality in the distribution of income, greater hardship for women, increased child labour, and the collapse of domestic industries causing growing unemployment and violation of labour standards (Badger *et al.*, 1996; Social Watch, 1999, cited in Kalisch, 2001; SAPRIN, 2002). In addition, SAPs had a long-term effect on the natural resource-base by increasing the allocation of protected areas to lodge development and hotel construction (Mchallo, 1994).

This was the context in which studies on the impacts of tourism in the 1980s and early 1990s had increasingly focused on the socio-economic and cultural consequences of tourism in LEDCs, where rapid, mostly unplanned and uncontrolled tourism operations and infrastructure development were reported to create inequality and increased poverty among local communities. Reports told of human rights abuses, displacement and eviction, child sex prostitution, child labour, slave labour, resource degradation and high levels of leakage (de Kadt, 1979; O'Grady, 1990; Monbiot, 1994; Equations, 1995; Keefe and Wheat, 1998; Madeley, 1996; Network First, 1996; Akama, 1997; Diaz Benevides, 2001).

Considering the immense socio-cultural, economic and political reach of tourism and its interconnection with a multiplicity of sectors nationally and internationally, some of the tourism impacts in LEDCs described could be explained by the overall structural imbalances that formed the backdrop to tourism development at the time. The majority of LEDCs introduced tourism development from a position of social and economic deficiency. This compounded a power inequality in international trade that already existed as a result of historical factors of unequal exchange.

The General Agreement on Trade in Services (GATS) – a 'level playing field' for trade in tourism?

Services have been growing in importance in modern economies and are increasingly traded internationally, contributing about 68% of world economy value added in 2003

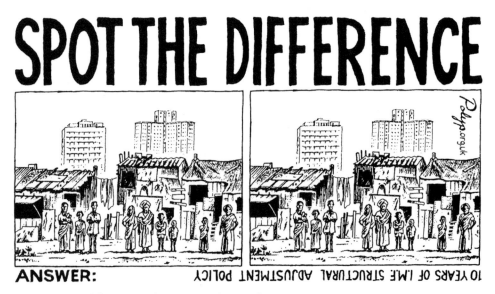

Fig. 6.2. Spot the difference (see http://www.polyp.org.uk).

(OECD, 2005). The GATS, administered by the World Trade Organization (WTO), is the first multi-lateral and legally enforceable agreement governing trade and investment in services and is considered the main instrument for facilitating free market access through liberalization and privatization of services (Kalisch, 2001).

Liberalization of services is a crucial aspect of globalization. It facilitates cross-border movement of companies, people and capital. The Agreement is intended to ensure a 'transparent' and anti-discriminatory level playing field by offering the opportunity to all its members to benefit from reciprocal rights when making commitments to liberalize their sectors. These reciprocal rights are deemed important for LEDCs in gaining access to industrialized countries' markets. LEDCs particularly the LDCs, are accorded special attention through provision for technical assistance and specific market opening commitments to industrialized countries in the area of technology transfer and access to computerized networks (World Tourism Organization, 1995; Kalisch, 2001).

Travel and tourism services are also included in the Agreement. As a major global export sector, tourism is currently the most open service sector: in 2005, almost 95% of the 160 members of the WTO had made commitments in tourism under GATS, over 115 of them LEDCs or transition countries (Adlung and Roy, 2005). Even before the introduction of the GATS, tourism services in LEDCs were largely liberalized but without such reciprocal rights. In theory, therefore, the GATS should enable those countries to achieve a fairer and mutually beneficial trading system. However, because of the historical power advantage of MEDCs, particularly in services, the GATS has been critiqued for being skewed to benefit mainly TNCs from MEDCs.

Box 6.1. The General Agreement on Trade in Services (GATS).

Liberalization

Liberalization under GATS is based on three specific pillars:

- market access (foreign-owned companies have free access to domestic markets);
- most favoured nation status (concessions granted to any one country must also be made available on a non-discriminatory basis to all other signatories of the Agreement); and
- national treatment (foreign investors must be treated on an equal basis with domestic investors, domestic investors must not receive any favourable treatment that could be conceived as protectionist).

Four modes of supply within GATS

GATS has identified four modes of supply for services which represent different forms of international trade:

- cross-border (services that are provided from abroad into the territory of another member country);
- consumption abroad (services consumed by nationals of one country travelling to another country);
- commercial presence (opportunities for foreign tourism businesses to establish a presence in another country, such as hotels, restaurants and tour operators);
- presence of natural persons (opportunities to move key personnel temporarily into foreign markets in order to provide a service there on behalf of the investing company, such as independent, self-employed suppliers or employees in the tourism/hospitality sector).

Tourism within GATS

Tourism in the context of GATS has been defined in a sector called 'Tourism and Travel-related Services' (TTRS). The four modes apply in tourism only in the following sectors:

- hotels and restaurants;
- travel agencies and tour operator services;
- tourist guide services; and
- other (unspecified).

Since the GATS was first launched in 1995, there has been deep concern, particularly among NGOs and civil society organizations, that a 'level playing field' for LEDCs may not be operative in a world where a large number of countries are at different stages of development. A 'level playing field' was considered impossible, when many economies were struggling with debt, economic dependency on MEDCs and the effects of SAPs (or their reformed successor, Poverty Reduction Strategy Papers or PRSPs, debt relief for heavily indebted poor countries; Equations, 1995, 2002; Badger *et al.*, 1996; Pleumarom, 1999; Seifert-Granzin and Jesupatham, 1999; Khor, 2001; Woodroffe, 2002; Font and Bendell, 2004; Plüss and Hochuli/Equations, 2005).

In the tourism sector, critics have levelled the following charges against the GATS (among others):

- The GATS provides legal leverage to large corporations who may operate against the interests of the host country. By incorporating a dispute settlement system whereby corporations can legally challenge government policies or regulation that may be deemed 'trade restrictive', the power of governments to protect their own small business sector, or impose social and environmental obligations on foreign investors is highly constrained (Kalisch, 2001, Plüss and Hochuli/Equations, 2005).
- There is evidence of national laws being adapted to assist foreign companies to invest, to the detriment of domestic providers (Equations, 2002).
- Foreign-owned TNCs are able to take over or eliminate budding smaller domestic providers who lack the resources, experience and expertise to compete with powerful investors (Pleumarom, 1999; Plüss and Hochuli/Equations, 2005). This will particularly affect women who tend to be highly represented in the informal sector of tourism as vendors, craft sellers and caterers (Williams, 2002).
- Investment and competition rules will make it impossible to ensure indigenous

and local control over tourism products (Williams, 2002).
- MEDCs are not reciprocating by opening their service sectors, instead they are restricting market access to LEDCs. This is particularly the case in tourism under the mode of supply for 'presence of natural persons' where trade barriers are created through restrictive immigration rules, e.g. when the presence of a professional, such as manager or tour guide from the country seeking market access is necessary to run an operation in another member country, which should provide reciprocal access rights, see 'modes of supply' in Box 6.1 (Kalisch, 2001).
- Subsidies are created by MEDCs for their domestic sectors, in the areas of technology, licensing and technical standard setting. This may affect the air transport sector where discrimination in the availability and cost of ancillary services may reduce the competitiveness of airline slot allocations and access to computer systems (UNCTAD, 1999; Kalisch, 2001).
- Access to communication channels and distribution networks, such as computer reservation systems (CRS) and global distribution systems (GDS) is regarded as discriminatory (UNCTAD, 1999). The main tourism distribution networks, such as Amadeus and Sabre, are essential components of airline marketing strategy. They are highly concentrated, and dominated largely by American and European airlines (Vellas and Bécherel, 1999; Kalisch, 2001).
- The GATS does not integrate sustainable development or human rights as identified in major international treaties and agreements.
- There is no provision for greater corporate transparency and legally binding accountability in trade practices (Kalisch, 2001).

In short, critics could argue that in an environment of uneven development and overwhelming power of TNCs, the agreement has the potential to threaten national sovereignty and increase rather than eliminate poverty and inequality.

It is beyond the scope of this chapter to discuss the GATS and tourism in detail and to analyse more recent research in this area. At this point, the discussion on the GATS mainly serves to illustrate the background that lead to the development of the concept on Fair Trade in Tourism. Since 1995, progressive rounds of negotiations where MEDCs have been urging LEDCs to open up their service sectors more rapidly (such as water, education and health), have failed to yield the desired results, because of opposition from civil society and many LEDC governments. The World Trade Organization has responded to civil society criticisms, emphasizing, for example, that 'domestic regulations are not considered as barriers to market access and national treatment under the GATS and, therefore, not subjected to trade negotiations' (World Trade Organization, 2009).

In 2001, a number of Latin American countries, including the Dominican Republic, Ecuador and Peru developed a draft Annex to the WTO's GATS on Tourism. It covers, among other points, safeguards against anti-competitive practices of tour operators based in tourist-generating countries (mainly industrialized countries). However, there is still a great deal of disagreement on this within the WTO and among civil society organizations (Plüss and Hochuli/Equations, 2005). It may take years to reach a consensus (International Centre for Trade and Sustainable Development, 2001).

Agents of Change

A greater awareness of ethical trade

In the 1990s, analyses of sustainable development and sustainable tourism mainly focused on issues of natural resource use and consumption, conservation and protection of biodiversity and ecosystems. The links between poverty, inequality and human rights abuses were rarely explored, particularly in relation to trade. However, globalization and the growing dominance of TNCs in LEDCs were increasingly being questioned and critiqued by NGOs and trade unions. Corporate practices in relation to child labour and sweatshop conditions, providing cheap products for wealthy consumers in MEDCs were exposed in the media, spawning consumer boycotts and consumer demand for more ethics in business. Ethical consumerism was beginning to be a force to be reckoned with by corporations who wanted to keep their reputation intact. The social dimension in terms of human rights and poverty gradually became an integral part of the drive towards sustainable development in key industry sectors. The concept of Corporate Social Responsibility (CSR) became an essential strategic framework for changing management practice towards greater social and environmental justice (Kalisch, 2002).

However, analysts and practitioners generally agree that there are numerous conflicting and vague definitions of sustainable development and CSR. In the context of perceived pressures from an increasing proportion of ethically influenced consumers (Mintel Market Report, 2001; Tallontire *et al.*, 2001; Kalisch, 2002), and in the fast and highly competitive business world, such ambiguity can often be used as a screen, using politically correct terminology in order to hide unsustainable practices for the purpose of competitive advantage, so-called 'greenwash'. This serves not only to undercut businesses with genuine credentials but also to bring the concept of sustainability into disrepute. Corporate accountability and reporting, ethical trading, Fair Trade and ecocertification have been voluntary initiatives by business or NGOs (adding business functions to their portfolio) that have spearheaded a more enlightened approach to trade practice in the absence of regulation. This approach aims to integrate ethical principles with business goals, addressing the interests of society as a whole rather than merely the narrow pursuit of profit and economic growth at all costs. It entails concrete methods for implementing, monitoring, measuring and publicly reporting on social and environmental performance, not only in the private sector, i.e. in business, but also in the public and voluntary sectors.

Tourism certification, ecolabelling and the Fair Trade label

In tourism, the social dimension of sustainable development was beginning to be expressed in the late 1990s through the development of community-based tourism, pro-poor tourism, responsible tourism and Fair Trade in tourism. Fair Trade in services, particularly in tourism, is still rare and under researched. The following section thus explores the implications of certification and ecolabelling within the framework of ecotourism and Fair Trade in commodities to assist with an analysis of Fair Trade in tourism.

Tourism certification and ecolabelling

Ecotourism seeks to provide tangible benefits for both conservation and local communities. Certification provides a system for monitoring and measuring those benefits (Honey, 2002), as a guarantee not only for consumers, but also investors, suppliers, employees, NGOs and governments. Certification and ecolabelling in tourism were responses to the challenge of 'greenwash' and corruption (Honey, 2002). They provide a welcome marketing tool for the multitude of small- and medium-sized businesses (SMEs) and microbusinesses that dominate the tourism sector. Ecolabels may help to differentiate them from the increasingly powerful TNCs. The overall aim is that an ecolabel will be recognized by consumers or distribution channels, and considered as added value, providing a competitive advantage in the market-place and creating consumer demand for environmental quality (Font and Harris, 2004). In this sense, an ecolabel can have the same effect as a brand name (Jha and Vossenaar, 1997).

On the positive side, tourism certification can act as a competitive marketing advantage for SMEs. It can serve as a tool for public education, raising awareness of sustainability and responsibility in tourism, as well as the need for more democratic and participative trading relationships,

with emphasis on local community control and empowerment rather than domination by corporate or governmental authority. While early approaches to ecolabelling had a focus on environmental issues, comparative studies of tourism certification initiatives carried out in 2003, using pro-poor tourism principles, found an increasing awareness of social standards for sustainability in tourism principles, codes and standards (Roe *et al.*, 2003; Font and Harris, 2004).

However, ecotourism has been critiqued as a 'Western-centric construct' (Cater, 2006) to promote sustainable tourism in the context of mass tourism, economic growth and modernization theory (Duffy, 2006).

Tourism certification programmes have not escaped criticism either. Critics claim that:

- Tourism certification schemes generally do not challenge existing structural inequalities in the international trade in tourism, which could arguably be creating or re-enforcing poverty and environmental degradation (Cleverdon and Kalisch, 2000). There is a risk, in LEDCs that they will be dominated by the interests of large-scale tourism corporations and MEDC agencies (Sasidharan *et al.*, 2002).
- They are deemed to be expensive and inaccessible to the poorest providers in the absence of relevant capital, complicated in terms of verification procedures, and dependent on consumer demand. Such demand is at best volatile, at worst non-existent.
- They have not served as a guarantee against 'greenwash'. Research has found that where the process is industry controlled, certification can be manipulated to suit business priorities (Synergy, 2000).
- The proliferation of different (often overlapping) national and international schemes causes confusion about the credibility of such schemes and consequent mistrust among consumers (Synergy, 2000; Honey, 2002; Fernweh, 2004).

- Certification could be perceived as a trade barrier by LEDC governments and as a tool for discriminating against small and microbusinesses without the resources to comply with the requirements of particular standards (Fernweh, 2004; Font and Bendell, 2004).

Fair Trade certification in commodities

While the success of tourism certification has been doubtful, Fair Trade certified products of primary commodities have attracted growing popularity. Fair Trade criteria for commodities such as coffee focus on a fair price, which includes an added premium to enable re-investment into community infrastructure and the direct relationship with the purchaser, excluding the need for middlemen, advance payments that enable small-scale businesses without assets and collateral to invest in production, and a long-term relationship with trading partners to enable collaboration on training, marketing and product development (Cleverdon and Kalisch, 2000). The standard setting and certification process at the European level is overseen by the Fair Trade Labelling Organization (FLO), in addition to national initiatives, such as the Fair Trade Foundation in the UK. Producers form an important part of the policy and decision-making process.

Fair Trade commodities have been steadily increasing their market share by gaining access to mainstream supermarket shelves, and influencing large corporations, such as the supermarket chains Sainsbury's and Tesco in the UK, to reconsider their trading practices as part of an 'Ethical Trading' initiative (Ethical Trading Initiative, 2000). Fair Trade marked products increased in value by 57% in 2000 over 1999 (Kalisch, 2002). Between 1998 and 2008, estimated UK retail sales in Fair Trade coffee increased tenfold, from 13.7 m to 137.3 m (Fair Trade Foundation, 2009).

The Fair Trade labelling process serves a dual purpose of providing direct market access for disadvantaged producers, thus increasing self-reliance and strengthening their bargaining position, and working towards readjusting the structural power imbalance in North–South trade relationships. In addition, it provides a human dimension to western consumption processes by linking consumers to the lives of producers as part of the marketing process in a world where consumers are increasingly alienated from the origins of the products they are consuming (Cleverdon and Kalisch, 2000; Paul, 2005). It offers consumers the chance to make a difference to global poverty and sustainable development through the choices they make while shopping (Fair Trade Foundation, 2008).

Fair Trading organizations are non-profit making and are motivated by a strong commitment to social equality and sustainable development. In the UK, Fair Trade originated in the collaboration of major NGOs, such as Traidcraft and Oxfam, who established a separate unit for trading operations with developing countries. While Fair Trade certification is a tool for marketing, generating consumer confidence in ethical standards, it is also a development initiative, based on participative principles (Paul, 2005). The concept of Fair Trade in commodities incorporates recognition of the unequal terms of trade for producers in LEDCs as a result of dependency in the North–South trade relationship and the power of corporations and middlemen to exploit small producers in remote locations.

Notwithstanding challenges that still exist for Fair Trade producers (Utting-Chamorro, 2005; Pirotte *et al.*, 2006), Fair Trade (in primary commodities) is regarded as economically efficient and has the potential to relieve poverty, by providing employment, choice and self-reliance (Cleverdon and Kalisch, 2000; Hayes, 2006). The security of a long-term relationship with traders helps to achieve credibility with bankers who are more inclined to provide loans for further investment (Cleverdon and Kalisch, 2000). Such an injection of capital can enable poor producers to turn the 'vicious circle of poverty'

into a 'virtuous circle of economic development' (Gamble, 1989: 9, cited in Burns and
Holden, 1995).

Fair Trade in Tourism

In 1996, the London-based NGO Tourism
Concern published 'Trading Places: Tourism as Trade'. It was the first study to
provide an analysis of international tourism
as an invisible service trade export in the
context of the GATS and the effects of SAP
reforms in developing countries. It argued
that tourism development in countries that
were implementing SAPs needed to be
considered in 'the light of a macro-
economic critique' (Badger et al., 1996: 25).
Such a critique needed to analyse the
effects of liberalization in tourism and
other sectors, enacted through the medium
of the GATS, from the viewpoint of LEDCs.
In its conclusion, the report raised the
question whether the concept of Fair Trade
in commodities, could feasibly be applied
to the tourism sector in order to address
globalization, human rights issues, poverty
and inequality.

The rationale for the focus on Fair
Trade was threefold:

1. The Fair Trade movement had made
substantial advances not only in creating
market demand for competitive products
based on ethical criteria, but also in raising
consumer awareness on injustices in trade
and developing the argument for a fairer
trade system with policy-makers within the
arena of international trade negotiations.
2. By taking the abstract idea of ethics in
trading into the tangible arena of product
development, creatively marketed to an
increasingly critical consumer base, it
attempted to provide a concrete and practical solutions-based, hands-on business
approach to the issues of poverty, injustice
and inequality. Such an approach had to be
taken account of in the business world
(where these issues were generally of little
importance at the time), particularly as Fair
Trade products were steadily increasing

their market share, successfully competing
with other conventional products.
3. By focusing on such a practical market-
oriented strategy for tourism, Tourism
Concern was aiming to combine campaign
rhetoric with innovative action.

After initial small grants from Voluntary
Service Overseas (VSO) and North London
University to launch consultation and
research on Fair Trade in Tourism in 1997,
Tourism Concern was successful in securing a grant from the European Social Fund
in 1999 for a 3-year awareness raising
project on Fair Trade in Tourism, with
matching funding from the UK Department
for International Development Tourism
Challenge Fund. British Airways later also
contributed a small grant, underlining
industry support for the undertaking. The
project's aims included the development of
criteria for Fair Trade in Tourism standards
and practice, based on consultation of an
NGO network and the creation of a
dialogue with the tourism industry, to
explore the implementation of Fair Trade
components.

Philosophy and methodology

The philosophical foundation for this work
was inspired by a critique of Fair Trade as
essentially a northern-led development
initiative, originated by radical activists and
student groups, religious and charitable
organizations in Europe and North America.
Its aim was, on the one hand, to challenge
neo-liberal trading practices of large multinational enterprises in developing countries
and, on the other benefiting poor southern
producers through 'trade not aid' (Kocker,
2006; Schmelzer, 2006), enabling them to
achieve greater self-sufficiency. It was
assumed by those groups that the worthy
goals of such an approach would naturally
lead to more equitable terms of trade and
better lives for southern producers (Kocker,
2006). Tourism Concern supported this
concept as a potential paradigm for an
alternative approach to trade in tourism.

However, it also questioned it for its Eurocentric elitist origins and its niche appeal. The methodology for developing a Fair Trade in tourism paradigm thus focused principally on participative consultation of grassroots stakeholders in LEDCs to establish what Fair Trade in Tourism meant to them. Therefore, Tourism Concern created an international multi stakeholder network on Fair Trade in Tourism, including representatives from industry, government, NGOs, community organizations and academia from both MEDCs and LEDCs.

The International Network on Fair Trade in Tourism

The International Network on Fair Trade in Tourism was formally set up in 1999, attracting 200 members within a year, supported from February 2000 onwards by an electronic group information and discussion tool in the form of a list server, which had 150 members by the time the project ended in October 2002. This process provided the opportunity to create not only a tool for consultation, but crucially a mass base of support, a platform for collaboration, and the exchange of knowledge and ideas. The Network enabled the alliance of groups from a diversity of national and organizational cultures, with a variety of (sometimes conflicting) values and worldviews. It comprised a myriad of different conceptual constructions, experiences and expectations, intent on a common purpose of improving the terms of trade in tourism for communities in LEDCs. As part of that process, Tourism Concern organized annual conferences over the course of the 3 years of the project in 1999, 2000 and 2002 in the UK and Africa, with a total of 175 participants. Representatives from community-based organizations in LEDCs came from The Gambia, Tanzania, Namibia, Philippines, Belize, Nepal, Kenya, India, Uganda, Malaysia and South Africa.

Outcomes from the Fair Trade in Tourism Project/Campaign 1999–2002

Pragmatists and ideologues

The main thrust of the initial discussions centred around the dynamic between the political and the practical level, the issue whether theory drives practice or vice versa, and whether it is possible to develop the one before engaging in the other:

- Should the Network concentrate on: (i) setting up a niche product label with Fair Trade in Tourism criteria; or (ii) influencing mainstream industry and the mass market?
- To what extent should Fair Trade in Tourism focus on political issues in tourism for grassroots communities, in terms of basic democratic rights, and the local impact of globalization, of which tourism is a major tool?

Among the key themes that emerged from the consultation process were the following:

- One of the most unfair aspects of tourism was the fact that the capital/product of tourism is public assets but the profit made from it is private: wealth should be turned into more public resources.
- The commodification of people, cultures and the natural environment, packaged and sold as a tourism product by foreign corporations, creates serious ethical and human rights challenges.
- The root causes of inequality were perceived as: a lack of access to capital, foreign and private ownership of resources, unequal distribution of benefits, control over the representation of the destination in tourism-generating countries, and lack of transparency of tourism operations, including price and working conditions (for further analysis see Cleverdon and Kalisch, 2000).
- It was stressed as important that Fair Trade in Tourism did not represent yet another 'museum piece' in tourism, like 'ecotourism', another model to be fronted by governments and industry to mollify critics and escape appropriate responsibility.

Other prerequisites for Fair Trade in Tourism were considered, such as:

- Democracy enabling communities to say 'no' to tourism, if they wished.
- Capacity-strengthening of local communities and the small businesses.
- A viable tourism product.
- Consumer pressure for ethical tourism.
- Focus on domestic markets as well as international markets.
- A recognition of the importance of mass tourism in the context of ethical planning and business practice, providing business and income in LEDCs.
- Greater awareness of the impacts of liberalization, whereby social, cultural and environmental standards should not be regarded as trade barriers.

Following the first meeting, Tourism Concern developed a set of draft principles and criteria for Fair Trade in Tourism as a basis for further consultation.

However, taking on board the complexity of development issues in tourism, the emphasis was less on setting up a Fair Trade Tourism kitemark[2] than on developing strategies for structural change, raising public awareness, capacity building among local communities, developing practical instruments for changing values and systems, and influencing government policy. NGOs were considered crucial agents in that process. Tourism Concern thus developed a set of recommendations for NGOs and community-based tourism enterprises in relation to the GATS, industry and governments (Kalisch, 2001). This was followed by a report aimed at mass package tour operators, translating development issues and principles of Fair Trade in Tourism into a business framework, such as the concept of Corporate Social Responsibility (Kalisch, 2002). The outcomes were a reflection of frontline research and an international process of consultation and decision making.

The process of creating principles of Fair Trade in Tourism was evolutionary and wide-ranging, involving a diversity of social and organizational cultures, nationalities and political perspectives. This provided strength to the arguments, which Tourism

Concern was presenting to key policy makers in the UK and Europe. It also strengthened the various groups involved in the International Network, who were able to carry the discussions further into the different global and local arenas of decision making on development, inspiring their own research and consultation processes. Many of the proponents of responsible, pro-poor, Fair Trade or community-based tourism were initially involved in the International Network on Fair Trade in Tourism.

Current initiatives on Fair Trade in Tourism

To date, the jury is still out on whether a Fair Trade Tourism certified kitemark would be effective in addressing the 'root causes of inequality' as determined by the International Network on Fair Trade in Tourism, either as a development or marketing tool.

Fair Trade Tourism in South Africa (FTTSA)

Fair Trade certification of tourism establishments has been realized in South Africa (Seif, 2002), ranging from whale-watching operations to game reserves and adventure tours.

Criteria include fair share, democracy, respect, reliability, transparency and sustainability. These criteria were determined on the basis of a 2-year consultation process with industry and local communities and a 1-year pilot and participative action research project (Kalisch, 2001; Seif, 2002). In 2009, FTTSA is planning to embark on a pilot project for Fair Trade travel packages to South Africa with funding from the Swiss government and in collaboration with partner organizations in Switzerland and Germany (Tjolle, 2009).

The International Fair Trade Labelling Organization (FLO)

Recent initiatives by the FLO to explore the feasibility of a Fair Trade label in tourism have revived the debate on this subject in

Europe, since the end of funding for the International Network on Fair Trade in Tourism in 2002. Between 2006 and 2008, FLO engaged in discussions with six NGOs from Europe (including Tourism Concern in the UK) and Africa to determine the extent to which conventional Fair Trade certification and licensing elements could apply to the tourism sector (Beyer/mas/contour, 2007).

FLO commissioned a feasibility report, which suggested various strategies in respect of two particular models: developing a pilot project with community-based tourism enterprises on the one hand and mainstream trade certification on the other, with further development of Fair Trade standards. However, these recommendations were not made without reservations based on the fragmented nature of the tourism supply chain, community-based tourism providers struggling with market access and commercial viability, and the difficulty of monitoring and setting a 'fair price' (Font, 2008).

Another report in 2007 (in response to the FLO consultation) by a group of consultants in Germany uses fair price as the key criterion for a Fair Trade analysis in the context of mainstream package tourism as opposed to community based tourism. They reason that community-based tourism only caters to a niche market and 'thus plays a minor role in international travel to developing countries' (Beyer/mas/contour, 2007: 8). The report highlights the complexities of setting a fair price in an industry as diverse as tourism and argues that 'the fair-trade labelling of package tours can only be considered plausible if all the core services in the destination included in the package deal meet the fair trade criteria' (Beyer/mas/contour, 2007: 17). This they deem doubtful and unrealistic at this point in time. Beyer's concern, is debatable, however, since currently some composite Fair Trade labelled commodity products, can carry the FAIRTRADE Mark even when not all of the ingredients are Fair Trade (Fair Trade Labelling Organization, 2009).

What does the future hold for Fair Trade in Tourism?

Ethical issues arising from the international and global promotion of tourism are closely interlinked with ethical issues arising from the promotion of the global economic system as a whole. Capitalism seems to have triumphed as the predominant world ideology, since the largest communist powers in the world, Russia and China, have opened their economies to the capitalist trading system. However, in the light of recurring economic crises, not least the global credit crisis of 2008, capitalism and free trade have been widely called into question. Critics lament the 'moral vacuum' of the economic system (Sunderland, 2008), which is deemed to promote a casino mentality to trading (Hertz, 2005; Randall, 2008). Calls for a fairer, more inclusive version of capitalism are assuming greater urgency among a movement of analysts from a wide variety of political credence (Hutton, 1996; Zadek, 2000; Sunderland, 2008).

So, in this changing public climate of greater ethical awareness what does the future hold for Fair Trade in Tourism? Is it just another 'museum piece', confusing to consumers and industry in the array of ethical, eco, pro-poor and responsible tourism concepts? Or does it have the potential to make a substantial difference towards creating a more equal and sustainable distribution of resources and a more ethical trading system in tourism, while providing value for customers?

Any approaches with an ethical purpose in tourism are beneficial if carefully researched and consulted upon through democratic participative processes. However, ethical consumers are still in the minority. Price, weather and convenience are still the highest priorities for most holiday-makers. Although the responsible tourism market has been growing, most recent surveys by Mintel (2007) reveal that ethical concerns and beliefs do not appear to be penetrating any further. This may be

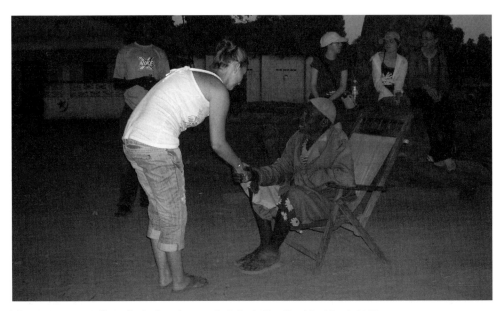

Fig. 6.3. Meeting village chief. Photo by Angela Kalisch, The Gambia, March 2008.

related to consumer confusion and a feeling of helplessness rather than being jaded. The lack of a credible and visibly marketed consumer product, widely supported by the media, government, industry and NGOs contributes to such confusion. Yet, Fair Trade in primary commodity products has captured the imagination of a growing number of people seeking more responsible ways of spending their money. Supermarkets with ethical policies, such as Waitrose and the Co-operative in the UK, have contributed to that. Research also suggests that there is potential among ethical grocery consumers for developing an interest in Fair Trade holidays (Mintel, 2007). Therefore, in order to capture this market a product needs to be created, an initiative to establish the mechanisms for changing trading and marketing structures in the tourism industry, possibly leading to Fair Trade certification. However, this is a complex and challenging process. Fair Trade holidays should not only be attractive to consumers but also bring substantial development benefits to local communities who are most affected by poverty and exploitation. In this sense, certification could be less important than effective policy intervention and the responsible marketing of such intervention. For example, in 2007, the UK-based Travel Foundation helped to change the distribution of tourism income to the Maasai in Kenya, who have suffered displacement and exploitation for over 30 years as a result of tourism development. The Travel Foundation worked with ground handlers and tour operators in Kenya to establish a new transparent ticketing and payment system for cultural visits to Maasai villages, which increased income to these villages by 800% during the first 6 months (The Travel Foundation, 2008). This new scheme is now marketed to UK tour operators with the help of practical guidelines to ensure take up of the system and responsible implementation.

Within mass tourism, tourism organizers and investors can be expected, or better still, be regulated to be publicly accountable for their social and environmental practices and performance. Studies on ethical consumerism have found that

> ... there is, a strong argument for integrating ethical concerns into the broader operations of a company rather than targeting a particular niche. If company claims can be backed

up by independently verified reporting, the potential for mainstreaming ethical concerns may be even greater.

(Tallontire, 2001: 27)

Moreover, the perception of tourism as a product deserves some serious critical analysis. On the one hand, the ethical implications of selling cultures, social relationships and the natural environment for private profit require some scrutiny. On the other hand, from the perspective of the consumer it could be argued that there is no tangible product as we know it. Instead, there are only loosely linked experiences. How could they be certified? Notwithstanding the challenges presented by this option, not least the interconnectedness of tourism with other sectors, practical initiatives to develop a Fair Trade Tourism certified product as a pilot project/experiment (with all its questions and complexities, and risk of failure) would advance the debate on market and industry viability, as well as development benefits for communities. '... real alternatives must grow from action and practical development experience, not from the minds of thinkers in the North' (Edwards, 1993: 173).

It would be fundamentally important that such initiatives originate from those stakeholders who are intended to benefit from it, in collaboration with partners in both MEDCs and LEDCs. They would need to incorporate the development of wider support structures for Fair Trade in Tourism, such as capacity-building and awareness raising for service and product providers in tourism receiving countries and inbound operators, as well as awareness raising and public information campaigns for consumers. A Fair Trade Tourism operation would require an institutional mechanism that is separate from but linked to a Fair Trade commodities organization. Research could either focus on the establishment of an alternative trade organization for tourism (or services), possibly modelled on or in collaboration with the newly reformed 'World Fair Trade Organization', formerly International Federation for Alternative Trade, or on a collaboration with a national or European Fair Trade labelling organization. It would need to focus specifically on promoting appropriate social standards and marketing of Fair Trade products in tourism, in conjunction with coordinating campaigns on Fair Trade in Tourism and human rights, linked to the wider issues of uneven development, international trade and sustainable consumption.

A practical initiative could also provide a more tangible basis for conducting more action research particularly with consumers, which is necessary to progress the arguments and to evaluate the potential development benefits of Fair Trade in Tourism. The pilot initiative on Fair Trade package travel spearheaded by FTTSA will make an important contribution in that respect. Ideological arguments are often high flying and conceptually inaccessible to the public and industry; so a tangible economic instrument that embeds such issues and is steeped in empirical evidence, while serving as a public education and marketing tool, helps to give substance to the arguments and build a strong supporter base.

However, in isolation, market instruments are unlikely to change the root causes of poverty and inequality. These originate in the historic patterns of power relations and domination over countries and resources by metropolitan industrialized economies. Fair Trade certification and an ethical niche product by itself, marketed to an elite, will hardly address the root causes of injustice as perceived by grassroots communities in LEDCs, relating to access to capital, ownership of resources, and distribution of benefits. Certification is also unlikely to shift the power dynamics of TNCs in the negotiation process between small and medium-sized domestic providers in developing countries (Buhalis, 2000), nor will it help microbusiness and informal sector traders (the poorest stakeholders that Fair Trade targets) to increase their gains from tourists and obtain access to international markets, because compliance with the financial and contractual requirements of the certification process would be unachievable for them.

The costs and complications of verification procedures would present serious obstacles. In addition, certification will have little meaning to indigenous people displaced from their land and homes by governments and tourism developers, or forced into prostitution through extreme poverty. These issues are all inextricably linked to the capitalist organization of the global economy and need to be addressed at local and global policy level. Governments, for example, need to use appropriate social policies to support measures for social ownership and for small domestic businesses to compete collaboratively in the face of domestic and foreign corporate power. They need to use their regulatory and negotiating powers to require responsible and ethical trading practices from domestic and foreign investors in the context of national and international laws and agreements. International trade agreements would need to incorporate provision for such powers. Policies and procedures within the World Trade Organization (in the context of the GATS) need to reflect the social and cultural issues generated by the trade in tourism. Fair Trade certification or ethical business practice should not be perceived as a trade barrier.

A Fair Trade Tourism label, in combination with a carefully researched mass based strategy might succeed in changing values and power dynamics among consumers, governments and businesses, towards a greater commitment to social justice. Such a strategy would need to include a process of advocacy, public education, capacity building, global networking and activism in equitable partnership between MEDC and LEDC stakeholders. However, it has to be recognized that this will always be an on-going struggle.

Conclusion

The purpose of this chapter was to analyse the opportunities for equitable trade in tourism and the developments of Fair Trade in Tourism in LEDCs, as spearheaded by Tourism Concern in the mid-1990s. The chapter argues that the forces of power and control within capitalism, the driving force of the tourism system, militate against an analysis that isolates market forces as a mechanism for greater social equality from the very power relations that are deemed to create that inequality. While the creation of Fair Trade Tourism initiatives may be constructive in progressing the research and debates on this issue, they should only be undertaken following appropriate consultation of the intended benefactors and in conjunction with mass based strategies to improve global policies for greater social justice and equality.

Ethical perspectives in trade and economic development are linked to values and beliefs. Structures that are deemed to promote ethical policies and practices, such as voluntary initiatives, codes of conduct, corporate reporting, or certification and labelling, indeed even regulation, are unlikely to change by themselves the root causes of inequality and injustice in tourism (or any other sector). Substantial structural transformation towards more equitable social, eco- and economic systems will only occur if the very values that lead to such causes change dramatically. It is likely that they will not change rapidly or voluntarily. Ultimately, as poverty, climate change and depletion of social and natural resources take their course, a more responsible approach to managing society will need to prevail by necessity, with or without certification.

Discussion Questions

1. How realistic is the expectation that TNCs in tourism could develop ethical policy and practice in developing countries?
2. How could Fair Trade Tourism certification address human rights issues arising from tourism development?
3. What are the key aspects of the trade in tourism that cause inequality?

Notes

[1]At the time of writing, in 2009, First Choice Holidays and Thomson Travel had been taken over by TUI AG and a German conglomerate Arcandor had a majority stake in Thomas Cook. Thomas Cook and MyTravel merged in 2009, Arcandor went bankrupt and another German corporation Rewe is considering taking over the stake.

[2]The Kitemark is a registered certification mark developed originally, and owned by the British Standards Institution (BSI). It is a symbol of quality and safety for consumers and businesses (BSI, 2009).

References

Adlung, R. and Roy, M. (2005) *Turning Hills into Mountains? Current Commitments under the GATS and Prospects for Change.* Staff Working Paper, Economic Research and Statistics Division, March, World Trade Organization. http://www.wto.org/english/res_e/reser_e/ersd200501_e.doc – 2005-04-15 – Text Version (accessed 21 November 2009).

Akama, J.S. (1997) Tourism development in Kenya: problems and policy alternatives. *Progress in Tourism and Hospitality Research* 3, 95–105.

Ascher, F. (1985) *Transnational Corporations and Cultural Identities.* United Nations Education and Scientific Organization, Paris.

Badger, A., Barnett, P., Corbyn, L. and Keefe, J. (1996) *Trading Places: Tourism as Trade.* Tourism Concern, London.

Barratt-Brown, M. (1993) *Fair Trade.* Zed Books, London.

Barratt-Brown, M. (1995) *Models in Political Economy,* 2nd edn. Penguin, Harmondsworth, UK.

Beyer/mas/contour (2007) *Fair Trade Certification in Tourism: Challenges, Conditions, and First Recommendations regarding Fair Pricing in the Tourism Branch.* Evangelischer Entwicklungsdienst, Bonn.

Bianchi, R. (2002) Towards a new political economy of global tourism. In: Sharpley, R. and Telfer, D. (eds) *Tourism and Development: Concepts and Issues.* Channel View, Clevedon.

British Standards Institution. (2009) Apply for a Kitemark. http://www.bsigroup.com/en/ProductServices/About-Kitemark/ (accessed 18 January 2010).

Britton, S. (1996) Tourism, dependency and development: a mode of analysis. In: Apostolopoulos, Y., Leivadi, S. and Yiannakis, A. (eds) *The Sociology of Tourism: Theoretical and Empirical Investigations.* Routledge, Abingdon, UK.

Buhalis, D. (2000) Relationships in the distribution channels of tourism. In: Crotts, J., Buhalis, D. and March, R. (eds) *Global Alliances in Tourism and Hospitality Management.* Haworth Hospitality Press, New York.

Burns, P. and Holden, A. (1995) *Tourism: A New Perspective.* Prentice Hall, London.

Cater, E. (2006) Ecotourism as a Western construct. *Journal of Ecotourism* 5, 23–39.

Cattarinich, X. (2001) Pro-poor tourism initiatives in developing countries: Analysis of secondary case studies, April, PPT Working Paper No. 8. http://www.propoortourism.org.uk (accessed 10 September 2007).

Cho, G. (1995) *Trade, Aid and Global Interdependence.* Routledge, London.

Cleverdon, R. and Kalisch, A. (2000) Fair trade in tourism. *International Journal of Tourism Research* 2, 171–187.

Cowe, R. and Williams, S. (2000) Who are all the ethical consumers? The Cooperative Bank, Manchester.

DeKadt, E. (1979) *Tourism: Passport to Development.* Oxford University Press, London.

Deloitte (2008) Tax services for the tourism, hospitality and leisure industry: Unlocking hidden value in tax, Deloitte Development. http://www.deloitte.com/assets/Dcom-UnitedStates/Local%20Assets/Documents/us_tax_hospitality_041308.pdf (accessed 01 September 2009).

Diaz Benavides, D. (2001) The viability and sustainability of international tourism in developing countries. *Symposium on Tourism Services,* 22–23 February. World Trade Organization, Geneva.

Dreze J. and Sen, A. (1995) *Economic Development and Social Opportunity.* Oxford University Press, Oxford.

Duffy, R. (2006) The politics of tourism in the developing world. *Journal of Ecotourism* 5, 128–144.

Edwards, M. (1993) 'Does the doormat influence the boot?': critical thoughts on NGOs and international advocacy. *Development in Practice* 3, 163–175.

Elliott, J. (2006) *An Introduction to Sustainable Development,* 3rd edn. Routledge, London.

Equations (1995) *Draft Statement on the General Agreement on Trade in Services.* Equations, Bangalore.

Equations (2002) Liberalising tourism under GATS: pitfalls for developing countries. In: Hanhoff, I. (ed.) *At Whose Service? Conference Proceedings*. Federal Environment Agency, Berlin, pp. 35–44.

Ethical Trading Initiative (2000) *Getting to Work on Ethical Trading*. Annual Report 1999/2000. Ethical Trading Initiative, London.

Fair Trade Foundation (2008) *The FAIRTRADE Mark Core standards and practice behind Fairtrade Labelling*. The Fair Trade Foundation, London.

Fair Trade Foundation (2009) Facts and Figures on Fair Trade. http://www.fairtrade.org.uk/what_is_fairtrade/facts_and_figures.aspx (accessed 10 June 2009).

Fair Trade Labelling Organization (2009) *Fair Trade Leading the Way*. Annual Report 2008–09. http://www.fairtrade.net accessed 30 May 2009).

Fennell, D. (2006) *Tourism Ethics*. Channel View, Clevedon.

Fernweh (ed.) (2004) *Tourism Interventions, Process Documentation 2003/2004*. Fernweh-Tourism Review, Freiburg.

Font, X. (2002) Environmental certification in tourism and hospitality: progress,process and prospects. *Tourism Management* 23, 197–205.

Font, X. (2008) Potential for a fair trade label in tourism: feasibility study. ESRC Seminar Series 1: Tourism, Inequality and Social Justice Fairly Traded Tourism, Centre for Leisure, Tourism and Society, UWE, Bristol.

Font, X. and Bendell, J. (2004) Which tourism rules? Green standards and GATS *Annals of Tourism Research* 31, 139–156.

Font, X. and Harris, C. (2004) Rethinking standards from green to sustainable. Annals of Tourism Research 31, 986–1007.

Gamble, W. (1989) *Tourism and Development in Africa*. John Murray, London.

Girvan, N. (1999) Globalisation, fragmentation and integration: a Caribbean perspective, Paper prepared for International Meeting on Globalization and Development Problems, Havana, Cuba, 18–22 January. http://www.geocities.com (accessed 15 June 2009).

Harrison, D. (1994) Tourism capitalism and development in less developed countries. In: Sklair, L. (ed.) *Capitalism and Development*. Routledge, London.

Hayes, M. (2006) On the efficiency of fair trade. *Review of Social Economy* 64, 447–468.

Hertz, N. (2001) *The Silent Takeover – Global Capitalism and the Death of Democracy*. William Heinemann, London.

Hertz, N. (2005) *I.O.U: The Debt Threat and Why We Must Defuse it*. Harper Perennial, London.

Honey, M. (2002) *Ecotourism and Certification: Setting Standards in Practice*. Island Press, London.

Hutton, W. (1996) *The State We're In*. Vintage, London.

International Centre for Trade and Sustainable Development (2001) Revised draft annex on tourism services tabled; many developing countries still sceptical, *Bridges Weekly Trade News Digest* 5, No. 32, 25 September. http://ictsd.net/i/news/bridgesweekly/6643/

Jha, V. and Vossenaar, R. (1997) Environmentally oriented product policies, competitiveness and market access. In: Jha, V., Hewison, G. and Underhill, M. (eds) *Trade, Environment and Sustainable Development*. Macmillan, London.

John, R. (ed.) (1997) *Global Business Strategy*. International Thomson Business Press, London.

Kalisch, A. (2001) *Tourism as Fair Trade: NGO Perspectives*. Tourism Concern, London.

Kalisch, A. (2002) *Corporate Futures: Social Responsibility in the Tourism Industry*. Tourism Concern, London.

Kanbur, R. (1990) *Poverty and Development. The Human Development Report* and *The World Development Report 1990*, University of Warwick and The World Bank, Policy, Research and External Affairs, Development Economics.

Keefe, J. and Wheat, S. (1998) *Tourism and Human Rights*. Tourism Concern, London.

Khor, M. (2001) *Rethinking Globalizarion*. Zed Books, London.

Klein, N. (2000) *No Logo*. Harper Collins, London.

Kocker, M. (2006) Sixty Years of Fair Trade – a brief history of the Fair Trade movement. IFAT Factsheet.

Korten, D. (1995) *When Corporations Rule the World*. Earthscan, London.

Lanfant, M-F., Allcock, J.B. and Brunner, E.M. (eds) (1995) *International Tourism: Identity and Change*. Sage, London.

Levine, D. (1988) *Arguing for Socialism: Theoretical Considerations*. Verso, London.

Madeley, J. (1996) *Foreign Exploits: Transnationals and tourism*. Catholic Institute for International Relations, London.

Madeley, J. (2003), Transnational corporations and developing countries: big business poor peoples. *The Courier ACP-EU* no. 196, Jan–Feb.

Mchallo, I. A. (1994) The impact of Structural Adjustment Programmes on the natural resource base: the case of tourism development. *UTAFITI (New Series)* 1, No. 2.

Meyer, D. (2003) *The UK Outbound Tour Operating Industry and Implications for Pro-Poor Tourism.* PPT Working Paper, No. 17. Overseas Development Institute, London.

Mintel (2007) *Holiday Lifestyles – Responsible Tourism – UK,* January. Mintel International Group Ltd, London.

Mintel Market Report (2001) *Ethical Tourism,* July. Mintel Market Intelligence, London.

Monbiot, G. (1994) *No Man's Land: An Investigative Journey Through Kenya and Tanzania.* Picador, London.

Mosedale, J. (2006) Tourism commodity chains: market entry and its effects on St Lucia.. *Current Issues in Tourism* 9, 436–458.

Mowforth, M. and Munt, I. (2003) *Tourism and Sustainability: Development and New Tourism in the Third World.* Routledge, London.

Network First (1996) *Inside Burma, Land of Fear.* Carlton UK Television.

O'Grady, A. (ed.) (1990) *The Challenge of Tourism: Learning Resources for Study and Action.* Ecumenical Coalition on Third World Tourism, Bangkok.

OECD (2005) *Services Statistics Coordination and Strategy.* OECD statistics directorate to UN statistics commission.

Paul, E. (2005) Evaluating fair trade as a development project: methodological considerations. *Development in Practice* 15, 134–150.

Pilger, J. (2002) *The New Rulers of the World.* Verso, London.

Pirotte, G., Pleyers, G. and Poncelet, M. (2006) Fair trade coffee in Nicaragua and Tanzania: a comparison. *Development in Practice* 16, 452–464.

Pleumarom, A. (1999) *Foreign Takeover of Thailand's Tourism Industry – the Other Face of Liberalization.* Third World Network Briefing Paper for CSD7, No. 2.

Plüss, C. and Hochuli, M./Equations (2005) *Perspectives on Tourism: Tourism and GATSi.* Ecumenical Coalition on Tourism, Hong Kong.

Polyp Cartoons (2009) http://www.polyp.org.uk/corporate-rule_cartoons/cartoons_about_corporaterule_and_democracy.html (accessed 4 October 2009).

Pro-poor Tourism (2004) Developing countries' share of the international tourism market. *Pro-poor Tourism Info-Sheets,* Sheet No. 4: Pro-poor tourism partnership. http://www.propoortourism.org.uk (accessed 17 June 2009).

Randall, J. (2008) *The City – Futures and Options,* Thursday, 18 September 2008, 9:00–9:45 (BBC Radio 4 FM).

Reid, D. (2003) *Tourism, Globalization and Development, Responsible Tourism Planning.* Pluto Press, London.

Roe, D., Harris, C. and de Andrade J. (2003) Addressing poverty issues in tourism standards: A review of experience. Pro-poor Tourism Working Paper No.14, Pro-Poor Tourism Partnership.

SAPRIN (2002) The Policy Roots of Economic Crisis and Poverty: A multi-country participatory assessment of Structural Adjustment. Washington: The Structural Adjustment Participatory Review International Network (SAPRIN). http://www.saprin.org/global_rpt.htm (accessed on 17 June 2009).

Sasidharan, V., Sirakaya, E. and Kerstetter, D. (2002) Developing countries and tourism ecolabels. *Tourism Management* 23, 161–174

Schmelzer, M. (2006) In or against the market – is fair trade a neoliberal solution to market failures or a practical challenge to neoliberal trade and the free market regime in general? Research Paper for Sociology 190, Peter Evans: Globalization, UC Berkeley, Spring 2006.

Seif, J. (2002) Facilitating Market Access for South Africa's Disadvantaged Communities and Population Groups through Fair Trade in Tourism, Fair Trade in Tourism South Africa/IUCN-South Africa and University of Chicago. http://www.icrtourism.org/library.shtml (accessed 4 June 2009).

Seifert-Granzin, J. and Jesupatham, D.S. (1999) *Tourism at the Crossroads: Challenges to Developing Countries by the New World Order.* Equations/Leinfelden-Echterdingen: Tourism Watch, Bangalore.

Sen, A. (1999) *Development as Freedom.* Oxford University Press, Oxford.

Sharpley, R. and Telfer, D. (2002) *Tourism and Development: Concepts and Issues.* Channel View, Clevedon.

Sheyvens, R. (2002) *Tourism for Development: Empowering Communities.* Pearson Education Ltd, Harlow.

Souty, F. (2004) *Passport to Progress: Challenges for World Tourism and Global Anti-competitive Practices in the Tourism Industry.* World Tourism Organization, Madrid.

Sunderland, R. (2008) Now is our chance to change capitalism for good. Let's Take it. *Observer*, 28 September 2008.

Synergy (2000) *Tourism Certification: An analysis of Green Globe 21 and Other Certification Programs*. World Wide Fund for Nature-UK, Godalming.

Tallontire, A., Rentsendorj, E. and Blowfield, M. (2001) Ethical consumers and ethical trade: a review of current literature, Policy Series 12. Natural Resources Institute, University of Greenwich, UK.

Tjolle, V. (2009) South Africa Fair Trade Tourism Packages Endorsed and Ready To Market. http://www.travelmole.com/stories/1136437.php (accessed 21 May 2009).

The Travel Foundation (2008) How UK tour operators can create positive change in Kenya for the Maasai tribe and wildlife conservation. The Travel Foundation Forum Meeting, 21 October.

UNCTAD (1999) Assessment of Trade in Services of Developing Countries – Summary of Findings. UNCTAD/ITCD/TSB/7, 26 August.

UNWTO (2009) Tourism Highlights, 2009 Edition. http://www.unwto.org/facts/eng/pdf/highlights/UNWTO_Highlights09_en_HR.pdf (accessed 26 January 2010).

Utting-Chamorro K. (2005) Does fair trade make a difference? The case of small coffee producers in Nicaragua. *Development in Practice* 15, 584–599.

Vellas, F. and Bécherel, L. (1999) *The International Marketing of Travel and Tourism: A Strategic Approach*. Macmillan Press, Basingstoke.

Watson, G.L. and Kopachevsky, J.P. (1996) Interpretations of tourism as a commodity. In: Apostolopoulos, Y., Leivadi, S. and Yiannakis, A. (eds) *The Sociology of Tourism: Theoretical and Empirical Investigations*. Routledge, London.

White Paper on International Development (2000) *Eliminating World Poverty: Making globalisation work for the poor*, December. The Stationery Office Ltd, Norwich.

Williams, M. (2002) The Political Economy of Tourism, Liberalization, Gender and the GATS, Occasional Paper Series on Gender, Trade and Development. Center of Concern – Global Women's Project, International Gender and Trade Network, Washington.

Woodroffe, J. (2002) GATS: *A Disservice to the Poor*. World Development Movement, London.

World Bank (2002) World Development Report 2001/2: Attacking Poverty: Opportunity, Empowerment and Security, online. http://siteresources.worldbank.org/INTPOVERTY/Resources/WDR/overview.pdf (accessed 16 June 2009).

World Tourism Organization (1995) *GATS and Tourism – Agreeing on Trade and Tourism*. WTO/OMT, Madrid.

World Trade Organization (2009) Misconceptions about the GATS, GATS Training module: chapter 8. http://www.wto.org/english/tratop_e/serv_e/cbt_course_e/c8s2p1_e.htm (accessed 30 August 2009).

Zadek, S. (2000) *Ethical Trade Futures*. New Economics Foundation, London.

7 Tourism and Human Rights

Stroma Cole and Jenny Eriksson

Introduction

This chapter examines the links between tourism and human rights. The rationale for tourism development in less economically developed countries (LEDCs) is to bring economic prosperity and a better standard of living. Frequently, however, the right of freedom to travel for the rich impacts negatively on the rights of people in destination communities. Following an introduction to tourism, globalization and human rights, this chapter examines how tourism impacts on labour and privacy rights, and the rights to water and housing. The chapter ends by making a business case for tourism companies to consider issues of human rights.

Human Rights

There is no universally accepted definition of human rights but they are the basic standards without which people cannot live with dignity (Donnelly, 2003). The United Nations defines them as inherent in our nature as human beings, the foundation for the quality of life in which individual dignity and worth receives due respect and protection and as the foundation for freedom, justice and peace (United Nations, 1948: preamble). The Universal Declaration of Human Rights (UDHR) is the first universal statement on the basic principles of inalienable human rights, adopted in 1948 by the UN General Assembly without a dissenting vote and proclaimed as a common standard of achievement for all peoples and all nations. The UDHR is the foundation of international human rights law and it sets out fundamental human rights to be universally protected.

Included are the rights to equality, well-being and health, as well as rights to privacy, to participate in culture, religion and education. Rights to freedom include rights to work and to join a trade union but also the right to rest, to leisure (tourism) and freedom of movement (to travel). Freedom from poverty is also a human right (Pogge, 2007).

Tourism Development

Tourism is considered to bring economic development as well as contribute to mutual

---

Box 7.1. Declaration on Human Rights with direct relevance to tourism.

- Universal Declaration of Human Rights, 1948;
- International Covenant on Economic, Social and Cultural Rights, 1966a;
- International Covenant on Civil and Political Rights, 1966b;
- Convention on the Rights of the Child, 1990;
- International Convention on the Protection of the Rights of All Migrant Workers and Members of Their Families, 1990; and
- Declaration on the Rights of Indigenous Peoples, 2007.

---

understanding and respect between peoples and societies. Tourism's potential contribution to development is the fundamental justification for governments and aid agencies encouraging the sector (Cole, 2008). While defining development has been subject to debate, present-day conceptions can be summed up as a multidimensional process leading to 'good change' and seen to embrace self-sufficiency, self-determination and empowerment, as well as improved standards of living (Scheyvens, 2003). Tourism is thus considered a positive contribution to the human rights of destination communities, freeing them from poverty, by providing work, well-being and opportunities to enhance cultural heritage.

Tourism's professed ability to bring freedom from poverty is further developed in the tourism literature, including recent work on pro-poor tourism.

- Small-scale, bottom-up, community-based developments present greater opportunities for control and profit by local people (Rodenburg, 1980).
- Many of the jobs in tourism are relatively unskilled, providing opportunities for women and other marginalized groups to earn money (Ashley *et al.*, 2001; Roe and Khanya, 2001).
- As tourism delivers consumers to the product, locals have a new market for their products and services. Thus tourism has the potential for linkages particularly to traditional livelihood occupations such as agriculture, fishing and handicraft production.
- Tourism can stimulate employment, the drive for young people to migrate to urban areas is reduced, leaving a more balanced population in remote rural areas and countering structural inequalities of income distribution (Britton, 1982: 183).
- Small-scale tourism places value on natural and cultural resources and can be developed without great capital investment in remote and marginal regions where a disproportionate number of the poorest people live.
- Tourism can stimulate small-scale and

micro-enterprises empowering previously disadvantaged members of communities, and further helping to alleviate poverty.

As discussed elsewhere (Cole, 2006), the development of small-scale tourism in poor remote areas has benefits that go beyond economic. Tourism can be a powerful tool to empower marginal communities. Many researchers have discussed how:

- Tourism brings about pride (Crystal, 1978; Mansperger, 1992; Van den Berghe, 1992; Boissevain, 1996; Adams, 1997; Cole, 1997; Erb, 1998).
- Tourism can enhance community cohesion (Sanger, 1988; Ashley *et al.*, 2001).
- Through tourism, communities can come to value their cultural assets.
- Tourism can lead to an increase in confidence and strengthen political identity (Swain, 1990; Johnston, 1992).

Tourism, it would seem, has the potential to bring dignity and alleviate poverty and therefore to enhance destination communities' human rights.

Globalization, Tourism and Human Rights

The majority of international tourism is controlled by multinational enterprises, powerful economic actors that wield significant political influence in developing countries (Hemmingway, 2004). These Trans-National Corporations (TNCs; often working through national subsidiaries that the TNCs set up) have oligopolistic, or near monopolistic, powers and can dictate terms in destinations (Bianchi, 2002). They have significant advantages over local companies, with access to financial, electronic, information and communication systems, as well as political lobbying powers (Mowforth *et al.*, 2008). They constantly monitor the environment to exploit changes in international costs and demand patterns, and having no particular loyalty can switch to a different destination as it suits them (Tribe, 2005).

International tour operators coordinate and control charter airlines and accommodation and through a vast network of affiliated companies and contracted suppliers use their powers to negotiate low prices. There is increasing consolidation of the major tour operators (there are now only two in the UK), who continue to buy up the small to medium specialists, capitalizing on their knowledge and loyal client bases. This leaves destinations at the mercy of even fewer companies. The ownership, control and therefore benefits of so much tourism accrue mainly to the rich industrialized nations and the privileged minority of state officials in destination communities. 'The rights of local people take second place to the needs and expectations of foreign tourists and the profits of the TNCs' (Mowforth *et al.*, 2008: 90). Tourism (especially to LEDCs) is based on unequal relations. Rather than alleviating the poverty tourism can exacerbate existing unequal, exploitative relationships and the poorest members of communities often feel the burdens hardest, frequently at the expense of their human rights.

So if tourism affects/denies/abuses the rights of local people in destination communities why is so little written about tourism and human rights in the tourism literature? A Google Scholar search on 'tourism and human rights' will come up with Tourism Concern's 10-year-old report that was 'designed to stimulate discussion ... and lead to positive action' (Tourism Concern, 1998: 3). However, the debate has not begun. The other relevant articles appear in human rights (Hemmingway, 2004) and ethics (George, 2007) literature. One recent exception is Lovelock's article in *Annals of Tourism Research*. His article about ethical decision-making among travel agents in New Zealand reaches conclusions that will disappoint human rights activists. The rights of tourists to travel were considered more important than destination communities' rights, even when travel agents suspected clients of travelling for sex with minors. Lovelock's conclusion: 'Tourism strongly supports the rights of the clients' (2007: 353) is echoed by Babu George who suggests, 'the rights of tourists are over-stressed and the rights of other

Fig. 7.1. Cartoon gratitude (see http://www.polyp.org.uk).

stakeholders, especially the local community members are under-stressed' (2007: 40).

All aspects of human rights: civil, political, economic, social and cultural are equally important, interdependent, indivisible and universal, but they have not been treated as such. In 1993, during the World Congress for Human Rights, this was reaffirmed. The human rights that had been divided into two separate covenants: the International Covenant on Civil and Political Rights (ICCPR) and the International Covenant on Economic, Social and Cultural Rights (ICESCR) were to be treated the same. Even so, the former is still given much more attention, legal status and weight then the latter (at least in the more economically developed countries (MEDCs).

Tourism is frequently under scrutiny for its harsh environmental impacts (as this is a part of the sustainability concept) but not from a human rights perspective. This, despite the direct and negative impact tourism can have on the rights of the local people in the destinations to attain a decent standard of health and well-being. The precedence of civil and political rights over economic, social and cultural rights is one of the reasons why human rights have not been acknowledged as an area that applies to tourist activities.

In the exceptional case of child sex tourism, the international community has acted toward this evil through the creation of laws and codes of practices, and focused on putting sex abusers behind bars. However, little has been done to address the reasons or causes behind the violations, i.e. the poverty of the children and their families and the uneven distribution of tourism profits.

Academics and textbooks have ignored the tourism and human rights agenda with the exception of books and articles about child sex tourism, perhaps the most heinous of all human rights abuses, and articles about Burma (e.g. Pleumarom, 2002). As tourism is largely taught in business schools, tourism is seen as an industry. Profit is the motive that drives business and the 'client is king' (Branson and Craven, 2002). The master–servant relationship of colonial times is replicated and has led to suggestions that tourism is a form of neo-colonialism (Bruner, 1996; Lea, 1988). So many textbooks and journal articles start about the size of the industry, the increasing number of tourists and the percentage of workers in the sector. This dominance of tourism as an industry rather than a system (George, 2007) may go some way to explaining the absence of human rights in the tourism curriculum.

Human Rights – Who is Responsible?

Under international law, the primary responsibility for the realization of human rights rests with the state. The responsibility requires three sets of obligations:

- to respect the freedom and dignity of the individual;
- to protect them against third parties; and
- to provide access to welfare covering basic needs such as food, shelter, education and health (Eide, 2004: 7).

However, in our increasingly globalized world, are individual states able to protect their citizens' human rights? The international economic and political pressures of globalization result in deregulation and privatization. With funding from international financial institutions such as the World Bank, the International Monetary Fund (IMF), the Inter-American Development Bank and the Asian Development Bank, LEDCs are persuaded to provide opportunities for TNCs. These powerful economic actors can act without duties to protect the rights of local communities. As Eide (2004: 42) suggests, the global market should be regulated through the application of environmental standards and human rights, by determined action of all the stakeholders involved.

Globalization should result in a global responsibility to assist in the creation of conditions for the full enjoyment of human rights. This responsibility is already spelled out in the UDHR, article 22:

> Everyone, as a member of society, has the right to social security and is entitled to realization, through national effort and international cooperation and in accordance with the organization and resources of each State, of the economic, social and cultural rights indispensable for his dignity and the free development of his personality.

This article can be read in conjunction with article 28 (see for example, http://www2.o hchr.org/english/issues/millenium-develop ment/achievement.htm and http://wwwuni versalrights.net/main/creation.htm), which emphasizes the importance of having a social and international order that can create the conditions for a global human rights culture to be achieved. It should not only be the responsibility of the state to ensure human rights; as the preamble to UDHR states, it is a responsibility for 'every individual and every organ of society'. Consumers (such as tourists) and TNCs not only have the rights to benefit from tourism but also duties to the local destination community, which they visit or function in (Muchlinski, 2001).

Among tourists, there is a growing awareness of environmental and social considerations and some tourists will reward companies that can show they are environmentally and socially conscious (WTO 1999). The liberal middle classes do not want their wealth to be dependent on the exploitation of the resources and labour of people on the other side of the world (Mowforth *et al.*, 2008), and they increasingly do not want to travel to destinations where people are having their rights violated in order to cater for their holidays. The industry is responding, concerned with public scrutiny it is beginning to appreciate human rights as part of corporate responsibility.

Labour Rights as Human Rights

Workers' rights and human rights are normally discussed as if they were two separate entities. But workers' rights *are* human rights. Work provides an element of human dignity as well as providing the remuneration important for securing an adequate standard of living (Smith, 2007: 279). The right to work has been spearheaded by the International Labour Organization (ILO) since its creation in 1919. It is enshrined in article 23 of the UDHR and further elaborated in article 6–8 of the ICESCR.

The right to work emphasizes the need to promote employment for all, but not just any kind of employment. Jobs and livelihoods have to be *decent* for the right to be fulfilled (ILO, 1996). Decent work entails: a just remuneration (a living wage); equal remuneration for work of equal value; safe and healthy working conditions; equal opportunity for everyone to be promoted in his employment; rest, leisure and reasonable limitation of working hours; periodic holidays with pay; and the right to form and to join trade unions (UN, 1948: 23, 24; UN, 1966b: ICESCR, 6–8). Forced or compulsory labor is classified as slavery and prohibited in the ICCPR (UN, 1966a: ICCPR: 8).

Migrant workers from the LEDCs are particularly vulnerable to violations of their right to decent work because many migrate because of poverty and the inability to earn or to produce enough to support themselves or their family (UN, 1990). Employers aware of this reason commonly exploit their vulnerability and treat them as low cost workers rather than humans that are equally entitled to the same rights as the workers from the MEDCs. The Convention on the Protection of the Rights of All Migrant Workers and Members of Their Families (ICPMW) is meant to reaffirm and secure the human right of migrants (UN, 1990).

Employment in the front-line in tourism is renown to be underpaid and highly stressful (Hall and Brown, 2006). As Tourism Concern's research into tourism labour (Beddoe, 2004) suggests, workers suffer from:

- long working hours;
- unpaid overtime;
- over-dependence on tips;

- stress;
- lack of secure contracts;
- poor training; and
- lack of promotion opportunities for locally employed people.

In many former colonies, the tourist–worker interaction is intersected by class, race and often gender inequalities. Workers are subordinate not just because of their occupational roles but also because of their status as a formerly colonized, often working class, frequently female, people of colour. Tourism work exaggerates and reinforces previous relations of inequality and emotional subordination (Kanemasu, 2008). In LEDCs, the line between servility and slavery is frequently crossed, as can be seen in the two case studies below.

Case 1: Gladys' story

Gladys is a fully qualified accountant but could not find a professional job, so she works as a shop assistant for a European Hotel North of Mombasa. She works a 6-day week, gets no sick or holiday pay. Her shifts are 8 h, during which she gets no breaks and cannot eat. Eating any food is charged at €12 or dismissal.

> Once a cook tasted a chicken's foot used to make soup, but not fed to guests. The security guard caught him and he was dismissed. We are not allowed to bring anything in, the guards at the gate check us … We don't eat anything at all, we get used to it … our stomachs adjust … Even the leftovers … they go to the cats or in the bin.
>
> I cannot afford the bus so I walk, except if I am on the late shift then I have to [use a bus], it's not safe for a woman to walk … The worst thing is we often get paid late so we have to borrow money, with the interest there is not enough [money to live on]… I know there are employment laws in Kenya that should protect us, but well, even unions are corruptible.
>
> (Interview with author, 2007)

Case 2: Cruise ships and violations of labour rights

The cruise industry is a multi-million-dollar industry and it is growing. In 2009, it is estimated that 13.5 million people took a cruise worldwide (Davies, 2009) and it is expected that the global cruise industry will reach 20 million passengers by 2012 (Mintel, 2005). One in every 12 package holidays booked in the UK is now a cruise, whereas it was only one in 26 in 1999 (Passenger Shipping Association, 2009: 3). People from all over the world are attracted to work on these cruises and they are needed for this industry to keep growing. Unfortunately, the cruise industry takes little responsibility over the welfare of its workers and operates under a system that makes it easy to exploit staff without being held accountable.

The system is called 'Flag of Convenience' (FOC) and it allows ship owners to register their cruises under foreign flags. This means that the state of which the flag belongs to is responsible for the protection and fulfilment of the human rights of both the ship's crewmembers and its passengers. Popular FOC states are Panama, Liberia and Bahamas. What these countries have in common is weak trade unions and labour laws and are known to ignore both international maritime standards and international human rights law. Popular cruises such as Carnival Corporation, Royal Caribbean, Star Cruises and Disney all sail under a FOC (ITF and War on Want, 2002: 26).

The International Transport Workers Federation (ITF) has long opposed this flag-of-convenience system, calling it worker exploitation (ITF, 2009). In 2002, after a large amount of complaints from crewmembers, the ITF, together with War on Want, a British Human Rights Organization, released a report 'Sweatships: what it's really like to work on board cruise ships' that highlights the daily human rights abuses of the crewmembers. Subsequent research in the industry confirms the grim picture (Torres and Rubadoux, 2006; Jenkins, 2007; Klein, 2008).

The workers suffer from:

- non-secure, short-term contracts;
- low wages and high costs, including illegal agents' fees to secure a job: money often has to be borrowed at high rates of interest;
- long working hours and high work intensity, leading to fatigue;
- poor management practices, including bullying and favouritism, racial and gender discrimination;
- high labour turnover, fatigue and inadequate training, giving cause for concern about safety; and
- employers who are hostile or resistant to trade union organization and collective bargaining.

Notable in the report is that racial and gender discrimination underpins the operations of many of the major cruise lines, from access to employment to rights at work. Unlike workers from MEDCs, workers from the LEDCs often have to pay illegal fees to crew agents used by the cruise lines, in order to secure employment. Many take high-interest loans to be able to do this and are therefore indebted before starting work and if anything goes wrong with the contract, the cruise ship worker and his/her family may find themselves in a spiral of mounting debt. This puts the workers in a vulnerable economic situation, which the employers reinforce by making the staff pay for their uniforms and many cruise lines also take an indemnity out of the wages from each employee, which is returned only at the end of employment and without interest. The economic dependency favours the employer as the employee is prevented from breaking their contracts no matter what conditions of work they experience. It is also commonplace that the employers hold on to their employee's passports, literally preventing the crewmembers from leaving the ship (ITF and War on Want, 2002: 15).

Migrant workers from the LEDCs cover the menial positions onboard and are often

moved around at the preference of the employer as the contracts rarely states what job they have been recruited for. The working hours are extreme; according to an ITF survey (ITF and War on Want, 2002: 15) of 400 cruise ship employees, over 95% were found working 7 days a week, over a third of the cruise workers work 10–12 h/day, and just under a third do as much as 12–14 h. Where there is no union agreement, overtime is recognized as regular working hours. For this hard work, waiters/waitresses can earn as little as US$45/month, bar tenders US$365 and hotel and gallery stewards between US$400 and US$480. In trying to gain a living wage, they compete for tips. This has created an internal system of charges where for example the waiter has to pay the cook to get his order prioritized. The work onboard is stressful and physically strenuous but crewmembers need to stay well, as the sick pay amounts only to a basic wage of US$45. Holiday pay is completely absent.

Not only do these practices violate the most fundamental rights of the workers but the practice described above cannot be defined as work at all as it amounts to bonded labour or debt slavery.

Meanwhile, the by-and-large white migrant workers from the MEDCs enjoy higher job positions, better wages, working and living conditions. This discriminative practice is highly visible because of the segregation of staff. Most of the crewmembers from the MEDCs are working and living on decks above sea level and enjoy a greater freedom of movement. Below sea level, crewmembers from the LEDCs are confined to cramped living and working spaces and face disciplinary action if they are seen on deck levels where they are prohibited from being (ITF and War on Want, 2002: 2).

For women, the situation onboard is particularly harsh, as they are also discriminated against because of their gender. Despite qualifications, they enjoy inferior positions to their male counterparts; mainly in jobs in contact with passengers such as waitressing. They are exposed to a highly sexualized environment where sexual harassment from fellow crewmembers and their superiors/bosses has become a normalized part of their working environment. Sexual harassment and rape of both female crewmembers and passengers are commonly swept under the carpet and the criminals are rarely prosecuted, as reported by an US-based maritime law firm (Lipcon *et al.*, 2008). Pregnancy and maternity rights are absent and women have had their contracts terminated when found pregnant (ITF and War on Want, 2002: 14).

In order to challenge discrimination onboard, as well as other illegal practices by the cruise ship company, seafarers have the right to form unions to bargain collectively for their labour rights to be respected and fulfilled. But cruise ship employers have been shown to be hostile to trade union organization and collective bargaining and a threat of instant dismissal hangs over those who try. ITF believes that solidarity between the workers is actively prevented through a 'divide and rule' strategy (ITF and War on Want, 2002: 13); the cruise lines employ as many different nationalities as possible and casualize work contracts, thus creating language barriers and preventing long-term relations forming. The constant struggle for making up wages with tips also creates a fierce individual competition detrimental to the solidarity between the cruise workers.

For 50 years the ITF has waged a campaign against the FOC system, demanding that ship owners take their responsibility over the welfare of its workers, their interests and rights, regardless of nationality. In 2006, the ILO adopted the Maritime Labour Convention. The convention sets out seafarers' rights to decent conditions of work and helps to create conditions of fair competition for ship owners. The known FOC states within the cruise ship industry; Bahamas, Liberia and Panama have all ratified the convention, though it will not come into force until 30 countries have signed it (ILOLEX, 2009). Meanwhile the ITF and War on Want report lists a set of recommendations for what action can be taken in solidarity with the cruise ship worker (ITF and War on Want, 2002: 30).

The Right to Privacy, Respect and Dignity

The notion of privacy refers to the sphere of a person's life in which he or she can freely express his or her identity, in relationships with others or alone (UN, 1994). Privacy covers both the physical and psychological integrity of a person and includes 'the right to personal autonomy'. The right to privacy also protects against arbitrary interferences with a person's family and home. The term family should be attributed to a broad interpretation to include all those comprising the family as understood in the society concerned (UN, 1988). Privacy can mean many things in different contexts: of people and peoples, cultures and nations. What constitutes an invasion of privacy differs according to these contexts and therefore has to be people-centred in order to be understood and respected.

The human right to freedom of expression and opinion is related to the right to privacy (Smith, 2007: 267), as this right is crucial for people to freely communicate their perceptions of privacy and with this, ensure their human dignity (Smith, 2007: 267). The right to privacy is protected in a variety of international human rights laws including the UDHR article 12, the ICCPR article 17, the Convention on the Rights of the Child (CRC) article 16 and the Declaration on the Rights of Indigenous Peoples article 12.

Undermining Dignity and Privacy in the Lower Omo Valley, Ethiopia

The principle of basic human rights includes an essential right to dignity and privacy. These rights are severely undermined when people and their homes are made into tourist attractions without their free, prior and informed consent, and without any intention to make them rightful stakeholders in a profitable industry. For over 10 years, the tourism industry and its clients have profited from the exploitation of the Mursi tribe of the Lower Omo Valley, Ethiopia (Steen, 2007).

The images of the Mursi wearing iconic lip plates and colourful dresses are, without their consent, seen plastered all over vacation brochures (e.g. Real Adventures, 1998–2009) and circulated among tour agents. The Mursi are sold as exotic cultural commodities to be visited, looked at and photographed, and it is a profitable business; thousands of private pictures of Mursi woman, men and children are circulating on the web as tourists and photographers are quick with uploading their cultural trophies for admiration or sale (Flickr; Photographersdirect).

For the Mursi, this means that their homes and private spheres are constantly subject to physical and psychological intrusion. In high season, external tour operators with non-local guides arrange trips to the same two or three Mursi villages, where 30 cars visit five or six times per week (approximately 90 cars per day) (Steen, 2007). The tourists are dropped off briefly to take pictures, leave a couple of Ethiopian Birr (less then 20 British pence) (Turton, 2004: 3) for his/her 'individual object' and jump back into their car and disappear. Not only is the Mursi's right to privacy of their person, home and family life shattered, but their right to have and maintain private relationships is also made difficult by the fact that they are not given any stake from the tourist industry and as a result have to compete fiercely for the few pence the tourists give for photographs (Steen, 2007). While the industry and the tourists continue to violate the rights of the Mursi, they are blamed for being aggressive to the tourists (Turton, 2004: 5, 6). The Mursi are asking for respect of their human dignity; they want tourism to be acted out on their terms and for their benefit. They do not want to be passive objects but active participants in the industry with the right to express their culture in the way that they choose. This was revealed in a workshop held in 2005 titled 'Tourism in South Omo: Questions of Social Sustainability', where 70 participants from 11 ethnic groups, youth and elders, throughout South Omo were brought together to discuss the issues about

present state of tourism and future imaginations from a community level. The idea of cultivating tourism from a grass-roots level was the most significant aspect revealed by these local perspectives (LaTosky, 2007: 8).

Stateless but Valuable: Kayan Women in Thailand

The same situation of exposure and exploitation for tourism purposes applies to the situation of the Kayan women and their daughters in Thailand. The Kayan are famous for their neck rings, a cultural attribute that makes their necks appear elongated. They are an ethnic minority group, refugees from Burma that have escaped grave human rights violations, and at the point of entry into Thailand are discriminated against because of the rings. They are separated from the other refugees and transported to specially built, artificial, 'long neck' villages where they serve as an all-year-round tourist attraction (Say Reh Soe, 2008). As stateless people, they are denied all forms of status, which would grant them basic rights, including refugee status. Those that have been granted resettlement abroad as refugees (in Finland and New Zealand) have been denied exit visas by the Thai authorities, as the Kayan generate income as tourist attractions for the local tourism operators, local government officials and village chiefs (New Frontiers, 2006; Parry, 2008).

The Thai authorities deny the Kayan refugee status, arguing that they are economic migrants that have 'chosen' to live outside the refugee camp to earn a good living from the tourism trade (Harding, 2008). But for the Kayan, the lack of status, even as economic migrants, means that they have no social security, they are not allowed to leave the tourist villages and consequently are denied the human rights:

- to freedom of movement;
- to free choice of work;
- to education; and
- to land and many other rights (Parry, 2008).

In fact, the Kayan seems to be denied the human right to have rights as a person, and as a literal expression of this, many Kayans have been trafficked as commodities for tourist exhibitions elsewhere in Thailand (New Frontiers, 2007).

The right to privacy is violated on a daily basis as up to 150 visitors are taken by Thai tour companies to each of the three Kayan (or Padaung) villages every day during high season (Tourism Concern, 2008). Tourists pay 250 baht (about £4) each as an entry fee to the village chief to walk around the village freely taking pictures of the Kayan women and children (Parry, 2008). The women and their families are supplied rice, chilli and cooking oil, and a monthly stipend of 1500 baht (£24) per set of neck rings (although many complain that if the tourists don't come they only get the rice) (Parry, 2008). They exist for the tourist dollar. The Kayan men, who do not have land to cultivate, are not of interest for the tourists and exist in the peripheries trying to sell textiles and handicrafts to generate income, the Kayans right to family life is therefore also violated.

Some of the younger generation Kayan are opposing their denigrating treatment as cultural exhibits for tourists in the artificial villages that they know are referred to as 'Human Zoos' (Harding, 2008). They have opposed the exposure of their private lives as seen all over billboards, brochures and postcards in Thailand and some of them have discarded their rings in the hope that by denying themselves the right to cultural expression (or the right to freely express their identity), they will have more freedom to move around, as they will not be attractive as exhibit-items for tourists (Harding, 2008).

Because of the consistent highlighting of the Kayan case by civil society organizations such as Tourism Concern, together with the United Nations High Commission for Refugees in Thailand, pressure has been put on the Thai government to take responsibility to respect, protect and to fulfil the human rights of the Kayan. Some Kayan have now been issued with exit visas and most villagers have been given the choice of entering the main refugee camp or remaining and working in

Fig. 7.2. Kayan woman shown alongside other attractions at Bangkok Zoo in an advertisement in Bangkok airport.

the tourist villages as economic migrants. As yet the Kayan do not have control over tourism in their villages, however, they do hope to be able to develop an encounter with tourists based on respect and dignity.

The Human Right to Water and the Impact of Tourism

Water is a critical resource for human survival and dignity; it is a fundamental, universal human need and basic human right. Water is an underlying determinant to health and is therefore connected to the human right to health, food, housing and ultimately to the human right to life (UN, 2003). Water is a necessity for agricultural production and millions of the world's poor, particularly in rural areas in subsistence agriculture, depend on water for their livelihoods (King, 2005: 3).

In order for the right to water to be fulfilled, it has to be sufficient, safe, physically accessible and affordable. The entitlements to water include the right to a system of water supply and management that provides *equality of opportunity* for all people to enjoy the right to water (UN, 2003: 4). Water is typically the responsibility of women in LEDCs; therefore women suffer to a greater extent when water resources are mismanaged, as many have to walk for several hours every day to find it (Hemmingway, 2004). Apart from increasing their workload, they lose out on their right to education – essential for strengthening their position in society and for efficient poverty eradication (Watkins, 2006: 47).

In popular holiday destinations, local inhabitants have to compete with the tourism sector over the access, allocation and use of water for their personal and domestic daily needs, as the tourism industry exerts an enormous strain on the water supplies (UN, 2006: 1). Locals also have to fight against the industry that pollutes much of the water it depends upon.

Continuing contamination, depletion and unequal distribution of water not only poses a direct threat to people's right to

health and life but it is also exacerbating existing poverty and is a source of conflict and societal instability (King, 2005). Priority in the allocation of water must be given to the right to water for personal and domestic uses, and for preventing starvation and disease.

As every tourist consumes between 300 and 850 l (De Stefano, 2004) of water per day, tourism development has become virtually synonymous with water depletion, scarcity and shortages:

> All around the Mediterranean, tourism has contributed to a severe lack of drinking water. In this relatively dry part of the world, the individual tourist consumes on average twice as much water as a local inhabitant. Due to the water shortage caused by tourism, the coastal communities are forced to produce drinking water out of seawater or to import expensive drinking water from elsewhere. Consequently, traditional economic activities such as agriculture, are marginalized by the lack of water.
>
> (Visser, 1999)

Moreover, extensive landscaping, water parks, swimming pools and golf courses are typical tourist facilities that require water during the dry season. On average, a golf course needs between 10,000 and 15,000 m^3 of water per hectare per year. The surface of a golf course lies between 50 and 150 ha, which means that the annual consumption of a golf course is around 1 million m^3 per year or the equivalent of the water consumption of a city of 12,000 inhabitants (De Stefano, 2004).

In the Alps, snow-making machines now suck up nearly as much water as Vienna, a city of 1.7 million people. In dry years, some Alpine villages have to get their water from fire trucks because mountain reservoirs are dry (Champion, 2008). In Kovalam, in the Indian state of Kerala, many hotels rely on water brought in by 10,000-l tanks from the nearby villages. Some villagers have sold access to their wells. Meanwhile, other villagers protest as the water table is lowered and fights have broken out because of water scarcity (Hickman, 2007). A similar story can be told from Zanzibar where the construction of a hotel has lead to the villagers' well being constantly exhausted, or in Goa where 50% of farming households have given up on agriculture because of water shortages (Solomon, 2008).

Apart from water depletion, the tourism industry is also known for polluting water sources because of its mismanagement of water and inadequate sewage systems, which is adversely affecting local people's health. In South India near to Ernakulam, the water theme park, Veegaland, is discharging chemically treated water into the surroundings, affecting agricultural land and causing skin irritations (Kamp and Mangalassery, 2005). In Kainakary near Alappuzha, pollution from an increasing number of houseboats for tourism has caused a decline in biodiversity and in fish stocks, as diesel from the motors and kerosene from the stoves leaks into the water. The locals who depend on the lake, river and canal water for cooking, cleaning and washing complain that even the fish taste of kerosene (Kamp and Mangalassery, 2005).

The Right to Housing: Tourism and Displacement

Housing is universally viewed as one of the most basic human needs deemed essential for good physical and mental health and for living a life in dignity. Housing is recognized in the UDHR where it proclaims the right of *everyone* to a 'standard of living adequate for the health and well-being of himself and of his family, including food, clothing, housing and medical care and necessary social services' (UN, 1948: 25: 1).

For housing to be a*dequate*, it has to provide more than just four walls and a roof over one's head; at a minimum it has to include: legal security of tenure; potable water and sanitation facilities; it has to be in a location that allows access to employment, schools and healthcare; it has to be habitable, culturally adequate and affordable (UN, 1991). The right to land is also recognized as being a critical element of the human right to housing, as inadequate housing often is the consequence of being barred access to land and common property resources (Kothari, 2007: 10). For indigenous peoples, a violation of their land rights poses not only a threat to their livelihoods but also to their cultural existence as their land forms an integral part of their belief system (Smith, 2007: 320). There is a systematic gender-specific violation of the right to an adequate standard of living as women are often denied the right to own and inherit housing, land and property (Kothari, 2007).

The right to housing and land is integrally related to other human rights such as the right to food, livelihood, work, self-determination, health, education and privacy. Forcibly evicting people from their homes is constituted being 'one of the most supreme injustices any individual, family, household or community can face', as it puts serious obstacles to the full enjoyment of all human rights (UN, 1996).

If people are displaced from their homes as a consequence of a natural disaster, the survivors have the right to return to their homes and places of habitual residence if they want to, with the assistance of the authorities (UN, 1998: 28:1, 29:2). If not, the authorities are obliged to provide adequate housing elsewhere. To make sure that the rehabilitation and housing corresponds to the needs of the survivors, it is of fundamental importance that the survivors' right to consultation and participation in the planning and managing process is fulfilled (UN, 1966a: ICCPR: 25; UN, 1998:28(2)).

Displacement of people because of large-scale development projects is prohibited unless it can be justified by compelling and overriding public interests (UN, 1998: 6:c). Can tourism development be of such a public interest that it justifies the displacement of people from their homes, communities, livelihoods and cultural identities?

Tourism can result in the displacement of people in a number of ways. People are evicted from their homes by either governments or developers. In other cases, they are forced to move because of environmental disasters or economic reasons. Frequently tourism causes dramatic price rises, and local people can no longer afford rents and are forced to migrate. In the worst cases, eviction includes people having a gun put to their heads to force them to surrender their lands as reported by Mowforth *et al.* (2008) in relation to a multi-million-dollar holiday resort development in Tela Bay Honduras. Or having their homes deliberately destroyed by fire, as occurred on the Island of Gili Trawangan in Indonesia (Dalton, 1995). More recently, land grabbing in Kenya by powerful tourism interests has led to one of the Siria Maasai tribe being shot and the rest burned out of their homes and chased off their tribal lands (personal communication, Tourism Concern, 2009).

More often people are given other land or places to live – however, this frequently uproots them from their social ties and economic livelihoods. The case of developments in Cairo is typical.

Losing it all in Cairo

In 1995, the Egyptian government wanted to beautify a part of the historic centre of Cairo by creating public open spaces and developing two luxury hotels and a commercial area. The project included rehabilitating an old cemetery Bab al Nasr, which was partly occupied by squatters. These residents were to be resettled on the fringe of greater Cairo. The local authorities arrived with the police and told the residents to pack their belongings. They had little time to salvage what they could. They were given plots in new desert settlements but there was no electricity and no water. In the city centre, they were close to their employment but from the new location they had to pay for transportation to the city; furthermore, many were hawkers and now had nowhere to sell their wares. Not only did they lose their homes and many of their possessions, they lost their source of income, social ties and community networks (Fahmi, 2008).

The Tsunami: Sri Lanka, Thailand, India

In December 2004, a tsunami hit the coasts of several countries in Asia, killing more than 230,000 people (Tourism Concern, 2009) and making more than a million homeless (Rice and Haynes, 2005: 6). A year after the disaster inhabitants in Sri Lanka, many of whom were still living in inadequate and temporary shelters, spoke of the 'Second Tsunami' as they saw their land being rapidly handed over to tourism developers (Rice and Haynes, 2005: 16). In fact, tourism played a big part in the post-tsunami reconstruction plans not only in Sri Lanka but also in Thailand and India. The tourism board in Sri Lanka expressed contention with the disaster, as it had created a 'great opportunity' for turning Sri Lanka into a world-class tourism destination (Rice and Haynes, 2005: 11). The human rights of the survivors were violated for businesses. The tsunami had cleared the beaches of houses and people and, under the guise of protecting people from another disaster, the governments started discriminatively to implement coastal regulation and buffer zones (CRZ), preventing local inhabitants from reconstructing their homes by the sea but allowing hotels and tourism-related businesses to do so. Foreigners were even allowed to buy land within the zones in Sri Lanka (Rice and Haynes, 2005:17). In Tamil Nadu, India, the authorities refused to give financial assistance to survivors wanting to rebuild their homes that were within the buffer zones (Rice and Haynes, 2005: 14) and in Thailand, the authorities attempted to evict fisher communities with customary rights to their lands while ignoring the private sector that were illegally reconstructing tourism amenities within the zones (Rice and Haynes, 2005: 13). In the tsunami-struck Pichavaram mangrove in the Cuddalore district of Tamil Nadu, the people were unable to return as the authorities had granted permission for developing their homes into an ecotourism area (Rice and Haynes, 2005: 22).

From the start, affected local communities have been denied their right to consultation and participation in the planning and management process of their rehabilitation and the reconstruction of their lives and livelihoods (Rice and Haynes, 2005; Interim Verdict, 2008: 6). Consequently fisher communities in Sri Lanka have been permanently but inadequately housed (if housed at all) inland, far away from the coast and their livelihoods. With no alternative ways of making a living and with no means of paying a return journey to the coast, the communities are now experiencing deep levels of poverty. Meanwhile, tourism amenities take up the space where they once used to store their boats and nets.

Five years after the tsunami, whole communities in Sri Lanka and India are still temporarily and inadequately sheltered and living conditions are inhuman, despite the outpouring of aid and assistance from the international community. In the Andaman and Nicobar Islands, survivors who are still in temporary tin sheds witness excess heat, leakages, noise, poor construction, disrepair and violation to their privacy rights, especially women (Interim Verdict, 2008: 6). In Tamil Nadu, India, the poverty is so grinding that women have been selling their kidneys for medical transplantation in order to survive (Klein, 2008: 499).

Meanwhile tourism development has blossomed in and around the southern states of India. In Kerala, the government has even diverted almost £10 million from the central government Tsunami Rehabilitation Programme (TRP) to Kerala Tourism Board. The survivors' rightful funds will instead be used for coastal beautification projects attempting to attract tourism, for areas not hit by the tsunami. One of the projects is the construction of an artificial reef in Kovalam, to attract international surfers; however, it poses a threat to the livelihoods of 500 fishermen (Mangalassery et al., 2009a).

A further threat to the entire coastal community across the country is the proposed Coastal Zone Management Plans, which, if implemented will privatize the coastal lands and let it be controlled by the tourism and fishing industries. The World Bank funded Emergency Tsunami Reconstruction Programme (ETRP) is encouraging its implementation through its programme (Interim Verdict, 2008; Mangalassery et al., 2009b).

A Business Case for Human Rights Considerations

In the UK, tourism is largely taught in business schools and students are taught that tourism is an industry rather than a system. Students engage in business modules and are taught financial management as an essential element of tourism management. Recently, environmental managment has become an element incorporated into some tourism business programmes, but how about the social performance of companies?

Despite globalization, deregulation and international economic influences, most human rights law respects states as the main vehicle through which rights are realized or denied (Hemmingway, 2004). States should take action against anybody that violates the rights and it is the states that are held responsible if they fail to control private enterprises whose behaviour deprives individuals of their rights. This is problematic in many LEDCs, where law enforcement is weak. As Hemmingway suggests 'due to the state-centric nature of international law TNCs are at liberty to operate to a large degree with impunity' (2004: 285). Furthermore, their collective might can overpower governments; for example, in 1999, the Gambian government outlawed all-inclusive resorts but under pressure from the European operators, the decision was reversed the following year.

However, consumers are changing, becoming more demanding and rewarding companies that have an environmental and social conscience (WTO, 1999). As many as eight out of ten people think companies are at least partially responsible for reducing human rights abuses and a number of firms are taking note (Amis et al., 2007). Driven by fear of public scandals, lawsuits and public boycotts or by gaining competitive edge, some leading companies are beginning to incorporate human rights as part of their corporate social responsibility (CSR) reporting.

As outlined by the International Business Leaders Forum (IBLF) (2006), there is a strong business case for having a human rights policy as part of a company's CSR and to champion good practice on human rights for the following reasons:

1. To safeguard reputation and brand image – at a meeting of major hotel chains brand image was the greatest reason they gave for the need to better understand their impact on human rights.
2. Gain competitive advantage – as a number of surveys have shown, increasing numbers of customers will choose ethical companies. Dealing with human rights issues will also make them attractive to partners, employees and governments.
3. Improve recruitment and staff loyalty – staff turnover and the consequences of costly training can be avoided if a company has responsible employment practices including transparent and appropriate policies on human rights.
4. Foster greater productivity – where workers feel valued and well treated, they are more likely to give their best to the company.
5. Secure and maintain a licence to operate – governments are increasingly looking for companies to have clear responsible policies to operate in their territory.
6. Reduce cost burdens – as well as savings on recruitment, from enhanced productivity and competitive advantage, being able to avoid litigation costs is becoming a reality companies cannot afford to ignore.
7. Ensures stakeholder engagement – engaging with stakeholders is a central tenet of sustainability. Trust and rapport with local communities and NGOs will be enhanced where a company has a transparent human rights policy.
8. Meeting investor expectations – as increasing numbers of investors are taking a close interest in responsible business prac-

tice and looking to put their money in ethical funds. This Socially Responsible Investment (SRI) has grown significantly to become an investment philosophy adopted by a growing proportion of investment institutions (Sparkes and Cowton, 2004). Having a human rights policy will allow access to these funds.

In 2003, the Global Reporting Initiative (GRI) completed its specific supplement for tour operators. In 2006, the United Nations World Tourism Organization (UNWTO) announced a tourism and human rights initiative to 'Create a framework to assist the tourism industry to address human rights within their own business operations' (IBLF, 2006) and to develop and adopt a specific set of human rights principles for the industry. In 2007, TUI appeared on the Dow Jones Sustainability Index. However, the UNWTO/IBLF project remains without results and TUI's sustainable policy triumphs climate, biodiversity and environmental reporting. What about the human rights? There are plenty of good reasons for tourism companies to take human rights issues seriously but it appears that few of them are as yet taking the issues on board. As Babu George suggests, 'sustainable tourism will remain incomplete without including the Human Rights of its stakeholders as one of its core constituents' (2007: 46).

Conclusion

This chapter has looked at the links between tourism and human rights. It has examined how tourism affects the human rights of people living in destination communities in a number of ways and has illustrated this through examining the links with employment, housing, water and privacy. This is by no means an exhaustive coverage but serves to demonstrate how the right to freedom and travel for the rich violates the rights of people in the destinations they visit. The chapter has also suggested that since tourism is usually taught in business schools, tourism is understood as an industry rather than a system, and for this reason, human rights issues receive scant attention in tourism texts and journals. The chapter ended on the business case for examining human rights and for their inclusion in companies CSR policies and reports.

Questions

1. What are the links between globalization and human rights abuses through tourism?
2. What can a tourist do to prevent their holiday abusing the rights of people in destination communities?
3. What human rights might you be abusing by having two showers a day on holiday?

Useful websites

http://www2.ohchr.org/english/law/index.htm#core (all human rights collected and easily linked).
http://www.bayefsky.com (straightforward guide to human rights conventions and subject matters within these and all countries' human rights ratifications).

References

Adams, K. (1997) Touting touristic 'primadonnas': tourism, ethnicity and national integration in Sulawesi, Indonesia. In: Picard, M. and Wood, R. (eds) *Tourism, Ethnicity and the State in Asian and Pacific Societies.* University of Hawaii Press, Honolulu, pp. 155–180.

Amis, L. Brew, P. and Ersmarker, C. (2007) *Human Rights: It is your Business. The Case for Corporate Engagement.* International Business Leaders Forum, London.

Ashley, C., Roe, D. and Goodwin, H. (2001) *Pro-poor Tourism Strategies: Making Tourism Work for the Poor. A Review of Experience.* Overseas Development Institute, London.

Beddoe, C. (2004) *Labour Standards, Social Responsibility and Tourism.* Tourism Concern, London.

Bianchi, R.V. (2002) A new political economy. In: Telfer, D. and Sharpley, R. (eds) *Tourism and Development: Concepts and Issues.* Channel View, Clevedon, pp. 265–299.

Boissevain, J. (1996) Introduction. In: Boissevain, J. (ed.) *Coping with Tourists. European Reactions to Mass Tourism.* Berghahn Books, Oxford, pp. 1–26.

Branson, R. and Craven, R. (2002) *Customer is King: How to Exceed your Clients' Expectations.* Virgin Books, New York.

Britton, S. (1982) The political economy of tourism in the third world. *Annals of Tourism Research* 9, 331–358.

Bruner, E. (1996) Tourism in Ghana: the representation of slavery and the return of the Black Diaspora. *American Anthropologist* 98, 290–304.

Champion, M. (2008) Water Hogs on the Ski Slopes. *Wall St Journal,* January 23, p. 6.

Cole, S. (1997) Cultural heritage tourism: the villagers' perspective. A case study from Ngada, Flores. In: Nuryanti, W. (ed.) *Tourism and Heritage Management.* Gadjah Mada University Press, Yogyakarta.

Cole, S. (2006) Cultural tourism, community participation and empowerment. In: Smith, M. and Robinson, M. (eds) *Cultural Tourism in a Changing World.* Channel View, Clevedon, pp. 89–103.

Cole, S. (2008) Living in hope: tourism and poverty alleviation in Flores. In: Burns, P. and Novelli, M. (eds) *Tourism Development Growth, Myths and Inequalities.* CAB International, Wallingford, UK.

Crystal, E. (1978) Tourism in Toraja (Sulawesi Indonesia). In: Smith, V. (ed.) *Hosts and Guests. The Anthropology of Tourism.* Basil Blackwell, Oxford, pp. 109–126.

Dalton, B. (1995) *Indonesian Handbook,* 6th edn. Moon Publications, Berkeley, CA.

Davies, P. (2009) Global cruise passengers to rise by 2.3%, Travelmole, 15 January http://www.travelmole.com/stories/1134067.php?mpnlog=1 (accessed 21 June 2009).

De Stefano, L. (2004) Fresh water and Tourism in the Mediterranean WWF http://assets.panda.org/downloads/medpotourismreportfinal_ofnc.pdf.

Donnelly, J. (2003) *Universal Human Rights in Theory and Practice.* Cornell University Press, New York.

Eide, A. (2004) Making Human Rights Universal: Achievements and Prospects. http://www.uio.no/studier/emner/jus/humanrights/HUMR4110/h04/undervisningsmateriale/eide.pdf.

Erb, M. (1998) Tourism space in Manggarai, Western Flores, Indonesia: the house as a contested place. *Singapore Journal of Tropical Geography* 19, 177–192.

Fahmi, W.S. (2008) Global tourism and the urban poor's right to the city: spatial contestation within Cairo's historical districts. In: Burns, P. and Novelli, M. (eds) *Tourism Development Growth, Myths and Inequalities.* CAB International, Wallingford, UK.

Flickr (2009) http://www.flickr.com/search/?q=mursi&w=all&s=int (accessed 24 June 2009). At the time of accessing 1807 photos of Mursi was found.

George, B. (2007) Human rights in tourism conceptualization and stakeholder perspectives. *Electronic Journal of Business Ethics and Organization Studies* 12, No. 2.

Hall, D. and Brown, F. (2006) *Tourism and Welfare Ethics, Responsibility and Sustainable Well-being*. CAB International, Wallingford, UK.

Harding, H. (2008) Burmese women in Thai 'human zoo'. *BBC News*, 30 January. http://news.bbc.co.uk/1/hi/world/asia-pacific/7215182.stm (accessed 24 June 2009).

Hemmingway, S. (2004) The impact of tourism on the human rights of women in South East Asia. *International Journal of Human Rights* 8, 275–304.

Hickman, L. (2007) *The Final Call*. Eden Project Books, London.

ILO (1996) About the ILO. http://www.ilo.org/global/About_the_ILO/lang--en/index.htm. Decent Work For All. http://www.ilo.org/global/About_the_ILO/Mainpillars/WhatisDecentWork/lang--en/index.htm (accessed 17 June 2009).

ILOLEX (2009) Convention N. MLC, 23 June. http://www.ilo.org/ilolex/cgi-lex/ratifce.pl?C186 (accessed 27 June 2009).

Interim Verdict (2008) National Peoples' Tribunal on Post-tsunami Rehabilitation: Housing, Land, Resources and Livelihoods, Chennai. http://www.hic-net.org/content/Jury%20Verdict.pdf (accessed 25 June 2009).

International Business Leaders Forum (IBLF) (2006) IBLF and UNWTO announces human rights initiative for tourism industry. http://www.iblf.org/media (accessed 28 September 2007).

International Transport Federation (2009) Flags of Convenience campaign. http://www.itfglobal.org/flags-convenience/index.cfm (accessed 21 June 2009).

ITF and War on Want (2002) *Sweatships*. http://www.waronwant.org/attachments/Sweatships.pdf

Jenkins, J. (2007) Crew and passengers pay price for fun on cruise liners. BBC Radio 4, 27 August. http://www.bbc.co.uk/pressoffice/pressreleases/stories/2007/08_august/27/fun.shtml (accessed 27 June 2009).

Johnston, B. (1992) Anthropology's role in stimulating responsible tourism. *Practicing Anthropology* 14, 35–38.

Kamp, C. and Mangalassery, S. (2005) 'Water Is A Human Right' Not To Be Compromised By Tourism! KABANI-UNEP Position Paper on Kerala experience. http://www.keralatourismwatch.org/node/18 (accessed 24 June 2009).

Kanemasu, Y. (2008) Weapons of the workers: employees in the Fiji hotel scene. In: Connell, J. and Rugendyke, B. (eds) *Tourism at the Grass Roots: Villagers and Visitors in the Asia-Pacific*. Routledge, London, pp. 114–130.

King, M. (2005) Water and Violent Conflict. OECD. http://www.globalpolicy.org/images/pdfs/052605water conflict.pdf (accessed 24 June 2009).

Klein, N. (2008) *The Shock Doctrine*. Metropolitan Books/Henry Holt, New York.

Kothari, M. (2007) Report of the Special Rapporteur on adequate housing as a component of the right to an adequate standard of living. General Assembly Resolution 60/251, United Nations.

La Tosky, S. (2007) Cultivating Tourism in South Omo. *In Focus*, autumn edition. Tourism Concern, London.

Lea, J. (1988) *Tourism and Development and the Third World*. Routledge, London.

Lipcon, Margulies, and Alsina (2008) Sexual Assault & Rape http://www.lipcon.com/areas_of_practice_assault_facts.php?source=blog (accessed 9 July 2009).

Lovelock, B. (2007) Ethical travel decisions. Travel agents and human rights. *Annals of Tourism Research* 35, 338–358.

Mangalassery, S., Rahman, S.A., Krishman, V. and Nair, P. (2009a) 'Water Is A Human Right' Not To Be Compromised By Tourism! KABANI-UNEP Position Paper on Kerala experience. http://www.keralatourismwatch.org/node/18 (accessed 8 June 2010).

Mangalassery, S., Rahman, S.A., Krishman, V. and Nair, P. (2009b) Are we headed towards a Destination Tsunami? Public Interest Research Series. Kabani, Kerala.

Mansperger, M. (1992) Yap: a case of benevolent tourism. *Practicing Anthropology* 14, 10–14.

Mintel (2005) The International Cruise Industry – Key Market Facts from Mintel, http://www.world-tourism.org/members/affiliate/eng/m_to_m/november27/MINTEL_1.pdf (accessed 21 June 2009).

Mowforth, M., Charlton, C. and Munt, I. (2008) *Tourism and Responsibility: Perspectives from Latin America and the Caribbean*. Routledge, London.

Muchlinski, P.T. (2001) Human rights and multinationals: is there a problem? *International Affairs* 77, 31–47. http://rru.worldbank.org/Documents/PapersLinks/human_rights_and_multinationals.pdf

New Frontiers (2006) *'Long Neck' Kayan Tired of Being Tourist Attractions.* Tourism Investigation & Monitoring Team, Penang/Malaysia 12, No. 4, July–August.

New Frontiers (2007) *Six Kayan Women Kidnapped For Show.* Tourism Investigation & Monitoring Team, Penang/Malaysia 13, No. 6, November–December.

Parry, R.L. (2008) Kayan 'Giraffe Women' trapped in Thailand by tourist trade. http://www.timesonline.co.uk/tol/news/world/asia/article3701576.ece. Times Online UK, 8 August (accessed 24 June 2009).

Passenger Shipping Association (PSA) (2009) The Annual Cruise Review. http://www.the-psa.co.uk/downloads/annual_cruise_review_08.pdf (accessed 21 June 2009).

Photographers Direct (2009) http://photographersdirect.com/buyers/search.asp?search=mursi&sz=0&maximages=40&l=on&p=on&s=on&w=on (accessed 24 June 2009). At the time of accessing, 208 pictures of Mursi for sale were found.

Pleumarom, A. (2002) How sustainable is Mekong Tourism? In Harris, R., Williams, P. and Griffin, T. (eds) *Sustainable Tourism, A Global Perspective.* Butterworth Heinemann, Oxford, pp. 140–166.

Pogge, T. (2007) Introduction. In: Pogge, T. (ed.) *Freedom from Poverty as a Human Right.* OUP/UNESCO, pp. 1–10.

Polyp (n.d.) http://www.polyp.org.uk

Real Adventures (2009) http://www.realadventures.com/listings/1128334_Omo-Valley-Tours-to-Ethiopia-Pharez-Ethiopian-Tour (accessed 24 June 2009).

Rice, A. and Haynes, K. (2005) *Post-tsunami Reconstruction and Tourism: A Second Disaster?* Tourism Concern, London.

Rodenburg, E. (1980) The effects of scale in economic development: tourism in Bali. *Annals of Tourism Research* 7, 177–96.

Roe, D. and Khanya, P. (2001) *Pro-poor Tourism: Harnessing the World's Largest Industry for the World's Poor.* IIED, London.

Sanger, A. (1988) Blessing or blight? The effects of touristic dance drama on village life in Singapadu. In: *The Impact of Tourism on Traditional Music.* Jamaica Memory Bank, Kingston, pp. 79–104.

Say Reh Soe (2008) The Plight of the Kayan, *Mizzima News*, New Dehli, India, 5 September. http://www.bnionline.net/feature/mizzima/4884-the-plight-of-the-kayan.html (accessed 24 June 2009).

Scheyvens, R. (2003) *Tourism for Development, Empowering Communities.* Prentice Hall, New York.

Smith, R.K.M. (2007) *Textbook on International Human Rights*, 3rd edn. Oxford University Press, Oxford.

Solomon, R. (2008) Goa, Our coast is not for sale. *In Focus*, autumn edition, Tourism Concern, London.

Sparkes, R. and Cowton, C. (2004) The maturing of socially responsible investment. A review of the developing link with corporate social responsibility. *Journal of Business Ethics* 52, 45–57.

Steen, M. (2007) A need for responsible tourism in the South Omo Valley. *In Focus.* Tourism Concern, London.

Swain, M. (1990) Commoditizing ethnicity in Southwest China. *Cultural Survival Quarterly* 14, 26–29.

Torres, J.A. and Rubadoux, C. (2006) The people and profits behind the port's cruise-ship party, *Florida Today*, 31 January. http://www.floridatoday.com/apps/pbcs.dll/section?category=NEWS07 (accessed 27 June 2009).

Tourism Concern (1998) *Tourism and Human Rights.* Tourism Concern, London.

Tourism Concern (2008) Padaung refugees trapped by tourism. *In Focus*, spring edition. Tourism Concern, London.

Tourism Concern (2009) Tsunami of Tourism. http://www.tourismconcern.org.uk/index.php?page=tsunami-of-tourism. Sri Lanka: http://www.tourismconcern.org.uk/index.php?page=sri-lanka

Tribe, J. (2005) *The Economics of Recreation, Leisure and Tourism*, 3rd edn. Elsevier, Oxford.

Turton, D. (2004) Lip-plates and the people who take photographs. *Anthropology Today* 20, 3–8.

United Nations (1948) *The Universal Declaration of Human Rights.* United Nations, New York.

United Nations (1966a) International Covenant on Civil and Political Rights, Office of the High Commissioner of Human Rights, Geneva, Switzerland. http://www2.ohchr.org/English/law/ccpr.htm (accessed 17 June 2009).

United Nations (1966b) International Covenant on Economic Social and Cultural Rights, Office of the High Commissioner of Human Rights, Geneva, Switzerland. http://www.unhchr.ch/html/menu3/b/a_cescr.htm (accessed 24 June 2009).

United Nations (1988) General Comments and recommendations 16 of art 17 of the International Covenant on Civil and Political Rights. Human Rights Committee, Office of the High Commissioner of Human Rights, Geneva, Switzerland. http://www.bayefsky.com/themes/privacy_general-comments.pdf (accessed 26 June 2009).

United Nations (1990) Fact Sheet 24, the Rights of Migrant Workers, Office of the High Commissioner of Human Rights, Geneva, Switzerland. http://www.unhchr.ch/html/menu6/2/fs24.htm (accessed 27 June 2009).

United Nations (1991) General Comment 4 The right to adequate housing of arts. 11: 1 of the International Covenant on Economic, Social and Cultural Rights, Office of the High Commissioner of Human Rights, Geneva, Switzerland. http://www.unhchr.ch/tbs/doc.nsf/(symbol)/CESCR+General+comment+4.En? OpenDocument (accessed 25 June 2009).

United Nations (1994) *Coeriel and Aurik v The Netherlands*, Human Rights Committee, Communication No. 453/1991. http://www.bayefsky.com/pdf/148_netherlandsvws453.pdf (accessed 24 June 2009).

United Nations (1996) Fact Sheet No.25, Forced Evictions and Human Rights, Office of the High Commissioner of Human Rights, Geneva, Switzerland. http://www.unhchr.ch/html/menu6/2/fs25.htm (accessed 25 June 2009).

United Nations (1998) Guiding Principles on Internal Displacement, Office of the High Commissioner of Human Rights, Geneva, Switzerland. http://www.unhchr.ch/html/menu2/7/b/principles.htm (accessed 25 June 2009).

United Nations (2003) General Comment 15, The Right To Water. 11 and 12 of the International Covenant on Economic, Social and Cultural Rights, Office of the High Commissioner of Human Rights, Geneva, Switzerland. http://www.unhchr.ch/tbs/doc.nsf/0/a5458d1d1bbd713fc1256cc400389e94?OpenDocum ent&Highlight=0,CESCR (accessed 24 June 2009).

United Nations (2006) Human Development Report Beyond scarcity: Power, poverty and the global water crisis. http://hdr.undp.org/en/reports/global/hdr2006/ (accessed 7 June 2010).

Van den Berghe, P. (1992) Tourism and the ethnic division of labor. *Annals of Tourism Research* 19, 234–249.

Visser, N. (1999) Inaugural address sustainable tourism development. http://www.mina.vomil.an/Duurzaam/ InaugAddrNV.html (accessed 28 September 2008).

Watkins, K. (2006) *Water, a shared responsibility*. Human Development Report. Palgrave Macmillan, New York. http://hdr.undp.org/en/media/HDR06-complete.pdf. (accessed 24 June 2009).

WTO (1999) *Tourism 2020 Vision Executive Summary*. WTO, Madrid.

8 Social Tourism for Low-income Groups: Benefits in a UK and Irish Context

Lynn Minnaert, Jane Stacey, Bernadette Quinn and Kevin Griffin

Introduction

In Ireland and Britain, it is still unusual to see tourism as a possible means to counter social exclusion, and thus as a potential part of social policy. However, providing access to tourism for groups unable to participate in the commercial tourism industry is not new. Since the Industrial Revolution, social tourism has been a means for low-income workers, children from inner city backgrounds, the sick and the elderly to enjoy a holiday away from home. More recently, attempts to tackle the social exclusionist nature of holiday practices are well advanced in many European countries such as France and Belgium, where social tourism for low-income groups is supported by public funding because of its ability to 'enable [individuals] to develop every aspect of their personality and their social integration' (European Economic and Social Committee, 2006: 3), thus linking it to wider social benefits for the individual and society. More recently, social tourism has gained prominence at pan-European level, appearing on the agendas of the European Commission, European Economic and Social Committee and the European Parliament.

This chapter seeks to provide an analysis of social tourism provision for low-income groups, focusing on the benefits of such provision. The chapter begins by defining social tourism and discusses issues in relation to holiday participation, poverty and social exclusion. A number of examples of social tourism provision from across Europe are also presented. The chapter continues with a presentation of the benefits of social tourism based on two empirical qualitative studies from Ireland and the UK. Both countries have limited social tourism traditions, particularly compared to a number of countries in mainland Europe, where social tourism provision is part of public policy. The studies were carried out independently, but have produced largely comparable findings, enforcing their validity and strengthening the argument for the introduction of social tourism policies and practices in each country respectively. The chapter concludes by presenting the potential relevance of social tourism on a social, economic and policy level.

Social Tourism

Simply put, 'social tourism' refers to initiatives that aim to include groups in tourism that would otherwise be excluded from it. Hall defines social tourism as 'the relationships and phenomena in the field of tourism resulting from participation in travel by economically weak or otherwise disadvantaged elements in society' (Hall, 2000: 141). A similar definition is used by BITS (International Bureau of Social Tourism): 'by social tourism, BITS means all of the relationships and phenomena resulting from participation in tourism, and in particular from the participation of social strata with modest incomes' (BITS, 2002).

In practice, social tourism usually refers to budget-friendly domestic holidays, or in some cases day trips to theme parks, museums and attractions. The term 'social tourism' is used in those countries with the strongest traditions of practice. More recent discussions have used the term 'Tourism for All', which was explicitly adopted by the English Tourist Board (1989) in order to 'avoid the downbeat implications of "social tourism"'.

In several countries and regions of mainland Europe (France, Flanders, Spain), social tourism initiatives are (co-) funded by public money – either via direct grants or public-private partnerships. In Anglo-Saxon societies like Ireland and the UK, the concept of social tourism is by comparison relatively unknown. It is not usually part of public policy and is mostly provided via charitable bodies. The main justifications for the provision of social holidays are the notion that everyone has the right to basic tourism provision on the one hand (EESC, 2006: 69), and on the other hand the assumption that 'social tourism clearly promotes integration, greater knowledge and personal development' (EESC, 2006: 76).

The justifications for social tourism tend to be based on the following principles.

Social rationale

- *Social right:* access to holidaying opportunities and the related benefits has long been understood as a social rights issue, as evidenced by various international declarations, dating back to at least as early as 1948 and including:
  - o UN Universal Declaration of Human Rights underscored that 'every one has the right to rest and leisure' (1948, Art. 24); and
  - o UN International Covenant on Economic, Social and Cultural Rights noted the right to periodic holidays with pay (1966, Art. 7d).

Specifically in the realm of tourism and access to holidays, the United Nations World Tourism Organization (UNWTO) has identified the individual's right to rest, leisure and holidays, declarations including the 1980 Manila Declaration and more recently in the 1999 Global Code of Ethics.

- *Social welfare and well-being:* according to Hughes (1991: 196), 'holidays cannot be dismissed lightly as a frivolous pursuit' but should be seen 'more as an investment in the well-being and social fabric' of society. The claim that non-participation in holidays is a social welfare issue with health and social care implications is particularly employed in the context of children and families (Haukeland, 1990, cited in Corlyon and La Placa, 2006). The value of leisure, as part of the individual and collective needs of a society, complementing work, reinforcing group or family relationships, providing therapy or even a preventative medicine to the pressure of everyday living is increasingly recognized by both governments and labour organizations (Shaw and Williams, 2002).

- *Social inclusion:* a further related argument employed to advocate for social tourism policy is social inclusion. Jolin (2004) asserts that social tourism, by its ambition to democratize tourism, contributes to the fight against inequality and exclusion and supports social cohesion.

Economic rationale

Economic as well as social benefits can be attributed to social tourism. The economic contribution of social tourism has been recognized by the European Economic and Social Committee (EESC), which states that social tourism is:

an effective way of including new groups of people in tourism-related activities, thus contributing to the growth of an economic sector which ... has a direct impact on the creation of wealth and jobs in the interests of society as a whole ... the industry itself must realise that such access, besides being a social responsibility, is a business opportunity and competitive advantage.

(EESC, 2006: 15–16).

These economic benefits can include:

- increasing business during off-peak times, e.g. government programmes assisting older people to holiday out of season, as in Spain;
- promoting and developing tourism in areas that may not otherwise attract tourists, as in France; and
- sustaining and reproducing a healthy labour force, as in the former Socialist countries of Eastern Europe (Cser, 2006).

Holidaying Participation

Holidaying has become an extremely important social phenomenon, involving millions of people throughout the world (EESC, 2003). Global tourism numbers continue to grow, with the UNWTO forecasting that international arrivals will rise to 1.56 billion by 2020. However, participation in tourism activities is by no means universal and relatively large proportions of people do not take holidays, for a variety of reasons (Shaw and Williams, 2002).

Aside from taste and desire to holiday, a number of factors account for differential holiday participation, including variations in income, time availability, gender, race and nationality (Davidson, 1996; Richards, 1998). Of these factors, economic constraints are the single most important factor responsible for non-participation in holidaying (English Tourist Board, 1985; Haukeland, 1990; Hughes, 1991; Eurobarometer, 1998; European Commission, 2001; Jolin, 2004).

Other factors that prevent people from having a holiday include (ETB, 1989; Shaw and Williams, 2002):

- illness and disability (physiological and psychological);
- mobility and access;

- family circumstances;
- caring for dependants; and
- problems associated with aging.

Many of these other constraining factors overlap with the economic variable in producing social marginality and exclusion (Temowetsky, 1983; Van Raaji and Francken, 1984; ETB, 1989; Seaton, 1992; Shaw and Williams, 2002).

While it has been argued that the advent of cheaper air travel, package tours and holiday camps has improved access for large sections of society (Pimlott, 1976; Thurot and Thurot, 1983), such institutional changes alone have been insufficient to date in ensuring equality of access to holidaying. Baum (2006) suggests that the reduction of purely financial costs does not necessarily facilitate social inclusion and access. Meanwhile, a number of researchers have pointed out that in addition to financial means, certain skills are needed to be able to access a holiday (Seaton, 1992; Gratton, 1990, cited in Shaw and Williams, 2002). Corlyon and La Placa (2006), for example, describe how the actual process of taking a holiday for those with little holidaying experience can be a difficult and stressful experience.

Thus, a dilemma is apparent. Holidaying has become a widespread social practice in advanced economies, like Ireland and the UK, as economic prosperity has created a situation where leisure is now regarded as an essential part of individual and community well-being (Dawson, 1988). However, holidaying is a socially exclusionist activity, with obvious inequalities in holiday participation evident. An important implication here is that as holidays have now become a significant part of contemporary life, involuntary non-participation may be an indicator of poverty (Hughes, 1991; Smith and Hughes, 1999) as it suggests an inability to 'participate in the commonly accepted style of life of the community' (Dawson, 1988), which is in line with the relativist notion of poverty.

Poverty, Social Exclusion and Holidaying

According to Oppenheim (1990: 3), 'poverty means going short materially, socially and emotionally. Poverty means staying at home, often being bored, not seeing friends, not going to the cinema, not going for a drink and not being able to take the children out for a treat, a trip or a holiday'. This definition of poverty reflects the broader understanding of poverty, which emerged in the latter half of the 20th century, beyond simple subsistence to acknowledge a person's right to exist in a socially meaningful way (Dawson, 1988).

Townsend's (1979) work on 'style of life' poverty was influential in expanding definitions of poverty to incorporate concepts of social well-being, quality of life and needs that extend beyond the physical and it is within this multi-dimensional, 'style of life' approach that leisure assumes a pivotal conceptual role (Townsend, 1979; Dawson, 1988). From this perspective, deprivation is not just about lack of money but also about exclusion from the customs of society. The higher the proportion of people in a society who have an item, the more likely individuals will feel deprived if they want it, but are not able to afford it (Eurostat, 2005). This more holistic view of poverty is linked to the concept of social exclusion. Rather than just emphasising financial poverty, social exclusion refers to:

- the inability to enjoy social rights without help;
- suffering from low self-esteem;
- inadequacy in their capacity to meet their obligations;
- risk of long-term relegation to the rank of those on social benefits; and
- stigmatization (Rodgers *et al.*, 1995: 45).

Poverty researchers such as Mack and Lansley (1985) and Oppenheim (1990) have shown that for many, holidays are perceived as a necessity rather than a luxury. More recently, research conducted on behalf of the Joseph Rowntree Foundation in the UK adopted a 'socially perceived necessities' approach to exploring poverty and social exclusion (Gordon *et al.*, 2000). It indicated that the general public holds ideas about the necessities of life, which are more wide-ranging and multi-dimensional than is ordinarily represented in expert or political analysis (Collins, 2006, citing Gordon *et al.*, 2000). People 'do not restrict their interpretation of "necessities" to basic material needs of a subsistence diet, shelter, clothing and fuel – there are social customs, obligations and activities that substantial majorities of the population also identify as among the top necessities of life' (Gordon *et al.*, 2000: 16).

Gordon *et al.*'s (2000) UK research found that 55% of adults maintained that a holiday away from home once a year (not with relatives) was a 'necessity'. However, 18% did not have a holiday, because of financial constraints. Furthermore, while 63% of parents in the UK considered a 'holiday away from home [for] at least one week a year' as a necessity for their children, the study found this to be the necessity that the largest proportion of children has to forego.

Significantly, the importance of taking an annual holiday away from home was recognized by the British Government in a new measure for assessing the extent of child poverty introduced in December 2003. This new measure incorporates the concepts of relative low income and material deprivation, the latter of which includes 'a holiday away from home at least once a year with his or her family' (Hazel, 2005).

A growing body of international literature provides support for Hobson and Dietrich's (1994, cited in Gilbert and Abdullah, 2002) assertion that there is an underlying assumption in modern society that holidays are beneficial in many ways. Generally speaking, holiday-taking is viewed as a mentally and physically healthy pursuit that increases quality of life. Richards (1998), for example, maintains that holidays are important not only because they provide an unbroken chunk of leisure time but also because the quality of time spent on holiday is different. Furthermore, holidays offer relief from time and place, which are the key constraints of everyday life (Richards, 1998).

A number of empirical studies in recent years have specifically focused on the benefits of holidays to those from disadvantaged backgrounds (English Tourism Board, 1976; Smith and Hughes, 1999; Voysey, 2000; Lewis, 2001; Ghate and Hazel, 2002; Gilbert and Abdullah, 2002; Wigfall, 2004). These studies provide evidence for the existence of real benefits, including:

- an essential break from (often stressful) routine and home environment;
- opportunities for social mixing and interaction with new people;
- increased life satisfaction, subjective well-being and enhanced quality of life;
- improved mental and physical health and well-being;
- opportunities for personal development through new experiences in new environments;
- improved self-image and self-esteem;
- refreshment and improvement of relationships; and
- establishing feelings of normalcy.

The benefits of holidays identified above are reflective of the holiday benefits identified in the general tourism literature (e.g. Mannell and Iso Ahola, 1987; Cohen and Taylor, 1992).

Furthermore, there is also evidence, albeit limited, to suggest that the benefits of a holiday extend beyond the time frame of the holiday itself, through the development of sustainable relationships and anticipation of a holiday having a positive impact on well-being (Smith and Hughes, 1999; Gilbert and Abdullah, 2002; Brimacombe, 2003; Wigfall, 2004). In addition, research on the benefits of holidays has extended beyond the individual/family realm, with some researchers suggesting that the benefits accruing to the individual and the family can contribute to financial and social benefits for society in general (Hughes, 1991; Hazel, 2005; Corlyon and La Placa, 2006). A survey of general practitioners (English Tourism Council, 2000) demonstrated that significant savings in government spending and reduced social cost could result from more, or more frequent, holiday-taking. It argued that this would:

- reduce the burden on health and social care services;
- lower the costs to the economy through sickness;
- reduce the support and intervention required by social services;
- enable individuals to make better use of opportunities available to them; and
- strengthen family and community ties.

However, a core societal problem is that holidaying is not experienced equally – the benefits of holidaying are inequitably distributed across societal groups. Ghate and Hazel (2002) found that holidaying is the first essential item of family expenditure sacrificed in poverty. Thus, it may be that the benefits of a holiday might be more strongly felt by certain groups, including those from deprived/disadvantaged backgrounds, those who are isolated, stressed, dependent, ill or materially deprived, as they are most in need of a holiday (Hughes, 1991; Smith and Hughes, 1999). A study by the English Tourist Board (1976: 5) concluded that 'it is a reflection of our [English] social policy that those who are most in need of the benefits that a holiday can bring are least able to take one'.

The benefits identified above provide support for Hughes (1991: 196) who concluded that 'if there are real benefits to be derived from a holiday (especially for the disadvantaged), and a holiday is a 'necessity', there may well be a good case for active financial intervention in order to bring holidays within reach of such deprived persons'. Meanwhile, Smith (1998) claims that the benefits of holidays are similar to the benefits put forward in favour of increasing access to sport and leisure activities on behalf of disadvantaged groups. Following this argument, there would appear to be a legitimate argument for including access to holiday-taking as part of social policy if it can be shown to provide similar benefits.

Social Tourism in Practice

Across Europe, access to holidays is facilitated by a wide range of actors, including the government, public organizations, employers, trade unions/work councils, social organizations/associations and the tourism industry itself, acting independently or in unison at national or regional level. The exact nature of assistance varies from initiatives assisting the target group to participate on a holiday to initiatives that focus on the availability of facilities that can meet the needs of the target group (Hughes, 1991; Jolin, 2004). Intermediary organizations, many of which are voluntary in nature, play a key role in both driving and disseminating overall provision.

'Tourism for All', an investigation conducted during the Belgian EU Presidency in 2001, revealed the large number and variety of initiatives and incentives, both financial and non-financial, available to those living in various EU states, with provision in some countries (e.g. France, Belgium, Spain) outweighing that in others, including Ireland and the UK. The following case studies profile some examples of social tourism provision throughout Europe.

Flanders, Belgium: Centre for Holiday Participation, Tourism Flanders

The central organization in social tourism provision in Flanders is the Centre for Holiday Participation, a publicly funded team within Tourism Flanders, the regional Tourist Board. This organization liaises between the public, private and social sectors. The private sector partners (hotels, guesthouses, attractions etc.) voluntarily offer discounts to socially excluded groups, to promote their product to a new target group or within the framework of corporate social responsibility. The Centre for Holiday Participation then communicates the reduced tariffs available to the social sector and the holiday-makers. The social organizations provide support for the holiday-makers and guarantee that the

system is not abused by vouching for their clients when the holiday application is made. The system operates with minimal expense for the government, and is based on voluntary cooperation and goodwill of the private and social sector.

France: holiday cheques

A national system of 'holiday cheques' or 'vouchers' operates in France, which can be used by beneficiaries on a wide variety of items including lodgings, dining, transport, leisure and culture. Employees are assisted in making regular savings, which are supplemented by employers and social organizations, which in turn benefit from reduced taxes and social contributions. The employee redeems the total value of the savings and supplementary contributions in the form of 'holiday cheques'. The economic impact of the holiday cheques is significant as it is estimated that total spending is four times more than the volume of cheques issued.

Furthermore, the value of expired holiday cheques is redirected to provide assistance to individuals or families who suffer from economic, social or cultural difficulties via holiday grants in the form of holiday cheques. This assistance is distributed by the ANCV[1] via a network of intermediary organizations, comprising social and charitable organizations throughout France, which are in permanent contact with those who are deprived and therefore in the best position to know their needs. This ensures the provision of support before, during and after the holiday.

Spain: holiday programme for older people and for the maintenance of employment in tourist areas

The Spanish IMSERSO[2] programme seeks to improve the quality of life of older people and address seasonality in the tourism sector. The programme provides older people with the opportunity to access holiday spells during the 'off season' in areas with a warm climate, undertaking cultural circuits and recreational activities through nature tourism. The programme is marketed through travel agencies by accredited companies following a tendering process. These agencies have equal access to a centralized computerized system, outlining the offers.

Financed through contributions by beneficiaries and public monies, the state recoups its contribution through cost savings (savings in benefits and subsidies) and earnings (e.g. income tax from economic activity generated, Value Added Tax (VAT), corporation tax, social security contributions). Because of the unique form of financing, which equally subsidizes all travellers rather than in proportion to the cost of the trip, the amount the state recoups in general exceeds the sum of its contribution.

UK: Family Holiday Association

Established in 1975, the Family Holiday Association (FHA) is a charity organization that seeks to ensure the inclusion of families living on a low income in holiday and leisure activities. FHA provides financial assistance to families in need who have not had a holiday in at least 4 years. The organization relies entirely on voluntary donations and the number of holidays it can offer is restricted by the funds it raises. Families are normally referred to FHA by social services, health authority staff and voluntary organizations.

The FHA approach promotes the idea of the 'family holiday' as a tool or mechanism for combating social exclusion and seeks to contribute to the Government's work in preventing the social exclusion of families. Specifically it aims to strengthen the ability of families to cope with their difficulties, strengthen their capacity to participate in and contribute to their community, and develop a model of holiday provision to families under stress that can be replicated in other areas of the UK.

Impacts of Social Tourism

The following section reports on empirical studies in Ireland and the UK, examining the impacts of social tourism on the beneficiaries. These studies were conducted independently of each other and the focus was on different target groups. The Irish study focused on children who had taken part in a child-only, child-centred group holiday, whereas the UK study focused on family holidays, both individual and in groups. Acknowledging the differential focus of the two studies, none the less both studies revealed considerable overlap and comparable findings, reinforcing the validity of their individual results. Both studies highlighted the social impacts of holidays in the following areas:

- break from routine and home environment;
- family benefits;
- social networks;
- self-esteem;
- learning new skills; and
- behaviour change.

Following a brief outline of the methodologies employed in each of the studies respectively, the comparable results are then discussed.

Methodology

Irish study[3]

The research represented the first attempt in an Irish context to analyse existing social tourism provision and develop an understanding of how tourism practices contribute to promoting social inclusion and create benefits for people living in poverty in Ireland. The research focused on a point in time in the lives of those living in poverty and as such, the emphasis is on 'well-being' rather than 'well-becoming'. Primary data collection focused on children and the guardians (parents/carers) of children who went on a child-only, child-centred holiday with one of three partner non-governmental organizations (NGOs). The primary research employed a number of qualitative techniques to examine the benefits that children, and by extension their families, derived from participation in these holidays. A multi-stage approach to data collection began with a series of in-depth interviews with key informants involved in policy and practice in a variety of social, community and child-related domains. Further data collection consisted of pre-holiday focus groups and post-holiday semi-structured interviews (within 2 months of the holiday) with children, their guardians and key informants. Some 75 children and 35 guardians participated in the first stage and 27 children and 16 guardians in the post-holiday stage. In total, 16 families participated in all stages of the research. In addition, photographs and drawings produced by the children during the holidays (using material supplied by the researchers) were used to generate discussions during the post-holiday interviews. The families who participated in this study were drawn from six geographically dispersed inner city and suburban areas in Dublin, each characterized by differing levels of social and economic disadvantage.

UK study

The study aimed to examine to what extent social tourism for low-income families benefited the beneficiaries after their return. The families who participated in the research had all been on holidays funded by the FHA. Most holidays were domestic and in fairly low-cost accommodation such as caravan parks. Both group holidays and individual holidays were represented. Qualitative methods were used: in-depth semi-structured interviews with partici-pants of individual holidays, and focus groups with participants of group holidays. Their 'welfare agents' – persons supporting the family such as health workers, charity workers and social workers – were inter-viewed individually. To examine the longer-term benefits of social tourism, the

research was semi-longitudinal: one round (40 respondents) took place in the month after the holiday, a second round (30 of the original 40 respondents) 6 months later.

Study Findings

In analysing the findings of both studies, a number of key common themes emerged, including: break from routine and home environment; family benefits; social net-works; self-esteem; learning new skills; and behaviour change. Each of these themes will be discussed below, illustrated by direct quotes from guardians, children and welfare agents who participated in the studies.

Break from routine and home environment

This common theme emerged strongly in both the Irish and the UK studies and is reflective of the reality that participants were drawn from areas characterized by economic and social disadvantage. The negative reality of the home environments and a desire for a break from this reality and the daily routine constituted a strong motivating factor in holidaying in both studies.

Two common underlying factors were observed across the two studies. The first related to safety and security concerns in relation to the home environment, for both adults and children. Violence, conflict and aggression of varying scales were dominant themes in both studies, as the following quotes illustrate:

> The worst thing about [home place] there's too many robbed cars, yeah, too many drug dealers ...
>
> (Young boy,[4] Ireland)

> Where my house is, there are a lot of drug users, and I didn't wanna leave the house ... the week we were going away there was scaffolding up as well, and I've got a back balcony, so someone could get up the balcony. But on the holiday I was more relaxed, and so was my son.
>
> (Parent, UK)

Boredom was also a common theme across the studies. In the Irish study, the lack of recreational opportunities available for children during the summer time caused frustration for most guardians, compounding the safety and security concerns. The study found that children tended to engage in passive indoor activities, played football or simply 'hung around' at home or on the streets with their friends.

In contrast with the negative conditions prevailing within the home environments, which created a series of push factors in the Irish study, the nature of the holidays created a strong motivational pull factor, as the holidays were action-packed, activity-filled, highly structured and child-focused:

> I would go every week … because it's very good down there [holiday destination]. You would rather live down there than live up in these flats.
>
> (Young girl, Ireland)

A related important finding of the Irish study was that the holiday afforded children the opportunity just to be children for a while. The holidays were great fun and eagerly anticipated, with the provision of diverse and varied activities and making friends enormously popular and enjoyable aspects of the holiday. Furthermore, children who were 'parentified' to varying degrees (assuming caring responsibilities normally associated with parenting/guardianship) were relieved of these responsibilities, which were a reality of their daily lives:

> It was great it was, making new friends and doing stuff every day and doing things that you didn't do before, all that is great, trying new things.
>
> (Teenage girl,[5] Ireland)

> He was worried about me because his father was there so automatically he was sort of 'Ma, are you alright?', you know, he sort of tries to protect me even though he is only 11.
>
> (Guardian, Ireland)

In the UK study, several respondents reported how being away from the daily routine gave them the time to think about their lives. The following participant, a female asylum seeker, reports:

> Most of the time you sit at home, you don't have anywhere to go, you just go to college twice a week. Then you come back in the house, you haven't got anything to do, nowhere to go, you have psychological problems. You can't think ahead. You become very stressed. So when you get a holiday like that, you go with your children, you meet different people, you go out, you are happy … you feel your life has changed a bit.
>
> (Asylum seeker, UK)

The welfare agents often commented on how the holiday, as a time to reflect, has been a motivation for the families to make changes to their daily lives:

> Because most of the parents here are so immersed in their own problems and issues that they can't see beyond that. Sending them on these holidays gives them that bit of time, that space away from their home environment, the turmoil in their lives. It's a good thing. I really saw the benefits.
>
> (Welfare agent, UK)

Family benefits

Both studies found that following the holiday, participants reported improvements in communication and overall family relationships, with knock on positive effects on the lives of the children and guardians.

In the UK study, which focused specifically on families, an improvement in this area was reported as a clear outcome of the holiday. The increase took the form of improvements in family relations, between the parents and the children, the adults as a couple or between siblings. In some cases, the holiday was also used to allow the children to adjust to new family members or a new family structure.

An improvement in the lives of the children was reported by the great majority of the participants and the welfare agents. This improvement can take many forms: the relationship between the parents and the child can improve, the child can make new friends and gain confidence, or the behaviour of the child can improve and have an effect on his or her school life.

Another aspect of this improvement, often reported by the welfare agents, is that some parents changed their parenting techniques after the holiday: they might spend more time with their children, play with them more, or communicate better. One example was that of a single father, who noted a big improvement in the communication with his teenage son after the holiday:

> It's a lot better yeah. He's certainly opened up more, at one time he wouldn't speak to anybody, like when you'd say, how was work. But now he's like 'I am doing this today', 'I am doing that today'. He's looking forward to go to college, and everything seems to be falling into place. He's happy now.
>
> (Parent, UK)

Another participant, who has a daughter with behavioural problems, reports a similar improvement:

> I am spending quite a lot of time with my little one now, quality time. Maybe it's just sitting down at home doing a puzzle, or sitting in the garden having biscuits together, at home. Or going out in the weekend, we had a good time in the weekend. And I didn't do that. But I have started taking her out and stuff. I didn't realize how good it would be, to have time together, just as a family, or just me and her.
>
> (Parent, UK)

The improvement in their relationship was still reported 6 months later:

> Last weekend we went up to London to the Lord Mayor Show. She did enjoy it, and she actually stayed with me, she did as she was told and held my hand. And that was the first time she actually ever done that, because normally she'd just wander off. But she took everything in, about everything that I was telling her.
>
> (Parent, UK)

The findings of the Irish study provide supporting evidence of these familial benefits, with intra-family relationships found to be strengthened by the separation, as guardians and children were better able to inter-relate more positively having had a break from each other. The mutual recognition that each had been missed was significant in reaffirming family ties. In general, the return of the children reinvigorated the home environment and refreshed relationships. Communication within the families was improved because of the flow of news and stories generated by the holiday, while one mother thought that the prizes children received on holiday helped guardians see their children in a new light.[6]

The further finding common across the two studies related to the inability to give their children a holiday constituting a source of guilt for guardians, which is strongly connected to their responsibility as a parent/guardian. In the UK study, many parents reported how the holiday had relieved them of a sense of guilt, and how they were proud their children now had had holiday experiences, just like their peers:

> We still think about the holiday all the time, for example, when a Butlins advert comes on the telly it's like 'we went there'. It's nice, because it lays the guilt off me, because we have all been on one family holiday in his life. So I don't feel so much of a failure.
>
> (Parent, UK)

Meanwhile, the Irish study found the intervention of the holiday organization functions to lessen the burden of responsibility guardians can feel in trying to adequately provide for their children's needs. Several guardians were conscious of the fact that the holiday agency was offering something that they themselves could not afford to give their children and welcomed this intervention, viewing it not only as beneficial to their children but as supportive to them also. Guardians also indicated that the children's holiday gave them a break/relief, although the majority had other caring responsibilities during the holiday period, for either elderly relatives or children who did not go on the holiday.

A holiday also provides lasting memories for the children and the adults:

> Tim had a picture taken with Bob the Builder, and that picture has the proudest place, it's paper thin now. He's always touching it, he's so proud of it. The parents are as well: we've taken them on courses and done things, and it's never that that comes up, it's always the memories of the holiday.
>
> (Welfare agent, UK)

Social networks

The social significance of the holidays, offering opportunities to meet and interact with new people, was a further benefit of the holidays, in contrast with the often limited social networks, which are a feature of participants' everyday lives.

One striking finding from the Irish study concerned the extent to which the children's geographical and social worlds were very limited, with little exposure to different areas, people and lifestyles. In contrast with their normally limited social worlds, on holiday, children encountered and engaged with children from other areas. The importance of 'making new friends' and reconnecting with friends made on previous holidays emerged strongly in both the pre- and post-holiday interviews. For several older children, obtaining mobile phone numbers and keeping in contact through texting and meeting up post-holiday was important:

> ... Made loads of new friends, we made friends with everyone down there ... I got all their numbers and we're meeting up Saturday in town.
>
> (Teenage girl, Ireland)

Often, the new friends lived in relative proximity, yet it was only through the intervention of the holiday that children managed to attain this modest broadening of their social worlds.

The families in the UK study also reported a feeling of exclusion and being alone. Meeting new people or strengthening ties with people the respondents already knew was often seen as an important benefit of the holiday. This benefit was most clearly achieved by the participants of group holidays: all of these reported to have extended their social networks and still to be in touch with other participants. The following volunteer highlights how important this aspect of the holiday was for the group he accompanied:

> Many are on benefits, they don't have many friends, other people are busy working so they don't even have time for them. So basically when they go on a holiday, they have this opportunity to make friends, to meet new people, to exchange addresses ... When they come back from the holiday, they can start from where they stopped.
>
> (Volunteer, UK)

Building self-esteem

The role of the holiday experience in building self-esteem, for both children and adults, was reported by both studies, as participants tried new things, were challenged in new (and appropriate) ways and developed confidence through new achievements.

Guardians in the Irish study identified the important role the holidays play in affirming self-worth and developing self-esteem as a key benefit identified by a majority of guardians. Significantly, the holidays studied constantly challenged the children in age- and socially appropriate ways, providing a very positive environment for the children to test their abilities and try new things, e.g. new activities, taking responsibility for/being a member of a team or acting as a mentor for the younger cohort. It should be noted that during the child-centred Irish holidays, a marked emphasis was placed on praising children, acknowledging and rewarding effort, and encouraging children to challenge themselves:

> ... Creates self-esteem and gives them courage to go out then with their friends instead of being bullied into the one place.
>
> (Guardian, Ireland)

In addition, for some children at least, participating in the holiday functioned as an important social statement, as it meant they were not excluded from the shared reporting of summer holiday activities that marks the return to school:

> So you can tell them about it ... normally we would just be sitting there ... yeah, you want to be saying ah I did this ...'
>
> (Teenage boy, Ireland)

The UK findings, meanwhile, show that social tourism can indeed boost self-esteem in certain cases, but that in other cases the low self-confidence of the participants makes it hard to enjoy certain aspects of the holiday.

Where individual holidays have positively influenced self-esteem, the participants have often described a sense of achievement of 'having done it alone'. One of the welfare agents for example described how she called one of her clients on the first day of the holiday and she proudly announced she had managed the train ride there without problems. Another welfare agent gave the example of a mother whose son has behavioural problems and whose confidence as a parent increased a lot on holiday:

> She was quite concerned about his behaviour before she went, 'what will I do with him when he starts in public'. I said 'do exactly the same as you are doing now with him', and she has actually got the confidence to take that forward now, if he screams in a supermarket, so what, she is really quite positive about that you know. If she can manage to take this child away and cope with him in front of all these holiday-makers, Asda or Tesco is not a problem then.

(Welfare agent, UK)

For some vulnerable participants, having to cope alone in an unfamiliar environment can cause anxiousness. For one respondent, a single father who was struggling before the holiday to find confidence as a parent, a holiday alone with three children to look after just proved too stressful. He saw the holiday as an attack on his self-esteem and came back more stressed. This indicates that finding the right holiday for the right family is an integral part of the holiday process if the holiday is to have positive outcomes for the family. Putting families through situations that are too challenging for them might hurt their self-confidence instead of boosting it. The right level of challenge needs to be found for the experience to be a positive and empowering one. This view is adequately expressed by one of the welfare agents:

> Without preparation and a bit of research into what they get when they finally get there, it

could be quite daunting for some families. I think it can take you back. Holidays are there to make you move on.

(Welfare agent, UK)

Acquiring and developing new skills

Both studies attest that the holidaying experience can provide opportunities to try new activities, learn new things and acquire new skills, challenging participants and leading to increased independence.

For the majority of children in the Irish study, opportunities to try out a range of new activities were central to the enjoyment of the holiday. Significantly, many of the activities provided opportunities for the children to take risks, to challenge and test themselves in controlled and appropriate contexts, in contrast with the home environments, which promote tendencies to engage in inappropriate risk-taking behaviour:

> ... All the different things, rock climbing and canoeing, even though I can't swim, trying new things.

(Teenage boy, Ireland)

Allied to this was the frequent suggestion from guardians that going on holidays encouraged children to develop a series of appropriate skills connected to self-reliance, independence and responsibility. The holiday experience was useful in helping children to develop maturity suitable to their age, to become more confident, to express themselves more clearly and to develop social interaction skills.

The UK study also showed that a holiday can provide opportunities for engaging in new activities and learning new skills. For many respondents, this was the first holiday in their life or in their adult life, so the holiday itself was a new experience. This holiday needed to be booked, suitcases needed to be packed and travel organized. For a large group of the respondents, these were new or fairly new activities, and this can thus be seen as a learning opportunity for new skills. The welfare agents often reported the families had increased their independence and skills by going away:

> You've got to book the holiday. And in an area like this, people are not used to doing things like that, they are used to having everything done for them. They go to Social Services if they run out of money saying 'my washing machine has cracked up, you've got to get me a new one'. They are not used to having a look around and finding the best buy and saving up for it ... it's quite a challenge.
>
> (Welfare agent, UK)

Behaviour change

Following the holiday, both studies report behaviour change of varying levels, with the semi-longitudinal nature of the UK study revealing greater levels of behavioural change. None the less, guardians in the Irish study, which focused on child well-being at a point in time, reported levels of positive behavioural change in their children post-holiday. Without exception, guardians thought the holiday had done their children a lot of good and considered their children to be 'happy', 'excited', 'in great form', 'more alive', to have 'come out of themselves' and to be 'just full of themselves'. Some children were reported to have come home 'more relaxed' and manageable:

> ... Settled him down ... he can be bold.
>
> (Guardian, Ireland)

A number of guardians reported that their children were acting more responsibly, helping more around the house and so forth. Interestingly, a few guardians acknowledged their own need to learn to give their children more independence – the provision of the holiday facilitated a modest 'letting go' of their children, in a way that was mutually beneficial.

In the UK study, it was found that the motivational quality of the holiday could, when adequate support was available, result in observable behaviour change. This effect was mainly reported in the longer term, 6 months after the holiday, by about half of the respondents. The research showed that holidays can change the aspirations of the participants and motivate them to achieve goals that appeared out of reach before. The following quotes are examples:

> The holiday gives them a little taste of what it could be like.
>
> (Welfare agent, UK)

> And with having had the holiday last year it's helped me ... I enjoyed it that much that it's helped me. It's shown me that if I want something I have to work hard and save for it.
>
> (Parent, UK)

This motivation was found potentially to lead to observable behaviour change on different levels. Many participants for example got a lot more involved in their support organization and enrolled for courses or one-to-one support. These opportunities were available to them before the holiday, but it was only after the holiday that they were taken up.

Two of the respondents in the UK study worked and both changed jobs following the holiday. One changed to a more flexible job, which allowed her to spend more time with her autistic son. The other respondent opened her own business. Several others drastically changed their budgeting habits. The main motivation behind this was the desire to save up for another holiday:

> I also think this budgeting thing ... they are so much more sorted with it. They know to get this, they need to do this, this and this. Whereas before it was waiting for either a cheque from somewhere or a rebate from somewhere. Whereas now, they know that if they want the holiday, they have to cut back here, or budget their shopping budgets, so it's definitely helped them. They haven't still physically got more money, they are just managing it better.
>
> (Welfare agent, UK)

To achieve drastic behaviour changes like these, the support from the welfare agent is a crucial factor: only in the cases where they had followed up the holiday with this support, these changes were achieved. This support can mean helping the family:

- before the holiday (packing, transport, financial planning, activities, choice of holiday type);
- during the holiday (in the case where welfare agents took a group on holiday); and
- after the holiday (helping participants to change certain areas of life).

Which level of change is 'adequate' depends on the individual participants, their skills and independence levels. This means that there is no one 'suitable' holiday format for social tourism: participants with great levels of independence may happily go on an individual holiday, whereas more vulnerable participants may benefit more from a supported group holiday.

different holiday types and participants (children-only versus family holidays) and were carried out independently. It was found in both cases that the holiday, as an opportunity for getting away from the home environment and its related lack of stimulation, can serve as a basis for personal and family development. This development can take different forms: a strengthening of the family unit; an increase in self-esteem or social contacts; learning new skills; and other forms of behaviour change. Examples of these benefits can be found in all respondent groups, from children of low-income backgrounds to families affected by human immunodeficiency virus (HIV) and from families that had suffered from domestic violence to guardians for children with disabilities. It is argued that such benefits, if harnessed, have the potential to have a knock-on positive impact on the community and society as a whole.

Conclusions

Social implications

The two studies presented in this chapter highlight the value of social tourism for low-income groups as being more than 'just a break away'. Each of the studies examined

Economic implications

Detailed cost-benefit analyses of social tourism are scarce at present and more

Summary Table: Comparable Empirical Social Tourism Benefits – Ireland and the UK

Impacts		Irish Study	UK Study
Break from routine and home environment	Safety and security concerns	*	*
	Boredom	*	*
Family benefits	Improved family relationships	*	*
	Improved family communication	*	*
	Relieved guilt of guardian in providing for family needs	*	*
	Lasting memories	*	*
Social networks	Broadening social world	*	*
	Meeting new people, extend social networks	*	*
Building self esteem	Opportunity to try new things	*	*
	Challenged in new and appropriate ways	*	*
	Develop confidence through new achievements	*	*
Acquiring and developing new skills	Opportunity to try new activities	*	*
	Opportunity to learn new things	*	*
	Opportunity to acquire new skills	*	*
Behaviour change	Positive behaviour change	*	*
	Behavioural change in the longer term, because of changed aspirations and goals[7]		*

research is needed to explore the impacts on revenue and employment generation in greater depth. European examples show that the sector can make significant contributions to employment and economic development, through an extension of the tourism season and tourism development in economically disadvantaged areas. The Spanish IMSERSO programme, for example, which subsidized holidays for older people outside the peak season with public funds, shows that social tourism can be economically sustainable. The Spanish State invests about €75 million annually in the programme, but through various tax mechanisms (VAT, tax on commercial and professional activities, corporate profits and income of physical persons), increased revenue from social security contributions and savings on unemployment benefits, the programme brings in some €125 million and is therefore economically highly profitable. Costs are recouped at a rate of €1.70 for every €1 invested in the programme (EESC, 2006).

Policy implications

On the basis of these results, social tourism can be presented as a potential measure to improve the quality of life of those living in poverty and reduce certain forms of social exclusion. Its apparent cost-effectiveness, when comparing the range of benefits a social holiday can bring with the rather limited cost of provision, also supports the argument for the inclusion of social tourism into public policy, as is already the case for many countries in mainland Europe. Being a positive measure, it has the ability to reach groups that are not usually involved in many of the support opportunities that are available to them and it can provide the motivation to change their situation. As with social supports in general, the manner in which social tourism holidays are provided is as important as the existence of provision itself, if not more so. It is essential that social tourism provision is appropriate to

the needs of the individual/family and achieves overall 'fit' within the context of other supports and services available to the recipient. In order to maximize the positive contribution of social tourism initiatives to the widest constituency of those experiencing poverty and social exclusion, the current provision in Ireland and the UK, which is dominated by the non-commercial private (charity/voluntary) sector, needs to be bolstered by greater support and involvement by both the public sector and the tourism industry itself, to facilitate an environment of 'tourism for all'.

Discussion Questions

1. Do you feel a holiday is a luxury or a right? Do you think governmental investment in social tourism is a justified use of public money?
2. Why do you think tourism is seen by the European Union as particularly meaningful and a right for all its citizens? What makes a holiday different from other products that people on low incomes often cannot afford, such as an MP3 player or plasma TV?
3. Social tourism is about more than lack of money – consider the range of factors that prevent individuals from accessing a holiday. How might the tourism sector in your area support and promote social tourism initiatives to the benefit of the tourism business and the wider economy and society?

Notes

[1] Agence National Chéques Vacances is a national organization established in 1982 which facilitates access to holidays for employees through the distribution of 'holiday cheques'.
[2] Spanish Ministry of Health and Social Policy Institute of Older People and Social Services.
[3] The Irish research was funded by the Combat Poverty Agency Policy Research Initiative.
[4] 'Young' boy/girl refers to children between ages of 7–12 years in Irish study.
[5] 'Teenage' boy/girl refers to children aged 13–15 years in Irish study.

[6]In the Irish study, prizes were distributed during the holiday on the basis of participation as much as success, and a conscious effort was made to ensure that all children won a prize.

[7]Observable only in the UK study because of its longitudinal nature, while the Irish study focused on a point in time.

References

Baum, T. (2006) Low-cost air travel: social inclusion or social exclusion? *Tourism, Culture & Communication* 7, 49–56.

Bureau International du Tourisme Social (2002) *Statutes*. BITS, Brussels.

Brimacombe, M. (2003) Wish you were here? *New Start Magazine*. http://www.newstartmaga.co.uk.

Cohen, S. and Taylor, L. (1992) *Escape Attempts: The Theory and Practice of Resistance to Everyday Life*. Routledge, London.

Collins, M. (2006) Exploring the experience and nature of deprivation in a disadvantaged urban community: a socially perceived necessities approach. Paper presented to the Combat Poverty Agency Research Seminar Series, 28 June, Dublin.

Corlyon, J. and La Placa, V. (2006) *Holidays for Families in Need: Policies and Practice in the UK – Final Report to the Family Holiday Association*. Policy Research Bureau, London.

Cser, Á. (2006) The role of trade unions in the social politic of tourism and in the introduction of the holiday checks at the places of work. Paper presented at the Tourism for All Conference, 17 January, Brussels.

Davidson, P. (1996) The holiday and work experience of young women with children. *Leisure Studies* 15, 9–103.

Dawson, D. (1988) Leisure and the definition of poverty. *Leisure Studies* 15, 89–103.

ETB (English Tourist Board) (1976) *Holidays: The Social Need*. ETB, London.

ETB (1985) *Holiday Motivations – Special Report*. ETB, London.

ETB (1989) *Tourism for All: a report of the working party chaired by Mary Baker*. ETB, London.

ETC (English Tourism Council) (2000) *Just what the Doctor Ordered*. English Tourism Council, London.

Eurobarometer (1998) *Europeans and their Holidays*. European Commission DG XXIII Enterprise policy, Distributive Trades, Tourism and Cooperatives, Brussels.

European Commission (2001) Outcome of the European Ministerial Conference 'Tourism for All'. http://europa.eu.int/comm./enterprise/services/tourism/policy-areas/bruges_conference.htm (accessed 25 May 2006).

EESC (European Economic and Social Committee) (2003) Socially sustainable tourism for everyone. *Opinion INT/173*, 29 October. EESC, Brussels.

EESC (2006) *Barcelona Declaration: Social Tourism in Europe*. EESC, Brussels.

Eurostat (2005) Material deprivation in the EU. *Statistics in Focus* 21/2005. Eurostat, Luxembourg.

Ghate, D. and Hazel, N. (2002) *Parenting in Poor Environments: Stress, Support and Coping*. Jessica Kinglsey, London.

Gilbert, D. and Abdullah, J. (2002) Holiday taking and the sense of wellbeing. *Annals of Tourism Research* 31, 103–121.

Gordon, D., Levitas, R., Pantazis, C., Patsios, D., Payne, S., Townsend, P., Ademan, L., Ashworth, K., Middleton, S., Bradshaw, J. and Williams, J. (2000) *Poverty and Social Exclusion in Britain*. Joseph Rowntree Foundation, London.

Hall, C.M. (2000) *Tourism Planning. Policies, Processes and Relationships*. Prentice Hall, Harlow.

Haukeland, J. (1990) Non-travellers: the flip side of motivations. *Annals of Tourism Research* 17, 172–184.

Hazel, N. (2005) Holidays for children and families in need: an exploration of the research and policy context for social tourism in the UK. *Children & Society* 19, 225–236.

Hobson, J.S.P. and Dietrich, U.C. (1994) Tourism, health and quality of life: challenging the responsibility of using the traditional tenets of sun, sea, sand and sex in tourism marketing. *Journal of Travel and Tourism Marketing* 3, 21–38.

Hughes, H. (1991) Holidays and the economically disadvantaged. *Tourism Management* 12, 193–196.

Jolin, L. (2004) L'ambition du Tourisme Social: un Tourisme pour Tous, Durable et Solidaire. http://www.bits-int.org (accessed 26 May 2006).

Lewis, E. (2001) *Evaluation of the Benefits of Recreational Holidays for Young People in Public Care*. The National Children's Bureau, London.

Mack, J. and Lansey, S. (1985) *Poor Britain*. George Allen and Unwin, London.

Mannell, R.C. and Iso-Ahola, S.E. (1987) Psychological nature of leisure and tourism experience. *Annals of Tourism Research* 14, 314–331.

Oppenheim, C. (1990) *Poverty: the Facts*. Child Poverty Action Group, London.

Pimlott, J.A.R. (1976) *The Englishman's Holiday: A Social History*. Harvester Press, Hassocks.

Richards, G. (1998) Time for a holiday? Social rights and international tourism consumption. *Time and Society* 7, 145–160.

Rodgers, G., Gore, C. and Figueredo, J. (eds) (1995) *Social Exclusion: Rhetoric, Reality, Responses*. International Institute for Labour Studies, Geneva.

Seaton, A.V. (1992) Social stratification in tourism choice and experience since the war: Part 1. *Tourism Management* 13, 106–111.

Shaw, G. and Williams, A. (2002) *Critical Issues in Tourism: a Geographical Perspective*. Blackwell Publishing, Oxford.

Smith, V. (1998) The relationship between poverty, holiday taking and social policy (with specific reference to low-income families). PhD thesis, Manchester Metropolitan University.

Smith, V. and Hughes, H. (1999) Disadvantaged families and the meaning of the holiday. *International Journal of Tourism Research* 1, 123–133.

Temowetsky, G.W. (1983) Holiday taking and socio-economic status in Australia. *Leisure Studies* 2, 31–44.

Thurot, J. and Thurot, G. (1983) The ideology of class and tourism – confronting the discourse of advertising. *Annals of Tourism Research* 10, 173–190.

Townsend, P. (1979) *Poverty in the United Kingdom*. University of California Press, Berkeley.

United Nations (1948) *Universal Declaration of Human Rights*. United Nations General Assembly, Paris.

United Nations (1966) *International Covenant on Economic, Social and Cultural Rights*. United Nations General Assembly, Paris.

Van Raaji, W.F. and Francken, D.A. (1984) Vacation decisions, activities and satisfaction. *Annals of Tourism Research* 11, 101–112.

Voysey, K. (2000) *Just What the Doctor Ordered – the Benefits of Taking Holidays*. English Tourism Council, London.

Wigfall, V. (2004) *Turning Lives Around: Evaluation Report of Family Breaks Pilot Project for Family Holiday Association*. Report for the Family Holiday Association, London.

World Tourism Organization (1980) *Manila Declaration on the Social Impacts of Tourism*. United Nations World Tourism Organization, Madrid.

World Tourism Organization (1999) *Global Code of Ethics for Tourism*. United Nations World Tourism Organization, Madrid.

9 Tourism and Welfare: Ethics, Responsibility and Well-being

Derek Hall and Frances Brown

Introduction

This chapter aims both to highlight some of the welfare dimensions of tourism and to suggest ways in which welfare can become a more important focus of tourism study, particularly through an emphasis on social responsibility. It looks at examples of welfare as applying to tourists, tourism destinations and tourism employees. Conclusions are drawn from this, and final questions posed.

Taking a 'welfare approach' to a study of tourism can help us to:

- focus on the distribution of benefits and dis-benefits resulting from tourism activity;
- identify where ethical and practical responsibilities in tourism development lie;
- highlight power relationships that underlie such responsibilities within tourism; and
- appreciate the wider, fragmented context within which tourism development processes take place.

In doing this, we hope to complement the sustainability debate in tourism. A number of critics of tourism and sustainable development, and of 'sustainable tourism' have argued that the sustainability debate may be a diversion. It is a diversion from acknowledging that mass tourism, far from fading, is growing, and that focusing on enhancing its benefits and reducing its negative impacts would be time and effort better spent. This does, however, assume that the continued growth of global tourism is, or can be, welfare-positive, which is a far from easy assumption to make.

'Welfare', as a concept and concern, is applicable to both mass and 'alternative' forms of tourism and their implications. In this sense, it is 'mode blind' and as such helps to draw us away from the divisive debates on the nature, applicability and value of 'sustainable' forms of tourism. There is a need to (re-)focus the debate on the impacts, (dis-)benefits and implications of tourism development more firmly upon:

- the ethical dilemmas behind individual and collective actions and behaviour;
- the nature and location of responsibility within (and affecting) the tourism sector; and
- the welfare trade-offs and outcomes of these.

This needs to be done while recognizing that tourism is part of wider social, economic, political, ecological and cultural processes. This means that it may be difficult and sometimes unrealistic to try to identify and isolate the specific influences and consequences of tourism development and activity from the outcomes of a wide range of other societal and environmental change processes.

Thus this chapter also highlights the need to recognize, accommodate and address the various trade-offs that tourism development processes incur. It emphasizes how attempts to increase the welfare of one set of participants may negatively affect the welfare of another. At the same time, major trade-offs may often relate to, and be driven by, basic inequalities that derive from the wider international system of political and economic dependency relationships.

What Do We Mean by 'Welfare'?

'Welfare' is defined by the *Chambers Twentieth Century Dictionary* as a 'state of faring or doing well: freedom from calamity, etc.: enjoyment of health, etc.: prosperity'. It can be regarded as a quality of well-being, which can be maintained, enhanced or threatened by interaction with external agencies. In the case of tourism, such external agencies may embrace the mutual relationships of tourists, tourism employees and employers, resident populations and environments, and include a wide range of private, public, voluntary and partnership organizations and structures that directly and indirectly, wittingly and unwittingly, interact with tourism processes.

Ideas of welfare owe much to the philosophy of utilitarianism, which, in its classical form as advocated by Jeremy Bentham, suggested that, as individual welfare is tied to human happiness, so public policies should aim to achieve the greatest happiness of the greatest number. Within this philosophical approach, an act can be considered morally right if it results in providing more pleasure than pain in comparison with available alternatives. Yet utilitarianism has been criticized because it has been thought to be unable to consider social justice. If happiness is maximized for the greatest good for the greatest number, it is likely that it will be achieved to the exclusion or detriment of a minority who will not share such happiness, at least not to the same extent.

None the less, welfare economists have adopted utilitarian assumptions to argue that an optimization of (social) welfare can be reached when one person's well-being can be improved while rendering others' no worse off; or if the total welfare of society is sufficiently increased to compensate fully those members adversely affected. This is known as a 'Pareto optimum'.

But international tourism is:

- a symbol of relative development and wealth; and
- a component of globalization, global inequalities and resource consumption.

In these roles it can seem to turn utilitarianism on its head by trying – perhaps ethnocentrically – to maximize happiness for minority (developed world) tourists at the relative expense of the majority (less developed world) 'hosts'. There are usually winners and losers in tourism and tourism development. Trade-offs between sectoral dimensions – economic, cultural, political, ecological – and between and within groups of 'stakeholders' – tourists, tourism workers, host populations and local authorities – mean that the achievement of any optimum which benefits all is virtually impossible to achieve.

The well-being of contemporary (Western) society can be thought of in relation to three models:

- consumerism: where 'well-being' is derived from the quantity and variety of material goods to which consumers have access;
- welfare-statism: where 'well-being' is secured from the quantity (if not variety) of public goods and services citizens receive as a right; and
- ecowelfarism: where 'well-being' results, organically, from the quality of the relations between people and between people and the natural environment.

In the important relationship between welfare, well-being and sustainability, evidence suggests that when individuals are more secure financially – but not necessarily wealthier – they are more likely to care about the well-being of future generations and of the environment. Focusing social and development policy on well-being rather than on per capita consumption can have positive implications for sustainability (Gowdy, 2005). This is an important consideration for a welfare focus in tourism.

Where does that leave 'welfare'?

Despite these qualifications, 'welfare' is perhaps the least inadequate single-word term to express the qualities under discussion. 'Welfare' can encompass social, behavioural, medical, psychological, cultural, economic, political, environmental and moral dimensions, and raises questions of resources, relationships and identity. The key components of welfare relevant to tourism analysis can include:

- health/freedom from disease and ill-health;
- physical safety and security/freedom from physical harm;
- emotional and spiritual well-being/freedom from stress and anxiety;
- financial security/freedom from poverty;
- mutual respect and support/freedom from exploitation;
- a healthy environment/freedom from environmental deterioration;
- access to appropriate accommodation/housing provision; and
- access to other necessary services.

'Well-being' is a term that has been applied occasionally in the context of tourism development, relating to qualities of enjoyment, achievement, personal relations, liberty, health, security and meaningful work, and most of these are applicable within a welfare focus for tourism. The similar terms 'life chances' and 'sustainable livelihoods' have been popular in development literature.

The currently fashionable notion of 'wellness' – an holistic combination of well-being and fitness, of physical activity combined with relaxation of the mind and intellectual stimulus – has become a popular tourism 'niche'. It also represents a greater individual and social awareness of (the need for) physical and psychological health.

In developed countries, more attention is being paid to the concept of *quality of life* (QoL), within which notions of welfare are a central part. In their turn, leisure and tourism are important contributors to this concept, both in their own right, and through their relationships with welfare issues.

At an individual level, QoL may be influenced by both specific and general aspects of:

- education;
- changes in family life;
- (changes in) employment;
- crime;
- religion;
- the role of the media in society; and
- globalization.

QoL can be related to the degree and way in which fundamental human needs are satisfied. These needs can be grouped into nine categories (Max-Neef, 1992):

- subsistence;
- protection;
- affection;
- understanding;
- participation;
- leisure;
- creation (self-actualization);
- identity; and
- freedom.

Society changes, not in its fundamental needs, but in the way it wants to satisfy those needs, and in doing this has embraced tourism.

Traditional economic indicators are poor measures of welfare, and as a consequence a number of attempts have been made to develop composite QoL measures. The Human Development Index (HDI) employed by the United Nations Development Programme is one of the most widely applied examples. Such indicators have helped development decision makers to move away from the dominance of economic considerations and to recognize the importance of social dimensions of capital and capacity. Our use of the term 'welfare' is less comprehensive than QoL or HDI, if only because tourism does not embrace all of the aspects of development policy that employ such terms.

Tourism as Welfare?

Much comment on leisure and tourism adopts a productivist approach, whereby work is viewed as the prime need in human existence. As part of leisure, tourism is seen as supporting the organization of work by providing opportunities for rest and relaxation. But this perspective sees tourism as contributing marginally to the QoL.

Yet studies of the relationship between leisure and work indicate a growing willingness by us to exchange money for more (and better quality) leisure time. The apparent desire for increased leisure and tourism consumption represents a wider shift in the focus of consumption in 'developed' societies away from physical goods and toward services and experiences. This suggests that welfare can be viewed increasingly in relation to individuals' ability to gain access to such services and experiences. Leisure time in general, and holiday time in particular, is recognized as offering a central set of experiences that people value as part of their QoL.

But while tourism participation has increased markedly, so also has the recognition that there exist a number of structural constraints on access to this participation (as seen in part one of in this book). Access to travel opportunities is not equally distributed, either within or between different societies, but is structured and constrained by variations in disposable income, discretionary time availability, gender, (dis)ability, nationality and a range of societal and personal factors.

Discussions of tourism and travel motivations have examined a range of seeking and escaping behaviours. A traditional view is that individuals seek an optimal level of stimulation, or optimal arousal, between too little stimulation (boredom) and too much stimulation (stress). Yet rather than being separate, the motives of seeking and escaping can be incorporated into the same tourism experiences. 'Old' tourism motivations, such as rest and relaxation, are being overlain with (not so) 'new' motivations, such as education, skill acquisition, fitness, culture and nature.

Although beach tourism remains the dominant form of tourism in much of the world, including Europe, many people's holidays appear to be incorporating an increasing number of different functions, with tourists shoe-horning ever more activities into their vacation time. In the past, holidays may have been havens of rest, but today they are increasingly an extension of the busy consumption patterns that characterize many people's lifestyles: they have become individualized, mechanized and competitive.

Holidays can provide three types of welfare enhancement:

- physical and mental rest and relaxation;
- space for personal development and the pursuit of personal and social interests; and, more dubiously,
- as symbolic consumption, enhancing status.

The last two of these are embraced by the rapidly growing phenomenon of 'volunteer tourism', which is promoted as an altruistic and self-developmental experience. But critics of this type of activity suggest that the interaction of 'self' with the 'other' in different cultural contexts may not meet idealized expectations, particularly as much 'volunteer tourism' is undertaken by relatively inexperienced young adults from Western societies during their 'gap' year between school and university.

Is such activity the result of an increasingly guilt-ridden society, reflecting a moralization of tourism (Butcher, 2003) as a result of (particularly young people's) disillusionment with modern (Western) society? While Butcher sees this reflected in the new moral tourist's external search for community and spirituality in the cultural and environmental 'other', an equally important trend is tourists' search within themselves.

In this way, spa and health holidays, and the more recent popularity of 'wellness' and holistic tourism, represent one end of a spectrum of welfare-conscious tourism activities that focus on the self. Medical tourism, where individuals travel to a destination purely or predominantly for the purpose of medical treatment, including surgery, has perhaps become the most widely publicized type of such self-focussed niche tourism (e.g. Connell, 2006).

Tourism has always been seen as a process of self-regeneration as well as relaxation, education or indulgence, and the growth of holistic holidays as one dimension of wellness has been notable. Holistic retreats tend to offer combinations of therapies and counselling, pathways to spiritual development, creative enhancement, and many other routes to the reconciliation of body, mind and spirit. The growth of the holistic tourism sector suggests a reinforcement of, or even return to, the desire to focus on the self rather than on the 'other' (Wang, 1999), the latter having gained attention during the Enlightenment and through experiences of the 'grand tour' in the 18th and 19th centuries.

Stakeholders: Who Are We?

A focus on stakeholders and their responsibilities is important for a welfare-centred approach to tourism. 'Stakeholders' are any individual or group influencing or affected by collective objectives, in this case the pursuit and development of tourism. Thus tourism stakeholders include tourists, tourism employees, the residents of tourist destinations, the suppliers of goods and services for use in tourism, the media, supranational, national, regional and local administrations, enterprises and business associations. The mutual obligations and responsibilities that stakeholders hold should, in theory, help decisions result in socially responsible action.

Power is an important element of stakeholding, both in terms of mutual responsibilities, and in the ability to translate proposals into concrete action. The power to deliver action implies that those in a subordinate role accept the primacy of those who are dominant, as, for example, in the relationship between accommodation providers in a developing resort and multinational holiday travel companies.

Ultimately, we are all stakeholders, at least from an environmental perspective. The impact that tourism and travel is having on the planet, most notably as a contributor to climate change, affects us all. Those of us in the 'developed' world each carry a heavy individual and collective responsibility to modify drastically our resource-intensive consumptive behaviour, of which tourism and travel is a major component.

This is the logical response to the United Nations World Tourism Organization's (UNWTO) call for 'stakeholders' to implement its *Global Code of Ethics* principles that declare 'sustainability' to be at their heart. But, like it or not, the UNWTO's approach – even its conversion to notions of pro-poor tourism (see also Chapters 6 and 10 this volume) remains locked within an ethos based on profit-generating, industry-expanding intentions. And for many observers, especially those from less economically developed countries (LEDCs), a global ethics code represents little more than tinkering around the edges of a juggernaut in need of radical re-appraisal. To appreciate this a little more, we can go back to the eight 'fundamental truths about tourism' that Bob McKercher (1993) recognized almost two decades ago (Box 9.1). These were published at that time when there appeared to be a lack of interest in the underlying reasons for tourism's negative impacts.

Box 9.1. Summary of McKercher's 'fundamental truths about tourism'.

1. As an industrial activity, tourism consumes resources, creates waste and has specific infrastructure needs.

2. As a consumer of resources, it has the ability to over-consume resources.

3. Tourism, as a resource dependent industry must compete for scarce resources to ensure its survival.

4. Tourism is a private sector-dominated industry, with investment decisions being based predominantly on profit maximization.

5. Tourism is a multi-faceted industry, and as such, it is almost impossible to control.

6. Tourists are consumers, not anthropologists.

7. Tourism is entertainment.

8. Unlike other industrial activities, tourism generates income by importing clients rather than exporting its product.

Source: McKercher (1993: 7), modified by the present authors.

Recognizing and understanding these 'fundamental truths' could be important in developing future sustainable tourism policies. By accepting these truths as a condition of tourism development, planners, policy makers and industry leaders could begin to develop effective policies to minimize their impacts. Some years later, McKercher's approach was modified by David Fennell (2000) who put forward the idea of five paradoxes of tourism (Table 9.1).

Table 9.1. Fennell's 'five paradoxes of tourism'.

The paradoxes	Our comments
1. Many tourists want to relax, act differently than at home, and thus do not want to be bothered to consider their impacts, which they may not be able to see, or are not aware of, anyway	Most of the tourism industry would not disagree with that. Despite McKercher's 'fundamental truth' 6 (Box 9.1), we are frequently told that consumers are becoming more ethically aware and motivated. Is this wishful thinking? Does this expose the gap between what people say, to reinforce their preferred self-image, and what they actually do?
2. People holidaying away from home are likely to have an overall greater negative impact than if they stayed at home, yet tourism has been enshrined as a human right	Rights need to be balanced by responsibilities
3. Local people want the economic benefits of tourism, and even some of the benefits of cultural exchange … but could manage much better without the actual tourists	Not all 'local people' are likely to want both or even either of these, in any particular place. Such benefits, although most usually financial, may be cloaked in terms of 'cultural' or 'social enrichment'. Crude economic tools such as cost–benefit analysis cannot represent the subjective (non-economic) value of 'social enrichment' or indeed of 'cultural erosion'
4. Tourists, not being their usual work-a-day selves, are not in a mode to be appropriate role models, yet may offer, in this inappropriate, atypical mode, the only opportunity for particular culture contact for local peoples	The 'responsibility of travelling' needs to be taken seriously both by those who travel and those who facilitate such travel: this should include global environmental as well as cultural considerations. The tourism industry, both in source and destination regions, could take a greater responsibility for the welfare of destination residents in the face of tourist activity. How far have codes of behaviour/conduct gained credibility in 'mainstream' tourism?
5. The economic rewards from tourism are likely to be divisive and their benefits polarized within certain social, employment and spatially located groups within wider society	Tourism is no different from any other economic sector in this respect. No pure egalitarian society has ever been achieved outside a few small communes

Source: Fennell (2000: 67), modified and developed by the present authors.

While to many of us with the benefit of hindsight, McKercher's and Fennell's offerings may be stating the obvious, they do emphasize realities that are still often overlooked, forgotten or ignored, namely that tourism is:

- an imperfect vehicle for human and environmental welfare within an imperfect world;
- far from being a democratic activity, even though it is often viewed in tourist generating societies as representing liberal values of freedom and democracy (see Hall, this book); and
- a heavily politicized and political activity.

As Brian Wheeller (2005: 267) points out:

> the actual development of tourism – the necessary wheeling and dealing – takes place in the real world ... [far away from] ... the protected dream world of textbook theory ... The question of corruption and the levels of intensity to which it is practised are conveniently ignored in the supposedly 'holistic', yet somewhat arbitrary, sustainable tourism vacuum.

And John Swarbrooke puts this into a wider context (Swarbrooke, 2003: 5–6):

> There is also a growing debate about the relationship between businesses in the tourism industry and ... their staff, customers and investors. This debate ranges far and wide including everything from salary levels to food safety to honest financial reporting. This interest ... is, of course, not just limited to tourism; it is a general concern fuelled by the numerous business scandals seen around the world in recent years. It clearly underpins the rise in interest in the concept of corporate social responsibility.

While government has a role as interest protector, a 'hollowing out' of the state and the dispersal of power to a multiplicity of unelected and semi-governmental agencies and business interests involved in the often fragmented 'governance' of regions, societies and environments, has resulted in a 'democratic deficit'. This means that governments are less able to protect their citizens from exploitation. This raises important questions concerning the ethical underpinnings of tourism processes and location of responsibilities for stakeholders' welfare.

Welfare and Responsibility in Tourism

The global tourism industry is fiercely competitive and dominated by transnational corporations, mainly based in developed countries. These organizations hold substantial power over the various suppliers of the tourism product, potentially creating unequal exchange and power relationships. They are forced to compete through international mergers and acquisitions, and are able to survive on small margins because of substantial economies of scale. This results in continuous new product development and aggressive marketing through lower prices. The resulting instability of the sector makes it difficult for companies to plan for a more sustainable future. In these circumstances, 'taking steps to behave more responsibly has traditionally received a predictably low priority' (Miller, 2001: 590).

Corporate social responsibility (CSR) is about forging stronger links between business and society and seeing companies directly improving the business environment. Specifically, it is claimed to be 'a commitment by business to behave ethically and contribute to economic development while improving the quality of life of the workforce and their families as well as of the local community and society at large (World Business Council for Sustainable Development, quoted in Kalisch, 2000: 2). This would appear ideally suited to benefit the welfare of tourism industry stakeholders. But tourism businesses would argue that they are severely limited in the range of social responsibilities that they can realistically undertake. Many would argue that tourism companies are no different from any other business, and to expect them to follow codes of conduct or CRS requests is unrealistic unless financial advantage or good public relations are involved.

Some specialist tourism operators view with suspicion such terms as 'responsible' (which can falsely raise expectation) and 'ethical' (which can be vague). Yet tourism sustainability cannot be achieved unless corporate bodies take greater responsibility towards society in general. Poverty alleviation and social equity – key themes of this book – would thus seem to be central to CSR.

For such approaches to represent a fundamental re-evaluation of tourism's role in relation to global equity there needs to be an – as yet apparently unrealistic – significant commitment to directly address the structural causes of global inequity.

Can stakeholders and companies negotiate a responsible path or is there a need for independent or regulatory organizations to guide and exert pressure for tourism development to be pursued for the collective good (however defined)? The CSR literature claims that companies can learn to be inspired by their customers and other stakeholders, and should combine this inspiration with the confidence to take socially responsible products beyond niches and into the mainstream. Once these products are in the mainstream, we are told, the evidence shows that they are unlikely to be rejected, and other companies may well imitate them. But these aspirations are based on a number of questionable assumptions (Hall and Brown, 2006: 160).

Pro-poor and fair trade tourism should represent important elements in the CSR debate, where the emphasis has shifted from short-term 'doing good' to finding 'win-win' situations. A fourfold typology of CSR approaches (Table 9.2), developed in the US emphasizes the range of 'superficial' and 'deep' strategies that can be adopted under the CSR banner.

The tourism industry in many respects mirrors the way in which contemporary business organizations represent a wide range of forms, activities, linkages and senses of corporate ethos, from the highly rigid and bureaucratic to the highly flexible and ad hoc. Distinctions have been drawn between surface and deep approaches to ethics in understanding the difference between the rhetoric concerning ethics and actual business practice. A surface approach to ethics, which is associated with self-interest, will not promote ethical behaviour. A deep approach, motivated by the desire to do the right thing, does have the potential to do so. The difference between the rhetoric and business practice suggests that most businesses either intentionally or unintentionally adopt a surface approach to ethics.

Is it therefore the role of tourism academics and students to take this issue up and emphasize that a deep approach to ethical concern and behaviour in tourism processes is essential? David Fennell (2008) considers that there is so much more we can, and should, do.

Although profound questions face tourism businesses in the choice of social responsibilities they can realistically

Table 9.2. Approaches to CSR.

Minimalist	Philanthropic	Encompassing	Social Activist
• Basic stakeholder support	• Project specific	• Looks beyond the immediate business stakeholder group to the broader community	• Approach is the foundation of the business
• Addresses aspects that are human resource-oriented	• Related to specific issues relevant to the organization	• Embedded in company values and management style	• Business is a catalyst for change
• Tokenistic	• Donations and gifts	• Seeks to lead change	• Seeks to effect change in others
	• Seeks to change		

Sources: Locke (2003), Ashley and Heysom (2005), and Hall and Brown (2008).

undertake, it is important that a company should be able to be assessed against a number of criteria in order that its ethical position and sense of (social and environ- mental) responsibility can be determined. Such ethical benchmarking criteria are brought together in Table 9.3. But how can such benchmarking criteria be brought into

Table 9.3. Ethical benchmarking criteria for tourism companies.

Criterion	Issues
Access and equity considerations	• Can the company represent, facilitate and accommodate a wide range of disabilities?
	• What is the company's policy on maternity rights and childcare facilities?
	• Does the company pay men and women equally?
	• Is there positive discrimination in favour of any particular (minority or disadvantaged) group?
	• Is there an equitable promotions policy?
	• Does it have a scheme to monitor the number of people it recruits from traditionally disadvantaged sections of the population?
	• Does it positively encourage survival and physical access for such groups?
	• Are its premises accessible to the (variously) disabled?
Client rights	• Does the company fully respect the rights of its clients – tourists – as recognized by international conventions?
	• Does it endeavour to provide full and impartial information?
	• Does the company make available client surveys and questionnaire responses?
	• Does the company respond promptly and effectively to client complaints?
Employees' rights	• Does the company respect its employees' rights to belong to a trade union?
	• Is there a constructive dialogue with the workforce?
	• Does management receive disproportionate benefits?
	• Are employees asked to work unacceptably long hours?
	• Are employees asked to work in unhealthy conditions or are put at risk of physical or mental injury?
	• Does the company have a proportionate part-time and seasonal workforce complement?
	• Is there encouragement and support for employee mobility and advancement?
	• Is there an appropriate (re-)training scheme for employees?
Human rights	• Does the company trade with countries or organizations with a poor human rights record?
	• Does the company research how tourism planning and development processes are executed?
	• Does the company positively support the participation of local people in deciding the nature and scale of tourism developments?
Exploitation of developing countries	• Does the company exploit developing countries, for example, by driving down wage and price levels?
	• Does the company ring-fence employment roles in developing countries for Western nationals?
Environmental	• What is the company's attitude to local sourcing, energy saving, renewable energy and recycling, conservation, organic agriculture, pollution and climate change?
	• Does the company recognize its role in combating climate change? Does it have a positive climate change policy?
	• Does the company have ethical codes of environmental behaviour for its employees, sub-contractors and clients?
Animal welfare	• Does the company recognize and respect animal welfare and the avoidance of inflicting suffering on animals?
	• Does the company positively contribute towards species conservation?

Sources: Winch and Watson (1992), and Hall and Brown (2008).

a practical scheme, and by whom should it be implemented? It is well known that certification schemes tend to be beset with operational and philosophical problems (e.g. Jamal *et al.*, 2006).

During the early 1990s, the UN Commission on Sustainable Development called for 'voluntary initiatives' in support of sustainable tourism development that would 'preferably exceed' accepted standards. This offered an important external stimulus to action. Since then, the development of electronic communication, has meant that negative publicity, such as that in tourists' and employees' web blogs, can move businesses to act. Twenty operators (including TUI, Thomas Cook and Accor) established, with UNWTO support, a *Tour Operators Initiative for Sustainable Tourism Development* website (http://www.toinitiative.org) in 2001 to detail company case studies of claimed 'sustainable' and 'responsible' activity. At the time of writing (November 2009), 17 companies were explicitly associated with the website: these included three from Morocco and one each from Brazil, Lebanon and Pakistan. These feature under headings that include 'integrating sustainability into the tour operators' supply chain' and 'TOI pilots: cooperation with destinations' (based in Brazil, Croatia, the Dominican Republic and Turkey).

Miller's (2001) examination of the role of CSR in tourism found that smaller companies better understood the destinations to which they took their clients and so had a heightened awareness of destination issues and problems, even if they were not in the best position to provide solutions to them. Larger tour operators, more financially able to take remedial steps, were so removed from the destination that they often lacked awareness of the issues and problems found there. There were, of course, exceptions to this simplistic generalization.

Yet it is clear that tour operators need to monitor in greater depth company performance and provide accessible outcomes of such monitoring to validate their claims for destination responsibility. Few tour operators appear willing to take action without external pressure to do so.

Although market surveys repeatedly indicate that consumers regard the environment as an important consideration, the gap between what respondents idealize and their actual behaviour is often substantial. Thus views are held that destination marketing that promotes 'sustainable tourism' probably results in more business, while market advantage forces companies to improve their ethical performance.

Conversely, as more tourism companies see the need to adopt the marketing clothes of social responsibility, so the concept loses its ability to provide market advantage, merely preventing companies becoming uncompetitive, and may thus be seen as a necessary extra cost. In this way, the over- and indiscriminate use of 'social responsibility' in tourism business literature renders the concept relatively meaningless and leaves stakeholders justifiably cynical, in much the same way that 'sustainability' marketing may be viewed.

Codes of conduct

One earlier response to the criticisms of tourist and tourism company behaviour was the creation of codes of conduct or behaviour. Three general guiding principles emerged in these: understanding the culture visited, respecting and being sensitive to the host population, and treading softly on the host environment. Again, companies were able to emphasize how such codes were being applied to the behaviour of their clients while minimizing adoption within the realm of their own business conduct.

A wide range of critical issues surround such codes in tourism:

- their very numbers and indiscriminate application has devalued their intrinsic worth;
- better coordination of and consistency between codes is needed to avoid confusing and conflicting messages being communicated;
- there are few data available on their effectiveness;

- the ethical purpose of a code may be subordinated to the role of a marketing rather than monitoring tool;
- few codes offer measurable criteria or conform to a widely accepted set of standards; and, most obviously,
- the existence of a code is no guarantee of ethical behaviour.

Within the tourism industry, evidence suggests that codes of practice and conduct can be used to deflect responsibility from company management either to employees, or more especially to tourists. That is not to argue that tourists should be absolved of responsibility for their behaviour in destination environments. But it suggests that codes of behaviour drawn up for tourists (although often not by tourists nor with such 'stakeholder' representation) may reflect an element of lateral displacement of responsibility both from tourism companies and from host destination authorities.

This raises the question of how far tourism wields power in different places, and whether it can realistically be a force for improving global welfare. There appears to be a contradiction here:

- we are often told that tourism does not have a loud voice or strong representation in government in the tourism generating, usually most developed countries: 'tourism' is often located within different state departments and ministries in different countries, may be moved from one to another over time, or may not be represented in name at all; yet
- in LEDCs and regions where tourism may play a much more significant, even dominant, role in the local economy, the power and influence of tourism, derived externally and/or from within, may be substantial, as in the case of Barbados. Here tourism has been seen to get special treatment. This has included not being closely scrutinized for its potentially damaging environmental impacts. Pugh (2003) refers to this as 'symbolic power', where an outer impression of rational consensus may hide the effects of power working behind the scenes.

Tourism as Well-being?

The common assumption that holidays are beneficial for those taking them appears to be supported by such contentions that 95% of British doctors recommend holidays as an alternative to medication, especially when patients have stress-related ailments. Australian research has indicated that most people enjoy a lessening of tension and fatigue after the first 4 or 5 days of holiday. Yet we have seen in recent years a marked growth in concern about tourism and risk, accidents, ill-health, terrorism, safety and security. This might suggest the limited or questionable welfare value of taking a holiday. More realistically, it represents three trends in international and domestic tourism:

- Tourism continues to grow, while tourists and the tourism industry continue to seek out new destinations and activities, so that more people are travelling to more and different places while pursuing different activities in those places, seeking out more distant and 'exotic' (and therefore unfamiliar) environments: tourists are penetrating ever more cultures and environments alongside other globalizing processes.
- Although tourism has tended to be characterized as largely risk-averse, certain tourism and recreation activities, such as adventure tourism, are becoming potentially more dangerous as more less-skilled and less well-equipped participants seek to share what may be seen as lifestyle determining activities. Partly as a result, risk assessment and management have become important considerations to protect the operator as much as the tourist.
- Whether true or not, the world often appears to many as a more dangerous place to be travelling in. As such, considerations of safety and security, following major violent incidents involving forms of transport and centres of tourism, have risen dramatically in the list of priorities for the industry and the regulatory frameworks within which it operates.

There are several elements in the cycle of tourist experience that have clear welfare implications. A tourist 'welfare cycle' (Table 9.4) can be comprised of:

- preparation;
- anticipation;
- the experience of travel; transport and the journey;
- the destination experience; and
- post-holiday syndromes.

In this chapter, because of space constraints, we concentrate on the first of these elements, preparation.

Preparation of the tourist

Maximizing tourist welfare requires a realistic appreciation of the opportunities and potential threats any destination or experience might offer, and being suitably prepared – physically and mentally – for them. If holidays are to enhance, or to at least maintain, the welfare of those taking them, there follow important considerations:

- What are the welfare consequences of such tourist aspirations for the other stakeholders in tourism processes, including other tourists?

- How far do behavioural, structural and other circumstances of the tourism industry condition such welfare attainment?
- How far do potential tourists receive the reliable and impartial sources of information about conditions in destination countries that they need to optimize both their own welfare and that of those they encounter?

Individuals are exposed to risk constantly, whether working, at leisure in the home or on holiday, near or far. The 1989 Hague Declaration on Tourism states that the safety, security and protection of tourists and respect for their dignity are the precondition for the development of tourism. But there are particular factors relating to travel, and to being in a foreign environment, which make tourists particularly vulnerable, and which demand appropriate preparation:

- transport risks: travelling poses specific risks related to transport accidents, hi-jackings, contracting deep vein thrombosis (DVT) or driving while jet-lagged (especially on the 'wrong' side of the road compared to home experience);
- unfamiliar environments: finding themselves in a new environment can render

Table 9.4. Components of the tourist welfare cycle.

Cycle elements	Key factors	Key concepts	Implications
Preparation	Availability of information	Security, safety, health, risk	Travel company information and communication practices
Anticipation	Travelling companions	Well-being	This is a less well researched area of potential tourist welfare and may be dominated by hidden emotions
Travel	Mode, time, distance	Stress, deep vein thrombosis, flexibility	Can be made much less stressful Can be an important part of the tourist experience
The destination experience	Motivation, behaviour, activities	Common sense	Tourist responsibility is critical
Post-holiday syndromes	Reflection	Re-circulation, readjustment	Wider modification of destination perceptions Readjustment can raise questions concerning the quality of home and work life

Source: Hall and Brown (2006: 46).

tourists vulnerable to unfamiliar bacteria, climatic or traffic conditions (Lawton and Page, 1997);

- targeting of tourists: in some destinations, tourists may be targets for criminal or terrorist activity (Richter and Richter, 1999);
- unfamiliar language: safety warnings and health information in a foreign language create additional risks for tourists (Smith, 1999);
- unaccustomed activities: holiday-makers may engage in activities they are unused to, and that increase their vulnerability (Page *et al.*, 2005). These might be a component of the holiday (skiing or hiking) or an activity undertaken 'because you're on holiday', such as excessive sun exposure, binge drinking or unprotected sex. Excess alcohol consumption can increase other forms of risk such as vulnerability to crime (see *Safety and security*, below).

In light of these considerations, the tourism industry's responsibility for addressing welfare considerations, particularly in the period before tourists depart or even commit themselves to a holiday, is coming under increasing scrutiny, alongside the responsibilities of public policy-makers and tourists themselves. However, both the industry and policy-makers seem reluctant to engage in public discussions about the risks associated with particular destinations or elements of tourism. This is perhaps unsurprising given the economic value of the industry, and its importance as a generator of foreign exchange. In this context, taking responsibility can mean in practical terms:

- ensuring that an adequate medical health infrastructure is an integral element of the development of tourist areas;
- tour operators and local authorities stipulating and enforcing minimum hotel standards, not least through regular auditing;
- tourists taking sufficient responsibility in their holiday behaviour to ensure that they do not expose themselves to unnecessary risks; and

- the application of appropriate monitoring systems in the control of travel-related diseases.

Since tourism quality and visitor satisfaction are usually directly linked to the experience of a visit, there are important implications for destination image, promotion and the encouragement of repeat visits. Thus for the welfare of tourists and destinations, it would seem logical for the tourism industry to take responsibility for the provision of adequate advice to inform intending travellers of the potential hazards, risks and type of health experiences they may encounter in particular tourism environments, and which can ultimately affect their (longer-term) QoL.

The tourism industry can play an important part in informing tourists about risks to health and safety. However, given the vertical integration of the tourism industry and the ownership of many travel agencies in generating countries by the travel conglomerates, retail travel agents are required to sell preferred products quickly and efficiently. These include those that offer higher commissions or bonuses to agents, cross-promotions or other incentives, and of course holidays of their parent company. There is little incentive for them to alert customers to any health or other hazards present at their destination.

The literature on the quality of travel agent advice focuses on the one-way communication process between the agent and the consumer. But communication is a two-way exchange process. The ability of the individual to articulate his or her own needs effectively must also play a key role in the information exchange process, especially if that person has special needs. Disabled traveller respondents have reported great variability in the quality of service provided by different agencies, as well as among different staff within the same agency. In one study (McKercher *et al.*, 2003) a small number described positive experiences, but most expressed low confidence in the sector. Such a failure to provide an adequate service directly affects the ability of tourists with disabilities to participate fully in travel (see also Chapter 1, this book).

A great deal of reassurance or uncertainty can rest with the quality and quantity of travel documentation provided. At least partly because of the perceived vacuum of information, some independent commercial organizations provide a health information service to potential travellers. The UK Medical Advisory Services for Travellers Abroad (MASTA, http://www.masta.org.uk), for example, runs a travellers' health line telephone service and website, travel shops and clinics, and produces a free guide to malaria protection which is distributed through a major pharmaceutical retailing chain. A Scottish Executive-supported public access website, www.fitfortravel.scot.nhs.uk, has been available for some time providing travel health information for people travelling from the UK. In 2003, a UK government-sponsored National Travel Health Network and Centre was opened in London to provide a public health and specialist travel health service, albeit exclusively to health professionals.

Social networks and social position are also significant in overcoming the information deficit. Information from friends and relatives, although low in credibility compared with more formal sources, can be more comprehensive. Research has suggested that tourists with higher levels of education will employ more information sources.

Industry concerns for tourist health and safety have tended to be reactive, and in response to large and newsworthy incidents or health scares. Such incidents, although serious in terms of their potential consequences, may be rare. But they may be temporarily highlighted by the media's propensity to focus on a dramatic event and then to move on to others before the first has been concluded: the *issue attention cycle* (e.g. Hall, 2002). In this way, when tourism risks are discussed, it is the newsworthiness of the risk and its consequences, more than the probabilities and outcomes involved, which may drive the debate.

At governmental level, the intricate and often hidden relationships between tourism (and trade) and politics (and international relations) that influence the provision of information, advice and support are not always favourable to tourism. National governments may impose travel restrictions on their citizens for economic reasons, such as temporary limits on the amount of money that an individual can take out of the country, or ideological, as in the US embargo on Cuba. In the case of visa or immigration restrictions on incoming tourists, they may result from broader policy decisions.

Political instability in destination areas, as a factor influencing tourist flows, may stimulate governments in tourism-generating countries to issue warnings or advice to potential tourists about travel to such destinations. For example, the US State Department issues detailed and up-to-date travel advice to tourists through its Citizens Emergency Center, and the Travel Advice Unit of the British Foreign and Commonwealth Office (FCO) advises tourists about potential political, health and other problems in over 100 different countries. In 2004, the FCO established a standing advisory council representing tourism stakeholders to help inform the production of its travel advisories, following a campaign from the pressure group Tourism Concern to ensure fair and balanced travel advice.

Such official advice varies in strength from precautionary to virtual bans on travel, the officially stated overriding concern being the health and security of the government's nationals abroad. Notionally this is an important and possibly vital welfare component of tourist preparation, which suggests that the issuing of travel advice should be non-political. However, the potential exists through travel advice for the governments of tourism-generating countries to influence, and disrupt, the structure and flow of international tourism, and thereby to exert economic and political pressure on destination countries (e.g. Sharpley *et al.*, 1996; Cole, 2008).

Government advice – perhaps transmitted via intermediary agencies – may be just one, albeit crucial, element in deterring tourists from travelling to particular intended destinations. But the presence of risk aversion behaviour in relation to the gathering of information by intending tourists before a trip has long been recognized. For example, an examination of the attitudes towards travel health risks held by (UK) international travellers attending a specialist travel clinic in Glasgow (Carter, 1998) found that:

- Europe and North America were perceived as safe;
- Africa was seen as dangerous and to be avoided; and
- Asia was constructed as simultaneously risky but also exotic and worth experiencing.

These travellers' accounts perceived danger within Africa as 'linked to random events beyond the control of the individual, such as blood transfusions'. By contrast, the dangers that travellers associated with Asia were perceived as more 'controllable', with two caveats: sexual contact should be avoided and food consumed with care. Through such acts of personal responsibility, travellers thought that the region could be 'made safe'. Yet for some male travellers these apparent gross stereotypes of place were further reinforced by the stereotyping of Eastern women in terms of their representing 'dangerous sexuality'.

Previous research had indicated that business travellers were more likely to have new sexual contacts than other tourists, and that these contacts were most often drawn from the host population of the region being visited rather than from among other travellers. Yet the scope for the uptake of health promotion aimed at modifying sexual behaviour in this group may be limited by the very ambivalence of these beliefs, particularly that of perceived sexual risk as being a passive threat almost 'beyond' their control. This would seem to highlight the need for sensitive pre-travel health promotional material that is targeted especially at business travellers. Such

materials should express awareness of the possibly complex interactions between the social construction of risky locations and likely eventual behaviour while visiting these areas. Understanding the underlying moral codes of different (mobile) occupation groups and classes could also be instructive.

The fact that travellers readily produced similar social constructions supported the view that an image is attached to 'regions', such as Africa, that culturally associates them with ideas of danger and ill-health for people in the West. This should be of some concern to governments and the travel industry promoting travel to locations outside North America and Europe.

More importantly, the cultural meanings given to the health threats of remote places is a dynamic process, and this needs to be taken into account in the preparation of information for travellers. If done successfully, travellers can be in a better position to minimize risks in the knowledge that they are not reinforcing existing myths liable to damage distant countries' images (and economies).

Welfare Considerations for the Destination

Those involved in developing tourism need to pay special attention to the ways that it can benefit destination resident populations. A welfare-centred approach to the question of tourism destinations, their residents and employees can assist an evaluation of the benefits and dis-benefits, the trade-offs between them and between residents and those involved in tourism.

The role and significance of tourism varies considerably within and between different local areas, and tourism interacts with other aspects of a destination's development sectors in diverse ways. Within this context, a focus is placed upon the ethical nature of interactions between the major tourism actors within the destination, with trade-offs, competitive and complementary roles being examined.

Crime at the destination is addressed in this context. An example of tourism employee welfare is then evaluated through the specific case of employment in the cruise line industry.

Drawing on a wide interpretation of 'destination resident' to include those working in the destination but not living there, we can recognize five types of 'states of (well-)being' that residents may experience in relation to tourism-related activities. These can be designated:

- *Competitive*, where residents, tourism workers and tourists compete for spatial and social resources, such as transport, including road and parking space, water and other natural resources, accommodation and property.
- *Complementary*, whereby the activities of tourists and the tourism industry complement those of residents, for example offering appropriate employment opportunities, helping to raise local skill levels or enhancing the quality of and access to local amenities.
- *Complicit*, where the values and aspirations of residents and mass tourism would appear to converge in opposition to external (often environmental) values, as in the case of the Akamas peninsula in Cyprus, where locals, including land owners and developers wanted to share the perceived benefits of mass tourism in opposition to environmental conservationists and governmental muddled thinking on 'sustainable tourism' (Ioannides, 1995).
- *Subverted*, where destination residents' values and practices are undermined to the detriment of both their cultural and social welfare, for example as expressed through health and diet, although this may be an inseparable part of wider processes of social and economic change, such as the spread of 'fast food' and an increase in obesity recognized in many 'developed' and 'developing' economies.
- *Subordinate*, whereby destination residents are explicitly subordinated to the tourism industry and may be unable to

express a dissenting voice to its presence and practices, as suggested for Barbados (Pugh, 2003).

In practice, of course, these categories may overlap and merge; situations are fluid, changing over time, and whether or not considered a 'community', residents' welfare interests and values can be far from uniform and consensual.

Safety and security

Specifically in relation to crime in tourism destination areas, much attention has been paid to tourists' experiences and fears, but much less to residents' experiences. According to earlier (particularly US) research, tourist areas appeared to suffer disproportionate amounts of crime, and within such areas tourists appeared be victimized more frequently than local residents. Reasons suggested for this included the fact that tourists are seen as an easy target – they may typically carry more than usual sums of money (although use of credit cards and hotel safe boxes might be thought to obviate this). They may also engage in 'risky' behaviours, may be ignorant of local languages, signs and customs, and lack local support groups.

There are two problematic issues here: different modes of crime exist, and tourism is difficult to isolate as an independent variable. Within tourism destination areas, five overlapping categories of crimes can be recognized:

- activities directed against tourists: the perpetrators may be local residents, tourism workers, criminals attracted to the area by tourism, or other tourists themselves;
- crimes committed by tourists: these may be aimed at residents, tourism workers or fellow tourists;
- crimes that occur through the illegal servicing of demands created by tourists;
- criminal activities, which relate to the growth and development of a destination

that has a tourist-dependent economic base; and

- criminal activity, which is independent of the nature of the tourist destination; most crime is directed against the resident population.

There are perhaps three basic reasons why it is often difficult actually to distinguish the influence of tourism, if any, on trends in crime and 'anti-social behaviour' in any particular place:

- tourism is part of wider social and economic development processes and often cannot be separated out: such processes may mask a significant or negligible tourism-related contribution;
- statistics are often poor, exacerbating the problem of identifying cause and effect; and
- conflicting trends tend to be reported from different destinations, for reasons possibly unclear because of the previous two factors.

For example, work in Queensland, Australia has resulted in mixed research findings (Prideaux, 1996). Reported crime rates in Cairns and the Gold Coast – both popular tourist centres – over a 10-year period suggested criminal activity had grown faster than the overall rate for the state as a whole and faster than population growth. By contrast, the Sunshine Coast, just 200 km north of the Gold Coast, with almost identical attractions, has had crime rates much lower than the state average. Two explanations have been put forward for this:

- Cairns and the Gold Coast have much higher levels of drug offences, and drug use is often associated with additional criminal activity; and
- promotional advertising for Cairns and the Gold Coast has often focused on images of semi-naked women and men, active nightlife and suggestions of uninhibited behaviour. The Sunshine Coast has not done this, and caters largely for families.

This emphasizes the need for destination residents to be able to take a more active part in decisions affecting the promotion and image formation of their home area in order to be able to influence tourism impacts on their own social and economic welfare. This is, of course, a long-recognized essential element of 'sustainable' tourism development.

When tourists' safety and security appear to be compromised, and particularly when this receives media attention, the knock-on effect of tourists' staying away can affect destination residents and workers substantially. The impacts of reduced levels of receipts and negative welfare implications for tourism workers may be felt both locally and nationally. Cooperation and coordination between local authorities and the tourism industry is vital in such circumstances. Yet when a high crime rate in New Orleans in the 1990s was clearly drawing attention and negative perceptions from potential tourists and conference planners, there was an apparent lack of tourism industry concern and cooperation in trying to overcome it. This severely hampered any alleviation of the situation, a fact not lost on the residents of that city.

The deterrent effect of conflict and civil unrest on tourism development is generally well documented. The rapid recovery of tourism economies following cessation of threatening activities has been noted in a range of destinations, including Cyprus, Sri Lanka and Northern Ireland. The supervision of media coverage of crisis and crisis management has become a core issue for tourism destinations. This was expressed when, following the bombing of a taxi-bus used by tourists and locals in the Turkish resort of Kusadasi, angry shop owners tried to prevent television news crews from filming the scene for fear that the negative images transmitted would discourage other tourists.

In Egypt, a 'self-induced' welfare threat to the tourism industry was emphasized by Aziz (1995), who argued that Muslim terrorist violence against tourists was a reaction to irresponsible tourism development. Safier (1994: 4) placed this within a wider context by arguing that 'when the forces making for inequality, division and disrespect reach a certain point, then the reactions can be correspondingly cumulative and ultimately dangerous to all'. As the globalization of tourism highlights, often unwittingly, social, economic and political inequalities, conflicts over resources and ethnic identity, the industry will need to express a tangible desire to maintain and enhance the welfare of destination environments. If not, the welfare of tourism and of those living, staying and working in tourism destinations will be threatened as they are held to ransom by those viewing the important economic role of tourism as a valid target through which to attack national governments, and as a symbol of dependent development through which to confront the current world order.

Working in Tourism

Because the welfare of tourism workers encompasses a range of issues in many different types of employment that contribute to the tourism experience, we have chosen just one sector where issues of inequality – stratification, race, class and income – are most common but may be rarely apparent to the tourist. This tourism sector is that of ocean cruise lines.

The welfare of tourism workers: cruise line employment

The pressure group Tourism Concern has pursued a number of campaigns for the improvement of the conditions of tourism workers (see Chapter 7). Examples of labour exploitation in tourism can include long working hours, unpaid overtime, overdependence on tips, stress, lack of secure contracts, poor training and lack of promotion opportunities for locally employed people.

While it is difficult to generalize from specific cases, certain sectors of the tourism and travel industry clearly depend upon low wage, informal, casual, part-time and intermittent labour sources, both in less developed and developed countries.

One important element of tourism's formal sector, dominated by ownership within the world's richest countries, is the ocean cruise line industry. Research into working conditions within this sector has been undertaken both by relatively dispassionate academics and by vested interests in labour unions. Their findings tend to be similar.

Ocean cruise tourism is a rapidly growing sector, and ocean cruise industry operations well exemplify major dimensions of globalization. The enormous scale of the ships symbolizes high concentrations of multinational capital. They spend much of their time in non-territorial waters, only briefly visiting favoured ports of call, and make cost savings by taking advantage of destinations that have cheap or low-tax fuel bunkering. Ocean cruise lines thus replicate the behaviour of land-based multinational corporations by driving down costs through playing off one low-cost, usually LEDCs, supplier against another.

Cruise ship crews may represent highly diverse labour forces originating from up to 50 countries on a large ship. Such globally recruited labour is usually stratified into three groups – officers, staff and crew – who have separate living quarters, segregated dining areas and different rules of engagement concerning interaction with passengers. They also enjoy vastly different pay levels, usually with a clear racial distinctiveness attached to the hierarchical divisions. The vast proportion – crew – are often drawn from LEDCs where pay rate expectations are low (e.g. Wood, 2004).

This pattern is found on most cruise lines, although some recruit more heavily from specific markets: Holland America Line, for example, relies heavily on Filipino and Indonesian crewmembers. Of the 114,000 who work on cruise ships around the world, about 70% are hotel/catering staff. They include the cabin stewards, bar staff, waiting staff, laundry workers, cleaners, chefs and kitchen crew, as well as receptionists and clerical staff. Also within this group are sound and light technicians, social hosts and play organizers for children. All of these are usually directly employed by the cruise lines, on fixed-term contracts, usually for between 6 and 10 months at a time.

A further 20% comprise the officers and crew who work in the deck and engine department. They include the greasers, fitters and mechanics, motormen, plumbers, deck cleaners and other non-officer ratings. Most of these are usually experienced seafarers whose working life is in the merchant marine, even if their repeat contracts are short. Other crewmembers, such as those working in the on-board shops, gyms, spas and beauty salons, or entertainers and musicians, are not the direct employees of the cruise companies but work for concessionaires or independent contractors.

Within these global and 'domestic' contexts, cruise line employees face a number of welfare-related issues. First, avoidance of national or international regulations is a major characteristic of cruise lines. 'Open registry', better known as the use of flags of convenience (FOCs), circumvents home country employment, wage, health, safety and environment laws, taxes and maritime regulations. Indeed, cruise development has been explicitly assisted by the climate of deregulation and availability of pools of flexible and cheap migrant labour. FOC ship crews are subject to the laws of the country in which the ship is flagged, and in most FOC countries, employment laws protecting the rights of workers are virtually non-existent.

This has been heightened by the fact that companies have responded to increasing competition by attempting to squeeze greater value from their workforce who may experience, for example, insecure, short-term contracts; low wages and high costs, including illegal agents' fees to get the job: money often has to be borrowed at high rates of interest, and if anything goes wrong with the contract, the cruise ship worker and his/her family may find themselves in a spiral of mounting debt; long working hours and high work intensity, leading to fatigue; poor management practices, including bullying and favouritism, racial and gender discrimination; high labour turnover, fatigue and inadequate training, giving cause for concern about safety; and employers who are hostile or resistant to trade union organization and collective bargaining (see also Chapter 7).

Royal Caribbean Cruise Lines, for example, although based in Florida, is registered as a Liberian corporation and it has been estimated that the company saves around US$30 million annually in avoiding payment of US taxes by registering its ships under FOCs. Such savings enable cruise ships to offer accommodation, meals and entertainment for substantially less than such a package would cost in most of the ports that they visit. In 2003, for example, North American Cruise Lines enjoyed a cabin occupancy rate of 95% compared with an average hotel room occupancy rate of only 59%.

Since '9/11', the FOC regime has come under closer global scrutiny. Long-existing campaigns against the system, waged notably by organized labour such as the International Transport Workers Federation (ITF) alongside campaigning NGOs such as War on Want, had previously achieved limited success, with just a few cruise ships signing agreements with the ITF. These agreements fall far short of negotiated union contracts – virtually the entire cruise sector being non-unionized – but seek voluntary compliance from companies in relation to the treatment of crew.

But emphasizing the interplay of global politics and economics with tourism welfare outcomes, China has been seeking access to overseas ship employment as a means of raising the country's maritime skills. By tapping a virtually inexhaustible source of cheap labour from the People's Republic, the cruise line industry could drive down crew wages and conditions even further.

Conclusion

In this chapter we have looked at some of the ways in which the concept of welfare can be applied in tourism to highlight inequalities, trade-offs, and winners and losers.

Although the tourism and travel sector, or at least various elements of it, has adopted notions of CSR and ethical codes of behaviour and conduct, these have tended to be superficial in their impact. The reality is that tourism is a business, or rather an enormous range of linked businesses, and welfare is still often seen as someone else's responsibility. As a consequence, the many gaps, shortcomings and inconsistencies that persist in the adoption of a responsible approach to tourism are detrimental to the welfare of tourism workers, destination residents and environ-ments, tourists and, of course, the tourism business sector itself.

Questions

1. Evaluate the major ways in which the concept of welfare can help us identify winners and losers in tourism development processes.
2. How far can individual tourism businesses pursue social responsibility and be financially successful?
3. Take two contrasting tourism products (e.g. a mass-market beach resort and an Amazon ecolodge): when examined through a welfare lens, which seems to provide the greatest good, and why?

References

Ashley, C. and Haysom, G. (2005) From Philanthropy to a Different Way of Doing Business: Strategies and Challenges in Integrating Pro-Poor Approaches into Tourism Business. ATLAS Africa, Pretoria. Available at: http://www.propoortourism.org.uk/Publications%20by%20partnership/propoor_business_ATLASpaper.pdf.
Aziz, H. (1995) Understanding attacks on tourists in Egypt. *Tourism Management* 16, 91–95.
Butcher, J. (2003) *The Moralisation of Tourism: Sun, Sand … and Saving the World?* Routledge, London.
Carter, S. (1998) Tourists' and travellers' social construction of Africa and Asia as risky locations. *Tourism Management* 19, 349–358.
Connell, J. (2006) Medical tourism: sea, sun, sand and … surgery. *Tourism Management* 27, 1093–1100.
Fennell, D.A. (2000) Tourism and applied ethics. *Tourism Recreation Research* 25, 59–69.
Fennell, D.A. (2008) Tourism ethics needs more than a surface approach. *Tourism Recreation Research* 33, 223–224.
Gowdy, J. (2005) Toward a new welfare economics for sustainability. *Ecological Economics* 53, 211–222.
Hall, C.M. (2002) Travel safety, terrorism and the media: the significance of the issue-attention cycle. *Current Issues in Tourism* 5, 458–466.
Hall, D. and Brown, F. (2006) *Tourism and Welfare: Ethics, Responsibility and Sustained Well-being.* CAB International, Wallingford, UK.
Hall, D. and Brown, F. (2008) The tourism industry's welfare responsibilities: an adequate response? *Tourism Recreation Research* 33, 213–218.
Ioannides, D. (1995) A flawed implementation of sustainable tourism: the experience of Akamas, Cyprus. *Tourism Management* 16, 583–592.
Jamal, T., Borges, M. and Stronza, A. (2006) The institutionalization of ecotourism: certification, cultural equity and praxis. *Journal of Ecotourism* 5, 145–175.
Kalisch, A. (2000) Corporate social responsibility in the tourism industry. *Fair Trade in Tourism Bulletin* 2, 1–4.
Lawton, G. and Page, S. (1997) Evaluating travel agents' provision of health advice to travellers. *Tourism Management* 18, 89–104.
Locke, R. (2003) *Note on Corporate Citizenship in a Global Economy.* Sloan School of Management and Department of Political Science, Massachussetts Institute of Technology, Boston, Massachusetts.
Max-Neef, M. (1992) Development and human needs. In: Elkins, P. and Max-Neef, M. (eds) *Real-life Economics: Understanding Wealth Creation.* Routledge, London and New York, pp. 81–102.
McKercher, B. (1993) Some fundamental truths about tourism: understanding tourism's social and environmental impacts. *Journal of Sustainable Tourism* 1, 6–16.

McKercher, B., Packer, T., Yau, M. and Lam, P. (2003) Travel agents: facilitators or inhibitors of travel for people with disabilities? *Tourism Management* 24, 465–474.

Miller, G. (2001) Corporate responsibility in the UK tourism industry. *Tourism Management* 22, 589–598.

Nalbantogly, G. (2005) Briton killed in Turkey terror blast. *The Sunday Herald (Glasgow)*, 17 July, pp. 1–2.

Page, S.J., Bentley, T. and Walker, L. (2005) Tourist safety in New Zealand and Scotland. *Annals of Tourism Research* 32, 150–166.

Prideaux, B. (1996) The tourism crime cycle. In: Pizam, A. and Mansfeld, Y. (eds) *Tourism, Crime and International Security Issues*. John Wiley & Sons, Chichester and New York, pp. 59–75.

Pugh, J. (2003) A consideration of some of the sociological mechanisms shaping the adoption of participatory planning in Barbados. In: Pugh, J. and Potter, R.B. (eds) *Participatory Planning in the Caribbean: Lessons from Practice*. Ashgate, Aldershot, pp. 118–137.

Richter, L.K. and Richter, W.L. (1999) Ethics challenges: health, safety and accessibility in international travel and tourism. *Public Personnel Management* 28, 595–615.

Safier, M. (1994) Potential and prospects for tourism in the world today. In Baskin, G. and Twite, R. (eds) *The Conversion of Dreams: Tourism in the Middle East*. Israel/Palestine Centre for Research and Information, Jerusalem, pp. 1–11.

Sharpley, R., Sharpley, J. and Adams, J. (1996) Travel advice or trade embargo? The impacts and implications of official travel advice. *Tourism Management* 17, 1–7.

Smith, G. (1999) Toward a United States policy on traveler safety and security: 1980–2000. *Journal of Travel Research* 38, 62–65.

Swarbrooke, J. (2003) Introduction. In: Swarbrooke, J., Smith, M. and Onderwater, L. (eds) *Quality of Life: ATLAS Reflections 2003*. ATLAS, Arnhem, pp. 5–7.

Wang, N. (1999) Rethinking authenticity in tourism experience. *Annals of Tourism Research* 26, 349–370.

Wheeler, B. (2005) Ecotourism/egotourism and development. In: Hall, C.M. and Boyd, S. (eds) *Nature-based Tourism in Peripheral Areas: Development or Disaster?* Channel View, Clevedon, pp. 263–272.

Winch, V. and Watson, R. (1992) *Responsibility in Business: Decisions, Issues and Ethics: a Case-study Approach*. Hodder & Stoughton, London.

Wood, R.E. (2004) Cruise ships: deterritorialized destinations. In: Lumsdon, L. and Page, S. (eds) *Tourism and Transport: Issues and Agenda for the New Millennium*. Elsevier, Amsterdam, pp. 133–145.

10 Pro-poor Tourism – Can Tourism Contribute to Poverty Reduction in Less Economically Developed Countries?

Dorothea Meyer

Introduction

For many of the world's population, the growing integration of the global economy has provided the opportunity for substantial economic and income growth and it is argued that without sustained economic growth there will be little hope of addressing poverty and inequality that is so pervasive (Dollar and Kraay, 2002; Rhodes et al., 2005). However, globalization has also increased the tendency towards inequality within and between countries (Flanagan, 2006). The tourism industry, by its nature, is probably one of the most globalized industries often characterized by relatively well-off 'northern' tourists travelling to exotic and LEDCs in the 'south' – accentuating the inequality between countries and possibly contributing to increasing the gap between the 'rich' and the 'poor'.

Over the past decades, discussions about the possibilities of tourism as a tool for development and poverty reduction in LEDCs have gained momentum – a key approach to this is the concept of pro-poor tourism (PPT). This chapter will illustrate the origins and ideas behind PPT by briefly illustrating issues and discussions related to tourism and development in LEDCs. This will be followed by specifying the meaning of PPT and its origins; and showing the PPT approach and strategies.

The chapter will conclude by illustrating some critique and challenges for the PPT approach.

The Situation: Tourism in Less Economically Developed Countries

International arrivals to less economically developed countries (LEDCs) have grown at an exceptional rate in the past two decades – now accounting for roughly 40% of total international arrivals globally (Box 10.1).

The dependence on this industry for many LEDCs is even more striking: in 2005, they accounted for 80% of total goods and services exports for Samoa, 70% for the Maldives, 56% for Sao Tome and Principe, and 43% for Vanuatu. Between 2000 and 2005, both annual international visitor arrivals and revenues for LDCs have grown rapidly, by 8.2% and 12.0% respectively (UNWTO, 2006). Subsequently, in recent years tourism has emerged as a key area of intervention for policy makers in LEDCs. Given its above average growth rate, it is viewed at local and national level as a route to broader development and shared growth and, as a consequence, tourism is included in the Poverty Reduction Strategy Papers (PRSPs) of more than 80% of low-income countries (Roe et al., 2004; see also Chapter 6 by Angela Kalish, this volume). Whereas tourism is becoming a key foreign

(eds S. Cole and N. Morgan)

Box 10.1. The growing significance of tourism to LEDCs.

- Since the 1950s, developing countries have received increasing numbers of international tourists, mainly from developed countries. International tourist arrivals have grown significantly faster in developing countries than they have in the EU or OECD countries. Developing countries had 292.6 million international arrivals in 2000, an increase since 1990 of nearly 95%. The subgroup of least developed countries (LDCs) had 5.1 million international arrivals in 2000. They achieved an increase of nearly 75% in the decade. This performance by developing countries compares very favourably with the growth of tourism to countries of the OECD and the EU, which achieved around 40% growth.
- Over the last 10 years there has been a higher rate of growth in the absolute value of tourism expenditure as recorded in the national accounts in developing countries than in developed countries. The absolute earnings of developing countries grew by 133% between 1990 and 2000 and in the LDCs by 154%, this compares with 64% for OECD countries and 49% for EU countries.
- The developing countries and particularly the LDCs secured a larger increase in the income per international arrival between 1990 and 2000 than did the OECD or the EU. The LDCs secured an increase of 45% between 1990 and 2000 and the developing countries nearly 20%, this compares with 18% for OECD countries and 7.8% for the EU.
- In developing countries the export value of tourism grew by 154% (between 1990 and 2000) second only to the growth in the manufacturing sector.

Sources: WTO (2002: 26–29), Roe *et al.* (2004).

---

exchange earner for many LEDCs and LDCs, it remains uncertain whether tourism can contribute to poverty reduction and most of all how best this could be achieved. Work on PPT by the Overseas Development Institute (ODI) has identified several reasons why tourism seems to be particularly relevant to poverty reduction and in achieving the Millennium Development Goals (MDGs). One of the key reasons is that tourism is often one of the only viable sources of growth and/or export earnings in many LEDCs – and it is growing strongly.

What is Poverty?

Whereas there is no commonly accepted definition of what poverty constitutes and how it should be measured, a simplistic way of defining poverty is by considering the financial income level below which people are described as poor. Hence so-called 'poverty lines' have been defined both by individual countries as well as international organizations. For the purpose of global comparison, the World Bank uses International Poverty Lines set at US$1.25 and US$2 per day (2005 Purchasing Power Parity terms). Poverty estimates released in August 2008 show that about 1.4 billion people in LEDCs, a quarter of the global population, were living on less than $1.25 a day in 2005 (Chen and Ravallion, 2008).

The conventional view of well-being was primarily linked to command over commodities, i.e. poverty was viewed largely in monetary terms. The highly influential work by Sen (1999), however, shows that poverty is a multidimensional phenomenon and arises when people lack key capabilities such as inadequate income and/or education, poor health, insecurity, low self-confidence, a sense of powerlessness, or the absence of rights such as freedom of speech. Sen's broader approach focuses on the capability of the individual to function in society that makes solutions to poverty far more complex than simply providing financial benefits. The World Bank's 'Voices of the Poor' study based on research with over 60,000 poor people in 60 countries, identifies a range of factors that people in LEDCs identify as contributors to poverty (Box 10.2).

These include:

- precarious livelihoods;
- excluded locations;
- physical limitations;
- gender relationships;
- problems in social relationships;
- lack of security;
- abuse by those in power;

- dis-empowering institutions;
- limited capabilities; and
- weak community organizations.

Poverty is related to, but distinct from, inequality and vulnerability (Haughton and Khandker, 2009). Inequality focuses primarily on the distribution of economic factors (such as income or consumption) across the whole population and requires a comparative analysis within that society; vulnerability on the other hand is seen as the risk of falling into poverty in the future and is a key dimension of well-being since it affects individuals' behaviour in terms of investment, production patterns, coping strategies, and in terms of the perceptions of their own situations.

Does Tourism Contribute to Poverty Reduction?

Since the development of mass-tourism in the 1960s, no consensus seems to have emerged whether the tourism industry can contribute to poverty reduction or, in fact, might actually exacerbate the inequality gap between 'hosts' and 'guests' and within destinations. The academic community seems to have maintained a rather pessimistic view regarding the sector's value as a tool for poverty reduction and continue to identify tourism as an *example par excellence* of increasing north–south dependencies. Academics critical of tourism as a tool for poverty reduction have adopted a (post)structuralist political eco-

nomy view arguing that unless major structural reforms of the tourism industry – and its guiding-force the global economic system – take place, the sector is unlikely to aid poverty reduction or reduce inequality (e.g. Bryden, 1973; de Kadt, 1979; Britton, 1982; Wilkinson, 1987; Brohman, 1996; Clancy, 1999; Duffy, 2002; Scheyvens, 2007; Schilcher, 2007). Scheyvens (2007, 2009), for example, argues that tourism might not be effective as a tool for poverty reduction but might instead increase the dependency of the 'south' on 'northern' transnational corporations (TNCs).

Several studies have shown that tourism can increase inequalities (Scheyvens, 2002, 2007), increase dependency on outward orientated growth (Brohman, 1996), exploit the workforce (Tourism Concern, 2004), lead to the displacement of communities (Akama, 1996, 2004; Mowforth and Munt, 2003) and contribute to conflict over scarce resources (Mbaiwa and Darkoh, 2009) – to name just a few of the widely discussed negative impacts of tourism development. A key concern has been that the global structures of the tourism industry, e.g. package tours 'manufactured' and sold by TNCs based in generating countries, made it impossible for LEDCs to reap the benefits from tourism development (Scheyvens, 2009). It has been claimed that 'leakages', i.e. money that leaves the destination to pay for imports necessary to sustain the industry, or monies paid to TNCs in the 'north' that never reach the destination, were exceptionally high in this

---

Box 10.2. What the 'poor' say about poverty.

Poverty is pain; it feels like a disease. It attacks a person not only materially but also morally. It eats away one's dignity and drives one into total despair.

Being well means not to worry about your children, to know that they have settled down; to have a house and livestock and not to wake up at night when the dog starts barking; to know that you can sell your output; to sit and chat with friends and neighbours.

A better life for me is to be healthy, peaceful and to live in love without hunger. Love is more than anything. Money has no value in the absence of love.

You grow up in an environment full of diseases, violence and drugs … you don't have the right to education, work or leisure, and you are forced to 'eat in the hands of the government'… so you are easy prey for the rulers. You have to accept whatever they give you.

Source: http://go.worldbank.org/H1N8746X10.

industry (e.g. Britton, 1982; Oppermann and Chon, 1997).

However, studies have also shown that leakages were not necessarily higher in tourism than in other industries (Page, 1999; Roe *et al.*, 2004) and that tourism at the same time can contribute to employment and income generation (Ashley and Mitchell, 2007), gender-equality (Anker, 1998; Scheyvens, 2002), education and knowledge exchange (Ashley *et al.*, 2001), inter-sectoral linkages (Belisle, 1983, 1984; Momsen, 1996; Torres 2002, 2003), entrepreneurship and small, medium and microenterprise (SMME) development (Kirsten and Rogerson, 2002), and nature conservation (Spenceley, 2008; Saarinen, 2009).

Whereas donors, (international) nongovernmental organizations ((I)NGOs) and technical assistance organizations stayed clear of promoting tourism as a development agent in the past, this has changed considerably since the UK Department for International Development (DfID) commissioned research into the possibilities of the tourism industry to contribute to poverty reduction (Bennett *et al.*, 1999). It was realized that tourism could provide the opportunity for a shift to non-farm economic activities in peripheral areas struggling to keep agricultural production afloat and that are, because of their isolation, unsuitable for large-scale export-orientated manufacturing (Farrington *et al.*, 1999; Ashley and Maxwell, 2001).

Weighing all these arguments up, it was suggested by Bennett *et al.* (1999) that the tourism sector actually had promising potential to contribute to poverty reduction in LEDCs for the following reasons:

- the market comes to the producers – thus providing additional sales opportunities in the destination;
- inter-sectoral linkages especially with agriculture, artisan production, and additional services can be created, which is essential for livelihoods diversification;
- tourism is generally labour intensive (although often less so than agriculture);
- tourism takes place in marginal areas –

areas where the majority of the poor live;
- tourism generally employs a high level of females, young people and unskilled or less-skilled individuals – a high percentage of the poorest of society fall into these categories;
- tourism has rather limited barriers of entry when compared to manufacturing or other export activities; and
- the tourism sector is already growing at a very high rate in many LEDCs.

The research undertaken by the Pro-poor Tourism Partnership (e.g. Ashley *et al.*, 2000, 2001) was instrumental in this new way of thinking about tourism. The UK-based ODI, for example, claims that the need – and opportunity – to harness markets for poverty reduction was particularly evident in tourism (Ashley and Mitchell, 2007; Mitchell and Ashley, 2009). Rather than just condemning tourism as a hedonistic, pleasure-seeking, 'white men's industry', practitioners and donors acknowledged that there was potential – whether this could and would be achieved was a rather different undertaking altogether.

As a consequence, in the past 10 years, many of the most influential development organizations (e.g. DfID, Netherlands Development Organization (SNV), International Trade Centre (ITC), Development Bank South Africa (DBSA), Kreditanstalt fuer Wiederaufbau (KfW), Gesellschaft fuer technische Zusammenarbeit (GTZ), Asian Development Bank (ADB), US government Overseas Aid Program (USAID), Australian government Overseas Aid Program (AUSAID), New Zealand government Overseas Aid Program (NZAID), International Finance Corporation (IFC), World Bank) invested considerable funds into how the tourism industry could be harnessed more effectively as a tool for poverty reduction – all adopting the ideas of PPT.

What is Pro-poor Tourism (PPT)?

The concept of PPT was first introduced in a report for the UK DfID in 1999 and was defined as 'tourism that results in increased net benefits for poor people' (Bennett *et al.*, 1999: ii). PPT fundamentally advocates tourism development and management that can help to reduce poverty in LEDCs. As such it is not a specific type of niche tourism such as for example ecotourism (with a primary focus on nature conservation) and community-based tourism (CBT; with a focus on community involvement in both benefits and decision making) – but instead it looks at all types of tourism and how these can contribute to poverty reducing. The PPT partnership argues that any type of company can be involved in PPT – a small lodge, an urban hotel, a tour operator, an infrastructure developer. The critical factor is not the type of company or the type of tourism, but that an increase in the net benefits that go to poor people can be demonstrated (http://www.propoortourism.org). In fact, PPT often focuses on how to change the existing mass-market practices rather than introducing yet another alternative type of tourism as it was realized early on that the greatest impacts on poverty reduction could be achieved by working with the mainstream players. Changes to these practices are not simply about increased employment opportunities but can particularly be found by working with suppliers such as local farmers of craft producers. Box 10.3 illustrates some of the underlying principles of PPT.

The Origins of PPT

The concept of PPT stems from two different but intertwined approaches to poverty reduction and improved livelihoods: the pro-poor growth (PPG) approach and the sustainable livelihoods (SL) approach.

Pro-poor growth (PPG)

PPT is based on the PPG assumption that economic growth is beneficial for development and should be encouraged as long as the 'poor' benefit over-proportionally (Ravallion, 2004). PPG is about changing the distribution of relative incomes through a growth process that favours the poor by enabling them to actively participate in and significantly benefit from economic activity. PPG is seen as the most important ingredient to achieve sustainable poverty reduction (Ravallion and Chen, 2001; Ravallion, 2004).

Some critical assumptions and tenets inform the PPG approach, including the following:

- growth is a means and not an end to development;
- economic growth is 'good' for poverty reduction (Dollar and Kraay, 2002);
- inequality limits the extent to which growth contributes to poverty reduction;

Box 10.3. Underlying principles of pro-poor tourism.

- Pro-poor strategies need to be complemented by the development of wider tourism infrastructure. A balanced approach is critical – if competitive products, transport systems or marketing do not exist, the industry will decline and so will any pro-poor strategy.
- Pro-poor principles apply to any tourism segment, though specific strategies will vary between, for example, mass tourism and wildlife tourism.
- Focus on expanding benefits, not just minimizing costs to the poor.
- Draw on lessons from other sectors (such as small enterprise, good governance, and poverty analysis) and apply these to tourism.
- Involve businesses in development initiatives and be commercially realistic.
- Do not expect all the poor to benefit equally, particularly the poorest 20% – some will lose.
- Learn by doing – the effectiveness of pro-poor strategies is not proven, but we won't know what can be done to reduce poverty through tourism until more concerted efforts are made.

Sources: Bennett *et al.* (1999); Ashley *et al.* (2001).

- policies can enhance the poverty reduction benefits of growth (Wiggins and Higgins, 2008).

The following two definitions for measuring PPG are commonly used:

1. *Relative Definition*: this compares changes in the incomes of the poor with respect to changes in the incomes of the non-poor and as such PPG is achieved when the distributional shifts accompanying growth favour the poor (McCulloch and Baulch, 1999; Kakwani and Pernia, 2000; Kakwani and Son, 2003; Klasen, 2003).

2. *Absolute Definition*: here growth is considered to be pro-poor if poor people benefit in absolute terms (Ravallion and Chen, 2001; Kraay, 2004), i.e. the aim is to achieve the greatest amount of poverty reduction possible through growth and progressive distributional change.

The relative definition focuses on reducing inequalities, whereas the absolute definition focuses on growth as a means for progressive distributional change. Whereas in principle policies related to the reduction of inequality are essential, they are of limited operational use if they impact on growth. The PPG approach is a major departure from the 'trickle-down' development concept, which assumes that the benefits of general economic growth will permeate to all sectors of society. As such both growth potential and PPG potential of the tourism sector need to be considered (Table 10.1).

The PPG approach not only gave the impetus for selecting the name 'pro-poor tourism', but is one of the two cornerstones of PPT – the other one is the SL approach.

Sustainable Livelihoods Approach

The SL approach, a concept that emerged from the agricultural development work undertaken and funded by organizations such as DfID, was applied in the late 1990s to tourism by the PPT Partnership. The aim was to move the focus 'beyond mere job

and cash income calculations' (Ashley, 2000: 8) by understanding the many issues that affect the lives of the poor. Similar to Sen's (1999) concept of *Development as Freedom*, the SL approach aimed to tackle the subject of poverty with an assessment of the capacities and assets of the poor and by learning about their strategies of coping and adapting. A livelihood comprises the capabilities, assets (including both material and social resources) and activities required for a means of living – it is sustainable when it can cope with and recover from stresses and shocks, and maintain or enhance its capabilities and assets both now and in the future, while not undermining the natural resource base (Scoones, 1998; Farrington *et al.*, 1999).

Farrington *et al.* (1999) argue that individuals pursue a range of livelihood outcomes such as for example health, income, reduced vulnerability, by drawing on a range of assets to pursue a variety of activities. The livelihood activities an individual chooses are only partly driven by their own preferences as they are influenced by their status of vulnerability and maybe most importantly by external policies, institutions and processes. People and their access to assets were at the heart of the livelihoods approach adopted by DfID in the late 1990s. The original DfID sustainable livelihood framework identified five categories of assets or capitals:

1. *Human capital:* skills, knowledge, health and ability to work.

2. *Social capital:* social resources, including informal networks, membership of formalized groups and relationships of trust that facilitate cooperation.

3. *Natural capital:* natural resources such as land, soil, water, forests and fisheries.

4. *Physical capital*: basic infrastructure, such as roads, water and sanitation, schools, ICT; and producer goods, including tools and equipment.

5. *Financial capital:* financial resources including savings, credit, and income from employment, trade and remittances (DfID, 1999: 1).

Table 10.1. Potential of tourism to contribute to pro-poor growth.

Positives	Negatives
Growth potential	
• Growing industry in less developed countries	• Requires substantial infra- and super-structural investment
• High foreign exchange earnings and GDP contributions	• Potentially high degree of leakage
• One of the few export/services sectors in which some poor countries have (or can develop) a clear comparative advantage	• Dependence on international networks, e.g. tour operators
• International linkages and technology transfer	• Highly vulnerable and marketing extensive industry
• High potential for inter-sectoral linkages and multipliers	
Pro-poor growth potential	
• Labour intensive (on average, more labour intensive than manufacturing)	• Disruption or expropriation of land, water, and other assets of the poor by tourism industry
• Employs a high percentage of women (relative to other industries in a given cultural context)	• Entry barriers to poor entrepreneurs: the industry is information/contact/marketing intensive
• Can involve more intensive use of un-skilled and semi-skilled labour	• Local economic linkages are often less than hoped: high transaction costs can be involved
• Can build on assets of the poor: their land and culture (land tenure and control over cultural commercialization are important)	• Cultural exploitation, unwelcome commercialization of culture
• Suited to some remote (i.e. poor) areas: contributes to spatially dispersed growth	
• Potential for involvement of a wide variety of enterprises, including small, medium and micro-enterprises (SMMEs) and informal sector. Because the customer comes to the product, local entrepreneurs gain opportunities for sale of other goods and services	
• Involvement of the poor can go beyond (migrant) employment in urban/industrial hubs: a variety of economic and decision-making roles are possible in dispersed locations	
• Non-commercial or indirectly commercial interests provide avenues for expanding pro-poor tourism strategies, e.g. ethical tourism niche, moves to responsible tourism and sustainable tourism; lodge managers who have made 'lifestyle choices' with destination commitment, and role of government in policy and planning	

Source: adapted from Ashley *et al.* (2001).

Early PPT research uses this SL framework as its key approach by exploring the use of assets and as such widening the range of livelihood options available. Ashley (2000) argues that tourism is often seen as a 'new rural activity for local people, and correctly perceived as risky' (2000: 17). Hence she recommends that tourism should be viewed as an *additional* activity to combine with existing livelihood activities, not as a substitute. She maintains that 'One of the most important ways in which tourism supports other activities is that it strengthens households' productive capacity by increasing skills and providing cash for investment (i.e. by boosting their asset base …)' (2000: 18). Ashley's research in Namibia, for example, shows that new skills gained from being employed in tourism could be transferred to other livelihood activities, that earnings from tourism were being invested in livestock and/or the development of SMMEs, and that tourism contributed greatly to non-financial benefits be it access to infrastructure (e.g. roads, telecommunication, water) or access to information, participation in decision making and empowerment (Box 10.4).

The SL approach according to Farrington *et al.* (1999) is based on the following two core principles:

1. *A focus on people*: analysis of people's livelihoods and how these have been changing over time; involvement of people and support for them in achieving their own livelihood goals; focus on the impact of different policy and institutional arrangements on people's livelihoods; and seek to influence these arrangements so they promote the agenda of the poor.

2. *Holism*: it is non-sectoral and applicable across social groups; it recognizes multiple influences on people, and seeks to understand the relationships between these influences; it recognizes multiple actors (from the private sector to national ministries, from community-based organizations to newly emerging decentralized government bodies); it acknowledges the multiple livelihood strategies that people adopt to secure their livelihoods; it seeks to achieve multiple livelihood outcomes, to be determined and negotiated by people themselves.

(Farrington *et al.*, 1999: 4)

PPT Strategies: Can they Contribute to Poverty Reduction and Increased Levels of Equity?

By using both the PPG approach and the SL approach, the PPT Partnership identified the following three broad intervention strategies to be applied to the tourism industry: (i) economic benefits; (ii) non-financial livelihood impacts; and (iii) enhanced participation and partnerships (Table 10.2).

The next section will illustrate two key research areas related to PPT: (i) changing business practice; and (ii) Value Chain Analysis (VCA).

Changing business practice

Early work by the PPT Partnership focused explicitly on encouraging the change of business practice within the mainstream tourism industry. It was acknowledged that whereas community-based tourism or CBT projects could empower communities to take part in the development and

---

Box 10.4. Sustainable livelihoods approach applied in Namibia tourism and wildlife.

In Namibia, SL analysis has been used to assess the tourism sector. The approach recognizes that tourism impacts on many aspects of livelihoods, and puts these as the priority concern. By contrast, conventional analyses of tourism tend to focus on macro-economic benefits, or environmental impacts, or negative social consequences. Fieldwork with communities combined with financial analysis led to identification of a vast array of positive and negative impacts. SL perspectives were used for pulling the results together. The findings indicate that:

- livelihood concerns vary between people and places, but go well beyond cash income, so donor/NGO strategies of maximizing local revenue through tourism are inadequate; coping with drought, access to grazing and veld foods, and maintaining local control were key issues;
- different types of tourism enterprise have quite different livelihood impacts;
- much can be done to enhance livelihood impacts of tourism; given the chance, people will adapt tourism to meet their livelihood concerns, so the important principle is to ensure local participation in planning; for the poor an expansion of informal sales and casual labour opportunities is more important than formal sector employment;
- livelihoods approaches can be informative at the international level, where tourism analysis has been dominated by macro-economic and conservation perspectives.

Also in Namibia, the Wildlife Integration for Livelihood Diversification (WILD) project used a wide range of participatory techniques to assess how different project options affected, or were affected by people's livelihood choices.

Source: Farrington *et al.* (1999), Ashley (2000).

Table 10.2. Pro-poor tourism strategies.

Increase economic benefits	Enhance non-financial livelihood impacts	Enhance participation and partnership
• Expand local employment, wages: commitments to local jobs, training of local people • Expand local enterprise opportunities – including those that provide services to tourism operations (food suppliers etc.) and those that sell to tourists (craft producers, handicrafts, guides etc.) • Develop collective income sources – fees, revenue shares, equity dividends, donations, etc.	• Capacity building, training • Mitigate environmental impacts • Address competing use of natural resources • Improve social and cultural impacts • Increase local access to infrastructure and services provided for tourists – roads, communications, healthcare, transport	• Create a more supportive policy/planning framework that enables participation by the poor • Increase participation of the poor in decision-making by government and the private sector • Build pro-poor partnerships with the private sector • Increase flow of information and communication between stakeholders to lay the foundation for future dialogue

Source: http://www.propoortourism.org.uk/strategies.html

management of tourism in their localities, they often failed to deliver significant poverty reduction impacts (e.g. Bennett *et al.*, 1999; Goodwin, 2006; Mitchell and Muckosy, 2008). The reasons for this were manifold and varied but three key factors were particularly important. First, many CBT projects were simply extremely small, i.e. maybe hosting only around 40 or 50 guests per year. Whereas this might have impacted significantly on a small community, it was seen as insufficient to contribute to poverty reduction at scale. The second and probably more important reason for the failure of so many CBTs was the fact that they were often initiated and managed by (I)NGOs or development agencies with relatively little knowledge of the workings of the international tourism industry. Many of these CBTs were not initiated based on researched market needs and most did not have access to the international distribution networks that were vital for bringing customers to the destination. In many cases a viable market access strategy was simply not considered while designing 'cute, green and community friendly' CBT products – which simply meant that customers could not be attracted – leading to the shattering of high expectations placed by communities on tourism. A third reason for the failure of many CBTs was that many were initially

funded by donor money, which generally had a short lifespan – after donors withdrew many projects collapsed.

In the early 2000s, the PPT team at ODI therefore focused on work with the mainstream private sector. The key assumption was that this would deliver poverty reduction impacts at scale by utilizing the market access power these companies could provide. The partly DfID/partly private sector-funded project *PPT Pilots in Southern Africa* hence worked with some of the largest tourism businesses in Southern Africa (i.e. Sun International, Southern Sun, Wilderness Safaris, Spier and Ker and Downey; see http://www.odi.org.uk/projects/details.asp?id=1103&title=pro-poor-tourism-pilots-southern-africa).

The types of intervention and successes varied greatly. Related to the Spier, Wilderness, and Sun City project sites, Ashley (2005) argues that interventions go well beyond conventional philanthropic donations. They included the outsourcing of services (e.g. laundry at Spier), the development of new products (e.g. craft production at Sun City) and new community ownership arrangements at Wilderness Safaris) (for detailed information on impacts, see McNab, 2005).

The two key impacts from this project were: (i) changes in company operational approach and strategy; and (ii) progress in actual implementation of linkages to poor neighbouring communities.

According to Ashley (2005), the PPT Pilots project has shown ten key challenges and factors that need to be in place to enable a change of business practice:

1. A champion who drives the process is essential, as is top management leadership.
2. Considerable amount of time input is needed, and therefore so is a staff member or facilitator who can do this.
3. Beyond the champion, wider buy-in across staff and management is needed.
4. Learn by doing: get practical and get going, and adapt from there.
5. The process is not just about changing company practice, but also changing attitudes to communities and local entrepreneurs.
6. A slow pace must be accepted, and expectations managed – without dampening enthusiasm.
7. Finding the right partners in the community is key. It is also often a difficult first step.
8. Combine a mentoring relationship with local partners, with commercial realism and quality standards.
9. Success lies in finding local linkages that help address current drivers of change in the company and complement core business concerns.
10. Partnership with others will be needed (Ashley, 2005; McNab, 2005).

However, the project has also revealed that financial impacts were relatively limited, i.e. those in employment or acting as suppliers might have seen significant benefits but impacts on a larger scale were scant. Ashley (2005), however, concludes that the potential to increase and multiply these linkages is significant. She maintains that if Spier, for example, can shift 10% of its procurement budget to local suppliers, the extra injection of R7.5 million into the local economy would be roughly equivalent to half the business' pay roll – thus indicating that rather than simply highlighting direct employment in the

tourism industry, a focus on procurement activity could provide significant PPT impacts.

The way in which individual accommodation providers can contribute to PPT is shown in a simplified manner in Fig. 10.1.

Most individual accommodation providers can contribute to PPT in four different ways: (i) *employment* (e.g. employment conditions, wages, in-house training); (ii) *sourcing and procurement* linkages with local suppliers (in particular SMMEs); (iii) SMME development and outsourcing of non-core business to SMME and collaboration and support to the informal sector; and (iv) *other types of partnerships* such as CSR-type community development initiatives.

The results of PPT interventions related to these four different areas are discussed in turn.

Employment

Ashley *et al.* (2005) show that wages to local staff contribute to over 70% of all cash earnings, whereas the UNWTO (2006) states that employment in the tourism industry was generally considered to be better remunerated and less labour-intensive when compared to traditional activities such as farming, despite the criticism of the working conditions in the tourism sector. Similarly, Lengefeld and Steward (2004) conclude from their research on all-inclusive resorts in the Caribbean that the majority of jobs were held by locals and whereas entry wages were based on minimum wage, employees earned about 50–70% more because of regular tips – considerably more than a local primary school teacher would earn. Additionally, employees often benefited from social and health insurances, free transport, free food and 120 h of compulsory training (Lengefeld and Stewart, 2004). The expansion of local employment and an improvement in working conditions can boost the staff morale, whereas customers are likely to enjoy a

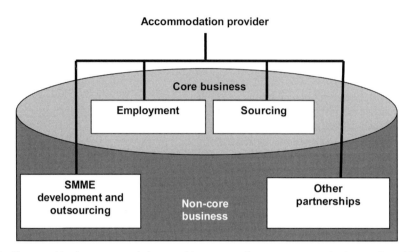

Fig. 10.1. Opportunities for accommodation providers to contribute to poverty reduction. (Adapted from Meyer, 2008.)

better service and are thus more likely to return and recommend the product – all of which is essential for business.

A change in recruitment procedures was a key intervention in the PPT Pilots programme in South Africa leading to a higher number of local people being employed and employees being selected on a more equitable basis rather than relying on local elite family members (McNab, 2005). The benefits from employment in tourism are not restricted to just employees but the UNWTO estimates that another four to ten family members benefit (UNWTO, 2006), and similarly local businesses profit from wages being spent on local goods and services.

However, employment often does not reach the poorest segments of society because of a generally low skills base and the lack of foreign languages.

Sourcing and procurement

Probably the biggest impact, however, is made by linking local businesses into the supply chain. This can include, for example, construction workers, carpenters and furniture makers, services such as guides, security personnel, gardeners, baby-sitters and hair braiders – but the greatest impact is likely to be achieved by creating linkages to local agriculture and fisheries, and craft producers. Whereas the poorest in society often do not have the skills and experience to obtain direct employment in the tourism industry, many are already engaged in agriculture and artisanal fisheries for their livelihoods. Tourism in fact is seen as providing good potential for livelihood diversification into the non-farm economy (Ashley and Maxwell, 2001).

Obstacles to increased inter-sectoral linkages between tourism and agriculture are manifold and frequently include: lack of quality and quantity; lack of storage facilities and transport infrastructure; limited knowledge of what is produced and what is demanded; limited communication between the two sectors; seasonality; insufficient marketing networks; bulk buying and preferential servicing – to name just a few (Meyer, 2008).

The PPT Pilots programme worked with Spier in South Africa to reform its procurement policies leading to eight new suppliers who earned US$90,000 within the first 10 months of cooperation and created 33 new jobs (McNab, 2005). An important element was continued business advice and mentoring provided by Spier.

Ashley (2005) argues that probably the most important factor in this cooperation was the willingness of Spier's managers to support the process.

Livelihood diversification via inter-sectoral linkages between tourism and agriculture offer tremendous opportunities that are frequently not tapped into – they not only provide income to local farmers but they can also considerably cut the import costs for tourism businesses, while providing a more authentic experience.

SMME development and outsourcing

Mainstream tourism businesses can get involved in PPT by helping local small-scale entrepreneurs with the set-up, management and establishment of market access for their businesses. Support to SMMEs can take a variety of forms from simply recommending their services to tourists to active involvement in their development via knowledge exchange and mentoring practices. This can involve a wide range of local stakeholders such as local business associations, as done in the case of ASSET in The Gambia (see Chapter 5, this volume), the informal sector and hawkers, or direct support to local entrepreneurs.

Spier and Southern Sun in South Africa contributed to SMME development by outsourcing their laundry and house-keeping departments, respectively, whereas Sun International helped set up a local hydroponic farm that supplies the Sun City resort with herbs and garnishes. Accommodation providers and tour operators also link up with local SMMEs to create excursion packages that tie-up several attractions that would independently not have enough potential to attract visitors – thereby also helping to disperse the benefits (Meyer, 2004). Tropical Ecological Adventures in Ecuador, for example, established joint products such as cultural and lifestyle experiences as well as home-stays with remote Amazonian communities, which increased the product appeal for potential tourists while contributing to local development (Braman and Fundación Acción Amazonia, 2001).

Other types of partnerships

Philanthropic donations are surprisingly common in the tourism industry and often include donations to schools and orphanages, sponsorships of students or even in kind donations such as the tourists' time or skills. However, philanthropic activities have also been criticized as 'paternalistic model of empowerment' (Mahony and van Zyl, 2001: 44). It is argued that these donations increase dependency and it would be more beneficial to contribute to empowerment by creating business linkages.

However, these critics often seem to forget that philanthropy can contribute to targeted priority needs of a community and thus a larger number of individuals, who might be unable to attain employment in the tourism industry, can benefit. Ashley and Haysom (2004) argue that in many cases, they provide a foundation for more substantial partnerships between the company and/or its clients on the one hand, and the local communities on the other.

In many countries, particularly in/around nature reserves in Africa, companies are at times forced to enter into formal business cooperation with communities. This is generally the case when the community is the legal landowner and operational agreements or even joint ventures are required. Roe *et al.* (2001) argue that in some instances, tourism businesses such as the South African company Wilderness Safaris voluntarily seek such business partnerships because they offer wide-ranging benefits such as a social license to operate, development of new products and improved customer experiences, increased staff morale, image enhancement and increased credibility; the community benefits from economic gains, improved infrastructure, a high proportion of local jobs, training and skills transfers, and supply and service opportunities.

Good relationships between the neighbouring communities and private business are vital for a hospitable tourism environment, if highly depending on the goodwill from neighbouring communities. This focus on tourism's contribution to broader local economic development rather than simply focusing on a narrowly defined tourism industry was followed up by proponents of PPT using the VCA related to tourism. It was realized that by just studying the poverty impacts from employment in a particular tourism business this would neglect the far wider impacts that can be achieved by looking at the whole, and very diverse and complex value chain with a particular focus on inter-sectoral linkages.

Value Chain Analysis (VCA) in tourism

One of the key concerns about tourism's potential as a tool for poverty reduction is that 'leakages' seem to be particularly high. 'Leakage' is a term used to describe the percentage of the price of the holiday paid by the tourists that leaves a destination in terms of imports or expatriated profits, or that never reaches the destination in the first place because of the involvement of 'northern'-based intermediaries. Several authors warn of the high reliance of the tourism industry on imports and thus the danger of unnecessarily high leakages (e.g. Belisle, 1983; Taylor *et al.*, 1991; Wilkinson, 1987). Diaz-Benevides (2001), for example, claims that between 40% and 50% of leakages occur in most developing countries. Leakages tend to be high when the local destination economy is weak and lacks the quantity and quality of inputs required by the tourism industry – this is a common situation in small island development states, which at the same time are often also highly tourism dependent destinations (e.g. Maldives, Seychelles, Caribbean and Pacific islands). However, leakages are not only a serious concern for small island developing states but also common in tourism destinations that are highly dependent on 'northern' operated package-tourism in general. Dieke (1993) estimates that leakage levels in The Gambia in the early 1990s were 77% for 'charter operations'. Leakages, however, are found in all

sectors and Page (1999) argues that leakage levels in tourism are not necessarily higher than in the manufacturing sector.

However, tourism also has the potential to create high multiplier effects from inter-sectoral linkages, i.e. the integration of local businesses into the supply chain (Fig. 10.2). The aim of creating linkages is to reduce the high import content in the tourism sector, which is achieved by substituting foreign imports with local supplies. In very broad terms, increasing backward linkages refers to increasing the collaboration and usage of other economic sectors and inputs in the country/region/destination, to stimulate the economy as a whole and to create synergy effects between different sectors.

One of the key aims of VCA is to detect notes within the supply chain where value from local supplies can be added. Porter (1985) argues that products pass through all activities of the chain in order and at each activity the product gains some value, i.e. the chain of activities gives the products more added value than the sum of values of individual activities.

Related to PPT, VCA has been extended beyond individual firms and applied to the whole supply chain and distribution network. Capturing the value generated for the poor along the chain and identifying supply/distribution-nodes where interventions to increase poverty impacts are possible is at the heart of the VCA used in tourism.

VCA focuses on the dynamics of inter-sectoral linkages and the way in which firms and countries are globally integrated, by shedding light on the income received to each mode within the supply chain. It enables researchers to go beyond a single sector (i.e. tourism) by focusing on inter-sectoral linkages (for the tourism sector especially important are agricultural and handicraft supplies) and allows greater integration between the formal and the informal sector (the informal sector being a key entry point of poor producers into the tourism industry, e.g. street vendors, handicraft sellers etc.). VCA is an analytical tool that helps to describe the workings of

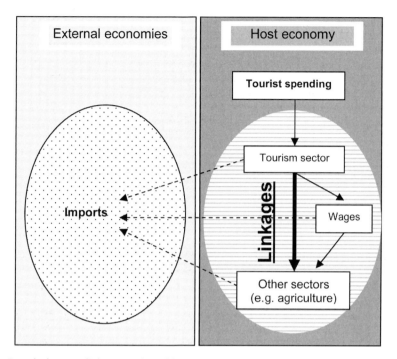

Fig. 10.2. From leakages to linkages. (Adapted from Meyer, 2008.)

the value chain in the destination but also in understanding the policy environment, which provides for the efficient allocation of resources within the domestic economy, and the way in which firms and countries participate in the global economy – which seems particularly important when studying international tourism.

Figure 10.3 shows a basic value chain in the tourism industry and common host destination inputs in LEDCs.

One of the distinct features of VCA research in development studies is its concern with distributional issues. Distribution has both power and income components. The former concerns the balance of leverage, which different parties have in determining the distribution of who does what in the tourism value chain and the returns which accrue to different parties (Kaplinsky and Morris, 2004). The latter is concerned with the actual distribution of the income from tourism activity. This focuses on issues such as barriers of entry, the measurement of income and profit-

ability, locality dimensions of the tourism value chain distribution, the make-up of recipients by class, gender, ethnicity, and the integration of SMMEs and the informal sector into the tourism value chains. VCA analysis related to PPT has been used to analyse the sequence of multiple and complex products and services across sectors that are delivered to tourists, which makes it possible to identify market-based solutions to improve opportunities and earnings for the poor. SNV for example uses it to link local farmers to international hotel chains, and works with handicraft producers to improve their product design and market share.

A study by Ashley (2006) compares the value chain in Ethiopia with Luang Prabang (Laos) and found that the former lacks numerous elements that are necessary for creating linkages. These include: limited opportunities for tourists to spend money; difficulties in changing money or using credit cards; limited interpretation skills by guides; handicrafts suffer from a lack of

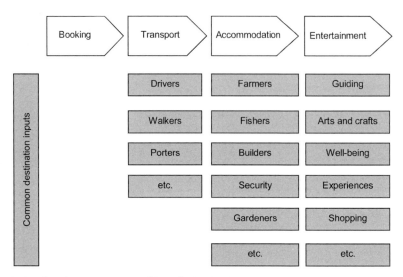

Fig. 10.3. Basic value chain in tourism and host destination inputs.

variety as well as quality; and the environment is not necessarily inviting for tourists to frequent local food stalls and restaurants.

Mitchell and Ashley (2009) argue that the particular value of VCA is that it allows the gathering of rich comparative data and that this in-depth description of what happens in the tourism supply chain in various destinations can inform policy makers to devise policy intervention mechanisms that might be valuable for other LEDCs. It was shown that the value chains and their development impacts varied considerably between destinations and that it would be meaningless to use development funds just because of tourism's inherent characteristics (i.e. labour intensity, gender profile or growth potential). The study compared the impacts of cultural tourism in Laos, Vietnam and Cambodia with surprisingly different results, i.e. whereas they did classify cultural tourism in Laos and Vietnam as pro-poor, only 7% of tourist spending reached the poor in Cambodia. When comparing inter-sectoral linkages they detected that in Cambodia the links to other economic sectors were generally very weak; in Ethiopia, on the other hand, characterized by limited import needs and a diversified agricultural sector,

around 13% of the total $55 million spent on food and beverages reached resource-poor food producers. Similarly, when comparing the pro-poor impacts of craft sales, it was found that spending on craft products in Laos was high because of the high quality of the products, the strong reliance on local materials and the well established distribution chains (i.e. $33 per visitor of which over 50% reached the poor); whereas in Cambodia only 5% reached the poor because production materials were largely imported and local traders were dependent on paying kickbacks to tour operators (Mitchell and Ashley, 2009). These findings confirm the value of VCA but also the need for strong attention being paid to the individual country contexts in which the value chains operate; understanding how and why a destination differs from another helps to identify the key factors differentiating tourism–poverty linkages.

Conclusion

Since the PPT approach was first introduced in 1999, it has come a long way in only a short time. Not only has the approach been made widely popular among practitioners and scholars in particular thanks to the work undertaken by the ODI and the PPT partnership, but it has also been adopted by influential organizations that work on tourism and development issues. The Netherlands Development Organisation SNV, for example, currently works with over 40 tourism advisors in Africa, Asia, Central and South America, and Europe who actively implement Pro-poor Sustainable Tourism approaches; key financial organizations such as the World Bank and the International Finance Corporation are aiming to roll out the PPT approach at scale; the United Nations Conference on Trade and Development (UNCTAD) has conducted a PPT-based global study of the developmental impacts of foreign direct investment in tourism; the UNWTO has established its Sustainable Tourism – Eliminating Poverty (ST-EP) programme; and many countries in Africa, for example, have included PPT in their PRSPs. The focus also has expanded in the past 10 years from working initially with individual businesses and CBT products to a wider destination development approach, which sees tourism as integrated into local economic development – and with this expanded focus, new methodologies have been incorporated such as VCA.

However, criticisms have been raised in the past and challenges lie ahead. Probably the first criticism was related to the term PPT itself. In 2002 a follow-up study was carried out by the PPT partnership to investigate if the first DfID-funded research project investigating the possibilities of PPT in seven case-study locations (i.e. Ecuador, Nepal, St. Lucia, Uganda, Namibia and two in South Africa) changed the activities and views of those practitioners and researchers involved. While the approach and the PPT strategies were praised by the majority of respondents, it was felt that the term 'pro-poor tourism', mainly based on development concepts, was initially an obstacle, as it provided little appeal to the industry, the consumers, governments or the 'poor' themselves (Meyer, 2003).

This also led to the second criticism of PPT, which was related to a widely felt uncertainty as to what PPT actually means. While the PPT partnership made it very clear at the beginning that PPT could relate to any type of tourism, from mainstream mass-tourism, over ecotourism, to CBT, academics as well as practitioners were overtly keen to push it into the CBT corner. In fact, much of the early work published by the PPT partnership focuses on CBT projects.

While PPT is valuable for an understanding of tourism's diverse poverty reducing impacts at the micro-level, it still seems insufficient in illustrating macro-level implications of tourism on poverty reduction. The focus on VCA is a very much welcomed first step in this direction but so far limited research has been undertaken that incorporates the many external forces that ultimately shape decision making such as for example the policy environment, local cultures and traditions, gender inequalities, the global political economy, and global policy networks. An understanding of these factors, however, is fundamental when aiming to develop a type of tourism that aims to contribute to poverty reduction. Probably the most common criticism of PPT is 'simply' that it so far lacks evidence that it can achieve impact on a large scale. The enrolment of powerful international organizations, practitioners and academics since the late 1990s, however, might indicate that when pulling heads and resources together, this evidence might hopefully be available in the near future.

This chapter set out to introduce the concept of PPT as a means to address inequality. Inequality, in particular economic inequality, is at the heart of PPT, which aims to promote tourism in LEDCs that results in increased net benefits for poor people. The development of this approach over the past decade was illustrated with examples given for two key applied research foci: (i) changing business practice by working with the mainstream tourism industry; and (ii) VCA as a means to understand how the participation and inclusion of marginalized people can be improved. While the PPT approach is still in its 'development stage' and further research is urgently needed, it is very encouraging to see that the ideas are being adopted by some of the key development *and* tourism organizations – maybe this gives an indication that the ideas are on the right track for considering tourism as a contributor to poverty reduction.

Questions

1. Can tourism be a sustainable approach to contribute to poverty reduction in LEDCs?
2. How would you convince an accommodation provider in a LEDC to adopt PPT strategies?
3. Should tourists from the 'north' take holidays in the 'south'?

References

Anker, R. (1998) *Gender and Job: Sex Segregation of Occupations in the World*. International Labour Organization, Geneva.

Akama, J. (1996) Western environmental values and nature-based tourism in Kenya. *Tourism Management* 17, 567–574.

Akama, J.S. (2004) Neocolonialism, dependency and external control of Kenya's tourism industry: a case study of wildlife safari tourism in Kenya. In: Hall, C.M. and Tucker, H. (eds) *Tourism and Postcolonialism: Contested Discourses, Identities and Representations*. Routledge, London.

Ashley, C. (2000) The impacts of tourism on rural livelihoods: experience in Namibia. ODI Working Paper No. 128. Overseas Development Institute, London.

Ashley, C. (2005) Facilitating pro-poor tourism with the private sector: lessons learned from 'pro-poor tourism Pilots in Southern Africa'. ODI Working Paper No. 257. Overseas Development Institute, London.

Ashley, C. (2006) Participation by the poor in Luang Prabang tourism economy: current earnings and opportunities for expansion. ODI Working Paper No. 273. Overseas Development Institute, London.

Ashley, C. and Haysom, G. (2004) From philanthropy to a different way of doing business: strategies and challenges in integrating Pro-Poor approaches into tourism business. Paper presented at ATLAS Africa Conference in Pretoria (SA), October.

Ashley, C. and Maxwell, S. (2001) Rethinking rural development. *Development Policy Review* 19, 395–425.

Ashley, C. and Mitchell, J. (2007) Assessing how tourism revenues reach the poor. ODI Briefing Paper. Overseas Development Institute, London.

Ashley, C., Boyd, C. and Goodwin, H. (2000) Pro-poor tourism: putting poverty at the heart of the tourism agenda. Natural Resource Perspective No. 51. Overseas Development Institute, London.

Ashley, C., Roe, D. and Goodwin, H. (2001) Pro-poor tourism strategies: making tourism work for the poor: a review of experience. Pro-Poor Tourism report No. 1, April 2001. ODI/IIED/CRT. The Russell Press, London.

Ashley, C., Warner, M. and Romano, J. (2005) Directions for private sector development instruments in Africa: 8 strategies for policy makers. Commission for Africa.

Belisle, F.J. (1983) Tourism and food production in the Caribbean. *Annals of Tourism Research* 10, 497–513.

Belisle, F.J. (1984) Tourism and food imports: the case of Jamaica. *Economic Development and Cultural Change* 32, 819–842.

Bennett, O., Roe, D. and Ashley, C. (1999) Sustainable tourism and poverty elimination: a report for the department of international development. Deloitte and Touch, IIED and ODI, London.

Braman, S. and Fundación Acción Amazonia (2001) Practical strategies for pro-poor tourism: TROPIC Ecological Adventures – Ecuador. PPT Working Paper No.6. ODI/IIED/CRT, London.

Britton, S. (1982) The political economy of tourism in the Third World. *Annals of Tourism Research* 9, 331–358.

Brohman, J. (1996) New directions for tourism in Third World development. *Annals of Tourism Research* 23, 48–70.

Bryden, J. (1973) *Tourism and Development: a Case Study of the Commonwealth Caribbean*. Cambridge University Press, Cambridge.

Clancy, M. (1999) Tourism and development: evidence from Mexico. *Annals of Tourism Research* 26, 1–20.

Chen, S. and Ravallion, M. (2008) The developing world is poorer than we thought, but no less successful in the fight against poverty. The World Bank Development Research Group. World Bank Publications, Washington.

de Kadt, E. (ed.) (1979) *Tourism: Passport to Development?* Oxford University Press, New York.

DfID (1999) *Sustainable Livelihood Guidance Sheets.* Department for International Development, London.

Diaz-Benavides, D. (2001) *The Viability and Sustainability of International Tourism in Developing Countries: Symposium on Tourism Services.* World Trade Organization, Geneva.

Dieke, P. (1993) Tourism and development policy in the Gambia. *Annals of Tourism Research* 20, 423–449.

Dollar, D. and Kraay, A. (2002) Growth is good for the poor. *Journal of Economic Growth* 7, 195–225.

Duffy, R. (2002) *A Trip Too Far: Ecotourism, Politics and Exploitation.* Earthscan, London.

Farrington, J., Carney, D., Ashley, C. and Turton, C. (1999) Sustainable livelihoods in practice: early applications of concepts in rural areas. Natural Resource Perspectives No 42, Overseas Development Institute, London.

Flanagan, R.J. (2006) *Globalization and Labor Conditions: Working Conditions and Worker Rights in a Global Economy.* Oxford University Press, Oxford.

Goodwin, H. (2006) Community-based tourism: failing to deliver? id21 insights 62. Institute of Development Studies, Brighton.

Haughton, J. and Khandker, S. (2009) *Handbook on Poverty and Inequality.* World Bank Publications, Washington, DC.

Kakwani, N. and Pernia, E. (2000) What is pro-poor growth? *Asian Development Review* 18, 1–16.

Kakwani, N. and Son, H. (2002) Pro-poor growth and poverty reduction: the Asian-Pacific experience. Poverty Centre Technical Paper Series, No. 01. United Nations Economic and Social Commission for Asia and the Pacific, Bangkok.

Kaplinsky, R. and Morris, M. (2004) A Handbook for Value Chain Research. IDRC, Ottawa.

Kirsten M. and Rogerson, C.M. (2002) Development of SMMEs in South Africa. *Development Southern Africa* 19, 29–59.

Klasen, S. (2003) In search of the Holy Grail: how to achieve pro-poor growth? Discussion Papers 096. Ibero-America Institute for Economic Research, Gottingen.

Kraay, A. (2004) When is growth pro-poor? Cross-country evidence. Policy Research Working Paper Series 3225. The World Bank, Washington, DC.

Lengefeld, K. and Stewart, B. (2004) All inclusive resorts and local development: sandals as best practice in the Caribbean. Presentation at World Travel Market, London, November.

Mahony, K. and van Zyl, J. (2001) Practical strategies for pro-poor tourism. Case studies of Makuleke and Manyeleti tourism initiatives. PPT Working Paper No. 2. http://www.propoortourism.org.uk

Mbaiwa, J.E. and Darkoh, M. (2009) The socio-economic impacts of tourism in the Okavango Delta, Botswana. In: Saarinen, J., Becker, F., Manwa, H. and Wilson, D. (eds) *Sustainable Tourism in Southern Africa: Local Communities and Natural Resources in Transition.* Channel View, Clevedon, pp. 210–230.

McCulloch, N. and Baulch, B. (1999) Assessing the poverty bias of growth methodology and an application to Andhra Pradesh and Uttar Pradesh. IDS Working Paper 98, Brighton.

McNab, D. (2005) Impacts of pro-poor tourism facilitation with South African corporates – monitoring and evaluation report of the Pro-Poor Tourism Pilots Project, PPT working paper.

Meyer, D. (2003) Strengths and weaknesses of a pro-poor tourism approach: results of a survey to follow-up pro-poor tourism research carried out in 2000–2001. PPT Working Paper No. 9. ODI/IIED/CRT, London.

Meyer, D. (2004) Outbound UK tour operating industry and implications for PPT in developing countries. PPT Working Paper No. 17. ODI/IIED/CRT, London.

Meyer, D. (2008) Pro-poor tourism: from leakages to linkages. a conceptual framework for creating linkages between the accommodation sector and 'poor' neighbouring communities. *Current Issues in Tourism* 10, 558–583.

Mitchell, J. and Ashley, C. (2009) Value Chain Analysis and poverty reduction at scale. ODI Working Paper 49. Overseas Development Institute, London.

Mitchell, J. and Muckosy, P. (2008) A misguided quest: community based tourism in Latin America. ODI Opinions 102. Overseas Development Institute, London.

Momsen, J. (1996) Linkages between tourism and agriculture in the caribbean. Paper presented at International Geographical Union Conference (IGU), August, The Hague.

Mowforth, M. and Munt, I. (2003) *Tourism and Sustainability: Development and New Tourism in the Third World.* Routledge, London.

Oppermann, M. and Chon, K.S. (1997) *Tourism in Developing Countries.* International Thompson Business Press, London.

Page, S. (1999) Tourism and development: the evidence from Mauritius, South Africa and Zimbabwe. ODI Working Paper. Overseas Development Institute, London.

Porter M.E. (1985) *Competitive Advantage: Creating and Sustaining Superior Performance*. The Free Press, New York.

Ravallion, M. (2004) Defining pro-poor growth: a response to Kakwani. One Pager, International Poverty Centre, United Nations Development Program, Brasilia, No. 4.

Ravallion, M. and Chen, S. (2001) Measuring pro-poor growth. Policy Research Working Paper, No. 2666. Development Research Group, World Bank, Washington, DC.

Rhodes, E., Warren, J.P. and Carter, R. (2005) *Supply Chains and Total Product Systems: A Reader*. John Wiley and Blackwell, New York.

Roe, D., Grieg-Gran, M. and Schalken, W. (2001) Getting the lion's share from tourism: private sector-community partnerships in Namibia. IIED Poverty, Inequality and Environment Series No 1. International Institute for Environment and Development, London.

Roe, D., Ashley, C., Page, S. and Meyer, D. (2004) Tourism and the poor: analysing and interpreting tourism statistics from a poverty perspective. PPT Working Paper No. 16. ODI/IIED/CRT, London.

Saarinen, J. (2009) Conclusion and critical issues in tourism and sustainability in Southern Africa. In: Saarinen, J., Becker, F., Manwa, H. and Wilson, D. (eds) *Sustainable Tourism in Southern Africa: Local Communities and Natural Resources in Transition*. Channel View, Clevedon, pp. 269–286.

Scheyvens, R. (2002) *Tourism for Development: Empowering Communities*. Prentice Hall, London.

Scheyvens, R. (2007) Exploring the poverty-tourism nexus. *Current Issues in Tourism* 10, 231–254.

Scheyvens, R. (2009) Pro-poor tourism: is there value beyond the rhetoric? *Tourism Recreation Research* 34, 191–196.

Schilcher, D. (2007) Growth versus equity: the continuum of pro-poor tourism and neoliberal governance. *Current Issues in Tourism* 10, 166–193.

Scoones, I. (1998) Sustainable rural livelihoods: a framework for analysis. Working Paper 72. IDS, Brighton.

Sen, A. (1999) *Development as Freedom*. Oxford University Press, Oxford.

Spenceley, A. (2008) *Responsible Tourism*. Earthscan, London.

Taylor, B.E., Morison, J.B. and Fleming, E.M. (1991) The Economic Impact of Food Import Substitution in The Bahamas. *Social and Economic Studies* 40, 45–62.

Torres, R. (2002) Toward a better understanding of tourism and agriculture linkages in the Yucatan: tourist food consumption and preferences. *Tourism Geographies* 4, 282–306.

Torres, R. (2003) Linkages between tourism and agriculture in Mexico. *Annals of Tourism Research* 30, 546–566.

Tourism Concern (2004) Holidays from hell. *TSSA Journal*, July/August. Transport Salaried Staffs' Association.

UNWTO (2006) *Tourism and Least Developed Countries: A Sustainable Opportunity to Reduce Poverty*. United Nations World Tourism Organization, Madrid.

Wiggins, S. and Higgins, K. (2008) Pro-poor growth and development. ODI Briefing Paper 33. Overseas Development Institute, London.

Wilkinson, P.F. (1987) Tourism in small island nations: a fragile dependency. *Leisure Studies* 6, 127–146.

World Tourism Organization (2002) Tourism and Poverty Alleviation. Madrid: UNWTO.

11 Urban Beaches as Social Tourism Installations: Case Studies of Paris Plage and Bristol Urban Beach 2007

Tim Gale

Introduction

Urban beaches have become a feature of many European cities in the summer months, on the pretext of providing an alternative recreational space for residents on low incomes. Accordingly, this chapter extends the discussion of social tourism in Chapters 3 and 8 to encompass the urban beach as a means of addressing, or compensating for, non-participation in leisure travel on the part of the least mobile in (post)modern society. It commences with a background to the development of urban beaches in the UK and continental Europe, before introducing Paris Plage and Bristol Urban Beach 2007 as, arguably, the best known and most recent examples thereof (at the time of writing). Through a combination of secondary and primary research (including a visitor survey), the chapter then evaluates the sustainability and social tourism credentials of the urban beach, ending with a commentary on the enablements and constraints to realizing more sustainable and inclusive forms of tourism through innovations such as this.

This chapter takes an innovative approach to exploring the prospects for promoting social justice (and environmental sustainability) in and through tourism, by focussing on case studies of urban beaches in the UK and Continental Europe, specifically Paris Plage and Bristol Urban Beach 2007. These particular examples of 'new'

tourism spaces and places are a feature of many European cities in the summer months (e.g. Rome, Berlin, Brussels, Amsterdam and Budapest and, elsewhere in the world, Brisbane and Tokyo), such that the urban beach now constitutes a phenomenon of sorts. Urban beaches may best be described as temporary installations of sand, grass and wooden decking adorned with palm trees, deckchairs, hammocks, beach huts and other seaside paraphernalia, in otherwise unremarkable or neglected urban environments (e.g. highways closed to traffic, disused wharfs, car parks, etc.). They are often found in cities seeking international recognition and/or with diverse and, possibly, disenchanted populations, given the public relations benefits and potential for social mixing afforded by these temporary public spaces. The prototype, Paris Plage, was conceived in 2001 as a recreational space for low-income residents of the city and its suburbs who could not afford a holiday at the coast, or anywhere else for that matter, and now attracts some three million visitors during the 6 weeks in which it is open to the public each summer. Elsewhere, I have argued that urban beaches such as Paris Plage are symptomatic of what Urry (1995) calls 'the end of tourism', or the de-differentiation of tourism and everyday life under disorganized capitalism as the form of society that has come to characterize the global North (Gale, 2009). This may be attributed to a paradigm shift in the mobility of people, goods and services, capital, information, governance and so on across national borders, which has seemingly brought the remote, the exotic and the 'other' closer to home with the result that people become for the most part tourists, 'whether they are literally mobile or only experience simulated mobility' (Urry, 1995: 148).

Theory aside, and notwithstanding the contradictions inherent in this proposition, what follows is an examination of the *social tourism* credentials of the urban beach (and the two examples mentioned above) or, put another way, its function as a surrogate tourism space for those who cannot travel for leisure, but would if they had the means – financial or otherwise – of doing so. Problems of definition aside (see Chapters 3 and 8), social tourism programmes are designed to address the various constraints that account for non-participation in tourism (e.g. low incomes, disability and ill health, cultural factors, etc.), and typically comprise financial support for disadvantaged individuals and groups, the operation of holiday savings schemes, and the provision of specialized accommodations and excursions. Their importance stems from the fact that a significant proportion of the population does not enjoy meaningful access to holidays, even in supposedly 'developed' countries such as the UK, where, annually, 35–45% of adults are reported as having not taken a holiday in the previous 12 months (Roberts, 2004). By virtue of their exclusion, the social benefits of holiday-making are denied to these people and their dependents, most notably:

- the ability to develop and maintain close relationships with friends and family;
- the ability to renew individual energy by means of removing oneself from stressful or mundane situations in every-day life; and
- the ability to self-actualize (achieving one's potential) and develop independence.

Accordingly, it is hypothesized that urban beaches and other temporary uses of space

in the city that are designed to s(t)imulate 'play', constitute innovative practice in social tourism (with some caveats to this proposition, which will be highlighted in the chapter's concluding paragraphs). In 'testing' this hypothesis, reference will be made to triple-bottom-line-sustainability as a concept of some significance and a context for understanding the arguments for promoting and consuming tourism(esque) experiences 'on one's own doorstep'.

Methods used in this study include an analysis of the various discourses in both print and electronic media that pertain to the case studies in question, observations undertaken at the sites themselves, and the salient results of a survey of visitors to one of these sites (namely Bristol Urban Beach 2007). Regarding the visitor survey, which yielded 116 usable responses, answers were sought to four overarching questions (or sets of questions):

1. Who uses the urban beach, and why?
2. How does it compare to a real beach? (Note that examples of seaside resorts in the region, such as Weston-super-Mare in this case, were mentioned in order to aid comparison.)
3. What do people most like and dislike about the urban beach?
4. How far and by what mode of transport did they travel to the urban beach, and how much was spent on their visit?

The empirical evidence generated by these methods is deployed in the discussion of urban beaches, sustainability and social justice in/through tourism that makes up the substantive part of this chapter. This is prefaced by a brief introduction to each case study, starting with Paris Plage.

Case Study 1: Paris Plage

The brainchild of the socialist mayor of Paris, Bertrand Delanoë, this is an annual event operating since 2002 that sees the closure to traffic of a 3-km section of the Georges Pompidou expressway alongside the Right Bank of the River Seine, from mid-July to mid-August (traditionally the time of year when those residents who can afford to do so leave the city for their summer vacation), and its transformation into a palm-fringed 'pleasure zone' (Fig. 11.1). It is widely regarded as the world's first urban beach, although evidence has come to light of an earlier example in Nottingham, England, in the early 1990s (A. Phelps, personal communication, 29 August 2007). Costing over €2 million, paid for by the city in partnership with public agencies and private sponsors, Paris Plage comprises:

- three distinct 'beaches' (four, now that it has been extended to the Left Bank of the Seine);
- a 28-m swimming pool;
- an adventure playground;
- a stage for open-air concerts;
- a venue for beach sports;
- numerous cafes; and
- a lending library.

As stated above, it attracts in the region of three million visitors and, like the tourist sites and destinations on which it is modelled, has spawned a variety of souvenirs and other merchandise (t-shirts, postcards, etc.).

Mayor Delanoë's vision for reuniting Paris and the Seine, hitherto divided by tarmac and traffic, was realized with the help of a scenographer, Jean Christophe Choblet, who modelled Paris Plage on traditional French resorts such as Deauville and Le Touquet. He was keen that the installation be accessible to all, especially less wealthy Parisians and suburbanites; indeed, the notion of social equity lies at the heart of the project, and Choblet has distanced himself from the many imitators of Paris Plage which, with a few exceptions, are private projects and not free of charge (Choblet, 2008). That said, this 'playground for the poor' also draws in a significant number of tourists – both nationals and foreigners – during one of the most popular times of the year for visiting Paris, providing them with a new and unusual vantage point from which to appreciate the city (while showcasing its politics). Of course, Delanoë and Choblet would have been aware of this from the outset and, even allowing for the tradition of providing holidays to the poor in France, it is unlikely that Paris Plage would have happened were it not for its novelty value in a place better known for its architecture and art galleries.

Fig. 11.1. A view of Paris Plage (c. 2005), looking west towards the Musée du Louvre.

Case Study 2: Bristol Urban Beach 2007

Resisting the corporate feel of other urban beaches (notably Birmingham's, which is sponsored by Monarch Airways), this was a community-led project delivered and managed by Demos, the so-called 'think-tank for everyday democracy', in collaboration with Zero Zero, a not-for-profit architectural practice and social enterprise, and Bristol City Council, the local planning authority. (It should be noted that, in addition to its statutory function, the Council were involved in an advisory capacity concerning matters of design, sustainability, community engagement and fundraising, and as a project enabler by providing a contribution to cover core costs.) Designed as an experiment in place-making and civic branding, and to showcase the creative arts and sustainable living, Bristol Urban Beach occupied an area of 1500 m² on a run-down site earmarked for development at Redcliffe Wharf in Bristol's Harbourside, between 21 July and 2 September 2007. It cost almost £170,000, and attracted an estimated 65,000 visitors – mostly families, office workers and the occasional *flâneur* from Bristol itself and the former County of Avon (numbering upwards of 2000 people per day when the sun was out). Deemed by all involved to be a great success, it addressed several of the Council's policy objectives in promoting:

- a thriving economy through increased visitor spend on site and in the surrounding area;
- health and well-being via participation in sport and other physical or cultural activities; and
- balanced and sustainable communities by providing outlets for cultural expression, opportunities for lifelong learning, etc.

More broadly, it demonstrated that these installations can be socially inclusive spaces attracting a variety of urban dwellers (including 'hard to reach' groups) who would not normally have reason to interact with one another, and also 'green' alternatives to flying or driving long distances

for sun and fun – in other words 'a beach within reach' (Demos, 2007).

Unlike Paris Plage, Bristol Urban Beach 2007 is not destined to be repeated in the near future. Demos and its partners have accomplished what they set out to achieve with the pilot project, namely by demonstrating what is possible when local people are actively involved in the production of public space and, without their involvement, Bristol City Council are reluctant to take solo responsibility for the delivery and management of another such installation on this site or, indeed, at a range of alternative locations in the Harbourside area that were put forward as suitable for temporary use as an urban beach.

Urban Beaches as a Form of Sustainable Tourism

Many readers will, no doubt, be familiar with the definition of sustainable development provided by the Brundtland Commission as 'that [which] meets the needs of the present without compromising the ability of future generations to meet their own needs' (World Commission on Environment and Development, 1987: 43). Fundamental tenets of sustainability include:

- the maintenance of ecological integrity and biodiversity;
- the meeting of basic human needs;
- keeping options open for future generations;
- reducing injustice; and
- increasing self-determination (Wall, 2000: 567).

One may be forgiven for wondering what this has to do with urban beaches which, as ephemera, stand in contrast to the more pressing concerns and long-term planning horizons set out in 'Our Common Future'. However, a cursory discourse analysis of statements concerning Paris Plage and Bristol Urban Beach 2007 taken from press releases, newspaper articles and the like, reveals something of how these installations correspond to established ideas about sustainable development and the environmental, social and economic dimensions thereof (Fig. 11.2). Here, by employing the convention of a Venn diagram, we can see that the urban beach is not just a marketing tool to encourage shoppers and tourists to spend (more) time and money on site and in the surrounding area, or a means of rebranding post-industrial cities as desirable places in which to work, rest and play in an era of 'tourism reflexivity' (Sheller and Urry, 2004: 3), worthwhile though these out-comes are. Rather, it appeals to a diverse constituency made up, on the one hand, of locals who for various income and struc-tural constraints cannot visit the seaside for real and, on the other, of more affluent residents, daily commuters and outsiders for whom it is an attractive, low-carbon alternative to leisure travel by car (and plane, if one accepts that such phenomena might help to promote 'staycations', a neologism for what used to be called domestic tourism).

The notion of a 'green beach' figures prominently in the prospectus for Bristol Urban Beach 2007, which makes reference to enterprises selling locally sourced food and 'eco-ethical' lunches. It is also borne out by the results of the above-mentioned visitor survey, notably the average distance travelled from home (8.3 miles, $n=84$), the average amount spent on purchases made at the beach (£5.83, $n=83$), and the mode of transport used to get there (Table 11.1). Respondents' postcodes were used to determine the first of these statistics, which confirms the local/regional appeal of the beach. The second is a relatively modest figure, most likely because admission was free, but it does hint at some money being injected into the local economy with, we might speculate, an attendant multiplier effect. (Also, increased footfall associated with the beach most likely resulted in additional expenditure in shops and restaurants and at other visitor attractions within the city centre.) The third suggests that the beach generated a significant amount of trips by car (35%), although other, more sustainable modes of transport are not far behind when grouped together

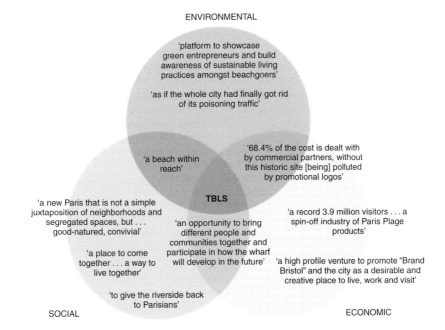

Fig. 11.2. Discourse about Paris Plage and Bristol Urban Beach, in the context of triple bottom-line sustainability (TBLS).

Table 11.1. Mode of transport used by respondents, Bristol Urban Beach 2007 Visitor Survey.

	Frequency	Percentage	Cumulative percentage
Walking (including wheelchair)	22	22.9	22.9
Car	34	35.4	58.3
Taxi	2	2.1	60.4
Bus or coach	27	28.1	88.5
Bicycle	5	5.2	93.8
Train	4	4.2	97.9
Other (n=96)	2	2.1	100.0

as can be seen in Table 11.1 (i.e. 'under one's own steam'/walking plus cycling, 28.1%; public transport/bus or coach plus train, 32.3%).

When asked how the urban beach compared to any real beaches with which they were familiar, a number of respondents identified the potential for reducing the need to travel by car and, in turn, one's carbon footprint, as indicated by the comments below:

> Bristol's beach lacks the donkey rides or candyfloss, but is a fantastic facility that saves going to Devon or Dorset where the nearest decent beaches are.

> Kids can play as though on a real beach and it's a safe and less expensive alternative to the seaside, certainly as petrol becomes more expensive.

> It's easily accessible, without using a car.

Others alluded to the socio-economic benefits of proximity to the urban beach, for example:

> There's better sand at the seaside, but it's good for families on low incomes.

Picking up on this theme, the relationship of urban beaches to broader policies and agendas of social inclusion is further explored in the next section.

Urban Beaches and their Social Tourism Credentials

Observations undertaken during fieldwork in 2005 and 2007 confirm the social tourism credentials of the urban beach. In the case of Paris Plage, various means of self-improvement were noted such as painting and writing workshops and taï chi sessions for the elderly; similarly, Bristol Urban Beach 2007 hosted a range of events such as art shows, salsa classes and talks/lectures. (These call to mind the 'rational recreation' movement in late Victorian Britain.) For both sites, admission was free, as were a number of the aforementioned activities, with commercial establishments kept to a minimum and chosen to complement the ethos of the beach. This resulted in a high degree of social mixing (something that has been diminished with the loss, through privatization, of public space in our towns and cities and of life from those spaces that remain), as articulated by La Pradelle and Lallement in their ethnography of Paris Plage:

> Businessmen in three-piece suits rushing from one appointment to another would cross paths with a handful of kids from the suburbs sauntering along in small groups 'to watch the girls in bathing suits'; elderly people sitting on the sides, as they would in a park, commenting on everything; and whole families settling on the sand with their picnic baskets, towels, and beach toys.

(La Pradelle and Lallement, 2004: 137–138)

Moreover, for these and other urban beaches, the sights, sounds and sensations of the real beach are recreated through the use of simple props, including water atomizers and the obligatory palm trees, encouraging liminal behaviour and a tolerance of proximity akin to that observed in popular coastal tourism resorts (see Shields, 1991, on the beach as a site of the carnivalesque). As witnessed first hand, this can lend itself to participatory activities and shared experiences that transcend class and other divisions (e.g. age, gender, race, etc.), helping to promote social cohesion and, reverting to the main theme of this chapter and of the book as a whole, access to tourism *for all* – if one accepts that these sites can provide something that approximates to a tourist experience for the majority of their visitors. On that note, the observed behaviour of visitors suggests that they are *performing* the beach; they walk on the asphalt and lay down on the sand as they would if visiting the seaside for real, while constantly being surrounded by reminders that they are not such as the absence of the sea and the texture of the sand. Of course, this is part of the attraction, but it does beg the question of whether urban beaches can offer a meaningful tourist experience (and, indeed, whether this matters to the majority of people who visit).

Statistically, the survey of visitors to Bristol Urban Beach 2007 revealed a few things of significance. Table 11.2 summarizes the salient characteristics of respondents (i.e. gender, age and ethnicity), where it can be seen that the majority were female (66%), aged 30–44 (40%) and White British (95%). Given that data were collected by a number of researchers at various times of the day, we can assume that this is a reasonably accurate reflection of the population of beachgoers. A broad range of age groups was attracted to the beach, but the anticipated diversity of users is best expressed by neighbourhood statistics (Table 11.3). These data were generated by asking each respondent for their postcode (95 of them obliged), and then converting this into an index of total deprivation (ITD) using a tool provided by the Office for National Statistics (UK) website (url: http://www.neighbourhood.statistics.gov.uk). This index is a composite of the income, employment, health, education, barriers to housing and services, crime and living environment deprivation indices for the postcode area in which the respondent lived, and ranged from 1 to 20 (where 1 was reserved for the least deprived areas and 20 for the most deprived). When grouped into quartiles, it became apparent that a majority of visitors were from more deprived areas (55%), the beach being located in a zone of transition between the gentrified central business district of Bristol and low-income neighbourhoods to the south and east. This suggests that the ambition of providing socially excluded residents of the city and its surrounding area with a satisfactory (albeit artificially generated) diversion or escape from everyday life appears to have been met. There was also a temporal dimension to visitation, with those from more deprived areas

Table 11.2. Gender, age and ethnic group of respondents, Bristol Urban Beach 2007 Visitor Survey.

	Frequency	Percentage	Cumulative percentage
Male	39	33.6	33.6
Female (*n*=116)	77	66.4	100.0
16–19	13	11.4	11.4
20–29	16	14.0	25.4
30–44	46	40.4	65.8
45–59	14	12.3	78.1
60–74	18	15.8	93.9
75+ (*n*=114)	7	6.1	100.0
White British	109	94.8	94.8
White Irish	1	0.9	95.7
Other white	1	0.9	96.5
Asian and white	1	0.9	97.4
Caribbean	1	0.9	98.3
African (*n*=115)	2	1.7	100.0

Table 11.3. Proportion of respondents living in less deprived and more deprived areas, Bristol Urban Beach 2007 Visitor Survey.

	Frequency	Percentage	Cumulative percentage
First quartile, 1–5 (least deprived)	18	18.9	18.9
Second quartile, 6–10	25	26.3	45.2
Third quartile, 11–15	30	31.6	76.8
Fourth quartile, 16–20 (most deprived) (n=95)	22	23.2	100.0

tending to visit during the middle part of the day, as opposed to early mornings or evenings.

While the above statistic points to the value of Bristol Urban Beach 2007 as a social tourism installation, it is the comments captured by the visitor survey that best illustrate this, a sample of which are included below:

> I've taken part in the Treasure Hunt and done some Kung Fu.

> The kids have played volleyball and had their faces painted.

> We've been sitting and talking since we got here.

> It's a nice spot to sit for a while and relax, without feeling isolated.

> It's a happy place with people having fun and chilling out.

> It's secure, and offers an opportunity for kids to play with other kids they don't know.

> It's a community thing. You get all different types of people coming here.

Relaxation, reflection and restoration, by means of a break from routine activities; social interaction, combating feelings of isolation for those who are often house-bound; opportunities to do something different, perhaps leading to new hobbies and interests and increased self-esteem; and the strengthening of family relationships through sharing 'quality time' – these are some of the benefits to individuals and families of visiting the urban beach that may be inferred from the above comments, all of which echo the arguments for providing holidays to disadvantaged groups (Hazel, 2005; Corlyon and La Placa, 2006; McCabe, 2009; Chapter 8, this volume).

Indeed, for one family with a disabled child and no access to a car, an afternoon at Bristol Urban Beach 2007 was the closest they had gone that year to enjoying the pleasures of the seaside (which many of us take for granted). Citing the practicalities of having to travel by public transport to the nearest resorts and the cost of entertaining the children once there as reasons for their non-participation, they would appear to be representative of a significant minority of city residents who rarely leave their local area, for whom the coast and countryside is 'out of bounds'.

However, notwithstanding the obvious benefits to those who cannot or do not travel for leisure purposes, a number of visitors to Bristol Urban Beach 2007 suggested that it was a poor substitute for the real thing:

> It's smaller and you can't paddle or swim.

> It's a bit of fun and doesn't really compare. A real beach provides a greater variety of attractions, plus natural features such as rock pools.

> There's no sea, and you wouldn't feel right trying to dress for the beach here.

It should also be acknowledged that a day trip is not the same as a long holiday or even a short break, although Corlyon and La Placa (2006) note that such trips can be as beneficial and, indeed, less stressful to organize. These sentiments were echoed by another respondent:

> The drive to the coast is a nightmare! Here, you can visit for an hour or two, rather than having to make a day of it.

Furthermore, with an urban beach there are few of the usual worries of being by the sea (e.g. risk of drowning), and less pressure to spend money in order to have a good time. We might even conclude that it is preferable to a real beach, on this evidence!

Conclusions

Suffice to say, this chapter has taken a somewhat unorthodox approach to addressing the question of how social (and environmental) justice can be achieved in and through tourism. It is written in the belief that the current era of cheap, uncomplicated long distance leisure travel is drawing to a close, as dangerous climate change, dwindling oil reserves, the economic downturn and global terrorism threaten to diminish our appetite for foreign holidays (Gale, 2008). Simultaneously, our towns and cities are broadening their cultural offer to include open-air theatres, outdoor ice-skating rinks and, as discussed here, urban beaches; it is the conjunction of these factors that opens up new possibilities for being a tourist without having to travel far from home for any great length of time (criteria that are enshrined in technical definitions of tourism). This marks a departure from the automobilities and aeromobilities that have come to characterize tourism, which is welcome news for the environment but also for the 'tourism-poor' – the main focus of this chapter – who cannot afford to travel any great distance or are prevented from doing so by other barriers to participation.

Critics of the urban beach cite the 'Disneyfication' of the city as an unwelcome consequence of these new public spaces, but much criticism of themed environments per se concerns the manipulation of design for financial gain (Ambler, 2009). Here, the use of cliché – the parasol set against the glare of the sun, the beach hut with its bright colours, the palm trees flanking the promenade – is motivated by a desire to convince visitors that they are 'at the beach', with a view to meeting new people or trying out something different (activities that are known to promote health and happiness). Furthermore, what is good for the individual, in evoking desired behaviours and outcomes that are so often missing from everyday life (and certainly the lives of the socially excluded), is also good for society, in reducing pressure on health and social care services and, quite possibly, the societal burden of drug abuse and crime. Hence, a modest investment in an urban beach can pay dividends further down the line, as with more conventional interventions in the name of 'social tourism' (such as those mentioned in the introduction to this chapter).

Naturally, it is difficult to sustain an argument about the benefits of urban beaches as social tourism installations without acknowledging evidence to the contrary. First, not all urban beaches can be described as such – some are designed to make as much money as possible from their visitors, others as animated billboards for their corporate sponsors. They are far removed from the altruistic agenda of Paris Plage and successive urban beaches cast in the same mould, such as Bristol Urban Beach 2007. Even in the case of Delanoë's 'pet project' there are tensions between its egalitarian origins and its appropriation as a chic hangout (although the installation is large enough for both to be accommodated), with a recent operation to remove vagrants begging on or adjacent to the site serving as a reminder that not all are welcome.

Second, routine practices and everyday norms in the city can only be interrupted and suspended for so long, and there comes a time when the sites in question must revert to their previous use (usually 4–6 weeks after the launch party). From that point onwards, would-be visitors will have to look elsewhere for things to do in their leisure time (assuming they have any to speak of), and at activities that may not be as meaningful to them as a visit to the urban beach. (In the case of one-off events like Bristol Urban Beach 2007, they are even denied the anticipation of it returning the following year.) Thus, as with the space itself, the benefits of visiting may be short-lived and not enduring (unless they are associated with a life-changing experience that transcends repeat visits to the urban beach). Finally, there is a need for further research to substantiate the above claims, not least in relation to the question of whether, and under what conditions, urban beaches and other such installations can fulfil visitors' aspirations for and expectations of the time they spend on leave from work or domestic duties.

To conclude, taking into consideration tourism's poor track record when it comes to sustainability and social justice (e.g. the loss of biodiversity in fragile natural environments, the displacement of indigenous peoples from their lands), we could be forgiven for thinking that 'the only sustainable form of tourism [is] to holiday at home' (Hall, 2005: 345). Fanciful though this may seem, and not disputing the fact that technology and imagination are incapable of replacing physical travel for all but a small minority, this chapter has shown how ideas and icons associated with tourism may be mobilized to provide genuine alternatives to travelling to other places in one's leisure time, benefitting both the environment and individuals who are normally excluded from participating.

Questions

1. Urban beaches are but one example of a 'new' tourism space or place, where sights and sensations associated with holiday resorts and the annual vacation are artificially recreated in everyday environments in/close to one's home town or city. Name some other examples.

2. Do urban beaches and other such simulations generate or suppress demand for physical travel?

3. What are the principal arguments for and against the urban beach as an environmentally sustainable, and socially inclusive, alternative to long distance leisure travel?

Acknowledgements

The author would like to thank Melissa Mean at Demos, Julie Witham at Bristol City Council and the editors of this volume, Stroma Cole and Nigel Morgan, for their assistance at various stages of the research process.

References

Ambler, M. (2009) Time and tide: urban beaches and the temporary construction of public space. Unpublished master's dissertation, Manchester Metropolitan University.

Choblet, J.-C. (2008) One of the fundamental ideas behind Paris Plage is social equity. http://www.eukn.org/romania/news/2008/08/interview-jean-christophe-choblet_1003.html (accessed 10 June 2010).

Corlyon, J. and La Placa, V. (2006) *Holidays for Families in Need: Policies and Practice in the UK*. Policy Research Bureau, London.

Demos (2007) Bristol Urban Beach: Your Invitation to Participate. http://www.demos.co.uk/files/File/bristol_urban_beach_intro.pdf (accessed 20 March 2010).

Gale, T. (2008) The end of tourism, or endings in tourism? In: Burns, P. and Novelli, M. (eds) *Tourism and Mobilities: Local-Global Connections* (pp. 1–14). CAB International, Wallingford, UK.

Gale, T. (2009) Urban beaches, virtual worlds and 'the end of tourism'. *Mobilities* 4, 119–138.

Hall, C.M. (2005) *Tourism: Rethinking the Social Science of Mobility*. Pearson, Harlow.

Hazel, N. (2005) Holidays for children and families in need: an exploration of the research and policy context for social tourism in the UK. *Children and Society* 19, 225–236.

La Pradelle, M.D. and Lallement, E. (2004) Paris Plage: 'the city is ours'. *The Annals of the American Academy of Political and Social Science*, 595, 134–145.

McCabe, S. (2009) Who needs a holiday? Evaluating social tourism. *Annals of Tourism Research* 36, 667–688.

Roberts, K. (2004) Leisure inequalities, class divisions and social exclusion in present day Britain, *Cultural Trends* 13, 57–71.

Sheller, M. and Urry, J. (eds) (2004) *Tourism Mobilities: Places to Stay, Places in Play*. Routledge, London.

Shields, R. (1991) *Places on the Margin: Alternative Geographies of Modernity*. Routledge, London.

Urry, J. (1995) *Consuming Places*. Routledge, London.

Wall, G. (2000) Sustainable development. In: Jafari, J. (ed.) *Encyclopedia of Tourism* (pp. 567–568). Routledge, London.

World Commission on Environment and Development (1987) *Our Common Future.* Oxford University Press, New York.

12 Justifying Tourism: Justice through Tourism

Freya Higgins-Desbiolles

Introduction

Justify – v.t. show the justice or rightness of (person, act, etc.); vindicate (of circumstances, esp. in pass.) be such as to justify; demonstrate correctness of (assertion etc.); adduce adequate grounds for (conduct, claim, etc.).

(*The Concise Oxford Dictionary*, 1976: 588)

Justice is a key issue of our times. We live in a world of spectacular wealth and yet millions live in abject poverty. We live in a time of progress, science and technology but these positives of human civilization have also contributed to a possible future of rapid and uncontrollable climate change, disproportionately felt by the poor who have least contributed to the problem. We also live in an era when more and more people of the more economically developed countries (MEDCs) can enjoy their holidays amid the exoticized underdevelopment and poverty of the less economically developed countries (LEDCs). These communities of the LEDCs are frequently compelled to 'host' these tourists and gear their infrastructure to the tourists' comforts despite their own poverty and underdevelopment in an effort to secure employment and foreign exchange in a world economy predicated on an unequal global trading regime.

However, tourism academics have rarely discussed tourism and justice (the rare exceptions include Hultsman, 1995; Scheyvens, 2002; Smith and Duffy, 2003; Fennell, 2006; Higgins-Desbiolles, 2008). Contemporary discourse on tourism in both the public and academic domains typically describes tourism either as a source of fun and/or fulfilment (Butcher, 2003) or focuses on its characteristics as an 'industry' delivering foreign exchange and jobs to communities around the globe (Smith, 1988). However, as I have described elsewhere (2006), at the founding of the modern tourism phenomenon in the mid-1800s with Thomas Cook's tours, tourism was seen as a potent social force of considerable significance.

In this chapter, I will analyse the complex relationship between tourism and justice, and assess the potential for justice through tourism. From the prism of climate change, unsustainable human demands on the natural environment, and poverty and human suffering, we may indeed need to justify our enjoyment of tourism. Examining tourism from a global justice perspective, I suggest that the benefits of globalization, which enable tourists from the MEDCs to enjoy holidays amidst the underdevelopment of the LEDCs also necessitate solidarity work to eradicate this very poverty and underdevelopment because the world is de facto becoming increasingly one place. While this sounds utopian in a world still viewed as a system of nation-states, my exploration of what I (2008) have called 'justice through tourism' shows that a multitude of efforts are underway to achieve this.

Tourism and Injustice

There is clearly a relationship between tourism and injustice. The negative impacts of tourism have been documented for decades, most vociferously by the non-governmental organizations (NGOs) concerned with tourism as well as certain critical academics. The literature in this vein is extensive and powerful, and comes from such sources as the Ecumenical Coalition on Tourism, the Tourism Investigation and Monitoring Team, Tourism Concern and academics and analysts such as Krippendorf (1987), McLaren (2003), and Turner and Ash (1976).[1] Some forms of tourism are inherently unjust and inequitable, for example when poverty and lack of opportunity compel people to sell that which normally would not be sold, found in such niches as sex tourism, organ-transplant medical tourism and poverty tourism. Rather than address the unjust nature of some tourism impacts or the exploitative nature of specific tourism niches, I will briefly highlight the global inequities on which the international tourism and travel industry are based, best exemplified in the relationships between the predominantly tourism-generating regions of the MEDCs and the tourism receiving regions of the LEDCs.

International tourism, particularly between the MEDCs and the LEDCs, exhibits increasing tensions of class polarization that result from regions of underdevelopment becoming incorporated into the global travel circuit as playgrounds for tourists from areas of conspicuous consumption. Such tension is most evident between tourists and their hosts, as tourists display wealth and consumption patterns unimaginable to some of the inhabitants of the poorer regions to which tourists are increasingly drawn in their search for 'authentic', 'exotic' or 'meaningful' experiences. Such a situation is evident in the work of Hutnyk (1996), who investigated 'poverty tourism' in Calcutta, India. He described the economic power displayed by poverty-gazing backpackers:

> The ability to move to conveniently inexpensive market and service centres through the facility of international travel yields a relatively high buying power with attendant ideological, habitual and attitudinal

> consequences – backpackers who can live like Rajas in Indian towns at low financial costs.
>
> (Hutnyk, 1996: 9–10)

Such discrepancies in wealth, power and status are particularly apparent in the tourism encounter as the tourist often comes 'face to face' with the poor. Crick has described this as 'leisure imperialism' and the 'hedonistic face of neo-colonialism' (1989: 322). That resentment is fuelled by this situation is apparent in the crime, violence, corruption and hostility that is apparent in many international tourism destinations of the LEDCs including Jamaica, India, Sri Lanka, Egypt and Indonesia. For instance, in a rare case of journalism that sought to explain the roots of violence against tourists, Levy and Scott-Clark (2006) explained how rapid societal changes brought on by tourism development have fuelled a 'violent crime wave' on the island of Koh Samui, Thailand. They note how this island moved from a sleepy backwater to hosting over one million tourists every year within the span of two decades, and how foreign and elite interests have come to dominate tourism (Levy and Scott-Clark, 2006). Levy and Scott-Clark refer to a submission made by Thai academics to the Thai government that describes a 'social and moral implosion' that has ensued as 'fewer than 20% of islanders have benefited from the boom, leading to "explosive tensions" between rich and poor residents, mainland Thais and foreigners' (2006).

However, the class polarization generated by tourism under capitalism is more complex than the gulf between tourists and host communities. Tensions are also exacerbated between locals at the tourism destination as different groups are affected differently by the onset of tourism. Tensions pit youth against elders and local elites against the masses (Dogan, 1989). Crick claimed:

> Benefits from tourism 'unlike water, tend to flow uphill' ... the profits go to the elites – those already wealthy, and those with political influence ... the poor find

themselves unable to tap the flow of resources while the wealthy need only use their existing assets (e.g. ownership of well-positioned real estate, political influence) to gain more.

(Crick, 1989: 317)

As discussed in Chapter 7 (by Cole and Eriksson), another key injustice frequently attributed to the pressures of tourism development is the dispossession of the local people. The NGO Tourism Concern has campaigned on human rights issues in tourism and has run specific campaigns on dispossession in places like East Africa and Southeast Asia. Mowforth and Munt noted:

Of all the problems experienced by local communities facing tourism development schemes, the most harrowing involve accounts of people being displaced. Such events normally reflect the distribution of power around the activity of tourism and highlight the powerlessness of many local communities. And it seems rare that displacement and subsequent resettlement of displaced people result in more even and equal development.

(Mowforth and Munt, 2003: 236–237)

Controversially, native Hawaiian academic Haunani-Kay Trask has condemned tourism as one form of environmental racism perpetrated on indigenous peoples (1993). Trask defined environmental racism as 'the practice of siting hazardous waste production and disposal in communities and in nations of color' (1993). In particular, she noted how the tourists drawn to her land for 'escape' on their holidays are 'participating in the destruction of a host people in a Native place' (1999: 137). Trask provided startling statistics on Hawaiian tourism: Hawaii hosts 35 tourists to every one native Hawaiian, which results in one of the highest tourist densities in the world (1993). The resultant crowding, pollution, pressure on Hawaiian resources, edging out of other endeavours such as fishing, agriculture and cultural pursuits, and economic inflation, result in indigenous Hawaiians leaving their homelands or trying to eke out survival on the margins of the tourism industry whose low wages leave many as

the working poor. In another powerful article, Trask has described how all of the significant public and private sector structures promote tourism growth:

In Hawaii, the destruction of our land and the prostitution of our culture is planned and executed by multi-national corporations, by huge landowners, and by collaborationist state and county governments. The ideological gloss that claims tourism to be our economic saviour and the 'natural' result of Hawaiian culture is manufactured by ad agencies, tour companies, and the state of Hawaii which allocates some $60 million dollars a year to the tourism advertising budget.

(Trask, 2000)

Finally, the most serious form of tourism's unjust impacts on the LEDCs is their forceful incorporation into the global trading system through their engagement with tourism in their hopes of harnessing tourism for development. Lanfant and Graburn argue:

[tourism] is a 'transmission belt' connecting the developed and the underdeveloped worlds. Tourism policy has become part of a global project which lumps together seemingly contradictory economic interests: the organization of vacations (an idea originating in rich countries) and the aspirations for development of economically weak societies. Thus 'free time' resulting from the exploitation of the surplus value of capital is put back into the calculation of economic productivity. Societies inexperienced with industrialization are re-oriented toward 'touristification'; tourism comes to be judged by economic and political criteria within the international framework, a vector for global integration.

(Lanfant and Graburn, 1992: 96)

As Kalisch discusses in Chapter 6, the global 'free' trade regime being established by the powerful MEDCs, the international financial institutions and powerful transnational corporation (TNC) interests are forcing a global integration, and tourism is a part of this agenda through the free trade agreement for the service sector, the General Agreement on Trade in Services (GATS). GATS is predicted to lead to greater concentration in the tourism sector as big tourism TNCs continue the trend towards vertical integration. This is very evident in places like Germany where the three leading tourism companies control 68% of the market (Berne Declaration and WGTD, 2004: 8–9). Simultaneously, GATS limits the capacity of LEDCs to control tourism for their own benefit:

> Designed to ensure that host governments, confronted with powerful transnational corporations who import their own staff and the majority of goods needed for their tourism operation, cannot compel them to use local materials and products to enhance the 'multiplier effect', or to take special measures to secure a competitive base for their domestic businesses.
>
> (Kalisch, 2001: 4)

With some notable exceptions (including Mowforth and Munt, 2003; Kalisch and Cole and Eriksson, this volume), the mainstream tourism literature over the previous three decades has tended to ignore these issues of injustice and tourism. While some tourism proponents have worked hard to promote the valuable economic potential of tourism, they have simultaneously downplayed the very real power differentials that are clear from political analyses. As Enloe claimed:

> Tourism is not just about escaping work and drizzle; it is about power, increasingly internationalized power. That tourism is not discussed as seriously by conventional political commentators as oil or weaponry may tell us more about the ideological construction of 'seriousness' than about the politics of tourism.
>
> (Enloe, 1989: 40)

A Theory of Justice and Tourism

There have been a small number of very significant contributions to discussions of the ethics of tourism. One of the earliest and more interesting was Hultsman's consideration of 'just tourism', which he suggested could mean 'fair' or 'proper' tourism or alternatively 'merely' tourism (1995:

560). In Hultsman's attempt to develop an ethical framework for tourism he focused on both the tourists' experience of tourism and the need to develop a 'principled' practice and 'ethicality' in tourism and ensuring that this imbues tourism curricula (Hultsman, 1995: 559–562). Absent from his analysis was any consideration of the receiving community or the justness or equity of relations between the tourists and the locals.

Fennell (2006) and Smith and Duffy (2003) considered the philosophical basis for tourism ethics and as part of these discussions analysed contributions of justice theory to the development of an ethics of tourism. These discussions include an application of Rawls' theory of justice (Smith and Duffy, 2003; Fennell, 2006), a consideration of rights discourse (Fennell, 2006), the contributions of feminist ethics and caring (Smith and Duffy, 2003) and communicative or discourse ethics (Smith and Duffy, 2003). Both of these analyses are brief and limited as the discussions of justice and tourism sit within books focused on the ethics of tourism. A key limit of both works is the focus on social justice or justice within societies and a failure to discuss the newer topic of international justice. This is a natural tendency, as we currently live in a world organized through nation-states and justice is most fully developed at the inter-societal level. However, this focus results in justice issues being discussed in more narrow terms. My focus in this chapter is more global, so I will instead engage with what could be termed global or international justice and assess its significance to international tourism.

It is widely agreed that one of the best conceptualizations of justice is offered by John Rawls in his 'theory of justice' (1972). Rawls viewed justice as the 'first virtue of social institutions' (1972: 3). Using a contractual and rationalist approach, Rawls explored justice as fairness and investigated the basic principles to which all within a society would agree. He suggested that the way to arrive at such principles is to imagine what rational individuals would choose as a just situation if they had no idea of their status or circumstances or, as Rawls terms it, they were shrouded by a 'veil of ignorance' that prevented them from being swayed by their selfish and particular interests (1972: 12). Rawls' principles are:

> First: each person is to have an equal right to the most extensive basic liberty compatible with a similar liberty of others.
>
> Second: social and economic inequalities are to be arranged so that they are both (a) reasonably expected to be to everyone's advantage, and (b) attached to positions and offices open to all.
>
> (Rawls, 1972: 60)

Rawls' main analysis was of distributive justice within society, asking what are the obligations that fellow citizens owe one another and what are the just bases for any inequality that may arise? Rawls accepted the reality that our current system is predicated on a system of nation-states and therefore his contractual theory of justice is largely about obligations within societies bound together by allegiance to the same social institutions. In this work, Rawls had little to say about the demands for distributive justice at the global level.[2]

Similar to Rawls' veil of ignorance, psychologist Lawrence Kohlberg explored the concept of 'justice as reversibility', which he suggested emanates from the 'one moral principle at the heart of ethics, the Golden Rule' (1981: xxxii). Kohlberg described this reversibility as 'put yourself in everyone else's place' and noted that it could also be called 'moral musical chairs' following the rules 'let everyone trade places before choosing and be willing to be in the worst-off chair' (1981: xxxii). Thinking in terms of global justice, could one imagine today switching places and being willing to put oneself in the 'worst-off chair' considering the premature death rates, hunger and poverty that characterize life for many in the LEDCs? Currently, those of us lucky enough to reside in the MEDCs enjoy our privileges and justify our enjoyment as the moral deserts of our industrious nations. Can an argument for

switching places through a commitment to global distributive justice be mounted?

Debates in global justice are ongoing but the theorization is still in its early stages (Brock and Moellendorf, 2005). However, some analysts participating in the debates on global justice argue that the key issue is distributive justice between nations or global distributive justice and these discussions are advancing rapidly. In his seminal article 'Famine, affluence, and morality', Peter Singer responded to a shocking famine in East Bengal in 1971 with a utilitarian argument that: (i) 'suffering and death from lack of food, shelter, and medical care are bad'; and (ii) 'if it is in our power to prevent something bad from happening, without thereby sacrificing anything of comparable moral importance, we ought, morally, to do it' (Singer, 1972).

In this argument, Singer claimed that the affluent have a moral duty to spend their excess income on famine relief and aid rather than unnecessary luxuries and this is an obligation not a matter of voluntary charity. The premise is there is no right to enjoy luxuries beyond all basic human needs when other sections of humanity are deprived and in danger. Singer's exposition provided a new moral vision for a more interdependent yet highly unequal world. If adopted, it might have assisted in helping the most vulnerable in the global community, but this world view was anathema to the materialistic, individualistic and neo-liberal orthodoxy.[3]

Thomas Pogge took another approach, arguing 'we – the more advantaged citizens of affluent countries – are actively responsible for most of the life-threatening poverty in the world' (2005: 30). This argument is based on a view that the global order and economy were established by gross injustices in the colonial period, which have allowed the peoples of the MEDCs to achieve their levels of affluence from the enslavement, impoverishment and exploitation of the peoples of the LEDCs, perpetuated by the current inequitable global trading system. Pogge stated:

> My main claim is ... that, by shaping and enforcing the social conditions that

foreseeably and avoidably cause the monumental suffering of global poverty, we are harming the global poor – or, to put it more descriptively, we are active participants in the largest, though not the gravest, crime against humanity ever committed.

(Pogge, 2005: 33)

Tourists and tourism are implicated in these crimes. According to Lash and Urry, 'international tourism is a process by which the affluent countries, having mined their own environments, now scavenge the earth to consume those of other people, particularly those environments consistent with images of "natural", "unspoilt", and "green"' (1994: 303). Additionally, tourists' demand for exotic holidays in LEDC destinations leads to an aesthetic of poverty, as exemplified in Hutnyk's (1996) work. This naturalizes a most inhumane situation as displays of obscene levels of wealth and excess occur in places of appalling and degrading poverty. The ideological assertion that tourists and the tourism industry that facilitates them are in fact 'pro-poor' in their efforts as their presence brings the market to the poor and gives them one of the few opportunities to make income can at best be described as wilfully ignorant. This masks the fact that the majority of LEDCs that bet their hopes for development on tourism are in fact subjugating themselves to continued underdevelopment in a global trading system established on inequitable foundations.

Tourism touted for its development potential to LEDCs integrates these nations in the global trading system on unequal terms, perpetuating their poverty and undermining subsistence. As Badger *et al.* have claimed:

> Power is increasingly in the hands of these large northern-based companies, who can direct flows of international tourists to particular destinations because of their high-tech globalised reservation systems. An estimated 80 per cent of all tourists travel with a tour operator package, so it is easy to appreciate the power of the tour operator vis-à-vis the host country.

(Badger *et al.*, 1996: 22)

Such package holidays result in high economic leakage, with the money staying in the MEDC generating economy and the LEDC economy receiving very little for hosting. Additionally, attracting these TNCs requires LEDCs to build infrastructure such as airports and roads, adding to the heavy debt burden that many of these countries are under. Enloe has described this as the 'tourism formula for development' and argued 'a government which decides to rely on money from tourism for its development is a government which has decided to be internationally compliant' (1989: 31). Analysts such as Pleumarom (1994, 1999) have pointed out a hidden agenda in the pressure placed on LEDCs to implement tourism strategies. This agenda includes achieving: debt repayments, sites for TNC investment, integration on unequal terms in global trading relationships, holiday opportunities for elite tourists but more importantly assimilation into the global capitalist order. As Fennell (2006: 102) stated, 'tourism is very much a justice issue', but as the foregoing analysis demonstrates, it is also particularly a global justice issue as well.

Justice through Tourism

While the relationship between tourism and justice is now clearer, it remains to be explored what justice through tourism might mean. There are clear indications in recent decades that some people are doing tourism differently. The alternative tourism movement has sought empowerment for local communities, meaningful experiences for tourists, protection for environments, and a more responsible and sustainable tourism sector. Lanfant and Graburn suggested alternative tourism could become 'the tourism in the promotion of a new order' (1992: 92) and justice tourism best exemplifies this vision. Holden described justice tourism as 'a process which promotes a just form of travel between members of different communities. It seeks to achieve mutual understanding, solidarity and equality among participants' (Pearce, 1992: 18).

One of the first analyses of 'justice tourism' was offered by Scheyvens, who described it as 'both ethical and equitable' and claimed it has the following attributes:

- builds solidarity between visitors and those visited;
- promotes mutual understanding and relationships based on equity, sharing and respect;
- supports self-sufficiency and self-determination of local communities;
- maximizes local economic, cultural and social benefits.

(Scheyvens, 2002: 104).

An even more comprehensive listing of key attributes is found in Scheyvens' extensive quotation from an Australian tour agency called Just Travel. 'Just travel' is described from the point of view of the traveller as providing:

- the knowledge that s/he is not an agent of oppression but is attempting to participate in the liberation process;
- a travel experience that will offer genuine possibilities of forming meaningful relationships with people of different cultures;
- an opportunity to experience firsthand what other people are doing to create new life possibilities for themselves and others; and
- adequate preparation for their travel.

(Wenham and Wenham, cited in Scheyvens, 2002: 104)

Additionally, just travel from the point of view of the tourist-receiving communities promises:

- Travellers will be people who are coming to share and not to dominate their lives.
- Local accommodation and infrastructure will be used. As far as possible the services of foreign-owned and operated companies will be avoided.
- Tourist sites and shows that degrade or debase the culture will be avoided. Opportunity will be given for local people to develop a real presentation of their culture with pride and dignity.
- Travellers will be required to observe standards of decency and will not be tolerated if their presence is offensive to local people.

(Wenham and Wenham, cited in Scheyvens, 2002: 104)

Scheyvens outlined five forms of justice tourism, which include:

- the 'hosts' telling their stories of past oppression;
- tourists learning about poverty issues;
- tourists undertaking voluntary conservation work;
- tourists undertaking voluntary development work; and
- revolutionary tourism.

(Scheyvens, 2002: 105–119)

However, it is problematic that some of the characteristics Scheyvens attributed to justice tourism overlap with what has been called responsible tourism. It may be helpful to view justice tourism as a continuum of activities focused on fostering more just relationships and outcomes in tourism, which ranges from responsible tourism on the more moderate end of the spectrum to transnational solidarity activism on the more extreme end (Fig. 12.1).

Transnational solidarity activism emphasizes active partnerships in overcoming injustice through supporting local communities facing human rights abuses and injustice in their efforts to overturn unequal power situations that entrap them. This transnational solidarity activism may also be described as justice through tourism and its participants called 'active justice tourists'.[4] Following Singer's and Pogge's arguments that global poverty is a key moral issue of our time, this analysis focuses on the more extreme end of the justice tourism scale. My argument here is that privileged tourists should justify their enjoyment of tourism by using their opportunities to work for justice and better living conditions for those who live in the places they visit.

To provide some insight into this little known phenomenon, I will provide a few examples that illustrate the range of actions for justice through tourism: an example of a community using justice through tourism to achieve its aims; an example of one organization arranging transnational solidarity opportunities; a profile of an active justice tourist; and a brief overview of justice tourism activism in global fora agitating for a more just form of globalization.

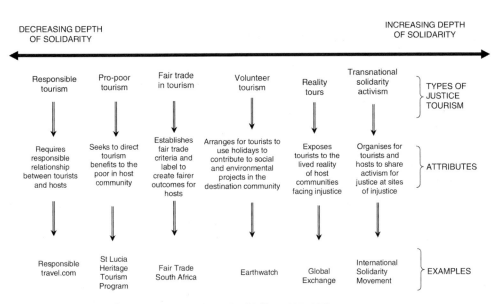

DECREASING DEPTH OF SOLIDARITY

INCREASING DEPTH OF SOLIDARITY

Responsible tourism	Pro-poor tourism	Fair trade in tourism	Volunteer tourism	Reality tours	Transnational solidarity activism	TYPES OF JUSTICE TOURISM
Requires responsible relationship between tourists and hosts	Seeks to direct tourism benefits to the poor in host community	Establishes fair trade criteria and label to create fairer outcomes for hosts	Arranges for tourists to use holidays to contribute to social and environmental projects in the destination community	Exposes tourists to the lived reality of host communities facing injustice	Organises for tourists and hosts to share activism for justice at sites of injustice	ATTRIBUTES
Responsible travel.com	St Lucia Heritage Tourism Program	Fair Trade South Africa	Earthwatch	Global Exchange	International Solidarity Movement	EXAMPLES

Fig. 12.1. Continuum of justice tourism (Higgins-Desbiolles, 2009: 338).

Examples of Justice through Tourism

The reality tours offered by the human rights organization Global Exchange (GX) serve as good examples of justice tourism experiences. Founded in 1988, GX is an American-based, international human rights NGO dedicated to 'promoting social, economic and environmental justice around the world' (Global Exchange, no date (n.d.) c). GX's vision states:

> We envision a people centered globalization that values the rights of workers and the health of the planet; that prioritizes international collaboration as central to ensuring peace; and that aims to create a local, green economy designed to embrace the diversity of our communities.
>
> (Global Exchange, n.d. a).

Its involvement in tourism is geared towards human rights education, citizen diplomacy, fostering just relationships and solidarity activism:

> The idea that travel can be educational, fun, and positively influence international affairs motivated the first Global Exchange Reality Tours in 1989. Our tours provide individuals the opportunity to understand issues beyond what is communicated by the mass media

and gain a new vantage point from which to view and affect US foreign policy. Travelers are linked with activists and organizations from around the globe who are working toward positive change. We also hope to prompt participants to examine related issues in their own communities.

> (Global Exchange, n.d. b)

Currently GX offers reality tours to over 30 countries in Latin America, Africa, Asia and the Middle East. Its portfolio of tours is varied and its aims are impressive:

> Participants learn about women's struggles in Afghanistan, the impact of oil exploration on Ecuador's indigenous communities, fair trade in Tanzania, the struggle for peace and justice in Palestine & Israel, and more. Global Exchange Reality Tours also provide opportunities for Americans to travel as 'citizen ambassadors' to countries like Syria, Iran, Libya, and Cuba, breaking down the stereotypes and misinformation that can lead toward hatred and war.
>
> (Global Exchange, n.d. c)

In addition to these tour itineraries around the globe that examine the fault lines of injustice and conflict, GX also organizes tours that coincide with the World Social Forum (WSF), a meeting of representatives of global civil society movements who gather to strategize ways to oppose corporate-led globalization (discussed further below). This particular tour is one of the more obvious examples of GX's commitment to use the tourism opportunity to work towards change in the global system.

GX provides participant comments on many of their tours as well as links to some of the many weblogs these participants have created to share what they have learned from their experiences. These provide some indication of the impact that GX's justice tours are having (Global Exchange, n.d. d). In particular, these commentaries show that many GX reality tour participants do embrace their responsibility to share their learning with others at the conclusion of their experience.

Another interesting example of justice tourism is the Community Leadership Program organized by the Australian NGO Oxfam Australia (formerly called Community Aid Abroad), which takes participants on an extended tour of India to learn about community development and to return committed to contribute to community development in Australia. Its vision statement reads:

> The vision for the Community Leadership Program not only encompasses a combination of workshops and project visits overseas but is hopefully an ongoing process of building effective community involvement in Australia around issues of human rights, international justice and sustainable development. To this end, participants will be encouraged to give some voluntary time in the 12 months following their return to become involved in locally based social justice issues.
>
> (Oxfam Australia, n.d.)

A distinguishing feature of this programme is the underlying ethos that people from developed countries can learn from the sound community development practices created by people in developing countries. The goal of this programme is to 'build a strong and effective supporter base in Australia and to be an integral part of a global movement for social justice' (Oxfam Australia, n.d.).

The Ladakh Project of the International Society for Ecology and Culture (ISEC) demonstrates another impact of justice through tourism. It can change attitudes of people who are 'subjected' to the impacts of corporate-controlled tourism. Ladakh is a region in the Himalayas with a strong, vibrant culture, which began to experience outside influence through the international 'development' process in the 1970s. Helena Norberg-Hodge of ISEC grew concerned that external influences such as the advice brought by development experts created 'idealised images of western consumer culture – undermining the local economy and eroding cultural self-esteem. The result has been increasing community and family breakdown, unemployment, sprawling urban slums and pollution' (ISEC, n.d.; Norberg-Hodge, 1991). So the Ladakh Project includes an educational and cultural exchange programme designed to provide the Ladakhi people with accurate insights into the lifestyles of the developed countries to counter the idealized images that tourists, expatriates, television and media often portray so that the people can make informed decisions about the future they wish to create for their community. The response of one of these Ladakhi reality tourists provides an interesting insight into the impact of this experience:

> Spending time in the West showed me a side of Westerners I never imagined. I found that they have lots of money but they don't have time for each other. Many of them are looking for community and a life closer to nature – a Ladakhi lifestyle!
>
> Stanzin Tonyot, ISEC's Farm Project Coordinator (ISEC, n.d.)

It is apparent that the phenomenon of justice through tourism works at numerous levels to foster transformations that are intended to spark changes for a more just and sustainable global order.

Justice through Tourism as a Tool for Communities Lacking Justice

The village of Beit Sahour near Bethlehem is significant to the Palestinian resistance. This village was known for its use of non-violent tax resistance during the first Intifada and it was instrumental in the use of alternative tourism for 'resistance and understanding' (Elias Rishmawi, cited in Stein, 1995: 18). In support of the latter effort, the Alternative Tourism Group (ATG) was established in 1995. It is a Palestinian NGO that offers 'justice tourism' experiences, which it describes as 'tourism that holds as its central goals the creation of economic opportunities for the local community, positive cultural exchange between host and guest through one-on-one interaction, the protection of the environment and political/historical education' (ATG, n.d.). In addition to this focus on the tourist and their experiences, ATG additionally encourages Palestinian tourism operators to avoid exploitative practices and to create an industry that benefits the Palestinian people. ATG's specific objectives include:

- to modify the tendencies of mass tourism in 'the Holy Land' to establish a more human-oriented tourism;
- to put foreign tourists in direct contact with the Palestinian population in order to help them develop a better understanding of Arab Palestinian culture and history;
- to break down the negative stereotypes of Palestine and its people that predominate in the West;
- to achieve more balance between the revenues of the Palestinian and Israeli tourism sectors by using Palestinian infrastructure (hotels, restaurants, transportation, guides, etc.);
- to augment the number of tourists visiting Palestine and increase the length of their stay in Palestinian areas;
- to develop among tourists a knowledge of Palestinian culture and the socio-political situation in Palestine;
- to encourage instructive and authentic meetings with the Palestinian people to develop among tourists an objective

understanding of everyday realities of the Israeli occupation; and
- to offer tourists the opportunity to share unique experiences with Palestinians through volunteer work with non-governmental organizations (olive harvesting, tree planting, etc.)

(Rami Kassis, 12 March 2009, personal communication)

Through these methods, the ATG 'seeks to promote a positive image of Palestine and its people and to contribute towards establishing a just peace in the area' (ATG, n.d.). Since 1995, the ATG has hosted more than 20,000 visitors to Palestine, among them 13,000 Christian pilgrims (Rami Kassis, 21 March 2009, personal communication).

International Solidarity Movement

The International Solidarity Movement (ISM) is a Palestinian-led movement committed to resisting the Israeli occupation of Palestine through the use of non-violent, direct-action methods. Founded by a small group of mostly Palestinian activists in August 2001, the ISM organizes for international solidarity volunteers to visit Palestine and through their presence support and strengthen the Palestinian popular resistance by providing the Palestinian people with international protection and a voice with which to get the Palestinian narrative on the Israeli occupation out to the world.

International volunteers are the key to the ISM strategy. According to the ISM, they provide:

1. **Protection**: an international presence at Palestinian civilian actions can ensure a degree of protection for Palestinians engaged in non-violent resistance.

2. **Message to the mainstream media**: the Palestinian struggle is not accurately reported by the mainstream corporate media ... People from all over the world that join us can reach out to their respective media and help dispel this notion.

3. **Personal witness and transmitting information**: international civilians joining

Palestinians can bear witness and return home to talk to their communities about what is happening.

4. Break isolation and provide hope: the occupation isolates Palestinians and cuts them off from the rest of the world and from each other. International civilians coming in, despite restrictions, send a message to the Palestinian community – 'we see, we hear and we are with you.' Hope that people acting together can change things is a cornerstone of our philosophy and message.

(ISM, n.d.)

The ISM is a Palestinian movement that seeks the support of international activists as a strategy to support its resistance to the Israeli occupation. ISM volunteers support the Palestinian resistance through:

- *Direct Action* – challenging crippling checkpoints and curfew, confronting tanks and demolition equipment, removing roadblocks, participating in nonviolent demonstrations, accompanying farmers to their fields and protecting families whose homes are threatened with demolition.
- *Emergency Mobilization* – escorting ambulances through checkpoints, delivering food and water to families under curfew or house arrest, assisting the injured or disabled to access medical care and walking children to school.
- *Documentation* – documenting and reporting to local and international media about the daily life under occupation and the countless human rights and international law violations by the Israeli military.

(ISM, n.d.)

Co-founder of ISM George Rishmawi stated:

Our goal is to help Palestinians do nonviolent resistance because when they do it without international accompaniment they are met with terrible violence. The international presence enabled many families, this October, to go to their fields and harvest their olives, and open roadblocks. When the army sees that they're watched, they are less free-handed in how they treat people.

You are all invited to Palestine. When they see internationals who have come, Palestinians feel hope, that others have come

to share their hardship. Hope is very important for a people who feel their pain ignored, their voice unheard, their land taken away every day.

(Rishmawi, 2004: 7)

That these solidarity volunteers might be critically injured or even killed has been acknowledged at the outset. As Rishmawi stated: 'when Palestinians get shot by Israeli soldiers, no one is interested anymore, but if some of these foreign volunteers get shot or even killed, then the international media will sit up and take notice' (cited by Kalman and Castle, 2004). One of the most well-known ISM activists is Rachel Corrie, because she was a youthful American killed by an Israeli 'Defence' Force bulldozer while trying to prevent it from demolishing a house in Gaza in March 2003 (more on Corrie as a 'justice through tourism tourist' follows). Since Corrie's death, other ISM activists have been injured, shot and killed (Fig. 12.2).

Despite the dangers and hardships, thousands of North American, British, European, expatriate Palestinian and even Israeli activists have volunteered to support Palestinians in their non-violent resistance through ISM. This must represent one of the most extreme forms of tourism on the planet and demonstrates the ultimate lengths to which committed people will go to turn their travel and tourism choices towards achieving justice for others in the global community.

Profile of a Solidarity Activist

Rachel Corrie was a justice tourist. She kept a diary and wrote numerous letters during her work with the ISM, and this was compiled into a book after her death. Her writing provides a useful insight into the way ISM activists witness Palestinian experiences and share their insights (Corrie, 2006). On 7 February 2003, after just 2 weeks in Palestine, she wrote:

I still have few words to describe what I see. I don't know if many of the children here have ever existed without tank-shell holes in their walls. I think even the smallest of these

Fig. 12.2. Activists from Viva Palestina aid convoy to Gaza enjoying a boat trip while protesting against the Egyptian Government's refusal to allow them to leave Aqaba, Jordan on 27 December 2009, the anniversary of the start of Israel's 'Operation Cast Lead' (Nicci Enchmarch).

children understand that life is not like this everywhere ... Nothing could have prepared me for the reality of the situation here. You just can't imagine it unless you see it. And even your experience is not at all the reality: what with the difficulties the Israeli army would face if they shot an unarmed US citizen, the fact that I have money to buy water when the army destroys wells, and of course, the fact that I have the option of leaving. I am allowed to see the ocean.

(Corrie, 2006: 29)

Corrie's work contains rich insights into the thoughts of the activist, the ways the activist interacts in solidarity with the local community with which they work and the ways they may view their own actions, as well as the ambiguities and fault lines that are ever-present working in such zones of inequity and injustice. Corrie obviously also hoped that others would follow her in her commitment to solidarity with the Palestinians and others suffering injustice in the global community. Shortly before her death, Rachel Corrie wrote to her mother:

It is my own selfishness and will to optimism that wants to believe that even people with a great deal of privilege don't just idly sit by and watch. What we are paying for here is truly evil. Maybe the general growing class imbalance in the world and consequent devastation of working people's lives is a bigger evil. Being here should make me more aware of what it means to be a farmer in Colombia, for example ... This has to stop. I think it is a good idea for us all to drop everything and devote our lives to making this stop. I don't think it is an extremist thing to do anymore.

(Corries, 2006: 49)

Writing a foreword to a book on the ISM, Edward Said noted the import of Corrie's example:

What Rachel Corrie's work in Gaza recognized was the gravity and the density of the living history of the Palestinian people as a national community, and not merely as a collection of deprived refugees. That is what she was in solidarity with. And we need to remember that kind of solidarity is no longer confined to a small number of intrepid souls here and there, but is recognized the world over.

(Said, 2004: xv)

Justice through Tourism on the Global Stage

Director of the ATG, Rami Kassis, has briefly discussed justice tourism from his experience of using tourism to effect change in Palestine. From his standpoint, Kassis observed a global dimension to this topic: 'justice tourism is a social and cultural response to the policy of cultural domination as reflected in the globalization of tourism' (Kassis, n.d.).

Activists in the newly emerging justice tourism movement have started aligning with the global justice movement through the annual gatherings of global civil society groups within the WSF convened since 2001 to advance their common concerns. The WSF opposes capitalist globalization and advocates for an alternative global-ization that is sustainable, economically just, people-centred and based on greater self-reliance than that currently fostered by neo-liberal globalization (WSF, 2004).

While tourism has long been criticized for its negative impacts, protest at a global level has only emerged at the WSF con-vened in Mumbai, India in 2004. At this meeting, tourism was put on the agenda of the WSF for the first time as a Global Summit on Tourism was held. The theme was 'Who really benefits from tourism?' The summit issued a call to 'democratize tourism!'. One NGO participant, the Ecumenical Coalition on Tourism (ECOT), called for a tourism that is 'pro-people' (ECOT, 2003). Attendees at the meeting released a statement of concern, which voiced similar concerns to the opponents of capitalist globalization, and formed a Tourism Interventions Group (TIG) (TIG, 2004). This group clearly positioned itself in opposition to the processes of capitalist globalization such as the General Agree-ment on Trade in Services and corporate-controlled tourism:

> We decided to strengthen and uphold the grassroots perspectives of tourism, which positions our interventions against those of the World Tourism Organization (WTO-OMT) (UNWTO), the World Travel & Tourism Council (WTTC) and other mainstream definitions of tourism policy and development. As the WTO-OMT (UNWTO) is now a specialised UN agency, we will address its new mandate and take forward civil society engagements to democratise tourism.

> A primary concern is the undemocratic nature of the ongoing negotiations in the

World Trade Organisation's General Agreement on Trade in Services (GATS) that are slated to end by January 2005. We stress the urgent need to bring in experiences from the grassroots on the environmental and social costs of tourism to inform the negotiating positions of governments and underline the need for a rollback in the negotiations.

(TIG, 2004)

However, the Tourism Interventions Group also made very clear what its movement was in support of, and this is very similar to the aims of other new social movements gathered at the WSF. They claimed:

> Highlighting tourism issues within a multitude of anti-globalization and human rights movements such as those related to women, children, *dalits*, indigenous people, migrants, unorganised labour, small island, mountain and coastal communities, as well as struggles related to land, water and access to natural resources, is crucial to sharpen local struggles and community initiatives of those impacted by tourism. Networking is at the core of future strategising to identify areas of common concern, forge alliances with like-minded individuals, organisations and movements and influence tourism policy agendas. Democracy, transparency and corporate and governmental accountability in tourism will be placed high on the agenda for concerted action and strategic interventions.

> We look forward to working in solidarity with local community representatives, activists and researchers from various parts of the world to strengthen our struggle and develop strategies for a tourism that is equitable, people-centred, sustainable, ecologically sensible, child-friendly and gender-just.

(TIG, 2004)

This gathering advocated:

- forming a solidarity campaign to secure the rights and interests of the people at the 'grassroots' who bear the impacts of tourism;
- concerted action to sensitize the UNWTO and the WTTC to the needs of ordinary people;
- petitioning the UN system to make the UNWTO (recently admitted into the specialized agencies of the UN) responsive to the civil society movement

which represents the people impacted by tourism rather than the beneficiaries of corporatized tourism;
• and investigating the impacts of GATS, leakages, structural adjustment, neo-liberalism and exploitative labour practices in order to develop an agenda to oppose corporatized tourism.

(ECOT, 2004).

This final example of justice tourism demonstrates that some wish to harness alternative tourism in the effort to secure a more equitable, alternative globalization. It remains to be seen how successful the TIG will be in drawing global attention to the negative impacts of corporate-controlled tourism and the positive potentials of justice tourism in securing a more just global order. However, the integration of the new social movement for justice tour-ism as represented by the TIG with the larger global justice movement provides a greater profile for this movement and increases the likely impact it can have.

Concluding remarks

Justice will only exist where those not affected by injustice are filled with the same amount of indignation as those offended.

(Plato)

The foregoing discussion provides an overview of some examples of tourism being harnessed for justice in the global community. It is by no means a compre-hensive portrait of the phenomenon and greater investigation is required. However, as has been demonstrated, certain individ-uals and organizations operating in the global community and concerned to estab-lish more just and equitable global relations have turned to tourism as one tool to achieve these goals.

However, justice through tourism has its ambiguities and difficulties. By its very nature, the tourism encounter is fleeting and the solidarity it can engender is limited unless conscious efforts are made to upset the power equation. Landy's research on activist tourists in Palestine reported:

One interviewee working in Palestinian tourism was sharply critical of activist tourism. While recognizing the good intentions behind it, she characterized it as a disempowering activity – a means for activists to portray themselves as heroes and then walk away from the situation, leaving locals to feel that political action is a seasonal foreign-orientated activity.

(Landy, 2008: 198)

Additionally, Mahrouse's analysis (2008) alerts us to examine this phenomenon critically. She has researched transnational solidarity activists similar to those of the ISM and she characterizes them as 'white/ Westerners as mediators of the Other's suffering' (Mahrouse, 2008: 89). She argued that these activists act as mediators as they try to make people back home aware of the injustices suffered by communities like Palestine. Using Arendt's theory of com-passion versus pity to assess whether these activists are successful in their efforts to act against injustice, Mahrouse demonstrated that the effort is problematic. As Mahrouse stated:

The important distinctions between the two centre on the relationship to the sufferer. In Arendt's view, a relationship of compassion is more or less an equal one and implies a sharing of suffering. Relationships of pity, on the other hand, re-enact the power differentials between the viewer and the sufferer, rather than disrupt them.

(Mahrouse, 2008: 98)

Mahrouse found in her research that when activists return home and tell of the suffering of people like the Palestinians visited on solidarity tours, because both the teller and the audience are both white/ western people of privilege, the teller potentially becomes the object of the compassion of their listeners, while their narrations only evoke pity for people like the Palestinians. Thus the activists' goals are potentially thwarted by the very power differentials their actions are attempting to address. While not nullifying the validity of the enterprise, it does problematize the effort of seeking justice through trans-national solidarity activism in a context of global inequities and chasms of injustice.

The only way such a situation is likely to be fully overcome is when the moral vision for global distributive justice and global solidarity spreads more widely throughout societies. At the moment, national borders serve as rather substantial demarcations of where suffering and poverty is considered the norm and where it is considered an anomaly. However, the forces unleashed by globalization are in fact steadily undermining these demarcations as evidenced in the rhetoric of 'one world' and cosmopolitanism. The global solidarity activists and justice tourists described here may be seen as a vanguard demonstrating a necessary transformation in consciousness required in our changing world. They also point the way to a necessary change in tourism and how it is done. Examining tourism from a global justice perspective, it is apparent that globalization enables tourists from the MEDCs to enjoy holidays amidst the more pristine environments and exotic cultures of the LEDCs, who are forced by their very underdevelopment to accommodate the demands of these MEDC tourists. The demands of justice in such circumstances commands all tourists of conscience to turn their efforts to global solidarity work, including during their holidays, because the world is de facto becoming increasingly one place in need of more equitable and just circumstances between all of its inhabitants. While this sounds utopian in a world still viewed as a system of nation-states, these transformations are underway and our ethical understandings need to evolve with these changing circumstances.

Tourism has undergone some startling and important transformations in the past three decades, most notably from the mass tourism phenomenon to the alternative tourisms of today. Simultaneously, the world has become a smaller place because of globalization and technology. And yet shocking poverty and suffering continues in a world of plenty. The MEDCs expect ever-growing levels of prosperity, while the LEDCs continue to seek development through tools such as tourism in vain because of a global trading system geared to their disadvantage. It is in this context of inequality and injustice that the active justice tourists undertaking justice through tourism experiences show how a most unlikely tool, tourism, can be turned to achieving some of the most important goals of our era, global justice and global solidarity. While the number of people and organizations that have made this transformation in consciousness may be currently minuscule, this does not diminish the importance of their examples nor the potential for them to be joined by others. If Edward Said is correct 'that [this] kind of solidarity is no longer confined to a small number of intrepid souls here and there, but is recognized the world over' (2004: xv), then we can look forward to a world of greater equality and justice where place of birth matters less and less to determining the quality of one's life.

Postscript

This chapter has been written in the shadow of an enormous tragedy in one of the world's poorest places, Haiti. On 12 January 2010, an earthquake of a catastrophic magnitude hit an area not far from the nation's capital, Port-au-Prince. At the time of writing, it is still not known how many dead and injured there are and what the costs of re-building will be. Yet as soon as one day after this tragic event, tourism analyst David Beirman was talking up the role of tourism in Haiti's future: 'The world tourism community has an opportunity, created by the current disaster to help Haiti emerge from its long nightmare. Donations and expressions of support are the right things to do in the short term but tourism is in a position to play a part in Haiti's longer-term route to recovery' (Beirman, 2010). In this rhetoric, we can see a continuation of the 'tourism formula for development' to which Enloe (1989) referred rather than the global solidarity that is needed to assist Haiti finally to emerge from centuries of exploitation and forced underdevelopment.[5] Only 7 days after the tragedy, it was reported with some dismay that cruise ships continued to dock: 'As a humanitarian crisis rages in Haiti, Royal Caribbean Cruise Lines continues to dock its ships in Haiti at Labadee, an exclusive private resort created to shelter tourists from the economic realities of this impoverished nation' (Koch, 2010). This site at Labadee has been described as a 'slice of Caribbean bliss surrounded by security fencing with all-you-can-eat buffets' (Lacey, 2007).

The inequities and injustice of contemporary tourism cannot be put in any starker relief than this. In a globalizing world, such strikingly unjust demarcations of poverty and suffering versus wealth and excess are becoming increasingly untenable.

Questions to Consider

1. Why is tourism a justice and equity issue?

2. What is justice tourism and what examples of justice tourism can you find in contemporary tourism and travel offerings?

3. The author argues that in an increasingly interdependent world, tourists of conscience should turn their holidays to efforts in fostering justice and poverty alleviation in the places they visit. How compelling do you find this argument?

Notes

[1]Elsewhere, I have provided a critique of the current impacts of tourism in my chapter 'Hostile meeting grounds' (2007), in which I explore the unjust economic, social and ecological impacts of tourism.
[2]Rawls weighed into the subject in his later work, The Law of Peoples (1999), but still viewed states as the key agents and argued that there are no strict requirements for global redistributive justice.
[3]However, if his moral imperative were taken seriously, it would not only relieve the poverty and suffering experienced in the LEDCs but would also undermine the destructive consumer lifestyle captivating the populations of the affluent MEDCs (Higgins-Desbiolles, in press).
[4]While these activists for justice might not recognise the label of 'justice tourists' as appropriate, they do fit the criteria of tourists often set out including: travelling a certain distance from their place of residence; temporarily staying in the destination community; spending money on goods and services within that destination community's economy; and then returning to their place of residence.
[5]Although the first colony to break away from slavery to establish the world's first black nation, Haiti was forced by military threats to pay compensation to France of 150 million francs (the equivalent of $25 billion today) for the loss of its colonial assets – a debt Haiti only finished paying in 1947. One source of Haiti's profound poverty is this completely repugnant action. If France was compelled to return these funds to Haiti, Haiti might be able to take its place with dignity among the community of nations rather than be presented as a perpetual basket case or worse, cursed peoples, in need of the charity and expertise of others.

References

Alternative Tourism Group (n.d.) *About us.* http://www.patg.org/index.php?page=1177263078 (accessed 11 June 2007).

Badger, A., Barnett, P., Corbyn, L. and Keefe, J. (1996) *Trading Places: Tourism as Trade.* Tourism Concern, London.

Beirman, D. (2010) How can tourism help Haiti? *ETurbonews*, 13 January. http://www.eturbonews.com/13829/how-can-tourism-help-haiti (accessed 13 January 2010).

Berne Declaration and Working Group on Tourism and Development (2004) The WTO General Agreement on Trade in Services and sustainable tourism in developing countries – in contradiction? http://www.akte.ch/pages/en/4_news/_aktion/Tourismus%20and%20GATS%20englisch.pdf (accessed 2 August 2005).

Brock, G. and Moellendorf, D. (2005) *Current Debates in Global Justice.* Springer, Dordrecht.

Butcher, J. (2003) *The Moralisation of Tourism: Sun, Sand ... and Saving the World?* Routledge, London.

The Concise Oxford Dictionary. (1976) 6th edn. Oxford University Press, Oxford.

Corrie, R. (2006) In: Rickman, A. and Vine, K. (eds) *My Name is Rachel Corrie.* Theatre Communications Group, New York.

Crick, M. (1989) Representations of international tourism in the social sciences: sun, sex, sights, savings, and servility. *Annual Review of Anthropology* 18, 307–344.

Dogan, H.Z. (1989) Forms of adjustment: sociocultural impacts of tourism. *Annals of Tourism Research* 16, 216–236.

Ecumenical Coalition on Tourism (2003) Concept paper for World Social Forum. Unpublished document. ECOT, Hong Kong.

Ecumenical Coalition on Tourism (2004) Recording of process, Activists Strategy Meeting on Tourism, 22–23 January 2004, YMCA, Mumbai, India. Unpublished document. ECOT, Hong Kong.

Enloe, C. (1989) *Bananas, Beaches and Bases: Making Feminist Sense of International Politics.* Pandora, London.

Fennell, D.A. (2006) *Tourism Ethics.* Channel View, Clevedon.

Global Exchange (n.d. a) *About Global Exchange.* http://www.globalexchange.org/about/ (accessed 25 January 2010).

Global Exchange (n.d. b) Global Exchange. http://www.globalexchange.org (accessed 25 January 2010).

Global Exchange (n.d. c) Global Exchange reality tours. http://www.globalexchange.org/tours/index.html (accessed 25 January 2010).

Global Exchange (n.d. d) Past participants share their experiences. http://www.globalexchange.org/tours/saying.html (accessed 25 January 2010).

Higgins-Desbiolles, F. (2006) More than an industry: the forgotten power of tourism as a social force. *Tourism Management* 27, 1192–1208.

Higgins-Desbiolles, F. (2007) Hostile meeting grounds: encounters between the wretched of the earth and the tourist through tourism and terrorism in the 21st century. In: Burns, P. and Novelli, M. (eds) *Tourism and Politics: Global Frameworks and Local Realities.* Elsevier, Amsterdam, pp. 309–332.

Higgins-Desbiolles, F. (2008) Justice tourism: a pathway to alternative globalisation. *Journal of Sustainable Tourism* 16, 345–364 .

Higgins-Desbiolles, F. (2009) International Solidarity Movement: a case study in volunteer tourism for justice. *Annals of Leisure Research* 12, 333–349.

Higgins-Desbiolles, F. (2010) The elusiveness of sustainability in tourism: the culture-ideology of consumerism and its implications, *Tourism and Hospitality Research* 10(2), 116–129.

Hultsman, J. (1995) Just tourism: an ethical framework. *Annals of Tourism Research* 22, 553–567.

Hutnyk, J. (1996) *The Rumour of Calcutta: Tourism, Charity and the Poverty of Representation.* Zed Books, London.

International Society for Ecology and Culture (n.d.) The Ladakh project. http://www.isec.org.uk/ladakh.html (accessed 30 June 2005).

International Solidarity Movement (n.d.) About ISM. http://palsolidarity.org/about (accessed 20 January 2009).

Kalisch, A. (2001) *Tourism as Fair Trade: NGO Perspectives.* Tourism Concern, London.

Kalman, M. and Castle, T. (2004) S.F. Jewish activist held as a security threat in Israel. *San Francisco Chronicle.* http://www.sfgate.com/cgi-bin/article.cgi?file=/chronicle/archive/2004/07/14/MNGBS7L5V71.DTL (accessed 3 March 2009).

Kassis, R. (n.d.) The Palestinians and justice tourism. http://www.patg.org/palestinians_and_justice_tourism.htm (accessed 19 July 2005).

Koch, L. (2010) Tourism and tragedy: cruise ships continue to dock in Haiti. *New York Destinations Examiner,* 20 January. http://www.examiner.com/x-23890-Long-Island-Budget-Travel-Examiner~y2010m1d20-Tourism-and-tragedy-Cruise-ships-continue-to-dock-in-Haiti (accessed 27 January 2010).

Kohlberg, L. (1981) *The Philosophy of Moral Development (Vol. 1), Essays on Moral Development Series.* Harper and Row, San Francisco, CA.

Krippendorf, J. (1987) *The Holiday Makers: Understanding the Impact of Leisure and Travel.* Butterworth-Heinemann, Oxford.

Lacey, M. (2007) Amid the woe, a Haitian paradise beckons, *New York Times,* 16 February. http://travel.nytimes.com/2007/02/16/world/americas/16haiti.html (accessed 27 January 2010).

Landy, D. (2008) Authenticity and political agency on study trips to Palestine. In: Lentin, R. (ed.) *Thinking Palestine.* Zed Books, London, pp. 189–205.

Lanfant, M.F. and Graburn, N.H.H. (1992) International tourism reconsidered: the principle of the alternative. In: Smith, V.L. and Eadington, W.R. (eds) *Tourism Alternatives.* John Wiley & Sons, Chichester, pp. 88–112.

Lash, S. and Urry, J. (1994) *Economies of Signs and Space.* Sage, London.

Levy, A. and Scott-Clark, C. (2006) Danger in paradise. *The Guardian,* 8 April. http://www.guardian.co.uk/weekend/story/0,,1748146,00.html (accessed 15 May 2006).

McLaren, D. (2003) *Rethinking Tourism and Ecotravel*, 2nd edn. Kumarian Press, Bloomfield, CT.

Mahrouse, G. (2008) Race-conscious transnational activists with cameras: mediators of compassion. *International Journal of Cultural Studies* 11, 87–105.

Mowforth, M. and Munt, I. (2003) *Tourism and Sustainability: Development and New Tourism in the Third World*, 2nd edn. Routledge, London.

Norberg-Hodge, H. (1991) *Ancient Futures: Learning from Ladakh*. Sierra Books, San Francisco.

Oxfam Australia (n.d.) Community leadership program. http://www.oxfam.org.au/CLP/index.html (accessed 2 November 2005).

Pearce, D.G. (1992) Alternative tourism: concepts, classifications and questions. In: Smith, V.L. and Eadington, W.R. (eds) *Tourism Alternatives*. John Wiley & Sons, Chichester, pp. 15–30.

Pleumarom, A. (1994) The political economy of tourism. *The Ecologist* 24, 142–148.

Pleumarom, A. (1999) Tourism, globalisation and sustainable development. *Third World Resurgence* 103, 4–8.

Pogge, T. (2005) Real world justice. In: Brock, G. and Moellendorf, D. (eds) *Current Debates in Global Justice*, Springer, Dordrecht, the Netherlands, pp. 29–53 .

Rawls, J. (1972) *A Theory of Justice*. Oxford University Press, Oxford, UK.

Rawls, J. (1999) *The Law of Peoples*. Harvard University Press, Cambridge.

Rishmawi, G. (2004) Helping to bring back hope. In: Sandercock, J., Sainath, R., McLaughlin, M., Khalili, H., Blincoe, N., Arraf, H. and Andoni, G. (eds) *Peace Under Fire: Israel/Palestine and the International Solidarity Movement*. Verso, London, pp. 3–7.

Said, E. (2004) The meaning of Rachel Corrie. In: Sandercock, J., Sainath, R., McLaughlin, M., Khalili, H., Blincoe, N., Arraf, H. and Andoni, G. (eds) *Peace Under Fire: Israel/Palestine and the International Solidarity Movement*. Verso, London, pp. xiii–xxii.

Scheyvens, R. (2002) *Tourism for Development: Empowering Communities*. Prentice-Hall, Harlow.

Singer, P. (1972) Famine, affluence, and morality, *Philosophy and Public Affairs* 1, 229–243. http://www.utilitarian.net/singer/by/1972----.htm (accessed 8 January 2010).

Smith, S.L.J. (1988) Defining tourism: a supply-side view. *Annals of Tourism Research* 15, 179–190.

Smith, M. and Duffy, R. (2003) *The Ethics of Tourism Development*. Routledge, London.

Stein, R.L. (1995) Remapping Israeli and Palestinian tourism, *Middle East Report*, Sept–Oct, pp. 16–19.

Tourism Interventions Group (2004) Who really benefits from tourism? Statement of Concern at the 4th WSF. http://www.e-alliance.ch/media/media-4589.doc (accessed 4 April 2005).

Trask, H.K. (1993) Environmental racism in Hawaii and the Pacific Basin, *ZMag*, Speech at University of Colorado at Boulder, 29 September. http://www.zmag.org/ZMag/articles/bartrask.htm (accessed 22 April 2003).

Trask, H.K. (1999) *From a Native Daughter: Colonialism and Sovereignty in Hawaii*. University of Hawaii Press, Honolulu.

Trask, H.K. (2000) Tourism and the prostitution of Hawaiian culture. *Cultural Survival Quarterly* 24, 30 April. http://www.cultural survival.org/publications/csq (accessed 7 November 2003).

Turner, L. and Ash, J. (1976) *The Golden Hordes: International Tourism and the Pleasure Periphery*. Constable, London.

World Social Forum (2004) World Social Forum 2004. http://www.wsfindia.org/whoweare.php (accessed 3 April 2005).

Conclusion: Tourism, Inequalities and Prospects

Nigel Morgan and Stroma Cole

As we have seen throughout this book, the undoubted benefits that tourism development can bring to under-empowered individuals, communities, regions and nations is increasingly being weighed against its negative environmental, social and cultural impacts. Such concerns over the tourism industry's ability to deliver holistic sustainability (recognizing ecological, social, economic and cultural considerations) and disquiet at its concentration of economic and political power in relatively few hands have been expressed by academics, policy makers and practitioners who have levelled much of their criticism at tourism's lack of social responsibility. At worst then, the tourism industry as a whole stands accused of unethical practice and of shoring up exploitation and at best, it is regarded as an imperfect mechanism for human and environmental welfare in an imperfect world.

Analyses of the causes of inequality in tourism are not new and many of the contributors here have rehearsed the arguments that highlight the underlying causes of inequity as unjust global systems, unfair international trade agreements and the workings of transnational corporations. For example, Stroma Cole and Jenny Eriksson (Chapter 7), Derek Hall and Frances Brown (Chapter 9), Dorothea Meyer (Chapter 10) and Freya Higgins-Desbiolles (Chapter 12) all neatly sum up the problem in their descriptions of how the global tourism industry is ferociously competitive

and dominated by transnational corporations, mainly based in developed countries. They explain how these organizations hold substantial power over various suppliers, especially in less economically developed countries (LEDCs), which are hugely reliant on tourism for their foreign exchange earnings. Such corporations compete through international mergers and acquisitions, and are able to survive on small margins because of substantial economies of scale. This in turn results in continuous product innovation and hardline marketing through lower prices. The resulting instability of the travel sector makes it difficult for companies to plan for a more sustainable future and taking action to behave more responsibly has traditionally been a low priority, so much so that many industry ethical codes are mere platitudes (Wheeler, 1994; Fennell, 2006, 2009).

However, as well as reflecting and producing inequality, tourism can also alleviate social inequality and play a part in reducing its impacts, both for the consumers of tourism and for its producers – those in destination communities that provide tourism products and services. For example, while tourism employs over 200 million people worldwide, it is a disproportionately important employment sector for women especially in LEDCs. Moreover, its size, rapid growth and diverse, dynamic and flexible nature mean that it is ideally placed to empower and advance women and it has done so in many countries and contexts. Women can find a voice and independence through their involvement in tourism activities – by becoming part of decision-making processes and carving out new roles in their families, homes, communities and within local power structures (Pritchard *et al.* 2007). We have seen in the preceding chapters just how tourism has the potential to act as a powerful force for creating more equal societies, both in MEDCs (Chapters 1, 2, 3 and 11) through social tourism and social inclusion initiatives and in LEDCs through social justice initiatives incorporating poverty alleviation (Chapters 5 and 10), fair trade (Chapter 6) and ethics, welfare-positivism tourism and human rights (Chapters 7 and 9).

In both tourism-generating regions and tourism-receiving communities, tourism is part of wider social, economic, political, ecological and cultural processes and ultimately of course we are all stakeholders in tourism, as its impact on our planet affects us all. One of the key reasons that solutions to overcoming inequalities in tourism have been overlooked is simply that tourism as an industry and a field of study has traditionally focused on those who participate rather than those who do not. Unlike the broader study of leisure where there has always been a concern with understanding non-participation, in tourism enquiry we are just beginning to consider the complexities of the problems. Also perhaps because tourism is easily dismissed as merely 'about fun' we have turned our backs on its human and planetary cost. When we're on holiday most of us simply want to relax, unwind and have fun and not concern ourselves with the impacts of our activities and behaviours. Yet at home as consumers, we are becoming more ethically aware and motivated (Harrison *et al.*, 2005). As a result, despite there undoubtedly being a gap between what people say and what they actually do, ethical practice is emerging as a key area of debate among tourism practitioners, policy makers, developers and tourists (Chapter 12, this volume). As we have seen, these debates include everything from the human

rights of cruise ship employees, to salary levels of climbing porters in Nepal, to local peoples' access to beachfronts and fishing waters in LEDCs, to demands for transparent financial reporting in multinational corporations. This interest is, of course, not peculiar to tourism but is a general concern fuelled by the numerous business scandals recently seen around the world and underpins the rise in interest in business ethics and the concept of corporate social responsibility.

Ethical business practice involves responding to situations that deal with principles concerning human behaviour in respect to the appropriateness and inappropriateness of all activities undertaken by a business. Tourism practitioners need to understand what 'good' ethics are and how to incorporate them in various activities, to show respect and acknowledge the basic human rights and dignity of all stakeholders and so better reach their audiences and gain trust. The adoption of ethical and socially responsible practices, regardless of the product offered or the market targeted, sets the benchmark for good business behaviour, resonates with contemporary consumers and of course demonstrates moral accountability. The universal establishment of human rights is the single most important political development of recent decades and the embedding of values based on human rights and equality principles in tourism business practice would signal a move towards justice tourism based on ethics, fairness and equity. However as Tourism Concern highlighted in its 2009 report *Putting Tourism to Rights*, all tourism stakeholders must move beyond paying mere lip service to ethics and social responsibility to take *meaningful* action, direct steps and establish new processes if real change is to happen.

As a collection, this book provides rich and diverse accounts of the different forms of inequality, exclusion or injustices related to tourism and presents new understandings of the ways in which social justice can be achieved in and through tourism. In so doing, the volume succeeds in unpicking complex processes to expose the relationships between tourism and inequality. More than this, however, its contributors have also reviewed international examples of socially responsible tourism to provide a bank of good practice cases for tourism students, educators and practitioners. Across its 14 chapters, a wide range of inter-related forms of inequality and routes towards social justice have been addressed. These include, but are not limited to, relations of class, nation, ethnicity, race, gender, disability and age as they relate to social justice initiatives incorporating poverty alleviation, social inclusion, fair trade, ethics and human rights. These analyses eloquently demonstrate how inequality in tourism is a multidimensional phenomenon arising from a lack of capabilities including, but encompassing much more than a lack of income. Exclusion from tourism participation in MEDCs where tourism is regarded as a social norm or a right also results from gender and age inequalities, racial, ethnic and ableist discrimination, and cultural fear and prejudice. What emerges from the studies presented here (as elsewhere) is that, frequently those most likely to need the benefits a holiday can bring, are the most likely to be excluded. The same factors are also central to creating inequality and injustice in tourism in LEDCs, but here they combine with other factors such as a lack of physical security and abuses by those in positions of power.

While the contributors here have reviewed and exposed such inequality and its causes, they have also endeavoured to consider how tourism can reduce the inequalities they explore. Across the chapters, a number of common themes have emerged, notably:

- the need for more nuanced understandings of the nature of the problems before effective solutions can be sought (e.g. Chapters 1 and 5);
- legislation alone does not guarantee equality or social justice (e.g. Chapters 1, 2, 4 and 5);
- education and attitudinal change are crucial change agents (e.g. Chapters 1, 3 and 5);

- partnerships between the private, voluntary and public sectors are extremely effective in providing solutions (e.g. Chapters 5, 8 and 10); and
- people can effect change through individual and group action and activism (Chapters 5 and 12).

When we first imagined this collection, our goal was to produce an accessible and above all affordable exploration of tourism's role as a site of injustice and its potential to address inequality. Neither of us wanted to produce a book that simply scoped and reviewed the problems of tourism and inequality; we wanted to produce a provocative text that also engaged with prospects for greater equality, one that would also ask 'what can be done' and 'is there another way'? We hope that this aim has been achieved and certainly, while the power dynamics of sexism, racism, ableism, international politics and so forth are rehearsed here, the contributors have eloquently urged us to see these relations through new lenses, to appreciate their complexities and to demand more in-depth understanding.

This book forms part of a growing debate in tourism scholarship and practice; there remains a considerable challenge to build a substantive body of knowledge that takes on the task of highlighting issues of justice, ethics, equality and responsibility in tourism. Yet too often 'research seems to be conducted for its own sake' (Walker, 2004: 1), with no positive impact on people's lives. We suggest that in developing this knowledge base tourism researchers link their endeavours to action beyond academia and thus aspire to advocacy scholarship that promotes human dignity, human rights and just societies. This is actually the essence of the emerging enquiry perspective of hopeful tourism scholarship (Ateljevic et al., 2007), which advocates an approach guided by moral agency, truth and responsibility. Hopeful tourism scholarship is closely entwined with what Tribe (2002: 322) has termed 'the idea of knowing-in-ethical-tourism-action ... Here reflection and action are integrated and where people act for the good of tourism societies. This is a move towards tourism stewardship ... and a fuller responsibility to the contexts within which tourism is practiced.' These notions are central to the hopeful tourism scholarship agenda, which has three key elements namely: the development of knowledge-based radical critiques of social settings and institutions; advocacy of human dignity, rights and just societies in tourism policy arenas; and the nurturing of reflexive, ethical tourism practitioners and policy makers of the future (Richards *et al.*, in press).

One of the main audiences for this text are tourism students and we need to reflect on why the growing critiques of tourism's low ethical standards and lack of social responsibility have taken some time to impact on industry practice. Tourism educators must shoulder some responsibility for this through their failure adequately to embed ethics, values and stewardship in their teaching and learning practice. Stewardship is a potent idea where thoughtful practitioners assume the responsibility for promoting the well-being of tourism's society and world and not just the profitability of individual firms (Tribe, 2002). In these times of environmental, social and financial crisis arguably caused by unethical and irresponsible management, perhaps we need a realignment of our approach to educating students for the tourism world (Sheldon *et al.*, 2009). Tourism academics must play their part in this and fulfil their role of educators in every sense of the word, moral as well as academic and practical. Yes, students on tourism programmes must learn the technical skills that will arm them for their careers, but they should acquire them along with strong values. Critical thinking and stakeholder consultation should be encouraged as well as intellectual rigour in teaching and learning practice. Words such as humanism, intelligence, professionalism, stewardship or responsibility cannot be simply words but must become actions carried into the classroom and beyond into the world of practice. At the very least, educators should re-affirm the idea that tourism operates as a system and remind

students of the inter-relationship between the environmental, ethical and political contexts and tourism business operations, while the incorporation of human rights concerns in human resource modules, ethical investment practices in finance curriculum and ethical dilemmas into management training should be the norm rather than the exception. In an increasingly complex tourism environment, management decision-making requires a rounded, well-informed view of the whole and an understanding that such decisions have ramifications for the well-being of society as well as individual organizations and corporations.

Certainly now seems to be the right time to reflect on the possibilities of such a paradigm shift as the dominant world system is at a crisis point and perhaps prevailing neo-liberal tourism systems face a potential 'regime change' (Holling and Gunderson, 2002). Thus, emerging paradigms and worldviews are growing in importance and these are seeking to generate transformative models for human development in a world dominated by post-9/11 security and political challenges, economic and financial collapses and the threats posed by climatic change. For example, resilience theory provides a new framework for analysing social–ecological systems in a world confronted by rapid change (Holling and Gunderson, 2002). Scholars in global change and resilience and sustainability studies are seeking conceptualizations and models that integrate the earth system, human development and sustainability based on a widely shared view that 'the challenge of sustainable development is the reconciliation of society's development goals with the planet's environmental limits over the long term' (Clark and Dickson, 2003: 8059). Tourism enquiry and practice needs to engage with such thinking and the international examples of socially responsible tourism provided here offer stories of hope for students, educators, activists and practitioners '... the kind of hope that employs all of our efforts in creating a mature vision of what's possible' (Judith, 2006: 14).

References

Ateljevic, I., Pritchard, A. and Morgan, N. (2007) Editors' introduction: promoting an academy of hope in tourism enquiry. In: Ateljevic, I., Pritchard, A. and Morgan (eds) *The Critical Turn in Tourism Studies: Innovative Research Methodologies*. Elsevier, Oxford, pp. 1–11.

Clark, W.C. and Dickson, N.M. (2003) Sustainability science: the emerging research program. *Proceedings of the National Academy of Sciences of the United States of America* 100, 8059–8061.

Fennell, D. (2006) *Tourism Ethics*. Channel View, Clevedon.

Fennell, D. (2009) Ethics and tourism. In: Tribe, J. (Ed.) *Philosophical Issues in Tourism*. Channel View, Clevedon, pp. 211–226.

Harrison, R., Newholm, T. and Shaw, D. (eds) (2005) *The Ethical Consumer*. Sage, London.

Holling, C.S. and Gunderson, L. (eds) (2002) *Panarchy: Understanding Transformations in Human and Natural Systems*. Island Press, Washington, DC.

Judith, A. (2006) *Waking the Global Heart: Humanity's Rite of Passage from the Love of Power to the Power of Love*. Elite Books, Santa Rosa, CA.

Pritchard, A., Morgan, N., Ateljevic I. and Harris, C. (eds) (2007) *Tourism and Gender: Embodiment, Sensuality and Experience*. CAB International, Wallingford, UK.

Richards, V., Pritchard, A. and Morgan, N. (In press) (Re)envisioning tourism and visual impairment. *Annals of Tourism Research*.

Sheldon, P., Fesenmaier, D.R. and Tribe, J. (2009) The tourism education futures initiative. *e-Review of Tourism Research (eRTR)* 7, 39–44.

Tourism Concern (2009) *Putting Tourism to Rights*. Tourism Concern, London

Tribe, J. (2002) Education for ethical tourism action. *Journal of Sustainable Tourism* 10, 309–324.

Walker, A. (2004). Introducing the growing older programme on extending the quality of life. In Walker, A. and Hennessy, C.H. (eds) *Growing Older: Quality of Life in Old Age*. Open University Press, Maidenhead, pp. 1–13.

Wheeler, B. (1994) Egotourism, sustainable tourism and the environment – a symbiotic, symbolic or shambolic relationship. In: Seaton, A.V. (ed.) *Tourism: The State of the Art*. John Wiley & Sons, Chichester, pp. 647–654.

Index

Page numbers in **bold** type refer to figures, tables and boxed text.

Wilson, D. B., Bouffard, L. A. & Mackenzie, D. L. (2005). A quantitative review of structured, group-orientated, cognitive-behavioural programs for offenders. *Criminal Justice and Behavior*, 32, 172–204.

Wincup, E., Buckland, G. & Bayliss, R. (2003). *Youth homelessness and substance abuse: Report to the drugs and alcohol research unit*. Home Office Research Findings No. 191. London: Home Office.

Wormith, J. S. & Olver, M. E. (2002). Offender treatment attrition and its relationship with risk, responsivity, and recidivism. *Criminal Justice and Behavior*, 29, 447–471.

Yalom, I. (1995). *The theory and practice of group psychotherapy (4th edition)*. New York: Basic Books.

Hollin, C. R. & McMurran, M. (1995). Series preface. In J. McGuire (Ed.), *What works: Reducing reoffending* (pp. ix–x). Chichester: John Wiley & Sons.

Hollin, C. R. & Palmer, E. J. (2004). *The special needs of women substance-using offenders*. Commissioned Report for the Women's Prison Estate, Home Office.

Hollin, C. R. & Palmer, E. J. (in press). Criminogenic need and women offenders: A critique of the literature. *Legal and Criminological Psychology*.

Hollin, C. R., Palmer, E. J., McGuire, J., Hounsome, J., Hatcher, R. & Bilby, C. (2005). *An evaluation of Pathfinder Programmes in the Probation Service*. Unpublished research report to the Home Office Research, Development and Statistics Directorate.

Home Office (2002). *Statistics on women and the criminal justice system*. London: Home Office.

Home Office (2004). *Reducing crime, changing lives*. London: Home Office.

Hope, T. (2004). Pretend it works: Evidence and governance in the evaluation of the Reducing Burglary Initiative. *Criminal Justice*, 4, 287–308.

Howden-Windell, J. & Clark, D. (1999). *Criminogenic needs of female offenders: A literature review*. London: HM Prison Service.

Howells, K. & Day, A. (2002). Readiness for anger management: Clinical and theoretical issues. *Clinical Psychology Review*, 23, 319–337.

Jacobson, N. S., Follette, W. C., Revenstorf, D., Baucom, D. H., Hahlweg, K. & Margolin, G. (1984). Variability in outcome and clinical significance of behavioral marital therapy: A reanalysis of outcome data. *Journal of Consulting and Clinical Psychology*, 52, 497–504.

Jacobson, N. S., Roberts, L. J., Berns, S. B. & McGlinchey, J. B. (1999). Methods for defining and determining the clinical significance of treatment effects: Description, application, and alternatives. *Journal of Consulting and Clinical Psychology*, 67, 300–307.

Jennings J. L. & Sawyer, S. (2003). Principles and techniques for maximizing the effectiveness of group therapy with sex offenders. *Sexual Abuse: A Journal of Research and Treatment*, 15, 251–267.

Jones, D. & Hollin, C. R. (2004). Managing problematic anger: The development of a treatment programme for personality disordered patients in high security. *International Journal of Forensic Mental Health*, 3, 197–210.

Kear-Colwell, J. & Pollack, P. (1997). Motivation or confrontation: Which approach to the child sex offender? *Criminal Justice and Behavior*, 24, 20–33.

Keijsers, G. P. J., Schaap, C. P. D. R. & Hoogduin, C. A. L. (2000). The impact of interpersonal patient and therapist behavior on outcome in cognitive-behavior therapy: A review of empirical studies. *Behavior Modification*, 24, 264–297.

Kendall, K. (2004). Dangerous thinking: A critical history of correctional cognitive behaviouralism. In G. Mair (Ed.), *What matters in probation* (pp. 53–89). Cullompton: Willan Publishing.

Kennedy, S. M. (2000). Treatment responsivity: Reducing recidivism by enhancing treatment effectiveness. *Forum on Corrections Research*, 12, 19–23.

Kennedy, S. M. (2001). Treatment responsivity: Reducing recidivism by enhancing treatment effectiveness. In L. L. Motiuk & R. C. Serin (Eds), *Compendium 2000 on effective correctional programming, Volume 1*. Ottawa, Correctional Services Canada.

Langan, N. P. & Pelissier, B. M. M. (2001). Gender differences among prisoners in drug treatment. *Journal of Substance Abuse*, 13, 291–301.

Laws, D. R. (1974). The failure of a token economy. *Federal Probation*, 38, 33–38.

Leschied, A. W. (2001). Implementation of effective correctional programs. In L. L. Motiuk & R. C. Serin (Eds), *Compendium 2000 on effective correctional programming* (pp. 41–46). Ottawa, Ontario: Correctional Service of Canada.

Lewis, S. et al. (2003). *The resettlement of short-term prisoners: An evaluation of seven Pathfinders*. RDS Occasional Paper 83. London: Home Office.

Lipsey, M. W. (1999). Can rehabilitative programs reduce the recidivism of juvenile offenders? An inquiry into the effectiveness of practical programs. *Virginia Journal of Social Policy and Law, 6*, 611–641.

Lipsey, M. W., Chapman, G. L. & Landenberger, N. A. (2001). Cognitive-behavioral programs for offenders. *Annals of the American Academy of Political and Social Science, 578*, 144–157.

Long, C. G. & Hollin, C. R. (1997). The scientist-practitioner model in clinical psychology: A critique. *Clinical Psychology and Psychotherapy, 4*, 75–83.

Lösel, F. (1996). Effective correctional programming: What empirical research tells us and what it doesn't. *Forum on Corrections Research, 6*, 33–37.

Lowenkamp, C. T., Holsinger, A. M. & Latessa, E. J. (2001). Risk/need assessment, offender classification, and the role of childhood abuse. *Criminal Justice and Behavior, 28*, 543–563.

Maguire, M., Raynor, P., Vanstone, M. & Kynch, J. (2000). Voluntary after-care and the Probation Service: A case of diminishing responsibility. *The Howard Journal of Criminal Justice, 39*, 234–248.

Mair, G. (2004). The origins of What Works in England and Wales: A house built on sand? In G. Mair (Ed.) *What matters in probation* (pp. 12–33). Cullompton: Willan Publishing.

Mann, R. E., Ginsburg, J. I. D. & Weekes, J. R. (2002). Motivational interviewing with offenders. In M. McMurran (Ed.), *Motivating offenders to change: A guide to enhancing engagement in therapy* (pp. 87–102). Chichester: John Wiley & Sons.

Marques, J. K., Day, D. M., Nelson, C. & West, M. A. (1994). Effects of cognitive-behavioral treatment on sex offender recidivism. *Criminal Justice and Behavior, 21*, 28–54.

Marshall, W. L. et al. (2002). Therapist features in sexual offender treatment: Their reliable identification and influence on behaviour change. *Clinical Psychology and Psychotherapy, 9*, 395–405.

Marshall, W. L. et al. (2003). Process variables in the treatment of sexual offenders: A review of the literature. *Aggression and Violent Behavior, 8*, 205–234.

Martin, D. J., Garske, J. P. & Davis, M. K. (2000). Relation of the therapeutic alliance with outcome and other variables: A meta-analytic review. *Journal of Consulting and Clinical Psychology, 68*, 438–450.

McGuire, J. (2002). Integrating findings from research reviews. In J. McGuire (Ed.), *Offender rehabilitation and treatment: Effective programmes and policies to reduce re-offending* (pp. 3–38). Chichester: John Wiley & Sons.

McMahon, G., Hall, A., Hayward, G., Hudson, C. & Roberts, C. (2004). *Basic skills programmes in the Probation Service: An evaluation of the basic skills Pathfinder.* Home Office Research Findings No. 203. London: Home Office.

McMurran, M. (2002). Preface. In M. McMurran (Ed.), *Motivating offenders to change: A guide to enhancing engagement in therapy* (pp. xii–xiii). Chichester: John Wiley & Sons.

McMurran, M. & McCulloch, A. (in press). Why don't offenders complete treatment? Prisoners' reasons for non-completion of a cognitive skills programme. *Psychology, Crime, & Law.*

Medical Research Council. (2000). *A framework for development and evaluation of RCTs for complex interventions to improve health.* London: Medical Research Council.

Merrington, S. & Stanley, S. (2004). "What works?": Revisiting the evidence in England and Wales. *Probation Journal, 51*, 7–20.

Miller, W. M. (1985). Motivation for treatment: A review with special emphasis on alcoholism. *Psychological Bulletin, 98*, 84–107.

Miller, W. M. & Rollnick, S. (Eds). (1991). *Motivational interviewing: Preparing people to change addictive behavior.* New York: Guilford.

Murphy, C. M. & Baxter, V. A. (1997). Motivating batterers to change in the treatment context. *Journal of Interpersonal Violence, 12*, 607–619.

NAPO (2001). AGM resolutions 2001. *NAPO News, 134*, 10–15.

O'Brien, M., Mortimer, L., Singleton, N. & Meltzer, H. (1997). *Psychiatric morbidity among women prisoners in England and Wales.* London: Office of National Statistics.

Ogloff, J. R. P. (2002). Offender rehabilitation: From "nothing works" to what next? *Australian Psychologist, 37*, 245–252.

Parsons, S., Walker, L. & Grubin, D. (2001). Prevalence of mental disorder in female remand prisoners. *Journal of Forensic Psychiatry, 12*, 194–202.

Pawson, R. (2002). Evidence-based policy: In search of a method. *Evaluation, 8*, 157–181.

Phillips, E. L., Phillips, E. A., Fixen, D. L. & Wolf, M. M. (1974). *The Teaching-Family handbook (2nd edition).* Lawrence, KS: University of Kansas Press.

Piper, W. E. et al. (1999). Prediction of dropping out in time-limited interpretive individual psychotherapy. *Psychotherapy: Theory, Research and Practice, 36*, 114–122.

Polizzi, D. M., MacKenzie, D. L. & Hickman, L. J. (1999). What works in adult sex offenders treatment? A review of prison- and non-prison based treatment programs. *International Journal of Offender Therapy and Comparative Criminology, 43*, 357–374.

Preston, D. L. & Murphy, S. (1997). Motivating treatment resistant clients in therapy. *Forum on Corrections Research, 9*, 39–43.

Raynor, P. (2004). The Probation Service "Pathfinders": Finding the path and losing the way? *Criminal Justice, 4*, 309–325.

Raynor, P. & Vanstone, M. (2001). "Straight Thinking on Probation": Evidence-based practice and the culture of curiosity. In G. A. Bernfeld, D. P. Farrington & A. W. Leschied (Eds), *Offender rehabilitation in practice: Implementing and evaluating effective programmes* (pp. 189–203). Chichester: John Wiley & Sons.

Redondo, S., Sánchez-Meca, J. & Garrido, V. (2002). Crime treatment in Europe: A review of outcome studies. In J. McGuire (Ed.), *Offender rehabilitation and treatment: Effective programmes and policies to reduce re-offending* (pp. 113–141). Chichester: John Wiley & Sons.

Reppucci, N. D. (1973). Social psychology of institutional change: General principles for intervention. *American Journal of Community Psychology, 1*, 330–341.

Reppucci, N. D. & Saunders, J. T. (1974). Social psychology of behavior modification: Problems of implementation in natural settings. *American Psychologist, 29*, 649–660.

Rex, S., Lieb, R., Bottoms, A. & Wilson, L. (2003). *Accrediting offender programmes: A process-based evaluation of the Joint Prison/Probation Services Accreditation Panel.* Home Office Research Study No. 273. London: Home Office.

Robinson, D. (1995). *The impact of cognitive skills training on post-release recidivism among Canadian federal offenders.* (Research Report No. R-41). Ottawa, Correctional Service of Canada.

Robinson, G. & McNeill, F. (2004). Purposes matter: Examining the "ends" of probation. In G. Mair (Ed.), *What matters in probation* (pp. 277–304). Cullomptom: Willan Publishing.

Rollnick, S. & Miller, W. M. (1995). What is motivational interviewing? *Behavioral and Cognitive Psychotherapy, 12*, 325–334.

Rutan, J. S. & Stone, W .N. (1993). *Psychodynamic group psychotherapy (2nd edition).* New York: Guilford Press.

Samstag, L. W., Batchelder, S. T., Muran, J. C., Safran, J. D. & Winston, A. (1998). Early identification of treatment failures in short-term psychotherapy: An assessment of therapeutic alliance and interpersonal behavior. *Journal of Psychotherapy Practice and Research, 7*, 126–143.

Seligman, M. E. P. & Levant, R. F. (1998). Managed care policies rely on inadequate science. *Professional Psychology: Research and Practice, 29*, 211–212.

Serin, R. C. (1998). Treatment responsivity, intervention and reintegration: A conceptual model. *Forum on Corrections Research, 10*, 29–32.

Serin, R. C. & Kennedy, S. M. (1997). *Treatment readiness and responsivity: Contributing to effective correctional programming.* Research Report, Correctional Service of Canada.

Sharpe, D. (1997). Of apples and oranges, file drawers and garbage: Why validity issues in meta-analysis will not go away. *Clinical Psychology Review, 17*, 881–901.

Sorbello, L., Eccleston, L., Ward, T. & Jones, R. (2002). Treatment needs of female offenders: A review. *Australian Psychologist, 37*, 198–205.

Tong, L. S. J. & Farrington, D. P. (2006). How effective is the "Reasoning and Rehabilitation" programme in reducing re-offending? A meta-analysis of evaluations in four countries. *Psychology, Crime, and Law, 12*, 3–24.

Van Voorhis, P. (1997). Correctional classification and the "responsivity principle". *Forum on Corrections Research, 9*, 46–50.

Van Voorhis, P., Spruance, L. M., Ritchey, P. N., Listwan, S. J. & Seabrook, R. (2004). The Georgia Cognitive Skills experiment: A replication of Reasoning and Rehabilitation. *Criminal Justice and Behavior, 31*, 282–305.

Walitzer, K. S., Dermen, K. H. & Connors, G. J. (1999). Strategies for preparing clients for treatment: A review. *Behavior Modification, 23*, 129–151.

Ward, T., Day, A., Howells, K. & Birgden, A. (2004). The multifactor offender readiness model. *Aggression and Violent Behavior, 9*, 645–673.

INDEX